RAVENCLAW READER

Ravenclaw Reader

SEEKING THE ARTISTRY AND MEANING
OF J. K. ROWLING'S HOGWARTS SAGA

ESSAYS FROM THE ST ANDREWS UNIVERSITY
HARRY POTTER CONFERENCE:

John Patrick Pazdziora and Micah Snell, Editors

Unlocking Press
Oklahoma City, Oklahoma

2015

Unlocking Press
328 NW 26th Street
Oklahoma City, Oklahoma 73103
www.UnlockingPress.com

Book Layout ©2013 BookDesignTemplates.com

Ordering Information:
Quantity sales. Special discounts are available on quantity purchases by corporations, associations, and others. For details, contact the "Special Sales Department" at the address above.

Ravenclaw Reader/ John Patrick Pazdziora, Micah Snell, Editors. —1st ed.
ISBN 978-0-9908821-0-7

Contents

*To Rebecca Pazdziora
and Jennifer Snell,
and everyone else who
has read a book they loved
to a child.*

Foreword
James Thomas

By the time I read my first *Harry Potter* book, the war was well under way. Battles were being waged on two fronts as the books were condemned, scorned, and maligned primarily by two groups: Harry Haters and academics. The former source of opposition came primarily from the U.S. as concerned and concordanced Christians armed themselves with the knowledge that sorcerers were condemned by God, albeit not often arming themselves with any knowledge of the books they were opposing. Moreover, a number of academics with impeccable pedigrees and impressive bibliographies—though, like the Harry Haters, usually without having read much or any of Harry's story—dubbed the books as "rubbish," unworthy of scholarly attention, and a waste of any intelligent reader's time.

Although these *Potter* wars were raging just over a decade ago, much has changed of late. Conservative Christian opposition has abated a good bit now that Harry's story has been told in full and after a few readers (or even non-readers) seem to have finally heard what John Granger, Connie Neal, and others had been saying from the beginning about the Christian context and symbols that are such a vital aspect of the books. Likewise, now that courses on the *Potter* books are offered in countless universities all over the world, now that numerous theses and dissertations are being written on the series, and now that academics come together occasionally to share analyses and ideas about the books, thus treating them as what they are—serious literature—this second front of the *Potter* wars seems to have abated as well. And yet, as we gathered a couple of years ago at the University of St. Andrews to share views on this rich literary series, there were a few flare ups on this front by some academics in the U.K. who seemed to wonder, perhaps even worry, that we were, alas, spending our time on a writer such as Rowling.

Spending our time—and a wonderful time it was—in the spring of 2012 at St. Andrews talking about the *Potter* books resulted in *this* book: a compilation of some of the papers presented on the literary elements, qualities, implications, and nuances of Rowling's books. On the final afternoon of the conference, as part of a panel fielding questions from the audience, I was asked my opinion of the future of academic attention to the *Potter* books. I am reasonably certain I was the oldest person in the room that day (I now often find myself in such rooms), and my immediate response was that *here* is the future of Rowling studies. Many who had presented papers at the conference, and many who are represented in this volume, are in the early years of their academic and scholarly pursuits. They had come together from all over the world; their analyses and interpretations of the *Potter* books varied considerably. Yet I think it is safe to say they all shared a passion for Rowling's books early on, and now their professional lives will reflect an ongoing and serious consideration of the books, resulting inevitably in more papers, articles, books, and reviews that will continue the discussion.

I believe this simply because the books are too rich, too deep, too personally meaningful to be forgotten or neglected by those who love books. That Rowling's work will endure and continue to elicit scholarly attention is, indeed, a prediction; and any academic who predicts enduring qualities for a contemporary work might be proved wrong—including an academic who is the oldest in the room. Yet it seems inconceivable to me that the *Potter* books would fade away in the future or fail to move and challenge readers in the coming generations. After all, Albus Dumbledore says over and over and in many different ways what the books are about, which is what *we* are about: love—just love. And whatever happens, whatever that flighty temptress adventure has in store for us, love will abide; and stories about sacrifice, love, and triumph over death itself surely will not die.

I have other reasons to believe that studies like those in this book will continue to be written as well. In *Harry Potter and the Half-Blood Prince*, Dumbledore finds the passage point in the cave "simply by looking and touching" the cave wall. Harry is not surprised at this low-key approach because he has "long since learned that bangs and smoke" are often not the signs of expertise. I believe we initially delight at the bangs and smoke of the *Potter* books and later, as re-readers or as scholars, we appreciate them for the looking and the touching. Surely, there is much, much more to see and to touch. Similarly, we as first-time readers feel the thrill of suspenseful moments and appreciate the ingenious solutions to the many mysteries Harry and the others solve; yet only later do we experience the deeper, unsolved and unsolvable mysteries of the heart inherent in the characters and the dilemmas they face. To use Gerard Manley Hopkins's phraseology, we move from perceiving *mystery* as "interesting uncertainty" to *mystery* as "incomprehensible certainty." And anything incomprehensible yet certain seems certain to interest or enliven readers and scholars for decades to come.

Having read the essays and responses which follow in this volume, I am convinced you will find each one compelling and thought provoking. John Patrick Pazdziora and Fr. Micah Snell have chosen well, selecting a number of studies which are indicative of the robust and burgeoning nature of scholarship on the *Potter* books. Yet some members of academia will remain unconvinced by this or any other book that such studies are noteworthy and worthwhile. Among them, the war will go on, and the battle to convince them to view these books as enduring literature will never be won. But among the current and future generations of scholars, in my view, that battle will never be fought.

James W. Thomas
July 2014

Introduction

In 1997, the world first met a boy named Harry Potter—a scrawny, mop-headed, dirty-faced boy with broken glasses and a lightning-bolt scar. His broken glasses were shortly fixed by his ever-resourceful friend Hermione. Fixing the scar would take ten years and seven books, spanning the horrific ordeals of school exams, multiple showdowns with a Dark Lord, and even asking a girl to the winter formal. Through all of these Harry, together with his enraptured fans, was growing up.

Pottermania and its shrieking obsession with J. K. Rowling's *Harry Potter* series (1997-2007) is remarkable in the recent history of children's literature. But it is less remarkable as a cultural phenomenon. The crowds, the queues, the costumes, the haircuts, the shipping wars, and the spoilers—these have all been seen and lived before. Harry Potter joins such pop-culture ranks as the Fifth Beatle (or Sixth), a Federation ensign working towards command of his own starship, a young Jedi knight in training, or—perhaps most pertinently—a Little Nell for the Noughties.

Cultural critics of the professional and armchair varieties will always find much to debate about these phenomena. Questions of why a particular work at a particular time creates a particular degree of hysteria deserve close scrutiny. But after the hype and hysteria are over—when the band splits up, the concluding book has been milked for more films than it is worth, and the cloth-bound editions are a penny apiece at Amazon.com—the work itself remains to be weighed and measured for its enduring worth in its own right and alongside others of its kind. Indeed, Harry's is merely the next face in the crowd of plucky underdogs-who-become-heroes, stretching back through DC, Marvel, Nesbit, Dickens, Hugo, Shakespeare, Mallory, Ovid, the Bible, and Homer to the earliest human impulse toward story. So the boy Harry Potter must find his place—or lack thereof—beside Ged and Christopher Chant, Jim Hawkins and Mowgli, Moomintroll and Alice. Rowling's *Harry Potter* books may be one of only a few manias in living memory, but they are one of many tales that have enchanted and delighted children. The simple question remains: How well do the *Harry Potter* books succeed as literature?

It is premature to judge the *Harry Potter* books with anything like finality: "the knife of demon Time the vivisector," to borrow Edwin Muir's phrase, has yet to preserve these stories or to destroy them. Those of us who met Harry Potter first will not live to see the judgement of Rowling by the ages. But this inevitable lack of historical perspective does not absolve the literary critics from considering the most influential texts of their own age. Loved or loathed or preserved as quaint enigma, *Harry Potter* will remain the definitive cultural literary text of the generation that read its way into the third millennium. Rowling's oeuvre will reside willy-nilly as an icon of the era of Steve Jobs, Oprah Winfrey, and George W. Bush.

The bulk of published attention to *Harry Potter* might superficially be judged by its interest in generating web site traffic. Between media outlets, social networks, fan sites, fan fiction sites, and even scholarly forums, the greatest commodity is the mania and its effects, or the derivatives of the source material, or the cultural icons spawned in the spinning outward. So the commercial success of this volume, despite the calibre of the included scholars and the quality of their work, may have less to do with its perceived credibility than whether Emma Watson is photographed holding a copy. The body of secondary literature that has steadily grown over the past fifteen years—represented in Rebecca Langworthy's extensive bibliography at the end of this volume—will likely never register one iota of the attention lavished on Daniel Radcliffe's next commercial failure.

Though *Harry Potter* has proven irresistible to scholarly writers and university classrooms, discussion of the texts as texts within the broader current of children's literature is a smaller, more struggling stream. This is partly the nature of the disciplines that drive roots into the soil of time. As the immediacy of cultural events wanes, the inevitable future of *Harry Potter* studies will be continued attention to the primary texts as enduring works of fiction. This will be measured not only by Harry's multi-generational popularity with readers, but also by literary-critical studies as long as they continue to analyze Rowling's work. This anthology, then, is an attempt to nurture scholarship that deepens our appreciation of *Harry Potter* as literature.

The anthology had its beginnings in an international conference, *A Brand of Fictional Magic: Reading Harry Potter as Literature*. Hosted by the School of English, University of St Andrews, in May 2012, it was the first academic conference in the United Kingdom dedicated to the *Harry Potter* books, and the first conference in the world to discuss them as literary texts. Contributions came from a cross-section of the academic world: undergraduates, distinguished professors, doctoral candidates, university administrators, and one irrepressible ten-year-old in full Gryffindor colours. Delegates came from universities in every corner of the globe including the UK, Ireland, France, Germany, the Netherlands, Sweden, Italy, Spain, the USA, Canada, India, the Philippines, Australia, and South Africa. The unifying goal that brought this eclectic, energetic gathering of academics together was to begin discussing the text of *Harry Potter* as a *text*. Put another way, it was the ideal critical desires to delight, to appreciate, and to understand. Enchantment in intellectualism is not dead, as the wide debate about the conference in British media outlets suggests.

It is no coincidence that J. K. Rowling has associated the search for understanding—the primary human inquisitiveness that underlies study of the humanities—with her own books, and her reasons for writing them. In her address to the graduating class of Harvard in 2008, Rowling offered a striking retrospective on the recently completed *Harry Potter* series, relating it not just to her undergraduate study in Classics, but to her work for Amnesty International. What unifies these three seemingly disparate elements is, according to Rowling, the empathetic use of imagination—the same empathy that allows one to get into an ancient mentality allows the experience of solidarity with sufferers and victims and the creation of imaginative worlds. Yet, significantly, it is not the exercise of imagination itself, but rather the act of empathy that makes these worlds worthwhile. Rowling explains:

> Unlike any other creature on this planet, humans can learn and understand, without having experienced. They can think themselves into other people's places.
>
> Of course, this is a power, like my brand of fictional magic, that is morally neutral. One might use such an ability to manipulate, or control, just as much as to understand or sympathise.[1]

---

[1] J. K. Rowling, "The Fringe Benefits of Failure, and the Importance of Imagination," *The Harvard Magazine*, 5 June 2008, http://harvardmagazine.com/2008/06/the-fringe-benefits-failure-the-importance-imagination 24 Feb. 14

This moral neutrality, both of Rowling's fictional magic and of the imagination, suggests a significant interpretive point for the *Harry Potter* books. Within the wizarding world, and through the dishevelled pedagogy of Hogwarts, Harry Potter must learn how to use magic responsibly for the betterment of society. This applies to the basic, technological use of magic. Spells such as the Imperius curse, which allow the caster "to manipulate, or control" another human, are rightly forbidden, as is jinxing objects to perplex muggles. But even skill in acceptable forms of magic does not a caring wizard make (consider, for instance, the respected and repugnant Dolores Umbridge). More importantly, Harry must learn, through the agency of his friends and his life experiences, to "think [himself] into other people's places"; this appears most in his increasingly complex interactions with Albus Dumbledore and Severus Snape. In these instances, the act of "thinking [...] into other people's places" becomes literal, both through the use of the Pensieve to provide external storage for memories and the fraught lessons on occlumency. In Rowling's imagined world, the external discipline of learning to use magic becomes an outward manifestation of the exercise of imagination.

There are, after all, many reasons for the close study of a literary text, whether to seek enlightenment from the masters of literary art, or to identify stereotypes and clichés in pulp writing, but surely the most basic, essential reason is that a text is fun to read and to talk about. This link between popular mania and critical analysis is too little acknowledged. For all the bewailing of the decline of English programs, the *Harry Potter* sensation forcefully demonstrates that people the world over still love to read books—to read them *and* write about them, to argue about them, and to speculate about how they will end, and skip with rage or delight when they end differently.

For good or ill, the Harry Potter series will form a vital component of future conversations about literature in the late-twentieth and early twenty-first centuries. A generation of young people, hipsters and homeschoolers alike, grew up with Harry, sharing his adventures as he discovered the delights and perils of the wizarding world. One of the revelations of the 2012 conference was that readers who were eleven when *Harry Potter and the Philosopher's Stone* came out in 1997 are now college graduates whose creative and critical work in or out of academia has been shaped in part by the imaginative empathy of J. K. Rowling. They found—as children always find, when they have given their hearts to a worthwhile book—that afterwards they knew their own world better too. The magic may be fictional, but the lessons learned and the imaginative empathy gained are real. Time will tell if one of the greatest impacts of *Harry Potter* is a generation of scholars who turn their clear eyes and full hearts to old texts in new ways—or new texts in old ways.

For now, *Harry Potter* studies has yet to validate itself—to the extent any legitimate endeavour can—in the eyes of both mainstream popularity and old guard academia. The media response to the conference occurred on a scale unnerving to a literary academic establishment more accustomed to being ignored than picked up by news agencies worldwide. The news stories and opinion pieces ran in two predictable veins: *Harry Potter* is awesome because people like *Harry Potter*! (and here is a brooding picture of Rupert Grint!), and J. K. Rowling is entertaining but certainly no William Shakespeare, so why are academics wasting their time on *Harry Potter*? Indeed, one expert harrumphed to a national newspaper that the conference organizers should be spending their time studying Shakespeare and Milton instead of silly children's books—blithely oblivious to the fact that, as the conference was going on, one organizer was a priest writing a dissertation on *The Tempest*, and the other was teaching a university course on *Paradise Lost*.

Reporters and bloggers for large outlets are seldom burdened with the need to be careful or constructive; none of the Rowling-is-no-Shakespeare sceptics troubled to mention the obviously fascinating parallel that in his day Shakespeare was considered too popular, too frivolous, and too undereducated to ever produce any work of enduring substance—and besides, getting rich from literary success (how dare he?) surely indicates a total lack of creative integrity. These two biases may not be substantiated, but the general critiques deserve reasonable attention at least in the short perspective.

Already the some of the general objections have been dismissed. Long before our book qualitative merits of *Harry Potter* have been sufficiently demonstrated to move beyond superficial claims the books are entertaining but worthless. Academic sceptics must now scoff in the faces of their own institutions, where, not only are dozens of universities offering classes on *Harry Potter* as literature that fill up with bright and interested students, but permanent faculty at universities as distinguished as Cambridge hold chairs in Children's Literature and direct terminal research degrees in the field. And, while our interests here are primarily literary, another revelation of the 2012 conference was that *Harry Potter* is being studied and applied as a common text for education, theology, psychology and counselling, multicultural studies, linguistics and translation, and surely more of which we are not even aware. The academic interest in *Harry Potter* has exploded any illusion of shoehorning the books into a School of English that cannot find any other pretence by which to garner attention.

The idea behind this book is to carry over the conversations among the scholars at the conference, and the broader conversation among readers and fans and critics of the series, into the texture of the book. Each chapter is followed by a short response essay from another scholar working on a similar topic. These should not be mistaken for rebuttals per se but rather a continuing of the conversation—suggestions for further directions in the literary study of *Harry Potter*.

The book begins with the three central elements of the series: education, death, and magic. Chapter one provides Jessica Tiffin's analysis of the silent curriculum of the series: the actual practice of education and pedagogy at Hogwarts. Tiffin suggests that not only is the actual schooling offered under Dumbledore's administration spectacularly awful, the enthusiasm with which child readers are relating this lopsided picture of education to their own school experiences is legitimate cause for concern. Joel Hunter's response situates the educational system at Hogwarts within Rowling's wider depictions of governance and society in the wizarding world. In chapter two John Dunne considers the series' presentation of death, both within the narrative and as an overarching theme. In particular he considers the inscription from St. Paul written on James and Lily Potter's gravestone in Godric's Hollow. In response John Granger offers some additional considerations about the book's presentation of mortality, distinguishing between "good" and "bad" forms death. In chapter three Siddarth Pandey analyses the types and uses of magic found in the wizarding world and their influence on the social structure. Vinitia Chandra responds with a consideration of the broader socio-political implications of magic in series.

From there the anthology turns to the narrative structure and genre study of the series. In chapter four, Garry MacKenzie brings a thoughtful examination of landscape in the books and the narrative space of the forest. He develops A. S. Byatt's critique of Rowling's forest, moving away from her more reactionary stance into a more careful consideration through comparison with other literary forests. The response from John Patrick Pazdziora focuses particularly on forests in children's literature and the use of the greenwood effect to imagine Arcadia. In chapter five, Joel Hunter uses Vladimr Propp's system of narratological functions to assess the structure of the series. Hunter argues that the most popular books in the series are the ones that adhere most closely to traditional folktale structure, while the least popular are those that deviate from it. In response Gabrielle Ceraldi suggests that not just the bones of narrative but also its flesh and blood play a significant role in reader preference. In chapter six, Sarah Cocita Reschan gives a reading of the series as young adult dystopia, and Amy Sturgis replies by setting the reading in the broader context of dystopia as a genre.

Narrowing the focus of the anthology, the next chapters turn to consider individual characters. In chapter seven, Timothy Bartel makes the case for the canonization of Neville Longbottom, presenting him as the character type of a confessor-saint. Maria Nilson replies with a portrayal of Neville as an atypical hero and accentuates his important, gender-bending role in Harry's community at Hogwarts. Joshua Richards takes on the puzzle of Severus Snape in chapter eight, suggesting that the Potions Master functions as the archetypal ogre-father in Rowling's use of Joseph Campbell's monomythic structure. Amy Sonheim offers a rejoinder that presents a psychoanalytic reading of Snape. In chapter nine, Rebecca Langworthy raises the question of the Dursleys and the troubling, often vicious portrayal of ordinary middle-class muggles in the series. The response essay by Travis Prinzi addresses additional political complexity of wizard-muggle relations, particularly in the interaction between the Minister of Magic and the Muggle Prime Minister.

In the concluding chapter, John Granger considers the ways in which the *Harry Potter* series enlarges and challenges our conception of literature, how it functions, and how it should be read. Tracing the series' use of literary alchemy, Christian symbolism, and ring structure, he suggests that it offers a transformative reading experience that engenders a deep, creative empathy in the reader. In reply, Josie Gabelman gives a spirited defence of playing make-believe.

A series of appendices edited by Joel Hunter provide detailed narratological analysis of all seven books for the curious. Rebecca Langworthy provides students and eager readers with a detailed bibliography of extant secondary literature on the Harry Potter books.

Our contributors to this anthology are enthusiastic, but they are also sincere. Their careful work has moved the conversation forward in meaningful ways and opened up both profound insights into Rowling's work as well as questions that trouble its overall profundity. The easier readings are falling away; forthright criticism is the best way by which to try *Harry Potter*'s true mettle.

In the spirit of fairness, we would like to offer the follow issues as a sampling of important problems in *Harry Potter* that go beyond the scope of our current project, but which we hope may stimulate future constructive analysis of the books:

1.   Music and poetry of a profound sort have no place in the Hogwarts' curriculum, or in the books themselves. This appears to be less a failure on Rowling's part to try and not succeed so much as an apparent failure to try and include them in any significant way.

2.   There are few apologists for Rowling's prose style. Whereas her ability to draw characters and dialogue is superb, critics of her prose are not easily answered. It is not evident that, given the age of her target audience, she has written at the highest level of her own competence, but proponents of her work would welcome defences against critics who say her stories are excellent but she cannot write—or edit.

3.   Probably the largest on-going area of study will be Rowling's relationship with her source material. To what extent was Rowling consciously engaging with and responding to the writings of Plato or Victor Hugo (just to name two possibilities) versus steeping in her literary heritage and doing her own creative work unwitting of the influence? Is Rowling a genius whose work should be considered primarily in its own right, or is she a considered snatcher up of trifles considered-or-no? The answers must be "yes" and "yes" to a great extent, but just how and to what extent remains a question where speculation must recede and first-rate work take over.

Ultimately, our hope is that this will provide clear, thoughtful statements in the on-going critical conversation about Harry Potter. We hope the dynamic interplay of voices and perspectives offer intriguing possibilities for further discussion. But where this conversation will go, and what will become of Harry Potter's brand of fictional magic, is for future readers and "the knife of demon Time" to decide.

John Patrick Pazdziora
Father Micah Snell
Pentecost 2014

CHAPTER 1

Learning, Understanding, Experience: Harry Potter and Pedagogy
Jessica Tiffin

In many ways, it is quite difficult to talk about Harry Potter. The phenomenon is so enormous, the readership so wide, and their identification with the narrative so strong, that the texts themselves are in danger of being erased by their effect. By a combination of design and fortuity Rowling's mixture of magical narrative, quest romance, mythic and folkloric elements, children's coming-of-age fiction and the old-fashioned school story has hit a cultural nerve. Hogwarts has become an icon: a removed, enchanted and in many ways beautiful space which carries all the connotations of comradeship, nurture, self-discovery and opposition to evil as well as its function as gatekeeper into a magical world.

In the generic mingling of the fantasy quest with the deliberate nostalgia of the school story, however, it is easy to lose sight of the essential identity of Hogwarts as a *school*, a space whose primary function is teaching and learning. One carries out of Hogwarts a sense of its glitter and charm, its function as a utopian locus of acceptance, magic and friendship in antithesis to the cold banality in which the institution of schooling is represented in a popular of Harry's upbringing, rather than any critical awareness of the nitty-gritty of education in its classrooms. This is a telling and significant issue, given the cultural currency of the series. Books with this degree of popularity and eliciting this degree of investment from their readers are clearly providing not just magical wish-fulfilment and images of agency, but resonance: something of a connection to and reflection of the lives of the reader. In Robert J. Helfenbein's analysis of education at Hogwarts he argues that "representations of teachers and schooling matter [...] the ways text reflect, at least to some degree, popular conceptions of governmental institutions, schooling, teachers and the ways in which they interact." [1] It is precisely this instrumental interaction between the ideal and the actual with which I am concerned. Formal schooling is a common experience to most children, and however diverse their schooling contexts, the learning process, and the interaction between students, school structures and teachers, must show some recognisable points of similarity. School-age readers of the series also experience it in the context of a world in which formal educational attributes, the ability to pass exams, are enshrined as a vital bulwark against the pressures of employment and earning power. In a series with this degree of popularity, the question is *what* images of schooling, and what kinds of judgements about learning, are being proffered to readers? And how are these images resonating with their own experience?

The reality is that in the Harry Potter series the view of education, of the act of *teaching* as well as assumptions about student learning processes, does not match the idealisation of so many other aspects. Despite the pleasures and rewards of Hogwarts, its operation as a source of warmth, validation and growth for Harry, the actual educational process, and the institutional culture of Hogwarts, are depicted in terms which too often reveal the institution and its teachers to be at best inconsistent or peripheral, and at worst fundamentally flawed. Worryingly, its readers clearly recognise and accept to some extent a learning experience which is characterised at various times by incomprehensibility, boredom, and even threat. Teaching is frequently ineffective and alienating to its students, and the knowledge it purports to teach often impenetrable; its function is secondary to the demands of what I choose to identify as the heroic plot, Harry's destined confrontation with Voldemort. In Rowling's Harvard commencement speech in 2008, she speaks of the value of human empathy as the ability to "learn and understand, without having experienced." [2] While she is concerned with the importance of imaginative empathy in her speech, nonetheless her phrasing is evocative of the central function of Hogwarts as an institution of formal learning, and in some ways denies the terms of Harry's heroic arc. The tension between learning and understanding on one hand, and active experience

---

[1] Robert J. Helfenbein, "Conjuring Curriculum, Conjuring Control: A Reading of Resistance in *Harry Potter and the Order of the Phoenix*," *Curriculum Enquiry* 38.4 (2008): 502.

[2] J. K. Rowling, "The Fringe Benefits of Failure, and the Importance of Imagination", Harvard Commencement speech 5 June 2008, *Harvard Gazette* 6 June 2008. Accessed 28 December 2011, http://news.harvard.edu/gazette/story/2008/06/text-of-j-k-rowling-speech/.

on the other, is important both in the depictions of education in the series, and in the generic intersections and clashes which underpin the narrative.

Varieties of dysfunctional learning

Various kinds of teaching failure are present across the series. The most obvious is probably found in Snape, the terrifying, bullying figure whose personal issues prevent him from imparting his knowledge of Potions to the bulk of the class. Harry and his classmates seem to learn Potions in spite of Snape, not because of him. The professor plays favourites with Slytherin students and has a disintegrating effect on insecure students such as Neville (*PoA* Ch 7); his classes are characterised not only by insufficient scaffolding and preparation for tasks (such as the Draught of Peace, *OP* 210), but by active physical threat. Hogwarts pupils are clearly expected to take in their stride burns, boils (*PS* 103), random shape-change (*CoS* 140-41), and other magical retributions for errors or clumsiness, as well as sarcasm and personal attacks from their teacher. Snape functions as the absolute antithesis of what is currently accepted as good teaching practice, and in fact his literary genesis is deeply Victorian: his most obvious antecedent is Dickens's Wackford Squeers, the monstrous schoolmaster in *Nicholas Nickleby* (1839) who operates as a caricature of the worst kind of Victorian educator. The difference, of course, is that Dickens was deliberately and critically highlighting abusive educational practices; Rowling is creating a romance villain. This is because, most importantly, Snape is deeply implicated in the heroic meta-plot of the series, in his Death Eater roots and his feelings for Harry's mother. His presence at Hogwarts is motivated by Harry's heroic identity, and his teaching function is clearly incidental. Like Quirrel, another poor teacher whose teaching efficacy is nearly paralysed by his own terror, Snape exists at Hogwarts as an indicator of Voldemort's power and purpose, an intrusion into the school's micro-environment of a wider world whose demands too often obscure and distract from the school's function as a *school.*

Professor Binns represents another teaching stereotype, that of the uninspiring teacher: his classes are simply boring, and his status as a ghost, while an entertaining play with the magical context, also points to the unexamined notion of teaching as a rote process, a habit divorced from any sort of investment of mental energy. "He had simply got up to teach one day and left his body behind him […]; his routine had not varied in the slightest since" (*CoS* 392). In an odd reversal of the Snape/Quirrel school of hiring teachers because of their relevance to the heroic meta-plot, Binns is exactly the opposite; his lessons lack any sort of awareness of the Wizarding World context of war and moral struggle or of the recurring problem of Dark Wizardry. History as a subject is dry-as-dust, a litany of names and dates without coherence or relevance to the students' real-world context. His classroom sessions are presented in exaggeratedly comic terms, with students dozing at their desks and writing down names more or less somnambulistically, and in this Binns can be categorised with teachers such as Gilderoy Lockhart or Sibyl Trelawney, comedy stereotypes whose amusement value overwrites the importance of the learning process and whose function as comic entertainment also trivialises the importance of teaching as a whole. While their effect is primarily comic, however, it should be noted that both Lockhart and Trelawney also fulfil important functions in the heroic meta-plot: Lockhart's vanity allows him to represent an archetype which warns Harry against a particular response to his own celebrity, and Trelawney has her place at the school solely because of her single genuine prophecy concerning, of course, Harry. Hagrid is another example in this framework; his importance to Harry as a supportive figure, and his own genuine love of the magical creatures of his subject, are coupled with insecurity and ineptness of teaching practice and a complete inability to control his classes. Whether they function as comic archetypes or necessary elements in the construction of Harry's heroic identity, these teachers are certainly not at Hogwarts because of any ability to teach.

Dolores Umbridge is yet another stereotype of poor teaching practice, although one perhaps more overtly linked to the current pedagogical landscape. She represents another facet of the heroic meta-plot intruding into the classroom: a Ministry desperate to deny the threat of Voldemort, and determined to disempower and suppress. While parodying the idea of theory taken to the point where it erases all practical application (*OP* 216-20), her classrooms also represent both mechanical teaching practice (reading and copying with the absolute denial of critical insight) and the antithesis of knowledge—in the Ministry's terms, ignorance is bliss. While Umbridge is clearly ignobly complicit with suspect bureaucratic processes, her lessons are in some ways horribly resonant with contemporary teaching experience in the sense in which teacher agency in the classrooms is too often undercut by resource issues or overly managerial intrusions by government bureaucracy. Her Defense Against the Dark Arts lessons, in their insistence on formulaic theory rather than practical application (*OP* 216-

219), are a reification of the Ministry's panicked denial of Voldemort's return, an interference predicted by Hermione's acute reading of Umbridge's welcome speech: "It means that the Ministry's interfering at Hogwarts" (*OP* 193). (They are also, of course, in their constitution of learning as a process of copying out of textbooks while the teacher absolutely forbids any kind of questioning or critical thinking, the antithesis of good teaching practice.) Belcher and Stephenson's *Teaching Harry Potter* makes this point powerfully in the American context,[3] but the truth is that too many education systems worldwide, under pressure from funding, overcrowding, or politically correct over-control, are to a greater or lesser extent in crisis. Umbridge thus stands, in the narrative, for a kind of recognisable despair: a sense in which terrible teaching practice is itself an inevitable outcome of higher organisational inadequacy.

Belcher and Stephenson's account notes the series' representation of archetypes and stereotypes of teachers and teaching: "we readers are definitely expected to *recognise* who is a good teacher and who is not."[4] "Good" teachers at Hogwarts clearly resist the Ministerial hijacking of their subjects (most notably Professor McGonagall, *OP* 286-7), but over the course of the series we cannot help but notice that even competent teaching has its limitations. McGonagall's classes present Transfiguration as complicated and almost impenetrable, and there is no real expectation that it will be accessible to the bulk of the class. Time and again practical Transfiguration classes end with only Hermione achieving the desired effect (*PS* 100, *GoF* 205, etc), and it is not clear how any action of McGonagall's fosters this. Lupin's Defence Against the Dark Arts classes seem to offer a better integration of theory and practice as well as presenting learning as interesting and vital. They are, however, angled towards student survival in the heroic meta-plot rather than learning for its own sake, and also open to disruption by it, as Lupin breaks off, for example, the boggart lesson in fear of Harry's response given his previous experience of Voldemort (*PoA* 117). In any case, the ingrained racism of the magical world—and, in fact, the threat Lupin constitutes to his own students in his werewolf identity—does not permit his continuation as a teacher despite his undoubted competence. The same problem applies to Mad-Eye Moody's compelling Defense Against the Dark Arts classes

---

[3] Catherine L. Belcher and Becky Herr Stephenson, *Teaching Harry Potter: The Power of Imagination in Multi-Cultural Classrooms* (New York, Palgrave Macmillan, 2011), 16-18.
[4] Belcher and Stephenson, *Teaching Harry Potter*, 20.

(*GoF* Ch 14), which are undermined by the revelation of his false identity; like Lupin, he seems to suggest that, while there are good teachers, they are not all they seem, and they cannot endure.

In addition to the problems of actual teaching, the Hogwarts curriculum itself presents some conceptual problems if considering the view of pedagogy promulgated by the series. To a large extent the magical curriculum is already a site of wish-fulfilment for students bored by Maths or English. The "Wizarding School" tradition refigures school content in idealised, magical terms which offer the appeal of power and excitement which are clearly meant to serve as an antidote to the humdrum and every-day. Magic thus overwrites the necessity, validity and relevance of the normal curriculum, subliminally suggesting that maths, writing skills, critical thought, biology, any broader context of history or geography, art or music, are unnecessary in a curriculum containing Transfiguration or Ancient Runes. While there are some clear parallels between Hogwarts and real-world subjects—Potions and Chemistry, for example, or History of Magic and normal History—the insularity and fantasy of the Wizarding World is affirmed by the suggestion that such mundane subjects are not actually relevant to wizards. Effectively, the Hogwarts curriculum comes down to Magic, Sport, and Heroism, the elitism of a magical curriculum echoed by the lionisation of Quidditch heroes (literally, given how often Gryffindor wins) and by the attention accorded to Harry's successes. Intellectual achievement is thus continually overwritten, in a process externalised neatly by the jewels in the house-point hourglasses, by sporting or heroic achievement. Moreover, this supports the focus of the heroic meta-plot on the active and real by denying the value of a humanist education in favour of learning skills in a purely utilitarian sense.

Erasure of the real-world curriculum is also too often the erasure of knowledge as a logical, apprehendable system. Subjects such as Charms are rote learning of words and gestures, with no sense of *why* they operate in the way they do (for example, the pronunciation and wrist movements for *Wingardium Leviosa, PS* 126); if there is a coherent theory underlying the difficulties of Transfiguration, it is clearly not reaching the students. Trelawney is not only an incompetent and hysterical teacher, but her Divination curriculum is spurious, ignoring any vital sense of the true prophecies which drive Harry's experience, but being presented, in her flaky person as well as in Harry and Ron's cheerful willingness to simply invent divinatory insights (*GoF* 193-4), as mere charlatanry. The position of Hermione's Arithmancy classes in the narrative is also interesting. We are never given a glimpse of how this arcane and demanding discipline actually works; it carries with it the same "Math is hard!" baggage as calculus does in the normal curriculum, an impenetrably difficult subject only understood by a few elite. Overall, magic itself is not a coherent system which is critically or consistently presented or investigated, and in this Rowling misses a great opportunity to mine the symbolic power of a magical system as a means of interrogating issues of learning, power and identity. Her writing can be contrasted with that of other fantasy writers presenting the learning experience of the young wizard; Ursula Le Guin, for example, offers in her Earthsea series a rigorous system of magic as naming which underpins Sparrowhawk's learning and insight.[5] It is clear that Rowling's text is not interested in the exploration of magic as systematic power, or anything other than the most superficial and entertaining sense of how one would go about learning it. Her focus on schooling, in fact, is not actually a focus on education.

Given the rather slender reed of teaching at Hogwarts, the process by which its students succeed in learning anything of their magical curriculum itself becomes somewhat magical; too often, and in particular with regard to the learning of students not in Harry's immediate circle, it takes place invisibly, outside the descriptions of classroom activities. If not actually assumed extra-narratively, a large proportion of the actual learning which goes on within the novels is extra-curricular, driven not by the acquisition of education as a worthy goal in itself, but by a simple need for survival. Harry's heroic challenges teach him and his friends a great deal more than the classroom does, as is seen in his preparation for the Tri-Wizard Tournament, his private lessons in the Patronus charm from Lupin, or in the DA classes in which desperate students take matters into their own hands—effectively, remedial sessions which gaps and flaws in the classroom experience render necessary. It is unclear how the gaps are filled by students outside Harry's exclusive group: we know little about the processes by which Hufflepuffs or Slytherins learn if they are not being driven by external quest pressures to seek knowledge through experience. This focus on Harry's learning fosters the tendency towards a celebration of elitism which is already inherent both in Hogwarts—only children with magical ability can enter the school or are capable of learning magic—and in the Wizarding World itself, al-

---

[5] Ursula K. Le Guin, *A Wizard of Earthsea* (Berkley: Parnassus, 1968).

ready an insular, highly powered elite characterised by general and often comic lack of knowledge about the broader world. It also underlines the value of practical ability rather than book learning, since study in the more formal sense is the attribute of Hermione, not of the hero himself. Clearly his time is too important: he should be doing, not studying, and formal learning is important only as far as it offers him support. The relegation of classroom discipline to Hermione parallels the divisions in the school itself: heroes are found in Gryffindor, doing great deeds, whereas Ravenclaw, whose students do take study seriously, is peripheral to the action. The marginalisation of students who study diligently and value educational achievement enacts something perilously close to the stereotype of the"swot," the high-achieving and academically-focused student traditionally lacking in social skills or popularity, who is most often the victim of both real-world and school-story jokes. This suggests that such students are less interesting than the active heroes, and reinforcing the casual quality of actual teaching with a clear devaluation of learning itself.

The notion of the active hero is thus in conflict with the system of formal classroom learning, but there is an argument for the failure of teaching, and the concomitant reliance on self-directed exploration and extra-curricular learning, as deliberate strategies to force young protagonists into discovery and growth. Critics such as Renée Dickinson suggest that the Harry Potter series simply relocates learning outside the classroom, and validly bypasses instruction and guidance to focus on learning by experience; following an argument first made by Jane Tompkins in 1996, she argues this is a process in which teachers "distance themselves from direct instruction approaches to the learning process, and act as facilitators rather than directors of the students' learning."[6] Similarly, Black and Eisenwein identify Hogwarts teaching as "a mix of progressive and existentialist ideas [...] Education is not separated from home or recreational life at the boarding school; rather, it continues through the day as life itself."[7] However, it is difficult to characterise Hogwarts teaching as an actual educational strategy given the paucity of textual evidence for a coherent theory of learning through action in the school. One could perhaps argue that McGonagall or Dumbledore take this approach, but too many of the professors are clearly incompetent

---

[6] Renée Dickinson, "Harry Potter Pedagogy: What We Learn about Teaching and Learning from J. K. Rowling," *The Clearing House* 79:6 (July/August 2006): 240.

[7] Mary S. Black and Marilyn J. Eisenweine, "Education of the Young Harry Potter: Socialization and Schooling for Wizards," *The Educational Forum* 66:1 (Fall 2001), 34.

teachers as well as dysfunctional individuals projecting their pathologies onto powerless students. Even Dumbledore withholds information for the student's own good, manipulating behaviour rather than empowering the individual's choice, a point which Dumbledore himself recognises in his apology to Harry (*OotP* ch. 37). Harry's confusion and despair during too much of the Horcrux quest points to the conclusion that withheld guidance is not necessarily productive. Above all, however, the comparative absence of viable formal learning opportunities in the series is important in the prevailing attitudes to, and expectations of, formal teaching it both recognises and entrenches.

It can be argued, therefore, that Rowling's insistence in her Harvard speech on the importance of the human ability to "learn and understand, without having experienced," is somewhat contradicted by the course of her novels, in which the emphasis is on experience, and usually Harry's experience, to the detriment of broader or more abstract notions of learning or understanding. The depiction of Hogwarts as a school environment—that is, an environment specifically dedicated to the self-conscious development of learning and understanding—is almost incidental to the other kinds of narrative which drive and define Harry's quest. I have chosen to attempt to understand this depiction of flawed teaching and learning at Hogwarts partially through the lens of genre.

Hogwarts and Genre

It is difficult, in the contemporary critical landscape, to invoke genre in any absolute or structuralist terms; nonetheless form and expectation underpin, in particular, the kind of text that Harry Potter represents. It functions as an accessible, popular narrative aimed at children, and offering the nice balance between familiarity and novelty identified by genre critics such as John G. Cawelti.[8] It also, in a postmodern landscape, demonstrates precisely the kind of flexible generic mixing and self-conscious play with expectations which is able to nod to reader familiarity with the tropes while adapting them freely to the modern context. The Harry Potter stories are obviously magical narrative, not only in their explicit concern with the magical, but in their depiction of a heroic journey through trials and challenges which allow the hero to confront and defeat evil and to achieve, via adventure and the testing imposed by that adventure, the vic-

---

[8] John. G. Cawelti, *Adventure, Mystery and Romance: Formula Stories as Art and Popular Culture* (Chicago: University of Chicago Press, 1976), 10-11.

tories and self-knowledge which are the object and focus of the quest. They are romance narratives, their parallels in the structures of fairy tale, the knightly quest of Arthurian romance, or the contemporary fantasy romance which follows a wizard through his growth to power. At the same time Rowling's texts offer the idealised depiction of a school environment in terms which seem most closely linked to the strongly-marked genre of the school story. The environment of Hogwarts is regressive, not just in the faintly medieval tinge lent by the magical elements, but in its recall of the school story narratives of the late-nineteenth to mid-twentieth centuries, e.g., *Tom Brown's Schooldays*, L.T. Meade, Angela Brazil, Greyfriars, Enid Blyton's Mallory Towers and St. Clare's, Jennings. In decoding the stories the readership of the Harry Potter series draws on recognition both of the fantasy romance tropes currently so prevalent in Western culture, and of a literary representation of the school experience which has very little to do with contemporary reality.

The antecedents of the Harry Potter series in magical quest romance are clear. Harry is the hero of destiny, endowed, in Northrop Frye's formulation, with abilities which set him apart from the normal individual.[9] His journey clearly exemplifies the function of romance narrative in exploring an essentially mythological environment in which the reductionist depiction of experience exposes romance as representation, "man's vision of his own life as a quest."[10] The roots of Rowling's stories—often explicitly referenced via names and plot elements such as three-headed dogs, a magician's hidden heart, a sword which recognises heroism, or a Divination teacher called Sibyl—are in mythology, folklore, fairy tale, and the medieval romance. Narrative in these contexts is external rather than internal, focusing on action rather than psychology or thought, and its clear-cut definitions are symbolic rather than mimetic. In the emblematic conflict between Harry and Voldemort, or between Death Eaters and the Order of the Phoenix, the framework and antecedents of the magical romance quest are clear. In his chivalric dedication to "good," his protective function, his embrace of self-sacrifice and his willingness to submit self to harm and danger in the service of an ideal, Harry functions as the questing knight of medieval romance.

---

[9] Northrop Frye, *Anatomy of Criticism* (Princeton: Princeton UP, 1957), 187.
[10] Northrop Frye, *The Secular Scripture: A Study of the Nature of Romance* (Cambridge: Harvard University Press, 1976), 15.

It is also significant that the series finds its genesis not only in the ancient forms of romance, but in the novelistic form of romance quest narrative represented by the contemporary genre of fantasy in its post-Tolkien, sword-and-sorcery incarnation. At the same time as he represents the hero—Galahad or Frodo or Aragorn—he is also the apprentice wizard whose narrative arc follows the process by which he comes to terms with his own power and the responsibilities of wielding it. This is a far more modern conception which parallels figures such as Ursula Le Guin's Sparrowhawk, whose growth as a magician beautifully encapsulates a symbolic grappling with his own flawed nature.[11] It reflects the translation of romance narrative into both the novel form as a whole, which is able to substantiate and psychologise the stripped-down narratives of romance and fairy tale, and specifically the children's novel, with its interest in the process by which a young hero acquires knowledge and agency.

And here, of course, learning is a central trope which is relevant to my exploration of the depiction of schooling at Hogwarts: the modern fantasy novel highlights the romance format's intrinsic predisposition towards the idea of learning, if only in the context of self-knowledge. Rowling's Harvard address speaks of the human ability to "learn and understand, without having experienced,"[12] but in fact the Harry Potter novels deny this: action is the testing ground which produces insight and growth. In the space and complexity of a novel there is some opportunity to externalise and explicate the process of personal growth, and to complicate the romance's tendency to moral reductionism, but psychological and moral realism contend continually against the constraint of symbolic forms. Above all, the idea of the quest as a space for learning and growth is complicated by the hero's identity as a figure of destiny: if an outcome is destined, how far is it possible to change yourself through learning? Harry's confrontation with Voldemort, regardless of how hard the narrative tries to emphasise his growth towards insight and choice, to some extent operates within the conceptual framework of inevitability. Thus, while he can learn to meet it effectively, he cannot learn enough to avoid it entirely. We know that he will confront Voldemort, because generic expectation dictates that the narrative can go no other way.

---

[11] Ursula K. Le Guin, *A Wizard of Earthsea* (Harmondsworth: Puffin, 1979).
[12] J. K. Rowling, "Fringe Benefits of Failure".

This element, perhaps, accounts to some extent for the marginalisation of formal learning experiences within the Hogwarts environment. It is also complicated by the drive in children's fiction towards isolating the protagonist: adult figures to some extent must be absent for the child to be able to experience, learn and grow on their own, and this absence is a repeated pattern across children's narratives from Dickens through to Disney.[13] It also, of course, reflects the isolation of the romance hero, the notion of test which is often individual rather than collective. Thus, while Dumbledore, McGonagall, and Lupin are all mentor figures to Harry, their mentorship is in many ways flawed, and the insights they offer are not sufficient for Harry to negotiate his challenges without frequent confusion, desperation and lack of clear goals. Their presence also does not adequately counterbalance the poor teachers who complicate or threaten Harry's existence. The experience of reading Rowling's series pulls up continual comparisons with texts such as Susan Cooper's *Dark is Rising* series, in which young Will's mentorship by Merriman Lyon provides a reassuring sense of guidance without sacrificing Will's independence as he grows into his powers.[14]

Given romance's rather different focus on learning through experience rather than teaching, it may seem discordant to couple the heroic quest with the school experience, but in fact there are more parallels than may at first appear. At its heart, the classic school story on which the environment of Hogwarts is built is not a realistic space; it demonstrates, in fact, similar elements of utopianism, nostalgia and reductionism to those found in romance. The public school experience which shapes and underlies Hogwarts is one which no longer exists, and which embodied, when it did exist, a removed and elevated ideal of privilege and difference highly congruent with the secret-magical-world fantasy of Hogwarts. Isabel Quigley's account of the English school story notes that "The public school was, by the end of the [nineteenth] century, an object of interest to those who had nothing to do with it, a symbol of romance,"[15] she characterises it

---

[13] See recent online discussions of this trope, including Leila Sales, "The Ol' Dead Dad Syndrome", *Publisher's Weekly*, Soapbox column (20 September 2010), http://www.publishersweekly.com/pw/by-topic/columns-and-blogs/soapbox/article/44502-the-ol-dead-dad-syndrome.html; and Julie Just, "The Parent Problem", *New York Times Book Review* (4 April 2010), 8.

[14] Susan Cooper, *The Dark is Rising* (London: Chatto and Windus, 1973).

[15] Isabel Quigly, *The Heirs of Tom Brown: The English School Story* (London: Chatto and Windus, 1982), 250.

as "burrowing deeper and deeper into fantasy."[16] George Orwell famously responds to the stirring school tales of the boys' weeklies of his time by suggesting that "that there are tens and scores of thousands of people to whom every detail of life at a 'posh' public school is wildly thrilling and romantic."[17] Rowling herself confirms the status of the boarding school as a fantasy of romantic rather than real experience by admitting, "I'm comprehensive educated—I've never even been inside a boarding school. I was asked recently whether I would have like to have gone to one. No, definitely not! But if it had been Hogwarts—yes, like a shot."[18]

The construction of a circumscribed school world in idealised terms is reflected in the school story's tendency to focus on the friendships, games and pranks of the students rather than the reality of education. This helps to foster the comic vein which has existed in the genre from early in its history, and which is a rich and appealing element in Rowling's writing; the Hogwarts experience echoes the fun inherent in the stories of P. G. Wodehouse or Rudyard Kipling's *Stalky and Co.* (1899), and in the caricatures and stereotypes of figures such as Billy Bunter and Jennings or the vivid satire of St Trinian's or Molesworth. The thread of comedy also, however, encourages the privileging of children's social bonds at the cost of undercutting and trivialising the process of education in the service of the story. The strongest elements that Hogwarts uses in its utopian view of the school are those of friendship—comradeship, alliance, recognition and peer support. This is particularly embodied in the sports system: Ken Watson notes the extent to which Thomas Hughes's "muscular Christianity" leads to "his adulation of athletic prowess, his ignoring of the intellectual side of school life,"[19] and this is clearly a powerful antecedent in the construction of Hogwarts. Against the lure of Quidditch, education in the sense of classroom

---

[16] Quigly, *Heirs*, 253.
[17] George Orwell, "Boys' Weeklies," Horizon (1940), Project Gutenberg text, http://gutenberg.net.au/ebooks03/0300011h.html#part9
[18] Jennie Renton, "The story behind the Potter legend: JK Rowling talks about how she created the Harry Potter books and the magic of Harry Potter's world," *Sydney Morning Herald*, October 28 (2001). http://www.accio-quote.org/articles/2001/1001-sydney-renton.htm.
[19] Ken Watson, "The Rise, Fall and Remarkable Revival of the School Story," in *Give Them Wings: The Experience of Children's Literature*, edited by Maurice Saxby and Gordon Winch (Melbourne: Macmillan, 1987), 197.

learning becomes opaque, an imposed and uninteresting formality when compared to the attractions of sport or friendships.

The school story's shifting of focus away from the classroom also means that
the considerable moral content of the classic story already tends towards the
kind of use made of it by Rowling under the simultaneous pressures of magical
romance. Mavis Reimer identifies "the older tradition of allegory that stands
behind the school story,"[20] in which "learning" is understood in far broader
terms: the child is encouraged to grow not necessarily in intellectual attainment,
but towards the self-discipline, self-knowledge and purpose required by the outside world of adulthood. Reimer argues for the "enclosed and self-sufficient"
world of the classic school stories,

> [...] with conflicts resolved within the terms of that world. In this, the
> school story is characteristic of children's narratives in general: they build pic-
> tures of concentrated worlds by explicitly mapping their geographies and
> boundaries; they demonstrate the principles by which power is exercised and
> distributed; they enact rules that assign morality and immorality to conduct;
> they institute the marks of belonging and exclusion.[21]

Hogwarts offers a clear parallel in the power struggles of teacher and house loyalties, Quidditch, and conflict between the students; it is, however, exaggerated
and at times disrupted by the nature of the outside world and the high stakes of
the conflict between the forces of good and evil. Hogwarts cannot continue to
function as a self-sufficient micro-environment given the larger world's location
of significant symbolic capital within the school, not only in the person of Harry,
but in the weaving of the histories and conflicts of the struggle against Voldemort into the lives of the pupils, their families, the teachers and the history of the
school itself. The moral polarities of the romance plot in some ways actually
inhibit moral development: there is an extent to which Hogwarts works firmly
against the notions of moral growth embedded in nineteenth and twentieth century school stories because of its house system. The Sorting Hat purports to
identify the nature and mode of learning of each student, but by so doing locks
them into an identity as surely as Harry is locked into his confrontation with
Voldemort. House allocation suggests that desirable qualities are not learned,

---

[20] Mavis Reimer, "Traditions of the school story", in *The Cambridge Companion to
Children's Literature*, edited by M.O. Grenby and Andrea Immel (Cambridge: Cambridge UP, 2009), 209.
[21] Reimer, 212.

they are innate, to be recognised rather than acquired or fostered: the narrative asserts that heroes are born in Gryffindor, not made, so that Hufflepuffs will always be supporting characters and Slytherins cannot be redeemed sufficiently to further the quest. Thus Hogwarts students can only grow and learn within a limited, pre-destined framework.

Rowling's use of school story traditions echoes their early roots in the moral concerns which shadow those of the romance plot, but her adaptations are even more interesting with regard to her depiction of actual teaching. Thomas Hughes clearly favoured escapade and sport over classroom achievements, but even so, the "Mr. Chips" stereotype of the insular bachelor teacher dedicated to teaching[22] acknowledges the importance of teaching in terms of relationships with and investments in students. Early girls' school story writers such as L. T. Meade could be relatively progressive in their depiction of actual education; Meade in particular insists repeatedly on her headmistresses being forward-thinking individuals who follow serious theories of education and are careful in their choice of teachers. Developing into the early twentieth century, the classic school story tends to use academic pursuits as an uninterrogated background to the exploits of their characters, but the overall effect is positive—that is, there seem to be more good than bad teachers in the pages of Enid Blyton or Angela Brazil. Mavis Reimer notes: "Criticism of schools as places of injustice, unhappiness and coercion have featured in narratives from the beginning of the genre, but such critiques have been a comparatively thin thread in the tradition."[23]

In some ways, Rowling clearly updates the classic school story, making it co-educational and allowing more of a focus on the individual rather than stressing conformity to rules and structures. However, despite its co-educational focus, Rowling's depiction of education is also regressive in that it ignores the updates to the genre made by more recent and critical contributions in the school story mode. Ken Watson comments on the extent to which realism and some degree of sophistication are features of school stories after the mid twentieth century, often replacing the exclusive fantasy of the public school with the more common day-school format, and dealing explicitly with the issues of race, class and disadvantaged upbringings which Rowling addresses only symbolically and

---

[22] Quigly, *Heirs*, 269.
[23] Reimer, 224.

in the broadest of terms.[24] (An interesting parallel here is Diana Wynne Jones's *Witch Week* (1982), whose school setting is more contemporary at the same time as its treatment of magical power is more nuanced.[25]) The development of the genre into the day school and also into the American experience persists as it develops into the television format, and Reimer remarks on the continued focus on peer interactions, rather than relationships with teachers, in television schools.[26] The constraints of the magical romance quest could be seen to partially dictate Rowling's investment in an outdated form of schooling, but such a correspondence is not inevitable—in its depiction of the interaction between a fantastic/heroic role and a normal school progression, the closest fictional ancestor to Hogwarts is possibly *Buffy the Vampire Slayer*'s Sunnydale High, which manages, despite its unabashed fantasy/horror elements, to normalise actual learning to a far greater extent than Hogwarts does.

Hogwarts as educational indicator

Overall, despite the identity of Hogwarts as a school, it is clear that education is not actually the point of the series. Rowling is interested in formal learning only as a backdrop to the hero's vital and world-embracing quest and his finding of a place in the magical world; the processes and goals of education are taken for granted by the series. While the narrative is presented as a heroic quest, bad teaching is seldom characterised as an evil to be overcome in the same way that Voldemort is. Struggles against various teachers, and against the challenges and terrors of a magical curriculum, in many ways echo and rehearse the greater struggle against Voldemort which Harry faces, but removing Snape or keeping Lupin are not tasks susceptible to heroic resolution in the same way that defeating Death Eaters is—that is, the organisational constraints of the institution are normalised in terms which removes agency from the students. Unlike the reign of Voldemort, poor teaching at Hogwarts cannot be tackled, but must simply be endured.

This largely neutralises the possibilities inherent in the interleaving of the school environment with the utopian resolutions of fantasy. Helfenbein argues

---

[24] Ken Watson, "The Rise, Fall and Remarkable Revival of the School Story," in *Give Them Wings: The Experience of Children's Literature*, edited by Maurice Saxby and Gordon Winch (Melbourne: Macmillan, 1987), 204-5.
[25] Diana Wynne Jones, *Witch Week* (New York, Beech Tree, 1997).
[26] Reimer, "Traditions" 220-221.

that the popular awareness inherent in the Harry Potter series also contains the possibility of resistance against a perceived status quo,[27] so enabling the reading of Rowling's texts as a deliberate educational dystopia. In the case of Hogwarts, however, the essentialist and symbolic elements of Harry's high fantasy battle against Voldemort tend to mask rather than opening for examination the much more mundane and real-world struggles taking place in the classroom. An interesting comparison for a more direct attack on poor teaching *per se* is found in Diana Wynne Jones's *Year of the Griffin* (2000), which offers a self-conscious depiction of an educational system gone badly awry because its focus is external, not on knowledge as holistic system or on the development of individual learner. The distortion of learning in Jones's magical university as a result of the artificial "quests" of the Tours is partially a commentary on a shifting in university processes towards career qualification or in schools towards standardised testing rather than learning for its own sake.[28] Unlike the Hogwarts environment, however, it brandishes the educational problem as a point of focus, not as an uninterrogated backdrop; it is thus far more able to offer resistance to the educational status quo.

On one level this tendency towards an unexamined dystopianism suggests that Rowling's own experience of a troubled British schooling system is one of disenchantment with its processes, but the true concern is in the recognition and identification of such elements by the series' legions of fans. Teaching and learning at Hogwarts reflect a world in which education is seriously in trouble—is engaged in what Belcher and Stephenson define as a process of "fighting difficult, uphill battles."[29] In many parts of the world—in Britain perhaps even less so than many other countries—education is in crisis. The varying demands of funding, regulation, political re-interpretation and socio-economic inequalities mean that many systems no longer have a coherent sense of educational purpose. Nor, in many cases, is there any realistic way to deliver a student-centred curriculum and process which puts individual development ahead of funding constraints, contested curricula or the emphasis on test scores. The lack of positive, definitive educational strategies in the Harry Potter novels reflects the lack of these strategies in a complicated and impenetrable world increasingly charac-

---

[27] Helfenbein, "Conjuring Curriculum", 20.
[28] Diana Wynne Jones, *The Year of the Griffin* (London, Gollancz, 2000).
[29] Belcher and Stephenson, *Teaching Harry Potter* 17.

terised by incoherence in the conceptualisation and administration of the educational process.

Beneath the charm and energy of the magical environment, then, Hogwarts conceals a set of assumptions about education whose negative elements are essentially unquestioned. Learning in a classroom, and the acquisition of knowledge and skills in mundane things such as history or mathematics, is often irrelevant and largely not enjoyable. The series assumes, and encourages its readers to become complicit in assuming, that subjects are not susceptible to true understanding, that learning is often a rote process, and that its transmission via the mechanism of teaching is irretrievably uneven, arbitrary and often elitist. Teachers who do succeed are giving their students practical skills useful in defeating evil rather than any integrated sense of knowledge within a system. Theory comes after practice if it comes at all, and too often the system of magic in Rowling's world is not actually systematic or entirely open to holistic understanding. Given the context of the school environment, a fantastic world in which the child's acquisition of magical power and community is presented in terms which directly address wish fulfilment and empowerment, it is tragic that the necessary adjunct to this is a system of formal education which is at most only partially useful, and more often must be circumvented in order for true learning to happen. It is also interesting in the context of Rowling's call for imaginative empathy, precisely because empathy is so much a central feature of good teaching, and because the Hogwarts environment is so powerfully characterised by not only the lack of teacher empathy for their students, but the lack of student empathy for formal learning.

I do not for an instant suggest that this analysis of the position of teaching and learning at Hogwarts should in any way impair our enjoyment of the series, or its achievements either as romance quest narrative, or as a compelling reinvention of the school story. What I am suggesting, however, is that the particular terms of Rowling's slightly unreflective engagement with the school story in concert with the magical quest—the simultaneously utopian and dystopian presentation of an educational environment—allow for readings which identify both the troubled educational context in which Rowling was writing the series, and the equal resonance with her huge readership of elements which reflect that educational context. I am arguing that the treatment of teaching and learning in the series is an integral and important aspect of the text. It suggests a popular environment which recognises and is receptive to images of the teaching and learning process which deny its centrality, minimise its achievements and take for granted the inevitability of poor teaching and poor student investment in the process. Important lessons, the series says, are only learned outside the classroom; the *Chamber of Secrets* quote which heads this paper demonstrates how utterly irrelevant formal classroom outcomes are deemed in their subordination to the heroic narrative. Fantasy is often a powerful and incisive record of the anxieties and desires of its time. To step aside from the magic and for a moment consider Hogwarts both as a popular fantasy icon and as a *school* demonstrates, I think, that across our education systems, something is very wrong.

Works Cited

Belcher, Catherine L. and Becky Herr Stephenson. *Teaching Harry Potter: The Power of Imagination in Multi-Cultural Classrooms*. New York, Palgrave Macmillan, 2011.

Cawelti, John. G. *Adventure, Mystery and Romance: Formula Stories as Art and Popular Culture*. Chicago: University of Chicago Press, 1976.

Black, Mary S. and Marilyn J. Eisenweine. "Education of the Young Harry Potter: Socialization and Schooling for Wizards." *The Educational Forum* 66 (1), Fall 2001

Dickinson, Renée. "Harry Potter Pedagogy: What We Learn about Teaching and Learning from J.K. Rowling." *The Clearing House* 79 (6), July/August 2006.

Frye, Northrop. *Anatomy of Criticism.* Princeton: Princeton University Press, 1957.

—. *The Secular Scripture: A Study of the Nature of Romance*. Cambridge: Harvard University Press, 1976.

Helfenbein, Robert J. "Conjuring Curricululm, Conjuring Control: A Reading of Resistance in *Harry Potter and the Order of the Phoenix*." *Curriculum Enquiry* 38 (4), 2008.

"J.K. Rowling's Books That Made a Difference, *Oprah Magazine*, accessed 5 May 2012, http://www.oprah.com/omagazine/JK-Rowlings-Books-That-Made-a-Difference/3.

Jones, Diana Wynne. *The Year of the Griffin*. London, Gollancz, 2000.

—. *Witch Week*. New York, Beech Tree, 1997.

Le Guin, Ursula K. *A Wizard of Earthsea*. Harmondsworth: Puffin, 1979.

Orwell, George. "Boys' Weeklies". *Horizon* (1940), Project Gutenberg text, accessed 6 May 2012, http://gutenberg.net.au/ebooks03/0300011h.html#part9.

Quigly, Isabel. *The Heirs of Tom Brown: The English School Story.* London: Chatto and Windus, 1982.

Reimer, Mavis. "Traditions of the school story", The Cambridge Companion to Children's Literature, ed. M.O. Grenby and Andrea Immel. Cambridge: Cambridge UP, 2009.

Maya. "Crouching Lion, Hidden Badger." Mistful's LiveJournal blog, accessed 1 November 2007, http://mistful.livejournal.com/37743.html.

Renton, Jennie. "The story behind the Potter legend: JK Rowling talks about how she created the Harry Potter books and the magic of Harry Potter's world," *Sydney Morning Herald*, October 28, 2001, accessed 6 May 2012. http://www.accio-quote.org/articles/2001/1001-sydney-renton.htm.

Rowling, JK. *Harry Potter and the Philosopher's Stone*. London: Bloomsbury, 1997.

—. *Harry Potter and the Chamber of Secrets*. London: Bloomsbury, 1998.

—. *Harry Potter and the Prisoner of Azkaban*. London: Bloomsbury, 1999.

—. *Harry Potter and the Goblet of Fire*. London: Bloomsbury, 2000.

—. *Harry Potter and the Order of the Phoenix*. London: Bloomsbury, 2003.

—. *Harry Potter and the Half-Blood Prince*. London: Bloomsbury, 2005.

—. *Harry Potter and the Deathly Hallows*. London: Bloomsbury, 2007.

—. "The Fringe Benefits of Failure, and the Importance of Imagination", Harvard Commencement speech 5 June 2008, *Harvard Gazette* 6 June 2008, accessed 28 December 2011, http://news.harvard.edu/gazette/story/2008/06/text-of-j-k-rowling-speech/.

Watson, Ken. "The Rise, Fall and Remarkable Revival of the School Story". *Give Them Wings: The Experience of Children's Literature*, ed. Maurice Saxby and Gordon Winch. Melbourne: Macmillan, 1987.

Hidden in Plain Sight
Response from Joel Hunter

Most readers of the Harry Potter series have not experienced the life of a student at a boarding school. Thus, the dystopic features of Hogwarts that are framed by the English class system—the hereditary privilege of a certain group of students, the multi-generational tradition of a family name attending a distinguished school—are romanaticized and subordinated to other social functions and effects of formal schooling. Jessica Tiffin richly expresses these attributes with devastating precision:

> [T]he Hogwarts curriculum comes down to Magic, Sport and Heroism, the elitism of a magical curriculum echoed by the lionisation of Quidditch heroes (literally, given how often Gryffindor wins) and by the attention accorded to Harry's successes. Intellectual achievement is thus continually overwritten, in a process externalised neatly by the jewels in the house-point hourglasses, by sporting or heroic achievement. Moreover, this supports the focus of the heroic meta-plot on the active and real by denying the value of a humanist education in favour of learning skills in a purely utilitarian sense. (6-7)

The Muggle equivalent of these elements is what Tiffin fears school-age readers of the series recognize and identify with in their own schooling. Curricular choices in subjects like math, reading and writing skills, science, or history are often governed by regimented standards tuned to standardized exams. The ennobling virtues of these subjects are sacrificed on the altars of funding constraints and dubious quantitative measures of teacher and school performance. And so the question Tiffin puts to Rowling is this: why have you not seized the opportunity to critically interrogate the values implicit in an educational system whose purpose is not to cultivate young people into an emancipatory life of intellectual

---

[1] Roger Waters, "Another Brick in the Wall (Part II)," *The Wall*, Columbia Records, 1979.

virtue and improvement, but to discipline and train future workers in a techno-
cratic middle class? For what is the magical curriculum as Rowling reveals it but
the instrumental knowledge of magical technology rather than higher aims of
inquiry for its own sake, self-knowledge, and awakening pleasure in learning
itself?

It is perhaps important that we probe this argument a bit more closely. That
the preponderance of the textual evidence supports Tiffin's characterization of
Hogwarts here and elsewhere in her essay is an unassailable fact. Rowling certainly does describe magical education at Hogwarts as one beset by deep systemic dysfunction. However, Tiffin's inference from this fact to certain effects
on younger readers is less obvious; namely, that the negative images of teaching
and learning in the Harry Potter series produce, or at least permit, an uncritical
judgment that such images mirror formal education in our world.

Tiffin's critical focus is on the image of Hogwarts as a school, a site of formal learning and classroom instruction, with clear depictions of its pedagogy,
curriculum, and institutional culture. She attributes at least part of the popularity
of the books and "the degree of investment from their readers" to more than
"just magical wish-fulfilment and images of agency, but resonance: something
of a connection to and reflection of the lives of the reader" (1). She tells us that
"it is precisely this instrumental interaction between the ideal and the real," the
dysfunctional educational environment and practices of Hogwarts and the educational experience of actual students who read the series, "with which [she] is
concerned" (2). She asks, "*what* images of schooling, and what kinds of judg-
ments about learning, are being proffered to readers? And how are these images
resonating with their own experience?"

At times, Tiffin seems to accept that these images *do* resonate with readers'
experience of schooling. "The lack of positive, definitive educational strategies
in the Harry Potter novels reflects the lack of these strategies in a complicated
and impenetrable world increasingly characterised by incoherence in the conceptualisation and administration of the educational process" (19). If the negative images of teaching and learning at Hogwarts resonate with students' own
experiences of schooling, then Tiffin implies that Rowling has a responsibility to
do more with the portrayal of formal learning than simply reproduce in magical
guise what is broken about our actual systems of education. She remarks several
times that Rowling fails to critically interrogate the dysfunctional education system represented by Hogwarts and that this "misses a great opportunity" (7),

shows a lack of interest "in the exploration of magic as systematic power" (7), takes for granted "the processes and goals of education" (17), and so on. She finds it "tragic that the necessary adjunct to [wish fulfillment and empowerment] is a system of formal education which is at most only partially useful, and more often must be circumvented in order for true learning to happen" (19), because, ultimately, Hogwarts exists "as an uninterrogated backdrop" to the hero narrative (16, 18). Tiffin's objection may be posed hypothetically: if Rowling depicts poor teaching and study habits, then is she obligated to attack them more directly?

Tiffin frequently attaches a derogatory sense to the "active hero" whose anti-intellectual virtues often are allowed to triumph over the system of formal classroom learning. "The notion of the active hero is thus in conflict with the system of formal classroom learning" (8). One response to this opposition between learning and action might appeal to the Nietzschean conceptual dichotomy of the Apollonian versus the Dionysian, the life-denying rational distance required by a life of ethics and reason, versus the life-affirming closeness of sensuous experience and chaos of the instincts. Apollonian Hermione is in dispositional opposition to Dionysian Ron, and it is in Harry's choices and actions that the two must be harmonized. Tiffin implies that the values Hermione represents are overwritten by Harry's practical ability and deeds, the effect of which is to lionize anti-intellectual virtues:

> The relegation of classroom discipline to Hermione parallels the divisions in the school itself: heroes are found in Gryffindor, doing great deeds, whereas Ravenclaw, whose students do take study seriously, is peripheral to the action. The marginalization of students who study diligently and value educational achievement enacts something perilously close to the "swot" stereotype, suggesting that such students are less interesting than the active heroes, and reinforcing the casual quality of actual teaching with a clear devaluation of learning itself. (9)

Ultimately, I find this the weakest part of Tiffin's argument. It seems that she is valorizing book-learning at the expense of wisdom and other virtues. Ravenclaw, like the other Houses, is far from monolithic. The same house that welcomes Ollivander and Luna Lovegood also embraces the vainglorious, manipulative Lockhart and weak-willed, but ambitious Quirrell. If the "swot" stereotype is one ditch to avoid in the representation of characters who take their studies seriously, then perhaps the other ditch is that of overweening regard for the virtues of the head over those of the heart. Knowledge puffs up, Rowling may be warning us would-be denizens of Ravenclaw. To accept this counsel does not entail a devaluation of learning.

As many readers have wondered, it is not obvious why Hermione is in Gryffindor rather than Ravenclaw. I think it is because Hermione treads wisely and steadily between the two ditches that border the life of the mind. "Books! And cleverness! There are more important things – friendship and bravery and – oh Harry – be *careful*!" (SS 287). So while Hermione is rightly recognized as "the cleverest witch of [her] age" (PA 346), she subdues her intellectual gifts for the even more difficult task of moral improvement. Her integrity, honesty, and courage do not exclude her relentless pursuit of learning and theoretical under-standing, they enable her to regulate the exercise of her intellectual life and the application of its fruits. Hermione does not sport the Blue and Bronze because she does not accept Ravenclaw's dictum that "the cleverest would always be the best" (GF 177). In an institution defined by division, Hermione transcends the Houses' exclusive identities, aspiring to be better than the best that any single House can claim.

Tiffin concludes with a suggestively elliptical assertion: "consider[ing] Hogwarts both as a popular fantasy icon and as a *school* demonstrates…that across our education systems, something is very wrong" (20). An unwritten, tantalizing *with...* invites us to consider at least two very different causes as the indicator of what Tiffin thinks is "very wrong" across our education systems. Is the popularity the series enjoys the disturbing indicator because it suggests that readers respond to the "wildly thrilling and romantic" details of life at Hogwarts, allowing it to override the judgment that Hogwarts is an utter failure as an actual school? If so, then it is understandable why Tiffin is concerned that readers thereby reward Rowling in spite of her failure to interrogate the dysfunctional system of formal education represented by Hogwarts. Or is the disturbing indi-cator that Hogwarts' utter failure as an actual school mirrors the negative as-sumptions about and experiences of the actual state of education in societies that have a significant number of Harry Potter readers? "The series assumes, and encourages its readers to become complicit in assuming, that subjects are not susceptible to true understanding, that learning is often a rote process, and that its transmission via the mechanism of teaching is irretrievably uneven, arbitrary and often elitist" (19). Does this not mirror the actual experience of many stu-dents and actual regressive pedagogical practices that "teach to the test" and prioritize performance on standardized exams? If so, then it is equally under-standable why Tiffin believes Rowling shoulders some responsibility to more directly attack the poor teaching and devalued status of book and formal class-room learning. If Rowling thinks Hogwarts curriculum, pedagogy and institu-tional culture somewhat reflect the realities of our educational systems, then does she owe us more than a laugh and a shrug in response to it, perhaps some-thing more sardonic like Waters's *The Wall*?

I think it is important to distinguish between the analytical and the normative claims in Tiffin's argument. Does the "charm and energy" of Hogwarts conceal "a set of assumptions about education whose negative elements are essentially unquestioned?" Tiffin thinks so; however, she considers the alternative reading of Robert Helfenbein,[2] who argues that the popular awareness of bad teaching inherent in the Harry Potter series "enables the reading of Rowling's texts as a deliberate educational dystopia" (18). Tiffin marshals a genre rebuttal to this counterclaim, arguing that the narrative demands and moral polarities of the Hogwarts saga as a romance quest narrative subordinate any critical response to education within the series, with Rowling allowing the utopian charms of Hog-warts to mask the devaluation of learning within formal education. I am not fully convinced by this genre argument because I think it proves too much. At the risk of too tangential an analysis, I will explain why.

Wizarding society is dysfunctional in all its institutions: the legal system, the financial system, health and welfare, law enforcement, government administra-tion, and so on. Tiffin's genre-based objection to the "uninterrogated backdrop" of Hogwarts schooling could be transposed to any of the social institutions of the wizarding world. Indeed, her scathing catalog of pedagogical abuses and the marginalization of learning within the culture of Hogwarts reminded me of Ben-jamin Barton's opening paragraph in "Harry Potter and the Half-Crazed Bureau-cracy." The depiction of the political sphere in the Harry Potter series includes a government that:

> tortured children for lying; designed its prison specifically to suck all life and hope out of the inmates; placed citizens in that prison without a hearing; or-dered the death penalty without a trial; allowed the powerful, rich, or famous to control policy; selectively prosecuted crimes (the powerful go unpunished and

---

[2] Robert J. Helfenbein and Sydney K. Brown, "Conjuring Curriculum, Conjuring Control: A Reading of Resistance in *Harry Potter and the Order of the Phoenix*," *Curriculum Inquiry* 38(4): 499-513, Sep 2008.

the unpopular face trumped-up charges); conducted criminal trials without defense counsel; used truth serum to force confessions; maintained constant surveillance over all citizens; offered no elections and no democratic lawmaking process; and controlled the press [...][3]

Despite the obvious tyranny of the political society in which Hogwarts functions, the Ministry of Magic, too, is a magical environment presented with a veneer of "charm and energy": memos flying from office to office, a massive seat of government concealed in the heart of Muggle London in plain sight, entry gained through public toilets, and so on. But are the negative elements of the Ministry essentially unquestioned? I do not think so. In the tradition of unsparing satire, the very lightheartedness of the depiction underscores rather than conceals the penetrating and devastating criticism of the Ministry inherent in the series.

"But Hogwarts is for kids while the Ministry mainly registers to older readers," so an objection to the comparison might begin. However, we do not experience the full force and extent of Ministry corruption and tyranny until *Order* and later; the children we grow to know through the first four books have grown themselves, have had to confront so-called "adult themes" of death and dying, social oppression, untrustworthy authority figures, and so on. Moreover, it is in *Order* where we see the Ministry intrude forcefully into Hogwarts. Gone are the amusements of the comically inept Binns, Lockhart and Trelawney (indeed, the latter character becoming a sympathetic and dramatic focal point when she is victimized and dehumanized by the dictatorial Umbridge). The underlying dysfunction of the educational system is brought into sharp relief by the reality of it being subordinate to the agenda of mostly invisible political forces and powers. The "charms and energy" of Hogwarts largely fall away halfway through the saga as Rowling's satire takes shape within the context of Harry's heroic journey. If the narrative demands of the multiple genres interwoven in the Harry Potter series obscure readers' critical response to the depiction of teaching and learning, we might reasonably expect the effects of genre to dull Rowling's commentary on the other social institutions that comprise wizarding society. Since genre does *not* seem to trump the implicit critique in these other cases, at least in the latter half of the series, and since education is one of these social institutions, then it seems Helfenbein is closer to the mark. Readers are perhaps

---

[3] Benjamin Barton, "Harry Potter and the Half-Crazed Bureaucracy," *Michigan Law Review* 104(6): 1523-38, May 2006: 1523f.

no more likely to be encouraged to accept assumptions about poor pedagogy and intellectual standards—even if they have experienced them—than they are about a government that operates in defiance of the principles of due process. Further scholarship might investigate the unanswered question that then remains: how do the narrative demands of the heroic quest romance and school stories coexist with, and perhaps even reinforce, the satire?

As we see the insulating layers of utopian and nostalgic elements crumble under the pressures dynamically unfolding after Voldemort's return at the end of *Goblet*, Rowling invites us to consider that the values and effectiveness of any educational institution are only as strong as the broader social context in which they are supported, ignored, or contested. Parenthetically, of the many things Tom Riddle and Harry Potter have in common, we cannot overlook their common success as Hogwarts students. As others have pointed out, Harry's sense of entitlement and privilege is cultivated in the same society that produced "Lord Voldemort" from the pathetic and wounded young man Tom Riddle.[4] Voldemort is not some malevolent alien entity beamed down into the middle of twentieth century England. The wizarding world is deeply complicit in the creation and success of Voldemort, and Hogwarts is not exempt from critical scrutiny for its role in shaping who he becomes and why.[5]

As the dystopic magnitude of wizarding society unfolds in *Order*, *Prince* and *Hallows*, readers may inevitably look back and ask "How did we ever get here?" only to find indicators of just how horrid Hogwarts schooling is in the first half of the series. Wizarding social institutions did not collapse overnight in virtue of the events that transpired in Little Hangleton graveyard; their brokenness was hid from us in plain sight all along because we, entranced like Harry, were still learning the ropes of this new society in *Stone*, *Chamber* and *Prisoner*. Rowling leaves it to her readers to imagine otherwise rather than deliver an unambiguous ideological alternative to oppression, tyrannical civil society, and the crisis in formal education.

---

[4] See, for example, Christopher Bell, "Riddle Me This: The Moral Disengagement of Lord Voldemort," in *Legilimens!: Perspectives in Harry Potter Studies*, edited by Christopher Bell (Newcastle upon Tyne: Cambridge Scholars Publishing, 2013), 43-65.

[5] I would argue that the "twinning" of Tom and Harry decisively subverts the apparent moral polarities of the overarching hero-villain narrative arc, and the magical quest romance becomes a conventional backdrop to the morally complex characterizations of protagonists and antagonists, and the institutional crises at all levels of society in which they are ensnared.

Works Cited

Barton, Benjamin. "Harry Potter and the Half-Crazed Bureaucracy." *Michigan Law Review* 104(6): 1523-38, May 2006: 1523-1538.

Bell, Christopher. "Riddle Me This: The Moral Disengagement of Lord Voldemort," in *Legilimens!: Perspectives in Harry Potter Studies*, edited by Christopher Bell. Newcastle upon Tyne: Cambridge Scholars Publishing, 2013: 43-65.

Helfenbein, Robert J. and Sydney K. Brown. "Conjuring Curriculum, Conjuring Control: A Reading of Resistance in *Harry Potter and the Order of the Phoenix*." *Curriculum Inquiry* 38(4), Sep 2008: 499-513.

CHAPTER 2

The Death of Death
in the Death of the Boy Who Lived:
The Morality of Mortality in Harry Potter
John Anthony Dunne

J. K. Rowling's riveting seven-part narrative relates to many common experiences throughout the world, which has undoubtedly contributed to the success of *Harry Potter*. Most notable among these common experiences is death. As John Granger has said, "Harry Potter is about love and death, but if I had to choose one over the other, I'd say the books are about death."[1] Indeed, the magic and mythology of *Harry Potter* are largely related to death, as in: (a) Harry's survival of the *Avada Kedavra* curse twice, (b) the Philosopher's Stone, (c) the Ghosts of Hogwarts, (d) the death and rebirth of Fawkes the Phoenix, (e) the phenomenon of *priori incantatem,* (f) the mythology of the Thestrals, (g) the zombified Inferi, (h) the portraits of deceased Hogwarts professors, (i) the Resurrection stone, (j) Horcruxes, and elsewhere. To get an important perspective on this, it is necessary to go back to the beginning.

Harry Potter was originally conceived in J. K. Rowling's mind during a train ride in June 1990 when her mother Anne was near the end of a decade long struggle with multiple sclerosis. Anne passed away later that year on 30 December 1990.[2] *Harry Potter* is therefore a story born in the pain and grief of bereavement. No doubt the vision of a boy wizard provided a welcome distraction from the domestic struggles in Rowling's life, but additionally, the pervasiveness

---

[1] John Granger, *How Harry Cast His Spell: The Meaning Behind the Mania of J. K. Rowling's Bestselling Books* (Carol Stream, IL: Tyndale House, 2008), 63. Cf. also Colin Manlove who notes that Harry Potter's "deepest theme is death." Colin Manlove, *The Order of Harry Potter: Literary Skill in the Hogwarts Epic* (Cheshire, CT: Winged Lion Press, 2010), 196.

[2] Sean Smith, *J. K. Rowling: A Biography* (London: Michael O'Mara, 2001), 97.

of death in *Harry Potter*—and the associated hope of transcending death—was most likely affected by Rowling's personal experiences.

Within the secondary literature on *Harry Potter*, the theme of death has been addressed thoroughly, yet one area where attention is lacking is on the moral value attributed to death.[3] The central question, then, is discerning whether there is a coherent presentation within *Harry Potter* regarding the goodness, badness, or neutrality of death. Although it has not been noted, it is precisely here where a tension emerges. The problem is created by the use of the Apostle Paul's words in 1 Corinthians 15.26 on the Potter tombstone in the chapter "Godric's Hollow" from *Deathly Hallows*—"the last enemy that shall be destroyed is death." The present study will therefore seek to demonstrate the tension between this epitaph and the rest of the *Harry Potter* series and suggest three possible ways to alleviate it.

Death in *Harry Potter*: A Tension?

1 Corinthians 15.26 is an appropriate place to start this enquiry into the morality of death for at least two reasons. First, Rowling has admitted that the epitaph about death as the last enemy is "the theme for the entire series."[4] Elsewhere she also stated that both the Potter epitaph and the inscription on the

---

[3] For select essays related to the theme of death in the Harry Potter series see e.g. John Granger, "The *Deathly Hallows* Epigraphs: *Aeschylus* and Penn Point to the Meaning of Harry Potter," in *Hog's Head Conversations: Essays on Harry Potter*, vol. 1, edited by Travis Prinzi, 43-63 (Allentown, PA: Zossima Press, 2009); *idem*, "The Triumph of Love Over Death," and "Victory over Death" in *How Harry Cast His Spell*, 63-76, 225-243; Charles Taliaferro, "The Real Secret of the Phoenix: Moral Regeneration Through Death," in *The Ultimate Harry Potter and Philosophy: Hogwarts for Muggles*, edited by Gregory Bassham, 229-245 (Hoboken, NJ: John Wiley & Sons, 2010); Jonathan L. Walls and Jerry L. Walls, "Beyond Godric's Hollow: Life after Death and the Search for Meaning," in *The Ultimate Harry Potter and Philosophy: Hogwarts for Muggles*, edited by Gregory Bassham, 246-257 (Hoboken, NJ: John Wiley & Sons, 2010); Michael W. Austin, "Why Harry and Socrates Decide to Die: Virtue and the Common Good," in *The Ultimate Harry Potter and Philosophy: Hogwarts for Muggles*, edited by Gregory Bassham, 258-270 (Hoboken, NJ: John Wiley & Sons, 2010); Elizabeth Baird Hardy, "Horcruxes in Faerie Land: Edmund Spenser's Influence on Voldemort's Efforts to Elude Death," in *Harry Potter for Nerds: Essays for Fans, Academics, and Lit Geeks*, edited by Travis Prinzi, 225-240 (Oklahoma City: Unlocking Press, 2011); J. Patrick Pazdziora, "'Just behind the Veil,' Death in Harry Potter and the Fairytales of George MacDonald," in *Harry Potter for Nerds: Essays for Fans, Academics, and Lit Geeks*, edited by Travis Prinzi, 241-268 (Oklahoma City: Unlocking Press, 2011).

[4] Nancy Gibbs, "Person of the Year 2007: Runners-up: J. K. Rowling," *TIME*, Wednesday, December 19, 2007.

tombstone of Kendra and Ariana Dumbledore taken from Matthew 6.21—
"where your treasure is, there will your heart be also"—together "sum up" and
"epitomize the whole series."[5] Second, the Potter epitaph on death appears to be
unambiguous. Death is an *enemy*, which presumably implies that it is bad or
evil. As an enemy, death is depicted as something that can be overcome. Yet is
the Potter epitaph alone sufficient to warrant the conclusion that death is presented as evil in *Harry Potter*? What might "defeating death" look like in the
series? Additionally, is "defeating death" actually commended anywhere? There
are at least three factors in the series that require a certain hesitation on our part
before concluding the matter.

First, certain statements seem to convey that death is morally neutral, or perhaps even good. As an example, in *The Sorcerer's Stone*, Dumbledore explains
to Harry that Nicholas Flamel had chosen to destroy the Stone that produces the
Elixir of Life, which Voldemort was pursuing through the possession of Prof.
Quirrell. Harry realizes that the destruction of the Stone means that Flamel had
consigned himself to death, but Dumbledore reassures him that Flamel's death
would be like "going to bed after a very, *very* long day" and more generally that
"to the well-organized mind, death is but the next great adventure."[6]

Second, at a few points in the narrative it is explicitly stated that there are
worse things than death. The centaur Firenze explains to Harry in *The Sorcerer's
Stone* that drinking unicorn blood can keep someone alive for a time, though it
places one under a curse. Harry asks Firenze curiously if death would be better
than being cursed forever and Firenze admits that it would be.[7] This is reminiscent of the Dementor's Kiss and the loss of one's soul, which Remus Lupin tells
Harry is certainly worse than death.[8] Similarly, in the duel between Voldemort
and Dumbledore at the end of *The Order of the Phoenix*, Voldemort declares that
there is nothing worse than death, yet Dumbledore asserts that Voldemort's failure to recognize that there are some things worse than death was his greatest

[5] Shawn Adler, "'Harry' Author J. K. Rowling opens up about books' Christian Imagery," *MTV*, October 17, 2007.
[6] J. K. Rowling, *Harry Potter and the Sorcerer's Stone* (New York, NY: Scholastic,
1999), 297. Referenced hereafter as SS.
[7] SS, 258.
[8] J. K. Rowling, *Harry Potter and the Prisoner of Azkaban* (New York, NY: Scholastic,
1999), 247. Referenced hereafter as PoA.

weakness.[9] Prof. Slughorn explains to the young Tom Riddle that "[d]eath would be preferable" to splitting one's soul into Horcruxes.[10]

Third, the quest for immortality is regarded as an evil pursuit. Colin Manlove is probably correct to note that Flamel's destruction of the Philosopher's Stone at age 665 is highly informative.[11] To live any longer would have been wicked (hence 666). The evil of immortality can be seen most clearly through the physical transformation that Voldemort undergoes in the process of creating Horcruxes, demonstrating that the pursuit of immortality is inhuman.

As a further development of the third point, an interesting perspective on the quest for immortality can be found in "The Tale of the Three Brothers", which contains the mythology of the Deathly Hallows.[12] Although the three brothers escaped death by building a bridge over a tumultuous river that had previously claimed many lives, they were unwittingly lured to their own deaths by magical items they presumed would help them achieve immortality. With the Elder wand it was believed that no one could defeat the possessor, with the Resurrection Stone it was thought that death could be mocked by the reversal of death, and with the invisibility cloak its owner could hide from death, although the concealment it offers is ephemeral. As Xenophilius Lovegood explained to Harry, Ron, and Hermione, the legend of the Hallows was that the possessor of all three would become the "master of death."[13] Yet attempting to transcend death in this manner is explicitly condemned within the narrative. Even the beloved Dumbledore falls prey to the lure of immortality in his attempt to gather the three Deathly Hallows as he admits to Harry in the aethereal "King's Cross station." This was part of Dumbledore's downfall and he admits that he was similar to Voldemort in this pursuit.[14] In this context Dumbledore declares to Harry:

---

[9] J. K. Rowling, *Harry Potter and the Order of the Phoenix* (New York, NY: Scholastic, 2003), 481.

[10] J. K. Rowling, *Harry Potter and the Half-Blood Prince* (New York, NY: Scholastic, 2005), 497. Referenced hereafter as HBP.

[11] Manlove, The Order of Harry Potter, 13.

[12] Dumbledore writes in his commentary that the main lesson of the tale could not be any more clear, "Human efforts to evade or overcome death are always doomed to disappointment." See J. K. Rowling, *The Tales of Beedle the Bard,* (New York: Scholastic, 2008) 94.

[13] J. K. Rowling, *Harry Potter and the Deathly Hallows* (New York, NY: Scholastic, 2007), 410. Referenced hereafter as DH.

[14] DH, 713.

You are the true master of death, because the true master does not seek to run away from Death. He accepts that he must die, and understands that there are far, far worse things in the living world than dying.[15]

As this brief overview suggests, many of the statements regarding death in *Harry Potter* do not appear to cohere with the Godric's Hollow epitaph, which asserts that death is the last enemy that will be destroyed. So how can we reconcile this apparent inconsistency? On the one hand, death is not the worst possible thing and the quest for immortality is an inhuman pursuit; on the other hand, as the Potter epitaph asserts, death is an enemy that ought to be defeated. How then is the epitaph to be reconciled with the broader perspective on death and become integrated within the narrative? There are at least three ways to help alleviate the tension caused by this apparent contradiction, which will be addressed in the following three sections of this study. The first point is determining precisely how death is mortal in the epitaph. Then subsequently the focus of the second and third points pertain to the precise referent for "death," noting the distinction between general and specific statements about death, and finally, noting the implications this has for viewing Voldemort as a personification of death—the last enemy. The remainder of this study seeks to demonstrate how these three points ease the tension previously outlined.

Death Is Mortal

The first way to alleviate the tension between the Potter epitaph and the broader sentiment of the *Harry Potter* series is to recognize the precise way in which death is depicted as mortal and therefore able to be defeated. Indeed, the tension is made explicit by the fact that Harry initially finds the Potter epitaph to be a "Death Eater idea."[16] The confusion arises because the Death Eaters are centrally concerned with seeking immortality in the present life, but this is not the perspective of the epitaph.

As Hermione explains in her interpretation of the inscription, "It doesn't mean defeating death in the way the Death Eaters mean it, Harry. [...] It means…you know…living beyond death. Living after death."[17] Hermione rightly admits that the sentiment of the epitaph does not cohere with the ideology of

---

[15] DH, 720-721.
[16] DH, 328.
[17] DH, 328.

the Death Eaters. In other words, she explains that it's not about a continued
immortality in this present life, since the defeat takes place "after death" and
"beyond death." Her interpretation is good as far as it goes, although it lacks
precision in regards to the original context of the citation. Yet we cannot fault
Hermione for this, since she was merely interpreting the text as presented on the
tombstone. The more relevant question is determining how Rowling has utilized
this text. Does she demonstrate a concern for the context of the citation, or is her
interest more atomistic?

Contextually, the Apostle Paul was not arguing *simply* for "living after
death" as Hermione stated—although that much is correct—but additionally, he
was concerned with *"life after* life after death."[18] That is to say, he was arguing
for bodily resurrection.[19] Certainly Rowling is not developing a nuanced perspective on the Christian doctrine of the resurrection in *Harry Potter.* However,
there may be a few hints along these lines in the remaining portion of the chapter on Godric's Hollow, such as: (a) when Harry thinks about "living after death"
in relation to his parents he thinks about *their bodies*—their moldering remains,[20] (b) Harry and Hermione visited Godric's Hollow on Christmas Eve—
likely evoking the Christian narrative connected to Jesus as the one who defeated death through his resurrection, and (c) Hermione magically creates "a wreath
of Christmas roses" for Harry to place at his parents' tombstone because all the
plants nearby were "leafless and frozen," which could provide suggestive resurrection imagery.[21] For the moment, judgment regarding Rowling's contextual
sensitivity should be suspended until the final section. However, the main concern of this study is not with the original context of 1 Corinthians 15.26, but
with the new narratival context that it has been placed within. Hermione's point
that the epitaph is about "living after death" is certainly closer to the meaning of
the passage than to the ethos of the Death Eaters, which is the main point to be

---

[18] This phraseology is borrowed from N. T. Wright, *Surprised by Hope* (London: SPCK,
2007), 148-152.
[19] The epitaph is taken from a larger section that comprises the Apostle Paul's apologetic attempt to convince the Corinthian church of the bodily resurrection of Jesus. The passage goes beyond posthumous existence, and envisions a time in which there is no more
death and a time in which the effects of death are removed: an era without corruption,
decay, or degeneration. Thus, death is described as an enemy in the original context because it is contrary to the role of re-creation and new creation that the Apostle Paul believes God is accomplishing through the resurrection of Jesus.
[20] DH, 328.
[21] DH, 329.

made here. Death is not defeated in the way that the Death Eaters suppose, that is, by becoming immortal *in this life.* As Hermione makes explicit—"living beyond death"—the defeat of death expressed in the Potter epitaph is not attained outside of death.

Death—A General or Specific Referent?

The second way to alleviate the tension caused by the Potter epitaph is to distinguish between *specific* and *general* statements about death. The statement about death as an enemy on the Potter epitaph is not focusing on individual deaths, but on death *generally.* Thus we could speak of degeneration and decay broadly. Conversely, seemingly positive or neutral statements about death in *Harry Potter,* such as the similarities between death and sleeping, are *specific* in nature, referring to an individual's subjective experience of death. Death is not the worst possible thing that an individual can experience, and if one approaches their own death with the proper mindset there is nothing to fear. However, when the perspective broadens outside of the individual's death, as in the Potter epitaph, death can be considered evil without contradicting the sentiment elsewhere.

When addressed in contemporary philosophical discussions, the morality of death can be addressed from the perspective of the survivors—those who experience bereavement—or with a focus on the subject, that is, the one experiencing death. In fact, arguments have been presented for both the goodness and the badness of death from specific/subjective experience. For instance, Thomas Nagel and others have suggested that death is bad because of what it deprives a person of, since it is the loss of life.[22] On the other hand, one philosopher has argued for the non-badness of death with an analogy from deafness. If a deaf woman walks by a poor performance of a Mozart symphony it is not bad to the deaf woman because she is unable to hear it.[23] In a similar manner, since death leads to non-existence and an "experiential blank"—as naturalists would af-

---

[22] Thomas Nagel, "Death," in *Mortal Questions* (London: Cambridge University Press, 1979), 3. So also, Anthony L. Brueckner and John Martin Fischer, "Why is Death Bad?" in *The Metaphysics of Death,* edited by John Martin Fischer (Stanford: Stanford University Press, 1993), 222.

[23] Stephen E. Rosenbaum, "How to Be Dead and Not Care: A Defense of Epicurus," in *The Metaphysics of Death,* ed. John Martin Fischer (Stanford: Stanford University Press, 1993), 123.

firm—it cannot be bad for the dead person because they do not experience anything bad.[24] This would cohere with Sirius' post-mortem discussion with Harry
mediated through the Resurrection Stone in *Deathly Hallows*. When Harry asks
if it hurts to die, Sirius denies it—"not at all" he says—and asserts that death is
"Quicker and easier than falling asleep."[25] Sirius' words convey the idea that
death's badness is linked to the harm or pain (in other words, evil) that it causes
a person. Yet it is clear that this perspective is intentionally narrow, focusing on
the specific/subjective experience of death and dying. To revert to the analogy of
the poor Mozart performance, it is still bad in actuality, regardless of the deaf
woman's inability to experience it as bad. This is why the *general–specific* distinction is a helpful one; there are different ways in which death can be both bad
and not bad depending on the perspective.

Therefore, the Potter epitaph from 1 Corinthians 15.26 only appears to be inconsistent with the broader *Harry Potter* series when it is not recognized as a
general and *universal* statement in contrast to the *specific* statements elsewhere.
The perspective of the epitaph that death is an enemy and therefore evil by consequence is not about specific incidences of individualized death, but refers to
death generally and universally. This helps to alleviate the tension between the
epitaph and the broader narrative of *Harry Potter.*

Death: The Last Enemy

The third way that the apparent tension caused by the Potter epitaph is alleviated—and the most crucial of the three points—is by recognizing that the Potter epitaph provides a perspective on Voldemort. When the epitaph is translated
into the narrative world of *Harry Potter* it is Voldemort who is the greatest enemy, and consequently, he becomes a personification of Death. (At this point in
the study "death" will designate empirical death, and "Death" will designate the
personification). As was mentioned in the previous section, the perspective of
the Potter epitaph regarding death is *general* rather than *specific*, and therefore,
by referring to this broad notion of death as "the last enemy" and speaking of its
future defeat, death appears to be depicted as a personified foe. This makes the
application of the Potter epitaph to Voldemort thematically appropriate. The as-

---

[24] Rosenbaum, "How to Be Dead," 122.
[25] DH, 699. Sleep as a euphemism for death is common in biblical literature (cf. e.g.
Matt. 27.52; 1 Thess. 4.13-15; 1 Cor. 15.6, 18, 20; Acts 7.60; 13.36; 2 Pet. 3.4).

sociation of a broad notion of death with a personification of Death can be seen, for instance, in the poetry of John Donne, "And Death shall be no more. Death, thou shalt die."[26] To be sure, Voldemort wears many hats. He can rightly be viewed as Satanic, the incarnation of Evil, a quasi-Hitler figure, and more. Yet his role as a personification of Death should not be missed. One of the closest articulations of this is from Joel Hunter, who asserts that Voldemort realized that:

> [. . .] to seek to master the eminent qualities of Death—power and invinci-bility—one must transform into something that Death cannot defeat. One must outdo Death at His own work. So in order to defeat Death Voldemort makes himself Death's pupil and servant. Voldemort is convinced by this inward-spiraling logic that he can turn the tables and become Death's master.[27]

As Hunter explains, Voldemort attempts to beat Death at His own game. Yet this could be pressed further to suggest that Voldemort becomes more than a mere "pupil and servant" of Death, becoming a personification of Death itself. Be-sides this minor quibble, it is clear from Hunter's comments that there is a strong affinity between Death and Voldemort. Seven points should be mentioned to help make the case that Voldemort is in fact a personification of Death.

First, the name "Voldemort" itself points in this direction. In French, *vol* means "to fly" and *mort* means "death." The word *de* is a preposition that can mean either "of" or "from." Thus, Voldemort's name means, "flight of/from death." Perhaps there is an intentional ambiguity at play with the use of *de*.[28] Voldemort is the *Flight of Death from death*, that is to say, Voldemort is a *mortal* personification of Death, as in the epitaph from 1 Corinthians 15.26, since death is there seen as defeatable. This coheres with Voldemort's quest for immortality, as he declares at the end of *The Goblet of Fire* that he has "gone further than anybody along the path that leads to immortality" and that his goal is "to con-quer death."[29] Thus, Voldemort, as personified Death, does not want to die, but

---

[26] Donald R. Dickson, *John Donne's Poetry*, A Norton Critical Edition (New York, NY: W. W. Norton & Company, 2007), 138-139.
[27] See Joel Hunter, "Technological Anarchism: The Meaning of Magic in Harry Potter," in *Harry Potter for Nerds: Essays for Fans, Academics, and Lit Geeks,* ed. Travis Prinzi (Oklahoma City: Unlocking Press, 2011), 120-121.
[28] This subtlety should not surprise us since Rowling studied French at the University of Exeter, spent her third academic year in Paris, and worked for Amnesty International in London as a secretary for Francophone Africa. See Smith, *J. K. Rowling,* 80, 87-88, 94.
[29] GoF, 653.

rather wants to take as many as he can along with him—to death. Misery loves company.

Second, Voldemort's followers are known as Death Eaters, implying that death provides their sustenance. When they have killed someone[30] the Dark Mark summons them with the magical spell, "Morsmordre."[31] This spell, like most of Rowling's spells, has a Latin background. A possible translation is "death bite" or "the bite of death," stemming from *mors* in Latin (and *mort* in French), meaning death, and *mordre*, meaning "bite" (in both Latin and French).[32]

Third, the way many people refer to death with euphemisms—such as "passing away," "kicking the bucket," and others—corresponds to the avoidance of Voldemort's name with "You Know Who" and "He Who Must Not Be Named." The fear of death in *Harry Potter* is in many ways akin to the fear of Voldemort's name. There are likewise a few instances in which the word "death" itself appears to be suggestively used as a euphemistic reference to Voldemort. In the Graveyard at the end of *The Goblet of Fire,* the revitalized Voldemort summons to Harry, "bow to death."[33] Also, note Rita Skeeter's comment about Harry—"he's looked death in the face"[34]—referring to the encounter when Voldemort killed his parents.

Fourth, death is specifically the *last* enemy in the Potter epitaph. Directly after Harry and Hermione read the inscription on the Potter Tombstone is the Bathilda Bagshot incident in which Voldemort utilized his snake Nagini as a trap.[35] At one point Harry passes into a visionary sequence in which he relives the encounter of Voldemort killing his family, although from Voldemort's perspective.[36] Since the previous chapter in *Deathly Hallows* ends with Harry finding his parents' tombstone and the citation from 1 Corinthians 15.26, it is probable that these chapters are to be interpreted together—being the record of

[30] PoA, 142.

[31] J. K. Rowling, *Harry Potter and the Goblet of Fire* (New York, NY: Scholastic, 2000), 128. Referenced hereafter as GoF.

[32] The suggestion that "Morsmordre" has a Norwegian background—and therefore means something like "mother killers"—is less likely because Rowling's studies in French and Classics provides a far better explanation, and "bite of death" is much more closely linked to the designation "Death *Eater.*"

[33] GoF, 660.

[34] GoF, 306.

[35] DH, 330-349.

[36] DH, 342-345.

what happened at Godric's Hollow. Thus, the notion of "the last enemy" could imply the sequence of destroying Horcruxes, which culminates in the battle with Voldemort—"the last enemy." This is probable because none of the remaining Horcruxes had been destroyed yet in *Deathly Hallows*, and the first one destroyed in the quest of Harry, Ron, and Hermione to destroy all the Horcruxes is dealt with just a few pages later in "The Silver Doe."[37] This notion of Horcruxes being related to how "the last enemy" is translated into the narrative is especially interesting because they are only created through death and therefore reinforce the link between death and Voldemort's "life."[38]

Fifth, apocalyptic imagery is associated with Voldemort. With the introduction of the *Harry Potter* series it is compelling that Voldemort's "death" is accompanied by shooting stars and the ominous presence of owls in the Muggle world.[39] Apocalyptic symbols such as these and other heavenly portents can be found throughout ancient apocalyptic literature and other texts that share the worldview of apocalypticism.[40] A few examples should be noted here. In the famous "Olivet Discourse" Jesus declares, "Immediately after the suffering of those days the sun will be darkened, and the moon will not give its light; the stars will fall from heaven, and the powers of heaven will be shaken" (Matt. 24.29 NRSV; cf. also Mk. 13.25, Lk. 21.25). Referring to the great dragon, Revelation 12.4a states, "His tail swept down a third of the stars of heaven and threw them to the earth" (NRSV).[41] Since the ultimate hope of apocalyptic thought was the transcendence of death,[42] the apocalyptic imagery at the outset of the *Harry Potter* series associated with Voldemort's "death" is highly suggestive, providing a further indication that Voldemort personifies Death.

---

[37] DH, 370-377.

[38] The link is also intriguing because Horcruxes are created through committing murder (HBP, 498).

[39] SS, 6.

[40] A standard definition of apocalyptic literature is this: "a genre of revelatory literature with a narrative framework, in which a revelation is mediated by an otherworldly being to a human recipient, disclosing a transcendent reality which is both temporal, insofar as it envisages eschatological salvation, and spatial insofar as it involves another, supernatural world." See John J. Collins, *Apocalyptic Imagination: An Introduction to Jewish Apocalyptic Literature* (Grand Rapids: Eerdmans, 1998), 5.

[41] Cf. e.g. Isa. 13.10; Dan. 8.10; Amos 8:9; Joel 2.10, 30-31; 3.15-16; Rev. 6.13; 8.12. See also *4 Ezra* 5.4-6; 7.38-41; *Sibylline Oracle* 5.512-531.

[42] John J. Collins, "Apocalyptic Eschatology as Transcendence of Death," *Catholic Biblical Quarterly* 36 (1974): 21-43.

Sixth, the structure of *Harry Potter* is such that the story begins and ends with the "death" of Voldemort accomplished through the death of another. In the beginning of the narrative it is the death of Lily that accomplishes this and at the end it is Harry's death. Thus, the death of Voldemort through another's death—the death of Death through death—functions as bookends to the entire narrative. This reinforces the problem with immortality in the narrative and the emphasis on the point that death cannot be defeated apart from death. To go further, it is possible to discern an antithetical correspondence in the graveyard scene at the end of *The Goblet of Fire*. In that pivotal scene Voldemort is given new life through the life-blood of Harry, which is the same protective blood of Lily—"[b]lood of the enemy...forcibly taken...you will...resurrect your foe."[43] The *Harry Potter* story begins and ends with the death of Voldemort through the death of Lily and Harry, and at the center—the moment when Voldemort regains his power, which provides an obvious turning point in the narrative—the life of Voldemort is regained through the life of Lily/Harry (their blood). Thus, structurally-speaking the death of Death (Voldemort) through another's death provides the bookends to the narrative that eases the tension within it. This observation could be utilized for a structural analysis of *Harry Potter*, contributing to observations regarding a macro-level chiastic structure, as in the work of J. Steve Lee,[44] or it could be utilized by those advocating a ring-composition of the series, such as John Granger.[45] It is beyond the scope of the present article to address issues of structure in any depth, but this observation is offered for the contribution of further structural analysis of *Harry Potter*, as neither Granger nor Lee mentioned this correspondence in their recent essays.

Seventh, and finally, is the nature of Harry's scar. As the final lines of *Deathly Hallows* state, "The scar had not pained Harry for nineteen years. All was well."[46] It is possible that this contains further influence from 1 Corinthians 15—the biblical chapter that contains the passage cited on the Potter tombstone. This additional influence of the broader context of 1 Corinthians 15 helps to

---

[43] GoF, 642.

[44] J. Steve Lee, "There and Back Again: The Chiastic Structure of J. K. Rowling's Harry Potter Series," in *Harry Potter for Nerds: Essays for Fans, Academics, and Lit Geeks*, ed. Travis Prinzi, 17-35 (Oklahoma City: Unlocking Press, 2011).

[45] John Granger, "On Turtleback Tales and Asterisks," in *Harry Potter for Nerds: Essays for Fans, Academics, and Lit Geeks*, ed. Travis Prinzi, 37-81 (Oklahoma City: Unlocking Press, 2011).

[46] DH, 759.

demonstrate that Rowling may not have been entirely atomistic in her use of 1 Corinthians 15.26.[47] At the very end of that chapter the Apostle Paul wrote, "Where, O death, is your victory? Where, O death, is your sting?" (1 Cor. 15.55 NRSV).[48] It is fitting that both 1 Corinthians 15 and the *Harry Potter* series conclude with an affirmation that death's sting has ceased. Harry's scar was his link with Voldemort. It was the piece of Voldemort inside of him—the piece of Death that stung him continually. As a personification of Death, the defeat of Voldemort is the ultimate transcendence of death in the narrative, and his sting has ceased.

Together these seven points help make the cumulative case that Voldemort is a personification of Death. Some of the points are stronger than others, but hopefully the collective case is found persuasive. Thus, death as an "enemy" in the Potter epitaph does not refer to individual experiences of death, but within the narrative context of *Harry Potter* it likely refers to the defeat of Voldemort. This provides perhaps the most helpful way to alleviate the tension outlined in this study.

Conclusion

As the present study has attempted to demonstrate, the tension caused by the citation of 1 Corinthians 15.26 is alleviated when it is recognized that the referent for death is a broad conception of decay and corruption, personified by Voldemort himself. This explains how death can be viewed as evil, in contrast to the positive/neutral statements elsewhere, and defeatable, despite the problems associated with immortality throughout, since death is defeated through death. In the Godric's Hallow epitaph, death is therefore both *moral* and *mortal*. Death's morality is evil because it is an enemy, and its mortality is associated with the fact that it is personified as a thing to be destroyed. Rather than seek immortality, one transcends death and becomes the master of death in the same way that Harry does, which is paradoxically through dying. Theologically, this is parallel

---

[47] Although if Rowling's use of 1 Cor. 15.26 is atomistic, it is only in regards to the anticipation of a bodily resurrection, since the Apostle Paul anticipates more than posthumous existence.

[48] This use of 1 Cor. 15.55 is itself a use of Hosea 13.14 from the Hebrew Bible, which contains similar wording: "Shall I ransom them from the power of Sheol? Shall I redeem them from Death? O Death, where are your plagues? O Sheol, where is your destruction? Compassion is hidden from my eyes" (NRSV).

to the accomplishment of the death of Jesus in the Christian tradition. Jesus is *Christus Victor,* the defeater of Satan, sin, and *death.*[49] This is why the present study partially borrows the title of the famous treatise by the Puritan John Owen, *The Death of Death in the Death of Christ.*[50] Rowling's narrative reflects her knowledge of the Christian tradition and utilizes Jesus' defeat of death as part of the paradigm. Her use of an explicitly Christian source (i.e. 1 Cor. 15:26) evokes this paradigm, even though the notion of bodily resurrection—found in the context of that source—is lacking from *Harry Potter.* The Christian tradition affirms that Christ defeated death through his own death and resurrection, even though humans continue to die. This corresponds to the narrative of *Harry Potter* since the story does not end in a paradisiacal state. All of our beloved characters will die. This is part of their plight as humans. Yet there is hope within the narrative; Harry's scar does not cause him pain anymore. Thus, the meaning of the citation in the narrative context of *Harry Potter*—"the last enemy that shall be destroyed is death"—points to this climatic accomplishment: Death/Voldemort died in the death of the boy who lived.[51]

Works Cited

Adler, Shawn. "'Harry Potter' Author J. K. Rowling opens up about books' Christian Imagery." MTV. October 17, 2007.

Austin, Michael W. "Why Harry and Socrates Decide to Die: Virtue and the Common Good." In *The Ultimate Harry Potter and Philosophy: Hogwarts for Muggles,* edited by Gregory Bassham, 258-270. Hoboken, NJ: John Wiley & Sons, 2010.

---

[49] For a discussion on parallels to the Christian doctrine of the atonement in *Harry Potter* see especially, Travis Prinzi, "Christ in the Forest: Aslan and Harry Walk to Their Deaths," in *Harry Potter and Imagination: The Way Between Two Worlds,* 101-118 (Allentown, PA: Zossima Press, 2008).

[50] John Owen, *The Death of Death in the Death of Christ: A Treatise in Which the Whole Controversy about Universal Redemption is Fully Disclosed,* reprint (Edinburgh: Banner of Truth, 1959).

[51] I would like to extend special thanks to Hillary Barthe for making a promise she couldn't keep that ultimately introduced me to Harry Potter, and to Nathaniel Warne, for a crucial conversation while on a pub crawl in Durham (UK) that helped give shape to the present article.

Brueckner, Anthony L., and John Martin Fischer. "Why is Death Bad?" In *The Metaphysics of Death,* edited by John Martin Fischer, 221-229. Stanford: Stanford University Press, 1993.

Collins, John J. "Apocalyptic Eschatology as Transcendence of Death." *Catholic Biblical Quarterly* 36 (1974): 21-43.

—. Apocalyptic Imagination: An Introduction to Jewish Apocalyptic Literature. Grand Rapids: Eerdmans, 1998.

Dickson, Donald R. *John Donne's Poetry.* A Norton Critical Edition. New York, NY: W. W. Norton & Company, 2007.

Gibbs, Nancy. "Person of the Year 2007: Runners-up: J. K. Rowling." *TIME.* Wednesday, December 19, 2007.

Granger, John. *How Harry Cast His Spell: The Meaning Behind the Mania of J. K. Rowling's Bestselling Books.* Carol Stream, IL: Tyndale House, 2008.

—. "The *Deathly Hallows* Epigraphs: *Aeschylus* and Penn Point to the Meaning of Harry Potter." In *Hog's Head Conversations: Essays on Harry Potter*, volume 1, edited by Travis Prinzi, 43-63. Allentown, PA: Zossima Press, 2009.

—. "On Turtleback Tales and Asterisks." In *Harry Potter for Nerds: Essays for Fans, Academics, and Lit Geeks,* edited by Travis Prinzi, 37-81. Oklahoma City: Unlocking Press, 2011

Hardy, Elizabeth Baird. "Horcruxes in Faerie Land: Edmund Spenser's Influence on Voldemort's Efforts to Elude Death." In *Harry Potter for Nerds: Essays for Fans, Academics, and Lit Geeks,* edited by Travis Prinzi, 225-240. Oklahoma City: Unlocking Press, 2011.

Hunter, Joel. "Technological Anarchism: The Meaning of Magic in Harry Potter." In *Harry Potter for Nerds: Essays for Fans, Academics, and Lit Geeks,* edited by Travis Prinzi, 105-134. Oklahoma City: Unlocking Press, 2011.

Lee, J. Steve. "There and Back Again: The Chiastic Structure of J. K. Rowling's Harry Potter Series." In *Harry Potter for Nerds: Essays for Fans, Academics, and Lit Geeks,* ed. Travis Prinzi, 17-35. Oklahoma City: Unlocking Press, 2011.

Manlove, Colin. The Order of Harry Potter: Literary Skill in the Hogwarts Epic. Cheshire, CT: Winged Lion Press, 2010.

Nagel, Thomas. Mortal Questions. London: Cambridge University Press, 1979.

Owen, John. *The Death of Death in the Death of Christ: A Treatise in Which the Whole Controversy about Universal Redemption is Fully Disclosed.* Reprint. Edinburgh: Banner of Truth, 1959.

Pazdziora, J. Patrick. "'Just behind the Veil': Death in Harry Potter and the Fairytales of George MacDonald." In *Harry Potter for Nerds: Essays for Fans, Academics, and Lit Geeks,* edited by Travis Prinzi, 241-268. Oklahoma City: Unlocking Press, 2011.

Prinzi, Travis. *Harry Potter and Imagination: The Way Between Two Worlds,* 101-118. Allentown, PA: Zossima Press, 2008.

Rosenbaum, Stephen E. "How to Be Dead and Not Care: A Defense of Epicurus." In *The Metaphysics of Death,* edited by John Martin Fischer, 119-134. Stanford: Stanford University Press, 1993.

Rowling, J. K. *Harry Potter and the Sorcerer's Stone.* New York, NY: Scholastic, 1999.

—. *Harry Potter and the Prisoner of Azkaban.* New York, NY: Scholastic, 1999.

—. *Harry Potter and the Goblet of Fire.* New York, NY: Scholastic, 2000.

—. *Harry Potter and the Order of the Phoenix.* New York, NY: Scholastic, 2003.

—. *Harry Potter and the Deathly Hallows.* New York, NY: Scholastic, 2007.

—. *The Tales of Beedle the Bard.* New York: Scholastic, 2008.

Smith, Sean. *J. K. Rowling: A Biography.* London: Michael O'Mara, 2001.

Taliaferro, Charles. "The Real Secret of the Phoenix: Moral Regeneration Through Death." In *The Ultimate Harry Potter and Philosophy: Hogwarts for Muggles,* edited by Gregory Bassham, 229-245. Hoboken, NJ: John Wiley & Sons, 2010.

Walls, Jonathan L. and Jerry L. Walls. "Beyond Godric's Hollow: Life after Death and the Search for Meaning." In *The Ultimate Harry Potter and Philosophy: Hogwarts for Muggles,* edited by Gregory Bassham, 246-257. Hoboken, NJ: John Wiley & Sons, 2010.

Wright, N. T. *Surprised by Hope.* London: SPCK, 2007.

Deaths that Destroy Death
Response from John Granger

I'm not sure of the courtesies involved in commenting on an essay that includes more than one reference to one's own writings. Please forgive me if I seem ungrateful or ungracious after such kindness from the author. Having said that, I'll do what I have been asked by the editors to do, namely, make a few points as clarification or continuation of this discussion of death in *Harry Potter*. I offer three thoughts on this subject for your comment and correction:

Fruits of the Tree: Ms Rowling was told by a bookseller in Canada on a trip she made before *Goblet of Fire* was published that customers were purchasing her books as gifts for those who were grieving for departed love ones or caring for those near death. The vendor said that the buyers reported that the message about "those we love never truly leaving us" was no small comfort to men and women unprepared by the loss of children, parents, friends, or spouse. Ms Rowling responded that this meant a great deal to her.

I mention this because it seems the story moral discussed in this essay, that death is mortal and to be transcended, is both a theme and, I'd say more importantly, an *experience* in the book. Hence its ability to serve as some comfort to grieving folk. We read about the survival of those we love, certainly, but we believe it, when we might find such Hallmark Card sentiments so much funeral home boilerplate elsewhere, because we have so entered into the story alongside and ultimately as "The Boy Who Lived" that his reassurance in Dumbledore's denouement scenes is also ours. This is Rowling's great achievement as a literary alchemist.

The death of Death by death? I think the obvious point I want to make here is implicit in the essay and will risk seeming boobish by saying it out loud in the hope that this will foster discussion in a different direction. In the formulation offered, "death of Death by death," the unwitting reader might think that *any death* destroys Death because the type of death that defeats the Dark Lord's personification of death is not specified. If this were true, of course, the Dark Lord would be defeated each time he had created a Horcrux. It is a specific kind of death that is powerful here, namely the sacrificial death made in love for another, even all others, and this is the moral of *Deathly Hallows* from epigraphs to epilogue with regard to death. Until we die to ourselves, which is to say, to our ego-selves or personae, and identify with the essence or *logos* within us, then our demise has no power over death (and we little hope of eternal life).

We see this in *Hallows* at the opening when Harry's Polyjuice Potion is golden and his wand on auto-pilot shoots out golden flames to defeat the Dark Lord. Harry is especially confused by this latter point because he's never heard of a wand acting this way. Harry as the Chosen One, whose very existence is predicated on the sacrificial love of his mother, however, has at his core the Light of the World (John 8:12, 1:9) that is Love (1 John 4:8). His task in *Hallows* is to identify with this alien core and die to his concerns as an individual. Which, in witnessing Dobby's sacrificial love and death, he understands at last on Easter morning at the bottom of a grave. This is the moment of death's defeat, if it takes a few more pages for all of that to play out!

Good, Evil, or Neutral: I think what I enjoyed most in this discussion was reading the ways in which death seems to be presented as an evil to be avoided at all costs, a good to be embraced, or a fate than which there are many worse things. The only point I would add is an alchemical footnote in support of Mr. Dunne's conclusion that the pursuit of individual immortality is necessarily evil, that the death which is good is the one that defeats that kind of narcissism, and that death per se, consequently, can be either good or evil.

The Hogwarts Saga's magic is the spell work of literary alchemy, in which the reader elides with the story hero/ine and is transformed within the narrative in shared catharsis, kenosis, and resurrection. This may seem to be an individual experience but, like the misunderstood mineralogical alchemy, literary alchemy specifically and the alchemy of literature in general is about the "suspension of disbelief," i.e., putting off our individual ratio-centric concern and identifying, activating our shared cardiac intelligence, the eye of the heart. This eye, as we see in the five different eye images in *Hallows*, are that essence with which Harry must identify to transcend self and defeat Death (John 12:24).

If I were to ask Mr. Dunne for an encore, I'd hope he would share what he thinks of death understood psychologically and spiritually, the greater deaths than physical death that Dumbledore and others refer to in the series. It is these deaths, I'm guessing, that are the key to Harry's ability to rise from the dead after giving himself up to the Dark Lord's Killing Curse and the deaths that destroy death we are invited to embrace.

Kenosis— emptying one's own will and becoming entirely receptive to God's will.

ontology - metaphysical
dealing with the nature of being

CURSE - Misha

LUCK - Andy

Capt - he was spared to be
able to donate lung

magic at it's deepest → unknowable
    M calls awe + wonder to ordinary life.
    M = imagination ?

CHAPTER 3

Between Knowing and Unknowing: Understanding the Fluid Force of Magic in the Harry Potter Series
Siddharth Pandey

The ontology of J. K. Rowling's fantastical world is fundamentally determined by the force of magic, an ostensibly supernatural entity that seeps, surrounds, and stimulates *Harry Potter*'s materiality in a variety of ways. This chapter is interested in charting some of the palpable and impalpable ways that collectively reveal the fluid basis of magic.[1] Perceiving magic as an intrinsic force of nature, the paper argues for a multi-layered understanding of magic that necessarily takes into account ideas of transformation, affect, and interiority. With these properties, the fluid supernatural force not only acquires the quality of a Deleuzean "becoming," it also resists the rigid categorization of a singular meaning and instead relates to the larger indeterminable ideas of unpredictability and ordinariness.

Broadly divided into two parts, the essay first focuses on the realm of the tangible to expose the corporeal basis of magic's expressions. It specifically sheds light on the use of human senses and the object world of *Harry Potter*, both of which serve as the most potent, discursive sites for Rowling to depict the palpable nature of magic. In the second half, the discussion tries to identify the

[1] Several of the ideas explored here were originally presented at the University of St. Andrews" two-day international conference on the *Harry Potter* phenomenon in May 2012. My heartfelt thanks to the conference organisers and fellow speakers for making it such a stimulating and memorable event. In particular, I am indebted to Dr. John Patrick Pazdziora and Fr. Micah Snell, whose excellent insights on the preliminary drafts of this paper helped tighten the argument and the overall shape. I am grateful to my friends, family, and teachers, who have shared so much of my enthusiasm all these years for J. K. Rowling's works. In particular, my deepest gratitude to a very dear friend and scholar, Abhija Ghosh, for those innumerable precious moments of "Harry Potter happiness." I am also grateful to the reviewers of my later drafts for their suggestions. Finally, my warmest wishes to J. K. Rowling, who magically changed my life forever.

multiple meanings of magic arising due to the differing uses and perceptions of various communities within Rowling's fictional world. It is here that I locate the author's understanding of magic within other conceptualizations of supernatural forces. In doing so, I show that the series desists from assigning a transcendental status to magic, and in fact argues for an ethical, everyday understanding of a force supposedly extraordinary.

The Corporeal Genesis of Magic

In their portrayals of the organic and the inorganic worlds, the *Harry Potter* narratives substantially experiment with the affective properties of human senses. That is, magic at the most general level acts in conjunction with the bodily, the corporeal. Every book of the series experiments and extrapolates the role of the human sensorium in order to render it fantastical. As an example, the narrativity of the first two books strongly depends on the capacity to see and to be affected by that seeing. Without having entered the magical world, in the first few paragraphs of the first book's first chapter, Rowling exposes the working of vision and its link to imagination and the supernatural. Describing Mr. Dursely's impression of oddness on his way to the office, Rowling writes:

It was on the corner of the street that he noticed the first sign of something peculiar- a cat reading a map. For a second, Mr Dursley didn't realize what he had seen- then he jerked his head around to look again. There was a tabby cat standing on the corner of Privet Drive, but there wasn't a map in sight. What could he have been thinking of? It must have been a trick of the light. Mr Dursley blinked and stared at the cat. It stared back. As Mr Dursley drove around the corner and up the road, he watched the cat in his mirror. It was now reading the sign that said Privet Drive- no, looking at the sign; cats couldn't read maps or signs. Mr Dursley gave himself a little shake and put the cat out of his mind...[2]

This introductory paragraph is significant because it succinctly foreshadows the subsequent emphasis of the books on maps, mirrors, signs, and everything else related to vision. Other examples manipulating vision abound as well. While Harry's eyes are frequently related to his mother's throughout the series, *staring* develops as a curious phenomenon that seems to exert some sort of mysterious influence. Not only do the books refer to the discerning gaze of Dumble-

---

[2] J. K. Rowling, *Harry Potter and the Philosopher's Stone* (UK: Bloomsbury, 1997), 8.

dore through his "half-moon glasses" and Snape's cold look piercing Harry and his friends, the stare of the Basilisk in *Harry Potter and the Chamber of the Secrets* and its various receptions by the four "petrified" victims also adds a deeper, sinister quality to the notion of gazing. Prior to this, in *Harry Potter and the Philosopher's Stone*, Harry's gaze vanishes away the zoo glass. Further, sight combines with desire and taste whenever Harry and his friends visit the Leaky Cauldron and pass by its many display windows exhibiting food and magical objects. Taste however develops into a strong category of its own with the regular descriptions of colourful, sumptuous food at Hogwarts and Honeydukes: "There were shelves upon shelves of the most succulent-looking sweets imaginable. Creamy chunks of nougat, shimmering pink squares of coconut ice, fat, honey-coloured toffees; hundreds of different kind of chocolate in neat rows."[3] Interestingly, in this description of Honeydukes, Rowling also talks of the "Special Effects sweets" that directly combine taste with other senses, such as the "tiny black Pepper Imps" that "breathe fire for friends" and "Ice Mice" which can make one "hear teeth chatter and squeak."[4] Touch too becomes magical and extraordinary, as for instance when students occasionally pass through Hogwarts's ghosts and feel "icy cold," and when Harry feels "strange to touch the Invisibility Cloak, like water woven into material," and most importantly, when it is revealed that Snitches have flesh memories and open with one's touch.[5] Likewise, the aural forever exerts a powerful presence: while Harry hears the traumatising screams of his mother on the nearing of a dementor in *Harry Potter and the Prisoner of Azkaban* as well as senses the disembodied voice of the Basilisk slithering through the walls of Hogwarts in *Chamber of Secrets*, Voldemort resounds through the school at the end of *Harry Potter and the Deathly Hallows*, spreading his message and fear with his snake-like, hissing voice.

The fantastical realm's indulgence in an excess of senses and their various effects may be understood in terms of the contemporary setting of the series. Unlike many traditional fairy-tales and supernatural stories that use a distant, ancient temporality with the staple "long time ago" beginning, Rowling's world

---

[3] J. K. Rowling, *Harry Potter and the Prisoner of Azkaban* (UK: Bloomsbury, 1999), 147.

[4] Ibid.

[5] Rowling, *PS*, 148; J. K. Rowling, *Harry Potter and the Deathly Hallows* (UK: Bloomsbury, 2007), 112-113.

exists parallel to our present world. In his scholarly work *A History of Senses: From Antiquity to Cyberspace*, Robert Jutte argues that our contemporary age rediscovers the sensual characteristics of the senses. The "rediscovery of the senses in the twentieth century" is connected to the emergent commercial pleasures, overstimulation in a post-industrial leisured society, management of colour, diverse ways of seeing, and an interest in extra-sensory perception such as the cyberspace.[6] All of these have led to the discovery of a "new pleasure in the body", the spread of "culinary pluralism", "the internalization of the sense of taste", "changing scent notes", mediums of "new listening", and "visual neo-cultures."[7] With the *Harry Potter* narratives paralleling our own world, Rowling's keen investment in exploring and magically renewing the emphasis on the sensorial appears both pertinent and dynamically sustained throughout the seven books. Interestingly, the "felt" experience does not even exclude ghosts, and therefore, Harry has to correct himself after facing Moaning Myrtle's anger ("Let's all throw books at Myrtle, because *she* can't feel it!" shrieks Myrtle) when he mistakenly conjectures that Tom Riddle's diary couldn't hurt her since "it'd just go right through you, wouldn't it?"[8] It is ironic that Voldemort, who otherwise desperately wants to escape the confines of his mortal body by becoming immortal, has to sustain himself by using others" body parts at the end of *Harry Potter and the Goblet of Fire*: the flesh of his servant Peter Pettigrew, the bone of his dead father, and the blood of his enemy, Harry, are the necessary components for his resurrection. The human body therefore becomes a significant discursive site at which the notion of the fantastical is frequently experimented and elaborated.

The proliferation of bodily effects and affects however does not remain limited to the domain of the human senses alone; it is also explored through the inanimate object culture of *Harry Potter*. That is, the sensorial excess characterising the force of magic also influences the inorganic realm, so that objects and spaces think, feel, mutate, and act on their own volition. It is noteworthy that not only special objects such as wands, Horcruxes, or the Pensieve, but even the most commonplace of everything existing seems to be constituted by the force

---

[6] Robert Jutte, *A History of the Senses. From Antiquity to Cyberspace* (UK: Polity Press, 2005), 237-321.
[7] Ibid.
[8] Rowling, *CoS*, 172.

of magic, so much so that their abundance makes the field of the extraordinary appear ordinary or naturalized. While some objects and spaces are enchanted, suggesting that someone has *worked* on making those objects "magical," several others seem to possess an enchantment of their own. And even when one would expect all of them to be *invented* entities, since they are objects and not naturally occurring material, they seem to defy the limits of their original invention and develop within themselves a conscious subjectivity.

For instance, the Ford Anglia in *Chamber of Secrets* is an enchanted Muggle car that flies, but later we are also made aware that the car thinks on its own, gets angry with Ron and Harry, and punishes as well as protects them. The Marauder's Map, introduced in *Prisoner of Azkaban*, despite being an invented object that shows all the whereabouts of Hogwarts, seems to have a mysterious, magical pact with the Room of Requirement introduced in *Harry Potter and the Order of the Phoenix*, so that only this particular room is invisible on it. That is, even though almost everything seems to be laid bare by the act of invention and controlling magic, an autonomy of the space and its magic still remains. The Room of Requirement in itself is a space that originates by "sensing" the needs of it user. A number of times, objects recognise their settings in which they are placed for a long time, or energetically perform their functionality and associate with their owners: If someone intends to displace them, or if the objects get into the wrong hands, a heightened consciousness regarding the dislocation is displayed on their part. Therefore, in *Order of the Phoenix*, when the members of the Order attempt to clean the house 12 Grimmauld Place, several objects of that house offer a stubborn resistance to their activity. Indeed, words such as "stubborn", "angry", "shrewd", "unpleasant", and others are frequently used by the author to depict the hypersensitivity of these objects. The grandfather clock for instance develops the "unpleasant habit of shooting heavy bolts at passers-by," and an "ancient set of purple robes" tries to "strangle" Ron "when he removed them from their wardrobe."[9] While the painting of Mrs. Black refuses to be removed from the wall by using a Permanent Sticking Charm on its own (just like the one hung in the office of the Muggle Prime Minister at the beginning of *Harry Potter and the Half Blood Prince*), the tapestry showing the Black family tree also offers a similar difficulty.

---

[9] Rowling, *OotP*, 110.

Further, the paintings override the act of their painter, whosoever he or she may be, by developing an interiority of their own, so much so that they begin to express human emotions that even practiced wizards find difficult to deal with. If the occupant of a painting decides to pay a visit to a different painting, such as the Fat Lady in *Philosopher's Stone*, one cannot do anything but wait for her to return.[10] Likewise, teapots go berserk and squirt tea when they happen to be in the hands of the wrong owner, and some books make the reader read them forever, so that "you just had to wander around with your nose in it, trying to do everything one-handed."[11] The strong implication that such behaviour is beyond control or repair is striking because it makes us wonder about the possibility of an added, autonomous property that supersedes wizarding capacity to control or pre-empt the consequences of such a property. Of course, it may be argued that someone cursed the objects in the first place. But it can also be said simultaneously that the objects develop an inherent power of their own accord as well, which is sufficient to hypnotise wizards and witches *forever*. That objects continue to perform themselves even after their owners die (as in the case of the teapot owned by a witch) or influence someone to behave in a particular way for an infinite period of time (as in the case of the books) attests to their unquantifiable behavioural powers. The degree of performance therefore seems to overpower the simple act of "external" placing of the curse. In other examples, metonymy also becomes crucial for demonstrating the interiority of objects, as for instance in the depiction of *Monster Book of Monsters*, which keeps eating itself and its other copies, and in the portrayal of *Invisible Book of Invisibility*, which cannot be seen.[12] It is as if the form of the book recognises its content and performs that recognition on a most literal level. Similarly, the Howler doesn't just convey the anger of the sender; it *becomes* the angry sender for that particular moment of eruption.

    It is this self-determinism of the inorganic world that makes the fantasy field of *Harry Potter* so enriching and fascinating. The perpetual focus on the liveliness of objects and spaces creatively and epically echoes the French philosopher Gilles Deleuze's blurring of the distinction between the organic and the inorganic, as well as his emphasis on the idea of a constant "becoming." "Matter," ac-

---

[10] Rowling, *PoS*, 116.
[11] Rowling, *CoS*, 28-29, 172.
[12] Rowling, *PoA*, 44-45.

cording to Deleuze, "offers an infinitely porous, spongy, cavernous texture without emptiness, caverns endlessly contained in other caverns: no matter how small each body is [...] surrounded and penetrated by an increasingly vaporous fluid, the totality of the universe resembling a 'pond of matter in which there exists different flows and waves.'"[13] This vaporous fluid lies at the heart of Rowling's idea of magic, which not only determines the constant metamorphoses of matter in the series, it *in itself* remains in a state of similar becoming, so that one can never point towards an essential, predetermined, fixed, singular identity of magic. I return to this point later as well.

Deleuze develops his philosophical idea of becoming through a broader terminological lens that he labels as the "fold." A trope invented to theorise non-human forms of subjectivity, the "fold" is a "continuous labyrinth [which] is not a line dissolving into independent points, as flowing sand might dissolve into grains, but resembles a sheet of paper divided into infinite folds or separated into bending movements, each one determined by the consistent or conspiring surroundings."[14] It seems to me that the fluid force of magic, acting both inwards and outwards with its various "bending movements," resembles this "continuous labyrinth," this "fold'; moreover, as Deleuze further observes, "force itself is an act, an act of the fold."[15] Movement indeed determines both the being and the experience of magic, so that Rowling's fictional world is forever embraced by a shiftiness. Thus, the staircases of Hogwarts frequently change directions and make it "very hard to remember where everything was, because it all seemed to move around a lot," and the Burrow, the Weasely household, also constantly "bursts with the strange and the unexpected"[16] :

> Life at the Burrow was as different as possible from life in Privet Drive. The Dursleys liked everything neat and ordered; the Weasely's house burst with the strange and the unexpected. Harry got a shock the first time he looked into the mirror over the kitchen mantelpiece and it shouted, "Tuck your shirt in, scruffy!" The ghoul in the attic howled and dropped pipes whenever he felt things were getting too quiet, and small explosions from Fred and George's bedroom were considered perfectly normal.17

---

[13] Felix Deleuze, *The Fold* (USA: University of Minnesota Press, 1993), 5.
[14] Ibid., 6.
[15] Ibid., 18.
[16] Rowling, *PS*, 98.
[17] Rowling, *CoS*, 37.

As if in an effort to provide a tangible form to an otherwise fluid and abstract identity of magic, Rowling develops what I would call an aesthetic of randomness or an aesthetic of disorderliness. It is this recurrent literary-visual trope that spreads throughout the universe of *Harry Potter* and makes the force of magic *known* in as palpable a manner as possible.

Intangible, Unpredictable, and Ordinary Magic

If on one hand, corporeality forms a platform for understanding magic, then on the other, Rowling also plays with an individuated idea of magic that goes beyond its sensorial grounding and works in conjunction with the emotional and the creative. Thus, even as her books refer to a wide range of spells and magical properties that need to be learned, their usage by wizards and witches often depends on their ability to master, and significantly, on their personal histories. So for instance, while the Patronus Charm helps one produce a guardian spirit to ward off the evil Dementors, its production essentially depends on the happiest memory of every individual. This emphasis on individuality and the implied difference between each wizard or witch lends magic a deeply particularised identity, even as the force of magic otherwise exists as a common medium. It is significant that other examples also emphasise this difference in a poststructuralist sense, so that the signifying system of magic is endlessly in a state of creative expression and development. Thus, when in *Order of the Phoenix*, both Dumbledore and McGonagall conjure chairs out of thin air at different moments, Rowling keenly notes the difference between the two manifestations to again hint at the uniqueness of material expression: "Professor McGonagall pulled her wand from the pocket of her dressing gown and waved it; three chairs appeared out of thin air, straight-backed and wooden, quite unlike the comfortable chintz armchairs that Dumbledore had conjured up at Harry's hearing."[18] Further, the Weasley brothers are constantly engaged in making new, attractive magical stuff. In another example from *Half-Blood Prince*, we encounter Snape's childhood book of potions that illustrates the transgression of proper rules and spells in order to create something new, something no one else has thought of. Thus, even while Rowling mentions that "precision" lies at the heart of making Potions, she creates a channel for an alternative in Snape's character to reach the same preci-

---

[18] Rowling, *OotP*, 415.

sion via individual genius.[19] Likewise, Dumbledore's Deluminator is wholly unique. These inventions, taken together with the subjective expressions of magic, testify to a profusion of creativity and cleverness.

Yet, even as magic at this deep level mingles with the expression of the human self, the self or the soul of the force of magic remains shrouded in mystery. In other words, while Rowling invests substantial detail into the devising of spells, jinxes, and hexes which are often intimately connected with the human senses and feelings, she also gives many instances where descriptions of magic simply cannot be accommodated within such acts of knowing, learning, controlling, or sensing. As the shuddering Dobby points out to Harry in *Chamber of Secrets*, "Albus Dumbledore is the greatest Headmaster Hogwarts has ever had. Dobby knows it sir [...] But sir... there are powers Dumbledore doesn't... powers no decent wizard" knows of or can imagine (18). Indeed, in *Half-Blood Prince*, Dumbledore himself is astounded by the discovery that Voldemort made seven Horcruxes. At the end of *Prisoner of Azkaban*, when Dumbledore explains Harry how the latter's saving of Pettigrew's life has created a bond between the two, he refers to magic "at its deepest, its most impenetrable" (311). Even within the "known" branches of magical studies, there is imprecision, and Fortune Telling, in the words of Hermione Granger and McGonagall, is "a very imprecise branch of magic" (190). Likewise, in *Deathly Hallows* Ollivander also acknowledges that it is not *exactly* known why a wand chooses its master, and that "wandlore is a complex and mysterious branch of magic" (400). This is again despite the fact that he and his previous generations have all been in the business of wand making for centuries. Through such examples, Rowling suggests that magic is *magical* precisely because it is, at its deepest, unknowable.[20]

I therefore again return to the idea of interiority that governs both the tangible and abstract realms of magic. If the force of magic has an indeterminable interiority, then it is tempting to align its ostensibly supernatural power with a certain notion of transcendence. But Rowling's genius fundamentally lies in resisting that very temptation, and it is this refusal to attach a transcendent, holy significance to magic that puts the pervasive force of the *Harry Potter* series in

---

[19] Rowling, *PS*, 190.
[20] Interestingly, in an interview, Rowling also revealed that "nobody knows where magic comes from." "Magic gene," http://harrypotter.wikia.com/wiki/Magic_gene (accessed April 30, 2013).

sheer contrast with other supernatural forces. While in Philip Pullman's fantasy trilogy *His Dark Materials* (1995-2000) the information and the working of the force of "Dust" is controlled by the dictatorial Church, in George Lucas's epic film saga *Star Wars* (1977-1983), the supernatural power of "Force," despite being a ubiquitous binding power, also has an inherent metaphysical aspect that is expressed most strongly in the holy words of the Jedi (the philosophical and most-trained wielders of Force): "May the Force be with you." Not only do such phrases implying a higher status of magic not exist in Rowling's world, it is also significant that the terms magic or "magical" are always written with a small "m," unlike the capital "D" or "F" in other cases. Only when the terms are used in titles or at the beginning of a sentence do they begin with a capital "M."[21] In his *The Chronicles of the Narnia* series (1950-1956), while describing the supernatural force as a collection of ancient rules and conduct, C. S. Lewis talks of a "Deep Magic."[22] And even while referring to a "magic deeper still," he adds a transcendent dimension by reversing Death.[23] It is significant that while comparing the "deeper magic" of Narnia with that of *Harry Potter*, Travis Prinzi finds a "strong parallel": like the love and sacrifice of Aslan, Prinzi asserts, "self-sacrificial love, first of Lily and then of Harry is the power that defeats Voldemort."[24] While I do not disagree with this observation, I want to point out that magic in the *Harry Potter* world does not and cannot reverse death. It is in this sense that even Lewis's magic attains a higher status than the ways of nature, whereas Rowling's does not.[25]

---

[21] Interestingly, while on one hand, "Dust" and "Force" have some aspect of "physicality" attached with them (Dust being made up of microscopic, conscious particles observable with the Amber Spyglass, and Force being the biological product of "midi-chlorians," microscopic life-forms residing within the cells of living things), then on the other hand, magic in itself contains nothing. This accounts further for its unknowability.

[22] C.S. Lewis, *The Lion, the Witch and the Wardrobe. The Chronicles of Narnia* (UK: HarperCollins, 1998), 142-152.

[23] Ibid., 171.

[24] Travis Prinzi, *Harry Potter and Imagination: The Way Between Two Worlds* (USA: Zossima, 2009), 33.

[25] Even as it is clear that there are obvious parallels between Aslan's and Harry's resurrection, it should be noted that Aslan's resurrection is first, due to "deeper magic," and second, more importantly, due to his prior knowledge of his resurrection, indicating the already written, known, and inscribed quality of "deeper magic': After he ressurects, Aslan points out that if the white witch "could have looked a little further back... she would have known" about the reversal of death (emphasis mine). (Lewis, *The Lion*, 171). This prior knowledge of the reversal is very different from the idea of "choice" that de-

Thus, magic's interiority, indeterminacy, and mystery remain earthly and within the laws of nature. This idea of magic is also different from Evelyn Underhill's philosophical rumination on magic, as she too speaks of a transcendent notion and quotes the nineteenth century French magician Eliphas Levi to support her claim: "Magical operations are the exercise of a power which is natural, but superior to the ordinary powers of nature."[26] But in Rowling, magical operations are an exercise of a power that is *both* natural *and* ordinary at the same time. Two critics, Roni Natov and Christopher Routledge, have dealt with the question of ordinariness in *Harry Potter* in some detail. While Natov relates Rowling's ordinary magic to real life in general ("magic calls wonder to the awe and wonder of ordinary life"), Routledge on the other hand cursorily mentions that magic appears ordinary to wizards and witches and then spends major part of his essay in making a link between the "mystery of ordinary life in *Harry Potter* with the mystery of the detective fiction genre."[27] However, I would approach magic's ordinariness by placing it within the philosophy of what constitutes the ordinary and the everyday itself.

For this, I find the critical reflections of the anthropologist Kathleen Stewart and the theorist Maurice Blanchot helpful. In her eminent work *Ordinary Affects*, Stewart explains that "ordinary affects are the varied, surging capacities to affect and be affected that give everyday life the quality of a continuing motion of relations, scenes, contingencies, and emergences. They're things that happen."[28] She further goes on to state that ordinary affects are "rooted not in fixed conditions of possibility but in the actual lines of potential that a something coming together calls to mind and sets in motion."[29] In effect, ordinary affects chart those trajectories "that forces might take if they were to go unchecked,"

---

termines Harry's return in the final book, and thus once again brings into focus human agency in Rowling's "magic."

[26] Qtd. in Evelyn Underhill, *Mysticism. A Study in the Nature and Development of Man's Spiritual Consciousness* (London: Methurn and Co., 1930), 161.

[27] See Roni Natov, "Harry Potter and the Extraordinariness of the Ordinary" in Ivory Tower and Harry Potter. Perspectives on a Literary Phenomenon, edited by LA Whited (USA: University of Missouri, 2002), 125-139; and Christopher Routledge, "Harry Potter and the Mystery of Ordinary Life" in Mystery in Children's Literature. From the Rational to the Supernatural, edited by Adrienne E. Gavin and Christopher Routledge (New York: Palgrave, 2001), 202-209.

[28] Kathleen Stewart, *Ordinary Affects* (USA: Duke University Press, 2007), 1-2.

[29] Ibid., 2.

and therefore "ordinary affects do not have to await definition, classification, or rationalization before they exert palpable pressures."[30] Rowling's fluid magic reflects this "potential" that surpasses "definition" or "classification" by remaining partly mysterious, partly knowable. Like Stewart, Blanchot observes that the everyday is "an experience that always escapes [and is] something inaccessible through knowledge."[31] "We cannot know it," the critic maintains, since it is the "unexperienced," and yet "we have always already seen it by an illusion that is, as it happens, constitutive of the everyday."[32] Thus, both Stewart and Blanchot are claiming that the ordinary is the pervasive, a pervasiveness that can both be known and yet not known, and this is what Rowling seems to be arguing for with her idea of magic too.

The notion of the ordinary (that which is and which is going to be) is therefore intrinsically tied with that of "becoming" that this essay earlier explored. Hence, Deleuze's fold is a symbol for Rowling's magic, for ordinariness, and consequently, for magic's ordinariness as well. It is noteworthy that in his review of Deleuze's *The Fold*, Nicholas Davey clearly points to the philosopher's anti-transcendental approach when he comments that in the concept of the fold, "transcendent all-embracing identity is replaced with an all-differentiating difference which recognises only a plurality of dissimilar conurbations."[33] So Davey observes that there is no "one" greater "Fold" fixedly determining the existence of "folds"; instead, it is "folds" that define being in terms of a seamlessly unfurling, unending, unpredictable variety. Similarly, with magic existing and expressing as an everyday force whose meaning(s) is both available and hidden but not transcendental, there is no one grander "Magic" but constantly proliferating "magics." By placing the ordinary within the ambit of fantasy, Rowling offers a strong critique to a fundamental assertion of fantasy authors and critics such as Ursula LeGuin and John Pennington who claim that "successful fantasy writers... know instinctively that what is wanted in fantasy is a dis-

---

[30] Ibid., 3.
[31] Blanchot in Amy Macdonald, "Book Review: Experiencing the Everyday in Maurice Blanchot's "Everyday Speech'," http://www.spaceandculture.org/2009/06/02/experiencing-the-everyday-in-maurice-blanchot's-"everyday-speech"/ (accessed April 27, 2013).
[32] Ibid.
[33] Nicholas Davey, "Book Review. The Fold," in *British Journal of Aesthetics*, Vol. 35, No. 2, 1995, 175-176.

tancing from the ordinary."[34] The ordinary is not necessarily the opposite of fantasy, the ordinary *is* fantasy.

It is this ordinary, undefined property of magic that the evil community of *Harry Potter* fails to grasp. Whereas magic is a ubiquitous force, it is the dark side that tries its best to make it a religion in a fundamentalist sense. The motto "Magic is Might" therefore appears in the final book when the ministry is taken over by Voldemort's followers, and the use of the term "might" forcefully counters the idea of magic's ordinariness. In a way, "Magic is Might" seems closer to the hallowed tone of "May the Force be with you" in *Star Wars*, a hallowedness that, as this paper has argued, Rowling deliberately resists. Voldemort and his supporters do not understand that magic and its teaching cannot be privileged for a few pure and mighty, since one can never exactly know how the force of magic works in the first place. The dark side is unable to acknowledge the simple fact that a magical gene may suddenly appear on its own in a wizard or a Muggle, and that no one can absolutely determine or control this "magical" suddenness. In other words, Voldemort lacks the power to acknowledge that magic is magical because it cannot be "pinned down." And yet, it is exactly this pinning down that he and his followers wish to achieve. Not only does Voldemort deliberately delude himself and others with the notions of blood purity (even as he himself is a half-blood), his servants also recognise the power of lying to support their self-imposed claims. Thus, in *Deathly Hallows*, when Umbridge inquires Mrs Cattermole "from which witch or wizard you took that wand," her victim finds it hard to explain what is otherwise a self-evident truth of magic: "'T-took?" sobbed Mrs Cattermole. "I didn't t- take it from anybody [...] It-it-it-*chose* me."[35] The italicisation of the word is Rowling's own doing, and the dialogue serves as a significant proof of the evil side's inability to comprehend the autonomy of magic. It is but natural, then, that "love," which is the most mysterious of all magic and defies the limits of comprehension, cannot be understood by Voldemort since he lacks it.

In the context of the Muggles, the word "magic" is firstly used for generating humour for the readers that results from the community's limited understanding of the term, exemplified by the exaggerated reactions of Muggles on hearing

---

[34] Ursula LeGuin in Pennington, "From Elfland to Hogwarts, or the Aesthetic Trouble with Harry Potter," in *The Lion and the Unicorn*, Vol. 26, No. 1, Jan. 2002, 84.
[35] Rowling, *HPDH*, 214.

"the M-word": "'WHAT HAVE I TOLD YOU,' thundered [Harry's] uncle,
spraying spit over the table, 'ABOUT SAYING THE M WORD IN OUR
HOUSE?'"[36] And secondly, for critiquing the lack of imagination in the Muggle
world whose importance Rowling has consistently stressed, both through her
books and her 2007 commencement speech at Harvard.[37] As Mr. Weasley points
out in *Chamber of Secrets*, "Muggles will go to any lengths to ignore magic,
even if it's staring them in face…"[38] In *Half-Blood Prince*, when the Muggle
Prime Minister questions the Minister for Magic on why his predecessors did
not tell him about their regular encounter with the magical world, his counterpart simply quips, "My dear Prime Minister, are *you* ever going to tell anybody?"[39] It is important to understand that Rowling's critique of Muggles should
not be directly taken as a harsh or condescending critique of *us* the human readers, even as we are the fictionally represented Muggles. At best, Muggles serve
as a rich literary trope, a construction, to enter a narrative that is primarily about
a secondary world. Rowling is no Swiftian misanthrope, and it is significant that
throughout her books she most rigorously argues for the power of love, notwithstanding its mystery. Love and friendship are essentially human aspects, and her
privileging of these over every expression of magic subtly suggests that she does
not assign a "higher" ontological status to wizards and witches. Rowling never
uses magic to "solve" the problems of the Muggle world, since that is not her
agenda. Problems exist in the magical world despite magic. In any case, as Ron
explains in the *HPCS*, "Most wizards these days are half-blood anyway. If we
hadn't married Muggles we'd've died out."[40] Surely, the magical community
would not exist had the alliance not taken place, unless, of course, the fluid force

---

[36] Rowling, *HPCS*, 8.
[37] J. K. Rowling, "The Fringe Benefits of Failure, and the Importance of Imagination,"
http://harvardmagazine.com/2008/06/the-fringe-benefits-failure-the-importance-
imagination/ (accessed July 8, 2012). Even when the word "magic" is used in the wizarding world, there is often a humorous double meaning encoded within it. For instance, the
name of Gilderoy Lockhart's autobiography *Magical Me* instantly conveys a sense of
arrogance and pompousness. Mrs. Weasely's cookbook named *One Minute Feasts—Its
Magic!!!* on the other hand seems to echo the Muggles" exclamatory use of the term
"magic." But in both the examples, we are also at the same time aware that the word
"magical" can equally refer to the fantastical force of magic that makes up the wizarding
world.
[38] Rowling, *CoS*, 34.
[39] Rowling, *HBP*, 12.
[40] Rowling, *CoS*, 89.

of magic suddenly reappeared once again, a return that neither the wizards nor the Muggles could ever prophesize or determine, since magic's magicalness exceeds predictability.

Conclusion

The force of magic is fluid because it affects the everyday existence of Rowling's fictional world in a seamless manner: it constantly enters, exits, pre-exists, and surrounds the animate, inanimate, and the realm of the abstract in unquantifiable, incalculable degrees, so much so that it becomes the ordinary, the natural. As a state or a medium that always inhabits the in-between, it essentially cannot have a technical detail. Hence an article on the popular online user-generated knowledge source Wikipedia asserts that "within the books, technical details of magic are obscure."[41] Made up magical rules can be broken; fundamental properties of mystery and indeterminacy cannot be tampered with. Thus, if according to some critics, "incoherence" does form a part of the magical system, I do not view it as equalising "aesthetic trouble."[42] Magic cannot be "coherent" simply because it itself is "magical," and the significance of the *Harry Potter* books lies in their successful creative experimentation with the unknown on an everyday level. If there is anything essential about the fluidity of magic, it is its ordinariness, its aversion towards transcendence, and its privileging of the most mysterious of human emotions, love; and in this respect, magic's humanist pull is most evident.

---

[41] "Magic in Harry Potter," http://en.wikipedia.org/wiki/Magic_in_Harry_Potter (accessed April 27, 2013).

[42] See John Pennington, "From Elfland to Hogwarts, or the Aesthetic Trouble with Harry Potter," in *The Lion and the Unicorn*, Vol. 26, No. 1, Jan. 2002, 78-97; Farah Mendlesohn and Edward James, *A Short History of Fantasy* (UK: Middlesex University Press, 2009), 174.

Works Cited

Davey, Nicholas. "Book Review. The Fold," in *British Journal of Aesthetics*, Vol. 35, No. 2, 1995.

Deleuze, Gilles. *The Fold*. Tr. Tom Conley. USA: University of Minnesota Press, 1993.

Jutte, Robert. *A History of the Senses. From Antiquity to Cyberspace*. UK: Polity Press, 2009.

Lewis, CS. *The Lion, the Witch and the Wardrobe. The Chronicles of Narnia*. UK: HarperCollins, 1998.

Macdonald, Amy. "Book Review: Experiencing the Everyday in Maurice Blanchot's 'Everyday Speech',"
http://www.spaceandculture.org/2009/06/02/experiencing-the-everyday-in-maurice-blanchot's-"everyday-speech"/

"Magic in Harry Potter." *Wikipedia*.
http://en.wikipedia.org/wiki/Magic_in_Harry_Potter

"Magic gene," http://harrypotter.wikia.com/wiki/Magic_gene

Mendlesohn, Farah and Edward James. *A Short History of Fantasy*. UK: Middlesex University Press, 2009.

Natov, Roni. "Harry Potter and the Extraordinariness of the Ordinary." In *The Ivory Tower and Harry Potter. Perspectives on a Literary Phenomenon*. Edited by L. A. Whited. USA: University of Missouri, 2002.

Pennington, John. "From Elfland to Hogwarts, or the Aesthetic Trouble with Harry Potter." *The Lion and the Unicorn*. Vol. 26. No. 1, Jan. 2002.

Prinzi, Travis. *Harry Potter and Imagination: The Way Between Two Worlds*. USA: Zossima, 2009.

Pullman, Philip. His Dark Materials: The Golden Compass. USA1997.

—. *His Dark Materials: The Amber Spyglass*. USA: Scholastic: Scholastic Point, 1995.

—. *His Dark Materials: The Subtle Knife*. USA: Scholastic Point, Point, 2000.

Routledge, Christopher. "Harry Potter and the Mystery of Ordinary Life." In *Mystery in Children's Literature. From the Rational to the Supernatural*.

Edited by Adrienne E. Gavin and Christopher Routledge. New York: Palgrave, 2001.

Rowling, JK. *Harry Potter and the Philosopher's Stone.* UK: Bloomsbury, 1997.

—. *Harry Potter and the Chamber of Secrets.* UK: Bloomsbury, 1998.

—. *Harry Potter and the Prisoner of Azkaban.* UK: Bloomsbury, 1999.

—. *Harry Potter and the Goblet of Fire.* UK: Bloomsbury, 2000.

—. *Harry Potter and the Order of the Phoenix.* UK: Bloomsbury, 2003.

—. *Harry Potter and the Half-Blood Prince.* UK: Bloomsbury, 2005.

—. *Harry Potter and the Deathly Hallows.* UK: Bloomsbury, 2007.

Rowling, JK. "The Fringe Benefits of Failure, and the Importance of Imagination." http://harvardmagazine.com/2008/06/the-fringe-benefits-failure-the-importance-imagination/

Stewart, Kathleen. *Ordinary Affects.* USA: Duke University Press, 2007.

Underhill, Evelyn. *Mysticism. A Study in the Nature and Development of Man's Spiritual Consciousness.* London: Methurn and Co., 1930.

Filmography

Star Wars Episode 1: The Phantom Menace. DVD. Directed by George Lucas. 1999. USA. 20th Century Fox. 2001.

The Ethics of Co-opted Reality
vs.
Fantasy in Children's Literature
Response from Vinita Chandra

S iddharth Pandey's essay, "Between Knowing and Unkowning: Understanding the Fluid Force of Magic in the *Harry Potter* Series," argues compellingly that the *Potter* series "desists from assigning a transcendental status to magic, and in fact argues for an ethical, everyday understanding of a force supposedly extraordinary." He supports this argument by pointing out that unlike traditional fairy tales that are located a long time ago (and might I add, in a land far, far away) the Potter series are situated in a world parallel to our present one, and the magic so completely inundates this world that "the field of the extraordinary appear(s) ordinary or naturalized" (54). I would like to take Pandey's thesis and the material he uses to support it and look at it from another perspective by locating it in the genre of Children's Literature—in which the adult author tries to recreate the magic of the child's world in its everyday ordinariness—and examine the interesting use of the term "ethical" that he uses in relation with this all-encompassing magic.

The idea of what constitutes the categories of childhood and Children's Literature has been shifting over the centuries. As many critics have pointed out, this is one genre that is defined not by its primary readership but by publishers, librarians, booksellers, and parents. Seth Lerer distinguishes "between claims that children's literature consists of books written *for* children and that it consists of those read, regardless of original authorial intention, *by* children."[1]

The aim of Children's Literature has been shifting over different time periods too; there is a perceptible shift in general from using storytelling with the purpose of educating and moralizing through to being taken the reader through a fantasy wonderland without giving a simplistic lesson to be learned at the end.

---

[1] Seth Lerer, *Children's Literature: A Reader's History, From Aesop to Harry Potter* (Chicago: The University of Chicago Press, 2008), 2.

The profusion of fantasy writing aimed at a readership of children and young adults in the last two decades. and its enormous popularity seen through sales of books, movies based on the books, accompanying video games, blogs, costumes, and so on, testify to a shift in reading preferences from Enid Blyton's children detectives and Nancy Drew's rationally solved mysteries, to a magic that goes beyond what can be understood through science and logic. As Pandey points out, the world of the *Harry Potter* series is immersed in everyday magic. What accounts for the popularity of fantasy in contemporary Children's Literature? To examine this question, I would like to glance briefly at Gramsci's theory of spontaneous hegemony[2] and the role of the child in society.

Gramsci's theory of dual power is one where power functions through the "political state" and "civil society." He places the educational system along with culture and religion in the domain of civil society. Gramsci argues that intellectuals work towards ensuring consensus and spontaneous submission in the social sphere. This "spontaneous consent," which ensures real domination, is what Gramsci defines as hegemony. In every society, then, building "spontaneous consent" in order to ensure domination starts almost as soon as a child is born and, along with the educational apparatus of formal schooling, the family, the religious community, and other peer groups, ensures that the child grows into an adult who learns not to question received notions, not to assert his or her individuality, and not to resist co-option into dominant cultural forms and ideology.

In the process of being co-opted into a hegemonic society, children must lose their sense of the magic and wonder of the world that is unfolding before them, which they are experiencing for the first time. Any individuality or creativity that transgresses the boundaries laid down by the dominant ideology must be discouraged. Children mature into adults when they learn to live by the rules of the adult world—rules that often go against everything they believe to be right. They must make their peace with a deceitful, corrupted "reality" and its arbitrary rules of what is "ethical", moral, humane, and what is not. "Ethics" that are determined by society must always be limited to the temporal and the spatial, and are always dictated by the dominant cultural formation and its ideology. In suppressing any individual, creative development of ideas or mores truly distinct

---

[2] Antonio Gramsci, *Selections from the Prison Notebooks of Antonio Gramsci.* Trans. Geoffrey Nowell Smith. Ed. Quentin Hoare and Geoffrey Nowell Smith (London: Lawrence and Wishart, 1971), 5-14.

from that of the social formation, civil society does not allow for any individual perception of morals or ethics.

Fantasy and magic in Children's Literature recaptures the wonder, the newness, the random, the arbitrary, the "not always already defined" and categorised, socialised adult world. Children's fiction uses the child's viewpoint to question received notions of the adult world; it uses fantasy and magic to recreate a world where the unexpected, the unscripted can happen. Kathryn Hume writes, "Fantasy is any departure from consensus reality."[3] Pandey argues,

> Rowling's fluid magic reflects this "potential" that surpasses "definition" or "classification" by remaining partly mysterious, partly knowable. [...] Stewart and Blanchot are claiming that the ordinary is the pervasive, a pervasiveness that can both be known and yet not known, and this is what Rowling seems to be arguing for with her idea of magic too. [...] The ordinary is not necessarily the opposite of fantasy, the ordinary *is* fantasy. (63)

Rowling's fantasy world, which is parallel to our own, offers a fantastical breaking of social hegemony, not by interrogating it through rational and intellectual debate but by replacing it with a fantasy and magic that cannot be understood and domesticated simplistically. It just has to be experienced.

Pandey points to a very interesting aspect of magic in the Potter series: he illustrates that Rowling's framing of magic always "plays with an individuated idea of magic that goes beyond its sensorial grounding and works in conjunction with the emotional and the creative. [...] Thus, even as her books refer to a wide range of spells and magical properties that need to be learned, their usage by wizards and witches often depends on their ability to master, and significantly, on their personal histories" (57-58). He gives the example of the Patronus Charm which helps one produce a guardian spirit to ward off the evil Dementors, and shows how "its production essentially depends on the happiest memory of every individual. This emphasis on individuality and the implied difference between each wizard/witch lends magic a deeply particularised identity, even as the force of magic otherwise exists as a common medium" (58). The fantasy world of magic is not an anarchic one, then, for its foundation is that of a "common medium"; however, to use it, every individual has to tap into his/her own individuality creatively and emotionally. While the Potter series is set in an edu-

---

[3] Kathryn Hume, *Fantasy and Mimesis: Responses to Reality in Western Literature* (New York and London: Methuen), 21.

cational institution that sets out to train a large number of children, the uncertainty of the fantasy world does not allow the Gramscian civil society's hegemony to function in it. In a world of shifting staircases, talking paintings, and invisible cloaks forming the day-to-day experiences of the students, the only ideology that exists is that of experiencing life in all its random arbitrariness, without any coercion to accept it unquestioningly.

Pandey's use of the word "ethical" in discussing the world of magic culminates in his treatment of the Dark Arts. Pandey writes, "Whereas magic is a ubiquitous force, it is the dark side that tries its best to make it a religion in a fundamentalist sense" (63). Voldemort's followers adopt the motto of "Magic is Might" and Pandey comments that "Voldemort and his supporters do not understand that magic and its teaching cannot be privileged for a few pure and mighty, since one can never exactly know how the force of magic works in the first place" (63). Unlike the production of a logical sounding ideology to manufacture consent in civil society, the force of magic can never be understood, and therefore can never be usurped by those in power to dominate the masses for their own purposes.

However, it is Pandey's equation of the "dark side" in the Potter series with institutionalized religion that I find fascinating. Institutionalized religion is fundamentalist when it does not brook any scepticism or doubt, and discourages all individual creativity and thinking. Religion has the power to co-opt that no other institution of civil society has because it can demand blind faith and acceptance of a creed that has already determined what is ethical and moral, and often positions itself as if under no obligation to explain its ethics, since at its foundation is a belief that a being higher than the human has ordained it. In the world of magic, Voldemort's attempts to concentrate power in the hands of the pure and mighty can never succeed because the nature of magic itself defies all rationalization and comprehension, and so his defeat is imminent. Institutionalized religion, on the other hand, continues to co-opt and use members of society by weaving an ideology of ethics, morality and the supernatural; when it becomes fundamental, rigid, inflexible, intolerant, then it inevitably leads to conflict and violence.

Rowling's parallel world of fantasy offers an alternative to both the dark side of the Potter world and the always-scripted, classified, rigidly defined society of our world through the oldest human virtues of love, friendship, and compassion.

Pandey writes, "Love and friendship are essentially human aspects, and her privileging of these over every expression of magic subtly suggests that she does not assign a 'higher' ontological status to wizards and witches" (64-65). Love and friendship, putting others over one's own Darwinian sense of survival, have always triumphed over the oppression of the dominating civil society; have even achieved victory over the might of the political state that stands in readiness to punish resistance to "spontaneous consent." The question of what is ethical can only be answered by stepping out of the education and socialization which makes us consent to everyday corruption, poverty, inequality, and violence as the "real" world; by attempting to retrieve the extra ordinary which has been made into the ordinary and the mundane. Children's Literature shows the constructed nature of this "reality" through whimsical fantasy. Pandey illustrates this beautifully when he quotes Rowling: "As Mr. Weasley points out in *HPCS*, 'Muggles will go to any lengths to ignore magic, even if it's staring them in face...'" (64).

Colin Manlove argues that there is no difference between the child and the adult, that the adult always carries the child within his/her repressed unconscious.[4] Children's Literature written by adults attempts to recreate the world of magic and wonder for children at one level, but also interrogates and critiques the arbitrary ethics, morals, customs, and mores of the adult world for an adult readership. In the past two decades, rapid developments in computer technology, the World Wide Web, the information highway, scientific discoveries, and such like have closed gaps in what we know, to the extent of trying to isolate the god particle. Fantasy fiction, which has become increasingly popular in this time period, offers a world where all answers and resolutions are fantastical, frustrating our desire for solutions that come in an array of pre-packaged options.

---

[4] Colin Manlove, *From Alice to Harry Potter: Children's Fantasy in England* (New Zealand: Cybereditions Corporation, 2003).

Works Cited

Gramsci, Antonio. *Selections from the Prison Notebooks of Antonio Gramsci.* Trans. Geoffrey Nowell Smith. Ed. Quentin Hoare and Geoffrey Nowell Smith. London: Lawrence and Wishart, 1971.

Hume, Kathryn. *Fantasy and Mimesis: Responses to Reality in Western Literature.* New York and London: Methuen, 1984.

Lerer, Seth. *Children's Literature: A Reader's History, From Aesop to Harry Potter.* Chicago: The University of Chicago Press, 2008.

Colin Manlove, *From Alice to Harry Potter: Children's Fantasy in England.* New Zealand: Cybereditions Corporation, 2003.

Liminality = Threshold

CHAPTER 4

The Roots and Rhetoric of the Forbidden Forest

Garry MacKenzie

The Forbidden Forest is one of the key locations for narrative development and character transformation in the *Harry Potter* books. It is a place where characters are tested, in particular Harry, from his first encounter with Voldemort in *The Philosopher's Stone* to his sacrifice at the hands of his foe in *The Deathly Hallows*. It is also a place where outcasts and fugitives can be free from the laws of wizard and muggle society, regardless of whether they are evil (Death Eaters, Aragog's spider clan), misfits (Grawp, the bewitched Ford Anglia), or figures whose relationship with mainstream wizarding is complex, such as the centaurs.

These aspects of the Forbidden Forest position it within a vast tradition of literature about or set in forests, and in this chapter I will explore a selection of these literary and cultural forests. I do not want to suggest that J. K. Rowling always has these precedents in mind when describing the Forbidden Forest, nor that an arboreal framework of allusions is crucial to enjoyment and understanding of the novels, but I do want to highlight some of the meanings of forests in literary culture and relate these meanings in turn to the *Harry Potter* books in order to open them up to dialogue with other works. In doing so I will examine claims that Rowling's world lacks spiritual or supernatural depth and will also suggest that her landscapes can be read in relation to contemporary environmental discourse. My concern therefore is with untangling some of the literary roots of the Forbidden Forest, but also with examining its rhetoric. By this I mean its literary presentation—how effectively its atmosphere and other attributes are created by the author. I will look at three main aspects of the Forbidden Forest:

its dangers, its relationship to society, and its environmental significance. First, however, I will demonstrate the importance of the Forest to plot and character development of the *Harry Potter* books.

The Forbidden Forest as a Place of Change

The idea of a forest as a place where characters face dangers and challenges, and from which they later emerge with a more developed sense of themselves or their situation, is far from unique to the world of *Harry Potter*. It is one of the most well-known tropes in fairy tales. In his essay about the defining landscape of the Grimms' Tales, the folklorist Jack Zipes begins with this summary:

> Inevitably they find their way into the forest. It is there that they lose and find themselves. It is there that they gain a sense of what is to be done. The forest is always large, immense, great, and mysterious. No one ever gains power over the forest, but the forest possesses the power to change lives and alter destinies.[1]

Zipes is talking about characters like Snow White and Hansel and Gretel, who find themselves lost in the forest and (sometimes misguidedly) seek the help of those who live there. Entering the forest is the narrative stimulus in many of the Grimms' Tales—in the forest the protagonist is faced with new people and situations and must transform aspects of their character if they are to survive and leave again. Cut off from the comforts of home and the conventions of society, they are no longer subject to norms such as feudal hierarchy and to some extent they are afforded an outside perspective on things which they had previously taken for granted. In Tales like "How Six Made their Way in the World" and "The Blue Light," for instance, soldiers (who were often regarded as social outcasts in early nineteenth-century Germany) acquire the means to advance to a higher status while in the forest and consequently gain revenge on the king who has treated them badly.[2] The forest of the tales represents ancient law and custom based on communal folk heritage; it is the landscape which the Grimms saw as the origin and unifying factor of German culture. Zipes suggests that the act of reading the Grimms' Tales is in some ways similar to entering the enchanted

---

[1] Jack Zipes, 'The Enchanted Forest of the Brothers Grimm: New Modes of Approaching the Grimm's Fairy Tales', *Germanic Review*, Vol. LXII, No. 2 (Spring 1987), 66.
[2] Zipes, 'The Enchanted Forest', 71.

forest—the Tales, like the forest, provide a space in which social and political change can be stimulated.[3]

Zipes' summary of the role of the forest in the Grimms' Fairy Tales could easily be applied to the Forbidden Forest of the *Harry Potter* series. In Rowling's books, as in the Tales, characters frequently enter the Forest and lose their bearings. Harry, Ron and Hermione often re-emerge from it with clues as to how they should fight to stop the annual crisis at Hogwarts. The Forbidden Forest is somewhere that wizards never really have power over—other creatures and mythologies hold sway there. The status of the Forbidden Forest has wider social implications both in wizard culture and, as I will suggest later in this chapter, our own.

The incursions into the Forbidden Forest tend to be briefer in the *Harry Potter* books than in the Grimms' Tales. Episodes rather than whole stories happen there. Nevertheless, journeys into the Forest become almost inevitable: in six of the seven novels in the series, Harry, Ron and Hermione (or at least one of these characters) find themselves in the Forest at a crucial stage of the narrative.[4] This pattern is established in *The Philosopher's Stone*: Harry, Hermione, Neville, and Draco are ordered to serve detention, and this takes the form of a dangerous task in the Forest, searching for an injured unicorn. In the middle of the Forest, where the path is almost impossible to follow through the tightly packed trees, Harry and Draco stumble across the clearing where a shadowy figure— Voldemort—is hunched over the dead animal. It attacks when Draco screams, and only the intervention of Firenze the centaur saves the two boys. At this moment, when Harry encounters Voldemort drinking unicorn blood, the reader immediately senses that the book is approaching its narrative climax. Harry has had his first real encounter since infancy with his enemy, and knows that he must act straightaway to stop Voldemort from returning to physical form. Thus he, Ron and Hermione attempt to safeguard the Philosopher's Stone in the next two chapters, the culminating scenes of the book.

---

[3] Zipes, 'The Enchanted Forest', 73.

[4] The exception is *The Half-Blood Prince*, in which the Horcrux cave and to a lesser extent the Room of Requirement function as places of revelation, threat and secrecy. This change slightly unsettles the narrative pattern we are accustomed to from previous books, and accompanies one of the most shocking moments in the series, the death of Dumbledore. It serves to give us further backstory about Voldemort, by revealing a sinister place from his past, and suggests that nowhere is safe from him, even Hogwarts.

We see a very similar structure in *The Chamber of Secrets*. In order to solve the mystery of the opening of the Chamber and the creature that has been Petrifying students, Harry and Ron enter the Forest on Hagrid's advice, following a trail of spiders. There they meet the giant spider Aragog and his many ravenous offspring, and learn that Moaning Myrtle's bathroom may be the way into the Chamber. Again they must act quickly to save the school. Near the end of *The Prisoner of Azkaban*, the time-travelling Harry and Hermione watch from the fringes of the Forest as earlier events unfold. From here they launch their attempt to save Buckbeak from execution and then Harry sets out to save Sirius, casting his first great Patronus charm.

From the pattern that is established in the first three books of the series, the journey into the Forbidden Forest becomes, if not inevitable, then at least a sign that the novel is approaching its climax and resolution. In *The Deathly Hallows*, the final book in the series, Rowling draws on the reader's awareness of the Forest's narrative significance by titling the climactic thirty-fourth chapter—in which Harry offers himself as a sacrifice in order to defeat Voldemort—"The Forest Again." Because we know that journeys into the Forest bring about important changes for the central characters and provide them with the knowledge they need to avert looming disaster at Hogwarts, this chapter title tells us that events are about to happen which will be crucial to the unfolding of the plot.

In the Forbidden Forest, the heroes gain a sense of what has to be done, and set out from there to protect the Philosopher's Stone, find the Chamber of Secrets, and rescue Sirius firstly from Dementors and later from Death Eaters at the Ministry of Secrets. They are changed by events which occur there and learn something about themselves and the threats they face.

I've drawn on the language that Zipes uses to describe the Grimms' enchanted forest in order to show some structural similarity between Rowling's Forest and that of Jacob and Wilhelm Grimm. I don't intend this similarity merely to illustrate the presence of an allusion, although the Grimms' Tales are a visible influence in the work of many children's writers, including Rowling. Rather, I think that this similarity is important because what is at stake in the Grimms' forest is also at stake in Rowling's Forest—access to the transformative influence of forces that exist outside the mainstream of urban, rationally governed society. In the *Harry Potter* books, these forces derive from the dangers and social position of the Forest, which I will discuss for the remainder of this chapter.

The Dangers of the Forest

It is frequently observed that Rowling draws on many literary archetypes in creating the setting, characters and plots of her books, and the Forbidden Forest is no exception. I have already looked at how its role in bringing about narrative change resembles that of the Grimms' enchanted forest, but the characteristics of the Forest also rely on earlier literary forests. In describing a large, dark, densely wooded place where wild creatures roam and people rarely stay for long, and in giving it an ominous-sounding name, Rowling is following the tradition of fairy tale woods, but also a tradition of forest literature that can be traced back to the Renaissance: the dark wood of Dante's *Divine Comedy* and the forest of physical and moral danger in Spenser's *The Faerie Queene*. Although the contemporary world isn't as densely wooded as it was when Dante, Spenser, or the Grimms were writing, the dangerous dark forest remains a potent motif both in literature and in other modern genres such as horror films. It might be taken for granted that a large, dark forest is inherently dangerous—a reader familiar with these precedents is likely to bring this assumption to their interpretation of Rowling's Forbidden Forest—but the extent of its threat in the *Harry Potter* series is debatable. In her infamous article, "Harry Potter and the Childish Adult," A. S. Byatt finds little to fear. She argues that the best recent children's literature contains:

> a real sense of mystery, powerful forces, dangerous creatures in dark forests. Susan Cooper's teenage wizard discovers his magic powers and discovers simultaneously that he is in a cosmic battle between good and evil forces. Every bush and cloud glitters with secret significance [...] Reading writers like these, we feel we are being put back in touch with earlier parts of our culture [...] Ms. Rowling's magic wood has nothing in common with these lost worlds. It is small, and on school grounds, and dangerous only because she says it is.[5]

It's easy for fans of the *Harry Potter* books to be overly defensive in the face of Byatt's blunt comments, but her point is reasonably astute. When you get below the surface, there isn't much mystery to the Forbidden Forest. Consider chapter

---

[5] A. S. Byatt, 'Harry Potter and the Childish Adult', *The New York Times*, 7 July 2003, http://www.nytimes.com/2003/07/07/opinion/harry-potter-and-the-childish-adult.html?pagewanted=all&src=pm, accessed 27 July 2012.

fifteen of *The Philosopher's Stone*, entitled "The Forbidden Forest," in which Harry encounters the Quirrell/Voldemort figure while on detention, as described above. Prior to this chapter, the reader has been given some information about the Forest, and this affects how we think of the setting when Harry and the others follow Hagrid into the trees. The first thing that the reader knows is that the Forest is out-of-bounds—Dumbledore has reminded all students of this at the term opening banquet, with Percy adding that it is "full of dangerous beasts."[6] Later, Harry follows Snape into the Forest and overhears him threatening Quirrell because, so Harry believes, Snape is after the Philosopher's Stone for his own nefarious ends. Snape tells Quirrell that he arranged they meet there so that their business may be kept private. These two incidents show that the Forest is off-limits for the student's safety and is somewhere that secret and ominous meetings can take place because they're hidden from sight. We have no real evidence yet, however, that this forest is forbidding as well as forbidden.

Then comes detention. Mr Filch leads Harry, Hermione, Neville and Draco into the Forest, gleefully warning them about its werewolves. Hagrid reassures them that they will be safe as long as they are with him and Fang, and as long as they don't stray from the path. Despite Filch's threats and Draco's fear, there is little about the Forest itself to instil terror. Admittedly it's dark, silent, and the path is narrow; there are mossy tree-stumps and tangled old oaks. But there is no sense that every tree has magical powers or spiritual significance of the sort that Byatt sees in Susan Cooper's fiction, or that the Forest itself is listening or has personality, like J. R. R. Tolkien's Fangorn.

In fact, Rowling's description makes the Forest seem unthreatening—in and of itself it fails to live up to the sort of danger that we might imagine a place with its name would have. This may be down to a failure on the author's part to generate a sufficient level of detail and atmosphere. There is real danger for Harry and his friends in the Forest, however, but it is important to note that this comes not from the wood itself but from the figures he meets there. The magic and the violence of the Forest come from these beings, not from the landscape. The centaurs, especially Bane, are wild and short-tempered, subject to different codes of conduct than humans, and often hostile to any suggestions of superiority by wizards. And Harry is in mortal peril when he encounters Quir-

---

[6] J. K. Rowling, *Harry Potter and the Philosopher's Stone*, (London: Bloomsbury, 1997), 95.

rell/Voldemort drinking unicorn blood in the clearing. An evil wizard hiding in the trees is a much graver threat to Harry than anything the natural world of the Forest can supply, however dark and off-limits it may be. The Forest is threatening because of what it contains—wolves, centaurs, Voldemort— rather than because of what it is.

In the final *Harry Potter* book, *The Deathly Hallows*, the Forbidden Forest is seen at its most dangerous, a lair of Dementors, werewolves, giants and Death Eaters. Again, the Forest provides the arena in which Harry faces his enemy, but does not itself take sides. It is not more inherently evil at this point than before—Harry must face wizards rather than the spirit of the place, and good still resides in the Forest, demonstrated for example by the centaurs who charge from the trees at the Death Eaters.

Byatt sees it as a fault that the Forbidden Forest is dangerous only because of the figures who dwell there, rather than because of its own magical properties. You cannot say that every bush there "glitters with secret significance." However, this isn't necessarily a failure: in the Grimms' Fairy Tales, characters who face dangers or undergo transformations in the enchanted forest are rarely changed by the forest itself (far more often they meet a witch or an animal with magical powers). Enchantments take place there because it is a space outside of the normal conventions and laws of society, rather than because the forest has a beneficent or malevolent will of its own. Rowling's Forest is hardly an exception to literary history. In fact, its dangers have huge literary precedent. In medieval romances, for instance, knights ventured into forests to face the monsters and wild men who lurked there. Their adventures often make the knights themselves go wild for a while before they return, strengthened by their experience, to the society from which they departed. They seek adventure in the form of rivals, and must contend with their own inner demons, but aren't bewitched by the innate power of the forest. Similarly, in Shakespearean comedies such as *As You Like It* and even *A Midsummer Night's Dream*, the transformative action that occurs in the forest is under the power of people, whether magical of not, who are encountered there. Forests are not wholly other, but rather places where people have lived, worked, gathered food and raw materials for centuries. Dangers come from people and animals, not from ancient, supernatural forces.

Forests are able to harbour these threats because of their location, removed from the centres of urban civilization, and the fact that their canopies and undergrowth offer an effective hiding place. The Forbidden Forest, like other literary forests, occupies a distinctive position in relation to society, which I will look at in the next section.

The Social Position of the Forest

If we return to the quote from Byatt's article, we see that she finds the Forbidden Forest tame because it is on school grounds. This isn't quite accurate: it may be geographically close, but its significance comes from the fact that it is outside the jurisdiction and conventions of Hogwarts. In *The Philosopher's Stone*, the centaur Bane calls it "our Forest"; in *The Deathly Hallows* it is outside the school's defences when the Battle of Hogwarts begins. It's a liminal place, a borderland between wizard society and wilderness, between the order imposed by Dumbledore at Hogwarts and the darker forms of magic which he and the institution tend to reject. This is why it is often home to wizards and magical creatures who want to hide. Snape and Quirrell have their secret meeting there in *The Philosopher's Stone*, Aragog and the wild Ford Anglia hide there in *The Chamber of Secrets*, as does Sirius (in dog form) in *The Prisoner of Azkaban*, and Voldemort sets up base camp there in *The Deathly Hallows*. Hagrid, a semi-outcast from Hogwarts, who is not allowed a wand and who is the first to be suspected of wrong-doing when the Chamber of Secrets is re-opened, lives in a cabin by the edge of the woods, and is more comfortable in the Forest than in the classroom.

The Forbidden Forest, sitting at the boundary of wizard society, is part of a long tradition of defining civilized, human order against wilderness as represented by dark and dangerous, though not especially remote, woods. In the ancient Sumerian epic *Gilgamesh*, the king of the city of Uruk fights the guardian demon of the nearby forest for the sake of his own and his city's glory. Similarly, the social order imposed by Pentheus, king of Thebes in Euripides' *Bacchae*, is literally torn apart by the frenzied followers of the god Bacchus in the nearby forest. Rowling may not have had these predecessors in mind, but like them her forest is close to civilization but outside of its law and order, and this positioning strengthens the landscape's importance to narrative and character development.

Another aspect of the Forest's liminality is what it tells us about character. From its first mention, students are instructed that it's out-of-bounds. Harry, Ron and Hermione nevertheless go there in almost every book in the series. They aren't afraid to break school rules (even the hard-working model pupil, Hermione) and their ability to think outside of regulations and norms becomes their strength as they resist the over-zealous Ministry of Magic in *The Order of the Phoenix* and the totalitarian regime of the Death Eaters in *The Deathly Hallows*.

The Forest may also be an appropriate location for their adventures for other reasons. The protagonists are teenagers, neither wholly child nor wholly adult. Across the books their awkward attempts at dating, their mood swings and their insecurities show that they are trying to work out their identities. Harry's search for father-figures as he closely follows the advice and examples of James Potter, Albus Dumbledore and Remus Lupin, is also part of this process—what pedagogical theorists describe as mimicry of the adult role-models from whom he is learning about himself and about the adult world.[7] The Forest, a place of metamorphosis, home to half-human creatures and talking spiders, where things are half-seen in the shifting light, is an appropriate place for the adolescent protagonists to encounter new ideas and try out different roles.

Returning once more to A. S. Byatt's article, she describes the Forbidden Forest as a "magic wood." Her intention is to belittle it—instead of the vast, untameable forests of northern Europe, Rowling gives us the quaint and relatively safe greenwood of English folk tales. However, the *Harry Potter* books take place in a Great Britain not so terribly different from the one in which the author lives. Harry would be hard pressed to find himself in woodlands similar in scale to the Black Forest.

The British forest, from Norman literature onwards, is depicted as a hunting ground set aside for the recreation of kings (the word "forest" probably derives from the Latin 'foresta', which refers to its legal status as "off-limits").[8] Norman enclosure of forests caused rural peasants a great deal of suffering and upheaval, and in response to acquisition by unjust rulers, figures such Robin Hood became

---

[7] Jan H.F. Meyer and Ray Land, 'Threshold Concepts and Troublesome Knowledge (2): Epistemological Considerations and a Conceptual Framework for Teaching and Learning', *Higher Education*, Vol. 49 (2005), 376.

[8] Robert Pogue Harrison, *Forests: The Shadow of Civilization*, (London: University of Chicago Press, 1993), 69.

the heroes of popular ballads. Paradoxically, the king's hunting ground was also the hiding place for criminals and outlaws as well as an essential place for ordinary folk to collect firewood, rear livestock and hunt. Robin Hood and his followers take advantage of the cover which the forest provides; Hood's surname alludes to his own concealment. As a mythical figure he remains popular today, mostly in the form of a swashbuckling, good-looking rebel, but in times when access to woodland was restricted for common people, such as the late eighteenth and early nineteenth centuries, English popular culture revived the Robin Hood figurehead in response.[9]

When characters in the *Harry Potter* books are on the run, they too find refuge in the forest. Harry, Ron and Hermione have their own Robin Hood adventure in *The Deathly Hallows*, constantly establishing temporary shelters while hiding from an unjust government—the Ministry of Magic as controlled by Death Eaters. Trees often provide them with cover, and like Robin Hood they are veiled, in their case by invisibility charms and Harry's invisibility cloak. A negative version of the Robin Hood figure is Voldemort, whom we are told hid himself in the forests of Albania after his first failure to kill Harry. When wizards find themselves subject to threat from their society they often go to a place which is outside the jurisdiction of that society—the forest. As well as wizards in hiding, the creatures that most wizards are scared of, such as thestrals, centaurs and Aragog's Acromantula, are free to roam there. Because it is off-limits, it becomes a sanctuary.

The Forest Environment

Mention of the Robin Hood stories inevitably draws attention to the connection between forests and folk identity. Robin was a champion of the common people, redistributing wealth and upholding virtues such as loyalty and fairness around which their society defined itself. In nineteenth-century Germany, the Brothers Grimm were also interested in finding the origins of German folk identity in stories about its forests. At the time when they were collecting and writing their Tales, the forest was seen by many as the great possession of the German people, to which all had rights of access. Laws were being passed which privat-

---

[9] Stephanie Barczewski, Myth and National Identity in Nineteenth-Century Britain: The Legends of King Arthur and Robin Hood, (Oxford: Oxford University Press, 2000), 7.

ized much of the forest, leading to a backlash which involved thinkers such as Karl Marx who, in his first publication about the material rights of the masses, appealed to similar sources as the Grimms did in arguing for the connection between the German people, tradition and forests.[10]

Issues of ownership and access are inescapably part of many forest folk traditions. As recent attempts to privatise British forests have shown, these issues remain unresolved and emotive today. There is a danger for any writer that reliance upon established motifs of forests as particularly enchanted or dangerous can lead to a failure to recognise that they have been, and remain, sites of conflict where real social and ecological exploitation have occurred, and where literature and myth often emerge from direct experience of this exploitation. Social and environmental exploitation are hard to separate, frequently occurring simultaneously. I do not wish to further pursue a Marxist reading of the *Harry Potter* books here, however, although an examination of class structures in the series could prove a fruitful direction for future study. I will instead conclude by suggesting a connection between the cultural heritage of forests and their ecological significance, and looking briefly at the Forbidden Forest through this environmental lens.

As campaigns relating to conservation and climate change have become more prominent in western society, forests have been ascribed a new meaning— as a synecdoche for the earth. When we speak of the "green planet" or of "green politics," we are using the colour of forests to represent the sum of ecological interactions both within these habitats and across the globe, and to express fears about environmental stability. Individual forests are also important to environmentalists—Amazonian deforestation, for instance, has provoked international calls for the sustainable use of natural resources. Furthermore, woodland is seen as an effective weapon for those fighting to protect the natural world—hence tree-planting is championed as a way to 'offset' carbon emissions and increase publicly-available green space. Literature about forests often contributes to these campaigns. The German philosopher Martin Heidegger, who has influenced a generation of environmental philosophers and literary critics, uses the image of walking in the forest as a metaphor for the process of thought, which he argues

---

[10] Harrison, *Forests*, 176-7.

is how we come to feel at home in the world around us.[11] The idea of getting "back to nature" is in part inspired by books like Henry David Thoreau's *Walden: or, Life in the Woods* (1854) and more recently Roger Deakin's *Wildwood* (2007). A wide range of poets including W. S. Merwin, Susan Stewart, and Sorley MacLean have written about the connection between the loss of wooded places and the loss of the cultural narratives that surround them.

Are there any signs of this forest-based environmental discourse in the *Harry Potter* books? Rowling offers no overtly environmental message in the series, and is not explicitly engaging with figures such as Heidegger or Thoreau. However, the environmental themes I have just touched on can provide a means of interpreting her representation of the Forbidden Forest.

To some extent, the Forest functions like a nature reserve, free from buildings and other signs of human presence. In the early books in the series, its animal inhabitants are generally left to their own devices. Characters express differing opinions regarding its worth. Hagrid, the closest figure in the series to a woodsman or park ranger, knows the Forest's paths well and has an impressive knowledge of its biodiversity. He treats its creatures—centaurs, thestrals, and even Acromantula—with a level of respect uncommon to wizards, who tend to ignore these creatures' existence. In fact, the first time we enter the Forest with Hagrid, in the excursion in *The Philosopher's Stone* which introduces the reader to his affinity with the place, he is working to protect its species by investigating the poaching of its unicorn population (an example of Voldemort simultaneously exploiting both natural resources and humans, in this case Quirrell, for his own gain). Hagrid's attitude contrasts with that of Dolores Umbridge in *The Order of the Phoenix*, who is "apprehensive" about entering the Forest and navigates it with difficulty. She and the Ministry she represents have treated it and its inhabitants with contempt, branding centaurs "filthy halfbreeds," beasts of "near-human intelligence" whom she suggests are only permitted to live in the Forest by the generosity of wizards, although it is actually their hereditary home.[12] It is fitting that her downfall is at the hands of these Forest inhabitants. The plot revolving around Umbridge's rule at Hogwarts, which contains some critique of

---

[11] See Martin Heidegger, '...Poetically Man Dwells...' in *Poetry, Language, Thought,* (New York: Harper Perennial, 2001), 211-227.
[12] J. K. Rowling, *Harry Potter and the Order of the Phoenix,* (London: Bloomsbury, 2003), 663-5.

recent British governments, may include a touch of scorn for political and corporate interests which disregard the rural environment; certainly Umbridge, the urban administrator, is unable to understand or appreciate the Forest and its creatures and her ignorance is a symptom of her ideological fervour.

Beyond the example of Hagrid, however, there is no suggestion in the *Harry Potter* books that the Forbidden Forest, or indeed other natural habitats, can and should be recognised for their inherent ecological worth. There is, further, little attention given to the potential costs to wizards themselves of environmental irresponsibility, except perhaps when the centaurs fight back in *The Deathly Hallows* after being maltreated by Death Eaters gathered in the Forest. Relying as it does on well-established tropes—the forest as dark, dangerous place, as refuge, as a place where character and plot transformations can occur— Rowling's Forest can at times appear one-dimensional when considered as an actual, complex ecosystem. In addition, Harry's adventures take place in a parallel version of contemporary Britain, and uncertainties about such matters as terrorism, governance and discrimination convincingly transfer from the real Britain into Rowling's fictional one, but environmentalism, despite its prominence in modern British society, is not much of an issue in wizard Britain. Although forests are landscapes where the troubled relationship between humans and nature is often manifested, evidence of this conflict in the books is limited to occasional acts by malevolent characters and there is no suggestion of local or nationwide environmental worries.

As I have shown above, forests play a significant role in western literature, particularly in folk tales. Representations of them are so common as to make specific instances of influence or allusion in the *Harry Potter* books difficult to assess, but the narrative significance of the Forbidden Forest, its liminal status and its role as a hiding place for outlaws establishes it within a long tradition. The relationship between the world of *Harry Potter* and its literary predecessors is certainly worthy of scholarly attention as it is important to consider why the series has been so popular and is so comfortingly familiar to so many readers. The Forbidden Forest is not a strikingly original creation, and is at times lacking in depth, for instance when we look closely at its supposedly threatening atmosphere or its potential as a place where environmental conflicts are foregrounded. Nevertheless, it is crucial to the unfolding of five of the books' plots. An awareness of the Forest's thematic importance and literary sources allows the reader to understand more clearly what is at stake for the various characters who enter it, and for those who fail to recognise its worth.

Works Cited

Barczewski, Stephanie, Myth and National Identity in Nineteenth-Century Britain: The Legends of King Arthur and Robin Hood, Oxford: Oxford University Press, 2000.

Byatt, A. S., 'Harry Potter and the Childish Adult', *The New York Times*, 7 July 2003, <http://www.nytimes.com/2003/07/07/opinion/harry-potter-and-the-childish-adult.html?pagewanted=all&src=pm>, accessed 27 July 2012.

Harrison, Robert Pogue, *Forests: The Shadow of Civilization*, London: University of Chicago Press, 1993.

Heidegger, Martin, *Poetry Language Thought*, trans. Albert Hofstadter, New York: Harper Perennial, 2001.

Meyer, Jan H.F. and Ray Land, 'Threshold Concepts and Troublesome Knowledge (2): Epistemological Considerations and a Conceptual Framework for Teaching and Learning', *Higher Education*, Vol. 49 (2005), 373-388.

Rowling, J. K., *Harry Potter and the Philosopher's Stone*, London: Bloomsbury, 1997.

—. *Harry Potter and the Chamber of Secrets*, London: Bloomsbury, 1998.

—. *Harry Potter and the Prisoner of Azkaban*, London: Bloomsbury, 1999.

—. *Harry Potter and the Goblet of Fire*, London: Bloomsbury, 2000.

—. *Harry Potter and the Order of the Phoenix*, London: Bloomsbury, 2003.

—. *Harry Potter and the Half-Blood Prince*, London: Bloomsbury, 2005.

—. *Harry Potter and the Deathly Hallows*, London: Bloomsbury, 2007.

Zipes, Jack, 'The Enchanted Forest of the Brothers Grimm: New Modes of Approaching the Grimm's Fairy Tales', *Germanic Review*, Vol. LXII, No. 2 (Spring 1987), 66-74.

The Suburbs of Arcadia
Response from John Patrick Pazdziora

T he forest is the place where the wild things are. Whether, on the other side, the child who enters it will discover a hot dinner waiting or the grim silhouette of Lonely Mountain is immaterial. The forest operates by its own rules, and its own law; the Wild Wood is an Otherland, and crossing into it is inevitable. Beyond its initiatory threshold lies the organic labyrinth of growing, and growing up. In the words of the great Michael Rosen: "We can't go over it. We can't go under it. Oh no! We've got to go through it!"[1]

So, with his engaging discussion of the roots and rhetoric of the Forbidden Forest, Garry MacKenzie has identified one of the key landscapes of children's literature, and of children's fantasy in particular. But where is Harry Potter's forest, exactly? At least three forests in the series play a significant role. Along with the Forbidden Forest, there is the Transylvanian forest that gives refuge to the disembodied Voldemort, and there is the Forest of Dean, where Harry and Hermione hide in *Deathly Hallows*, where they are reunited with Ron, and where Harry undergoes his baptismal vision of the Silver Doe.[2]

The dark woods on the edge of Hogwarts, and the darker wilderness of Transylvania, are logical enough as landscapes in a magical world. But the Forest of Dean appears, at first blush, to bear out A. S. Byatt's complaint that Rowling's magic woods are tepid, sanitized affairs. As Hermione implies when she mentioned that "I came camping here once, with my mum and dad,"[3] the real-life Forest of Dean is a prime holidaymaker's destination. A quick glance at a recent Visitor Guide reveals the classic charm of a domesticated wilderness, replete with "a network of enticing tracks and paths", championship golf on "excellent greens and challenging holes", "the International Centre for Birds of Prey", "a

---

[1] Michael Rosen, *We're Going on a Bear Hunt* (London: Walker Books, 1993), pp. 5 et al.

[2] For a detailed discussion of the symbolic role of the forest within the larger framework of the series, cf. Travis Prinzi, *Harry Potter and Imagination: The Way Between Two Worlds* (Allentown: Zossima, 2009), 111-112, 125-126.

[3] J. K. Rowling, *Harry Potter and the Deathly Hallows* (London: Bloomsbury, 2007), 297.

top quality offering of food and drink", and "one guarantee of FUN!"[4] While
hiding from Death Eaters, Harry and his comrades would also need to hide from
horseback riders, birdwatchers, sport enthusiasts on "one of the UK's longest zip
wires", children clamouring for a ride on Thomas the Tank Engine, the Father
Christmas grotto, and BBC film crews shooting historical dramas.[5] Admittedly,
even BBC film crews can hardly fill all 200 square miles of the forest at once,[6]
but it seems that the Forest of Dean's "remoteness and unspoilt natural beauty"[7]
is only for a given value of "remote" and "unspoilt."

But Rowling's use of the Forest of Dean is hardly arbitrary: she lived near
the forest for much of her childhood. As she recalled in a 1998 article called
"The Not Especially Fascinating Life So Far of J. K. Rowling":

> When I was nine we moved to Tutshill near Chepstow in the Forest of Dean.
> We were finally out in the countryside, which had always been my parents'
> dream, both being Londoners, and my sister and I spent most of our times wan-
> dering unsupervised across fields and along the river Wye.[8]

This common-sense connection between her "parents' dream" and her own "unsupervised wandering" raises a curious point about the type of forest found in
the Wizarding World. The grown-ups want the children to inhabit a pastoral
world of free play and exploration of nature. Yet the children's unsupervised
play is still to some extent controlled by their parents; the child is not wholly
unsupervised, and, like Max, returns home to find supper waiting. This is the
landscape of *Winnie-the-Pooh* rather than *Babes in the Wood*; it engages with

---

[4] *Forest of Dean & Wye Valley: Visitor Guide 2014* (Cokeford: Forestry Commission
England, 2014), 2, 6, 25, 27, http://www.visitforestofdean.co.uk/system-
images/files/VG%20layout%202014%20LR(2).pdf, accessed 10 January 2014.
[5] Ibid., 4, 6, 13, 21, et al.; cf. "Filming at Puzzlewood," *Puzzlewood: A magical day out
in the Forest of Dean*, http://www.puzzlewood.net/filmingatpuzzlewood.htm, accessed 10
January 2014; "Puzzlewood News 2013," *Puzzlewood: A magical day out in the Forest of
Dean*, http://www.puzzlewood.net/puzzlewoodnews.htm, accessed 14 January 2014:
"Santa has decided to hide away in his house in Puzzelwood this year. His naughty rein-
deers are all over the woods and we need your help to find them."
[6] "Tourist Information and Travel Guide for Forest of Dean in the English County of
Gloucestershire," *Royal Forest of Dean .Info* (2011),
http://www.royalforestofdean.info/forest-of-dean/, accessed 10 January 2014.
[7] "J K Rowling," *Forest Web: The Virtual Guide to the Royal Forest of Dean* (2009),
http://www.fweb.org.uk/local-history/15-J_K_Rowling, accessed 8 January 2014.
[8] J. K. Rowling, "The Not Especially Fascinating Life So Far of J. K. Rowling,"
Accio Quote, 16 February 2007,
http://www.accio-quote.org/articles/1998/autobiography.html, accessed 8 January 2014.

nature through unstructured play, not actual subsistence. So the nine-year-old Rowling explored the Forest of Dean in the care of her parents; Harry, Ron, and Hermione explore it under the benevolent if curmudgeonly oversight of Severus Snape and the portrait of Phineas Nigellus.

The "unspoilt" aspect of the Forest of Dean, then, is the recollection of free play in a natural environment. The landscapes of childhood are always vaster and grander in memory than in grown-up fact, and it is the child's vision that matters for Rowling in *Harry Potter*. Even A. S. Byatt grudgingly admits the series' shrewd "child's eye view."[9] This, indeed, counts more for the series' success than Byatt cares to admit: Rowling's writing may meander but it never patronizes. It is the child's own experience of the world, rather than grown-up formulations of it, that ultimately matters in the stories.

This is as it should be. The best writers of children's literature—the writers whose works deserve to be called simply *literature*—attain a deep, resonant empathy with their child readers. They create stories that children enjoy and like to read or have read to them, and which, just as importantly, revivify the childlikeness of the grown-ups who are obliged to read them aloud several times an hour. But such literary proficiency is only attainable through a grown-up mastery of craft, a grown-up awareness of others, and a grown-up empathy. It is the grown-up's imagination of childhood that is being narrated, a distinction sharply apparent when the best stories written for children are contrasted with the stories children tell themselves. The defining feature of children's literature is this experience of dedoublement: being at once thoroughly identified with the child protagonist, whilst simultaneously standing apart as an adult observer.

To a certain extent, any work of children's literature becomes a dream of a lost Arcadia. Because the task of writing children's literature is the province of the adult, the adult seeks to harmonize through narrative the dichotomy between their grown-up self and the child they once were, or the children they now care for. And yet, because they themselves have grown, they are all too aware that childhood itself is a sort of greenwood—a liminal and transient state. The narrative becomes one of dream-consciousness and escape. In this sense, the green-

---

[9] A. S. Byatt, "Harry Potter and the Childish Adult," *The New York Times*, 7 July 2003, <http://www.nytimes.com/2003/07/07/opinion/harry-potter-and-the-childish-adult.html>, accessed 10 January 2014.

wood effect applies to every landscape in children's literature. Any writer for
children celebrates the individual moment of childhood preserved in their story,
and its childish wonder at newly discovery in the world. But they cannot help
but understanding the fleetingness of childhood, like Lewis Carroll recalling and
lamenting the Golden Afternoon of wonder and play. The players must eventually leave the greenwood, and Alice wakes from Wonderland.

MacKenzie compares the forests in *Harry Potter* with the forests of the
Brothers Grimm, giving the wandering heroes "access to the transformative influence of forces that exist outside the mainstream of urban, rationally governed
society." The forests in Grimm, however, form the primary *topos* of the tales. In
a fairy tale, the story begins when the threshold of the forest is crossed, and ends
when the forest and its effects are ultimately eluded; the forest is the whole of
the netherworld, the katabatic landscape of the hero's moral and physical dilemmas and quests. In *Harry Potter*, the forest serves only a secondary, episodic
topos. A more precise analogue to the forest in Grimm would be the whole of
the Wizarding World itself. The Wizarding World, with its trains and broomsticks and banks and civil servants and, above all, its boarding school, is the
enchanted fairy wood through which Harry must pass, where he seeks and finds
his fortune, and from which, ultimately, he never returns. The forests are a part
of the Wizarding World, in the way a castle or cottage might be part of the forest
of Grimm. But, paradoxically, they are not actually the enchanted forest itself.

Perhaps the Wizarding World could be best described as a suburban greenwood. The Forbidden Forest is present within the Wizarding World, true, but it is
present in much the same way the Forest of Dean is present in modern England:
a relic of an older time, carefully stewarded for the enjoyment of modern people
in modern ways, whether they prefer wilderness trails or Father Christmas grot-
toes, informed by relatively modern sensibilities concerning the environment.
For good or ill, the old Greenwood has vanished, in England and the Wizarding
World alike. Thus Harry Potter's Arcadia has been suburbanized, with an im-
mensely desirable private school which guarantees a comfortable career in the
civil service. All the structures which a suburban child unwittingly assumes to
constitute the world are present: the school, the grocery store, the bank, and so
on. But in the Wizarding World they become the gothic towers of Hogwarts, the
lively sweets of Honeydukes, the lofty dungeon of Gringotts. The suburban
world is glamourized, glittering and enchanted.

It is precisely at this point where Byatt's criticism of Rowling breaks down. By-att laments that Rowling has neglected to imitate Susan Cooper and create a dark forest where "[e]very bush and cloud glitters with secret significance." And, as MacKenzie points out, the bushes and canopies of the Forbidden For-est—and the Forest of Dean, for that matter—are little more than stage dressing; the real action is played out between the characters interacting with each other, and not through engagement the forests themselves as forests. But if, as I sug-gest here, the Wizarding World as a whole is analogous to the greenwood of Grimm, then Byatt's position becomes more tenuous. In *Harry Potter*, Rowling chooses not to create Arcadia from a mythic wilderness—a landscape which very few people in the Western World have genuinely encountered in the past century—but an Arcadia from a glamourized suburb, out of the bits and bobs of her child readers' everyday lives. To demand of this world the anthropomorphic, mythical pantheism of Yeats's *Celtic Twilight* and its imitators is to miss the boldly enchanted landscape Rowling has in fact created; to decry the fact that Harry encounters perfectly ordinary bushes in the Forbidden Forest would be like complaining that Snow White finds seven perfectly ordinary little chairs in the dwarfs' cottage. One cannot help but feel that Byatt—forgive me—has missed the forest for the trees.

Works Cited

Byatt, A. S. "Harry Potter and the Childish Adult," *The New York Times*, 7 July 2003, <http://www.nytimes.com/2003/07/07/opinion/harry-potter-and-the-childish-adult.html>, accessed 10 January 2014.

"Filming at Puzzlewood," *Puzzlewood: A magical day out in the Forest of Dean*, http://www.puzzlewood.net/filmingatpuzzlewood.htm, accessed 10 January 2014

Forest of Dean & Wye Valley: Visitor Guide 2014 (Cokeford: Forestry Commission England, 2014), 2, 6, 25, 27, http://www.visitforestofdean.co.uk/system-images/files/VG%20layout%202014%20LR(2).pdf, accessed 10 January 2014.

"J K Rowling," *Forest Web: The Virtual Guide to the Royal Forest of Dean* (2009), http://www.fweb.org.uk/local-history/15-J_K_Rowling, accessed 8 January 2014.

"Puzzlewood News 2013," *Puzzlewood: A magical day out in the Forest of Dean*, http://www.puzzlewood.net/puzzlewoodnews.htm, accessed 14 January 2014:

Rosen, Michael. *We're Going on a Bear Hunt*. London: Walker Books, 1993.

Rowling, J. K. *Harry Potter and the Deathly Hallows*. London: Bloomsbury, 2007.

—."The Not Especially Fascinating Life So Far of J. K. Rowling," *Accio Quote*, 16 February 2007, http://www.accio- quote.org/articles/1998/autobiography.html, accessed 8 January 2014.

Prinzi, Travis. *Harry Potter and Imagination: The Way Between Two Worlds*. Allentown: Zossima, 2009.

"Tourist Information and Travel Guide for Forest of Dean in the English County of Gloucestershire," *Royal Forest of Dean .Info* (2011), http://www.royalforestofdean.info/forest-of-dean/, accessed 10 January 2014.

CHAPTER 5

Folktale Structure, Aesthetic Satisfaction, and the Success of *Harry Potter*

Joel Hunter

By the time the fourth book in the *Harry Potter* series, *Goblet of Fire*, had been consumed by the reading public in 2001, academe had begun to respond to the global Potter phenomenon and started constructing a significant body of secondary literature. Whilst this literature is multidisciplinary, the research more or less coalesces into two scholarly areas with their attendant questions: what are we to make of Potter as a *literary achievement* and as a *cultural phenomenon*? In their own ways and with their own methods, the question that drives both of these investigations and persists into the present day is this: *Why has the Harry Potter series of books been so popular?* This is the explicit question to be answered in this essay, and to do so we have developed a hypothesis based on the theory and methods of formalist folklorist Vladimir Propp.[1]

Introduction

The body of scholarship on the Potter series which is concerned either implicitly or explicitly with the question of why the series has been so popular includes a wide variety of methods of literary analysis in narratology and semiotics, including metanarrative analysis, structural and poststructuralist critiques, historicist and new historicist readings, psychoanalytic critiques, postcolonial, Marxist, critical race and gender theories, and so on. Our approach is

---

[1] The results of the research discussed in this essay were originally presented on May 17, 2012, at the conference "A Brand of Fictional Magic: Reading Harry Potter as Literature," in St Andrews, Scotland.

one of many abstract frameworks seek and use a formal system of description. It is important to discuss the advantages as well as the limits of this approach.

Propp's structuralism is formalist. This distinguishes his methods from those of other structuralist approaches, such as that of Claude Lévi-Strauss. In his introduction to the *Morphology*, Alan Dundes characterizes Lévi-Strauss' structural analyses as "paradigmatic" wherein stories are organized according to a matrix of paradigmatic thematic units, typically expressed in a set of binary oppositions such as life/death, male/female, sacred/profane, good/evil, and so on. Paradigmatic structuralism is, in short, a theory of literary *meaning*. Propp's structuralism, in contrast, is a theory of literary *form* rather than content. It is unconcerned with basic units of meaning outside the specific text at hand, and thus avoids the knotty problems of semiotics. Dundes describes Propp's approach as "syntagmatic," that is, the combination of basic units in a specific linear sequence. So, for example, in the sentence "Harry looked at the snake," one would analyze the combination "Harry" and then "looked at" and then "the snake." Substitutions one might make for any of these units—for example, "approached" for "looked at" and "Ronan and Bane" for "the snake"—are irrelevant. The basic units in the folktale according to Propp are a set of 31 functions of the *dramatis personae*, which comprise the narrative's "grammar," and the analyst's job is to identify and describe the "syntax" of the tale with these functions.

Propp's formalist approach is *a way to begin* to answer our leading question of Harry Potter's popularity. The advantage of this approach is that its methods are empirical and inductive; the results we have obtained are reproducible by a similarly trained analyst. However, there are two cautionary notes it is important to raise about this. First, as has been pointed out by others,[2] the simplicity of Propp's theory and the temptation to treat it as a universal typology for all stories can lead to analysts misinterpreting or distorting Propp's schema, the tale being analyzed, or both. To arrest the tendency for our analyses of the *Harry Potter* series to be either too reductive or too complex, we established analysis and review protocols to limit the possible misapplication of Propp's very specific parameters for the functions and the schema as a whole. Second, Propp's approach abstracts the tale from its social and cultural contexts. This is a well-

---

[2] David Bordwell, "ApProppriations and ImPropprieties: Problems in the Morphology of Film Narratives," *Cinema Journal* 27, no. 3 (1988): 5-20.

known problem with formalist theories, but it is particularly important for one to know what the results show and what they do not about the Harry Potter series. They do not unearth *all* that can and should be shown about the meaning and artistry of the Hogwarts saga. But we do argue that our findings are sufficient to account for the popularity of the series, and even more significantly, *the popularity of the individual books in the series relative to each other*.

Children all over the world hear many folktales and like to hear their favorite ones again and again. By the time they become readers the narrative sequence common to many of these stories has been mapped onto their minds. Tales "go" a certain way. Specific actions should be present for it to "work" for the listener or reader. Irrespective of whether we define the *Harry Potter* series of books as a folktale according to other literary criteria, we should not be surprised that they are scaffolded like other stories in bestselling fiction, graphic novels, movies, and so on. If the *Harry Potter* series of books did *not* harmonize with Propp's schema, then we would have to look for others reasons that readers are so easily and effectively drawn into the story. Since Propp himself warns the reader that there are "thousands of other tales not resembling fairy tales," it is imperative that we not presume the *Harry Potter* series *is* a folktale, even if it is reckoned so under different definitions of folktales. Since superficial resemblances of a few story elements to Propp's functions may be justly disregarded, we formulated and followed a set of procedures that constrained our analyses and interpretation to Propp's schema as he intended it.

Thus, other factors relevant to explaining the popularity of the *Harry Potter* series notwithstanding, we argue that it is sufficient to explain its popularity with a Proppian analysis. Our hypothesis is, in other words, that the popularity of the *Harry Potter* series can be accounted for by the books' narrative structure, in particular, their concordance with a linear sequence of elements typical of folktales as outlined by Vladimir Propp. The aesthetic satisfaction with any particular book in the series should positively correlate to that book's folktale structure as enumerated in Propp's system of 31 functions of *dramatis personae*. In other words, readers will report *less* aesthetic satisfaction the less concordance obtains between the book's actual morphology and Propp's schema; readers will report *more* aesthetic satisfaction the more concordance obtains between the book's actual morphology and Propp's schema. Moreover, the aesthetic satisfaction of the *series* of books also concords with the folktale structure of the Hog-warts saga when it is analyzed as a single tale.

Overview of Propp's Theory

Vladimir Propp was one of the leading figures of the Russian formalist school of literary theory. His seminal work, the *Morphology of the Folktale*,[3] was published in 1928, but not translated into English until 1958. By that time the winds of theory had shifted in other directions in both Russia and the West. Nevertheless, since the 1960s, this work has inspired a number of studies in multiple disciplines among English-speaking scholars. Its applicability to the folktales of other cultures, to other kinds of folk narrative, to the learning and transmission of fairy tale structure in children, and to performance, non-folklore literature, and other cultural materials has been examined.[4] See, for example, Misia Landau's application of Propp's schema to accounts of human evolution.[5] Such versatile applications of Propp's theory to narratives of widely divergent types, authorship, and aims have established the context in which the present study grew.

Propp found that the magical folktales of his native Russia conformed to a schema of thirty-one functions.[6] He derived this schema from a systematic analysis done on a set of 100 stories in the collection of fairy tales compiled by Alexander Afanasyev, and produced symbolized representations for about 50 of those to demonstrate in abstract description the repetitive and uniform structure of such tales. These morphologies enable the folklorist to do comparative analysis *within* individual tales and *among* multiple tales:

---

[3] Vladimir Propp, *Morphology of the Folktale*, 2nd edition, ed. Louis A. Wagner, trans. Laurence Scott (Austin, TX: University of Texas Press, 1968).
[4] Alan Dundes, "Introduction" to *Morphology of the Folktale*, xiv-xv.
[5] Misia Landau, *Narratives of Human Evolution* (New Haven: Yale University Press, 1991), x-xi and 3-16.
[6] Propp, *Morphology*, 25-64.

Symbol	Function Name	Function Description	Group
α	Initial Situation	Not a function. Enumeration of family members, future hero introduced by mention of name or status, etc.	
β	Absentation	One of the members of a family absents himself from home	Preparation
γ	Interdiction	An interdiction is addressed to the hero	
δ	Violation	The interdiction is violated	
ε	Reconnaissance	The villain makes an attempt at reconnaissance	
ζ	Delivery	The villain receives information about his victim	
η	Trickery	The villain attempts to deceive his victim in order to take possession of him or of his belongings	
θ	Complicity	The victim submits to deception and thereby unwittingly helps his enemy	
A	Villainy	The villain causes harm or injury to a member of a family	Complication
a	Lack	One member of a family either lacks something or desires to have something	
B	Mediation; The Connective Incident	Misfortune or lack is made known; the hero is approached with a request or command; he is allowed to go or he is dispatched	
C	Beginning Counteraction	The seeker agrees to or decides upon counteraction	
↑	Departure	The hero leaves home	Transference
D	The First Function of the Donor	The hero is tested, interrogated, attacked, etc., which prepares the way for his receiving either a magical agent or helper	
E	The Hero's Reaction	The hero reacts to the actions of the future donor	
F	Provision or Receipt of a Magical Agent	The hero acquires the use of a magical agent	
G	Spatial Transference Between Two Kingdoms, Guidance	The hero is transferred, delivered, or led to the whereabouts of an object of search	
H	Struggle	The hero and the villain join in direct combat	Conflict
J	Branding, Marking	The hero is branded	
I	Victory	The villain is defeated	
K	Misfortune Liquidated	The initial misfortune or lack is liquidated	
↓	Return	The hero returns	Return
Pr	Pursuit, Chase	The hero is pursued	
Rs	Rescue	Rescue of the hero from pursuit	
o	Unrecognized Arrival	The hero, unrecognized, arrives home or in another country	
L	Unfounded Claims	A false hero presents unfounded claims	
M	Difficult Task	A difficult task is proposed to the hero	
N	Solution	The task is resolved	
Q	Recognition	The hero is recognized	Recognition
Ex	Exposure	The false hero or villain is exposed	
T	Transfiguration	The hero is given a new appearance	
U	Punishment	The villain is punished	
W	Wedding	The hero is married and ascends the throne	

We may illustrate how to apply Propp's system with a simple and familiar tale: "The Three Bears." The functions of the *dramatis personae* corresponding to the narrative elements will be given in square brackets [ ] in **bold** type.

Three bears live together in a house in the woods. They each have a porridge bowl, a chair and a bed [**Initial Situation**]. The Three Bears go for a walk in the woods [**Absentation**]. The Old Woman comes to the Three Bears' home, looks in the window, and peeps in the keyhole [**Reconnaissance**]. The Old Woman discovers that the Three Bears are not at home [**Delivery**]. The Old Woman eats Wee Bear's porridge, breaks his chair, and sleeps in his bed [**Villainy**]. The Three Bears return home. Wee Bear finds the Old Woman in his bed [**Mediation, The Connective Incident**]. The Old Woman wakes, jumps from the window, and runs away [**Misfortune Liquidated**].

We note that this tale consists of only two *dramatis personae*: the Three Bears are the heroes (of the victim type) and the Old Woman is the villain. In the schema of 31 functions, Propp designates each function with a symbol. The symbolized representation of "The Three Bears" is:

$$\alpha\ \beta\ \varepsilon\ \zeta\ A\ B\ K$$

Thus, "The Three Bears" is a tale consisting of six functions (the Initial Situation, α, is not a function according to Propp). None of its functions is out of the sequence established in Propp's schema.

Propp argued that two further structural laws follow from his morphological study of tales: (3) that the sequence of functions is always identical and (4) that all fairy tales are of one type in regard to their structure.[7] Since the sequential progression of functions is always the same, there develops a single narrative axis in all folktales. The position for a given function is always the same in every tale, though a particular function need not be present at all. These two morphological laws are central to our study and assessment of the Harry Potter series of books.

Propp and the Potter Saga

The possibility of applying Propp's schema to the Harry Potter series has been noted before. The first instance found in the literature is Joan Acocella's review of the series up to the then-released *Goblet of Fire*.[8] Acocello claims that

---

[7] Ibid., 22-3.

[8] Joan Acocella, "Under the Spell; Harry Potter explained." The New Yorker, July 31, 2000). John Granger also noted Acocello's article in *How Harry Cast His Spell: The Meaning behind the Mania for J. K. Rowling's Bestselling Books* (Carol Stream, IL: Tyndale House, 2008), 21.

Rowling was successful because of her "utter traditionalism," and Acocello proceeds to tick off a string of literary genres that many readers have identified. She then connects this literary borrowing to Propp, whose schema of functions she deems a list of "just about every convention ever used in fairy tales." She lists six of the functions and fills them in with plausible story elements from *Philosopher's Stone*. However, Acocello applies Propp's theory loosely, especially the four morphological laws, treating the functions precisely as conventions and without respect to the formal organization that is central to Propp's schema. Indeed Acocello equates Propp's functions to archetypes, which is an unhelpful confusion of literary approaches.

Slavic folklore scholar Jann Lacoss[9] applied Propp's schema to *Philosopher's Stone* and *Goblet of Fire*. After a brief paragraph of introduction to Propp, Lacoss claims that "[t]he Harry Potter series seems to employ these same functions, although not always in the proper order (in the Harry Potter series, they are actually quite often in the same order as in magic tales)."[10] She is quite correct here, as our own analyses confirmed (albeit with significant variation from Lacoss's tables, discussed in APPENDIX III). She also correctly claims that "each book follows the sequence, and the overall plot of the series also appears to do so." This is quite prescient given that Lacoss was working only with the series through *Goblet of Fire*. Furthermore, she speculates as we do that the language of tales "may be learned and sublimated from childhood. Thus when the books were written, Rowling had an instinctive 'road map,' so to speak, for creating an engaging tale to which children (and adults) could easily relate."[11] Like Lacoss, we are not arguing that Rowling followed this structure intentionally. It is more likely that, like the Potter readers enthralled for reasons of which they are unaware, Rowling unconsciously followed the "cultural script" of folktales in writing the saga.

---

[9] Jann Lacoss, "Of Magicals and Muggles: Reversals and Revulsions at Hogwarts, in *The Ivory Tower and Harry Potter: Perspectives on a Literary Phenomenon*, ed. Lana A. Whited (Columbia, MO: University of Missouri Press, 2004), 67-88.

[10] Ibid., 85.

[11] Ibid.

Testing Our Hypothesis: Aesthetic Satisfaction of *Harry Potter* Readers

An online survey was prepared and administered (see APPENDIX I). We distributed the survey to students who had completed our Harry Potter course at Arizona State University and to colleagues hosting Harry Potter-related academic and fan sites worldwide. The response size was 599. Respondents first answered whether or not they had read all of the books in the series. Those re-responding "No" were discarded from the data set (N = 13). Next, respondents were asked the number of times they had read through the entire series. This indicates the probable familiarity the reader has with the story details of the series. These levels of familiarity are denoted as follows: A *Novice* has read the series only once (N = 67); an *Amateur* has read the series more than once but fewer than five times (N = 251); an *Aficionado* has read the series more than five times but fewer than ten (N = 118); a *Savant* has read the series more than ten times (N = 90). Respondents then selected the rank order of the books in the series from least aesthetically satisfying (1) to most aesthetically satisfying (7). Responses with fewer than five of the seven ranking positions selected for the individual books were discarded (N = 60). The total response size analyzed was 526.

We have summarized our results from the survey of aesthetic satisfaction of Harry Potter readers in Tables 1 and 2. Table 1 shows the mean scores (on a scale of 1, representing least aesthetic satisfaction, to 7, representing greatest aesthetic satisfaction) of the survey responses to each book in the series by the different levels of reader familiarity:

Reader Familiarity with the Series		*Stone*	*Chamber*	*Prisoner*	*Goblet*	*Order*	*Prince*	*Hallows*
Novice	N = 67	3.8	3.2	4.6	4.0	3.7	4.3	4.9
Amateur	N = 251	3.6	2.9	4.7	4.0	3.7	4.3	5.0
Aficionado	N = 118	3.5	2.5	4.9	4.0	3.6	4.2	5.4
Savant	N = 90	3.8	2.5	4.7	3.6	3.9	4.1	5.5
All	N = 526	3.6	2.8	4.6	4.0	3.7	4.3	5.2
Rank in Aesthetic Satisfaction (all readers)		2	1	6	4	3	5	7

Table 1:   Summary of survey results showing the mean scores for aesthetic satisfaction

Table 1 shows that for all readers, regardless of their level of familiarity, *Deathly Hallows* is the most aesthetically satisfying book and *Chamber of Secrets* is the least aesthetically satisfying book. Table 2 shows the response by *mode*, which shows the score most frequently assigned by respondents to the given text. A mode of "1" indicates that "1" was the most frequently assigned value out of all possible values '1' through '7'.

Reader Familiarity with the Series	Stone	Chamber	Prisoner	Goblet	Order	Prince	Hallows
Novice	5	2	7	4	4	6	7
Amateur	2	1	7	5	1	6	7
Aficionado	3	1	7	5	1	6	7
Savant	4	2	7	4	1	6	7
All	3	1	7	4	1	6	7

Table 2:   Summary of survey results showing the mode for aesthetic satisfaction

The findings in Table 2 bear some further comment. We are interested in the extremities of the data. At the upper end of the range, the value indicating *highest* aesthetic satisfaction, both *Prisoner* and *Hallows* were chosen more frequently and consistently by readers as the most aesthetically satisfying tales in the series. At the low end of the range, the value indicating *least* aesthetic satisfaction, both *Chamber* and *Order* were chosen more frequently—though not consistently—as the least aesthetically satisfying tales in the series. For Novice readers, none of the books in the series achieved a mode of '1'; '2' was the lowest mode and it was assigned to *Chamber*. Aesthetic judgment hardens among the Amateur and Aficionado readers; two books indicate a mode of '1' and two books indicate a mode of '7'. Two modes do not appear in their rankings ('3' and '4' for the Amateur; '2' and '4' for the Aficionado). For the Savant, aesthetic judgment softens for *Stone* and *Chamber*. Only *Order* retains a mode of '1' for the Savant whilst *Prisoner* and *Hallows* retain their modes of '7'. Lastly, it should be pointed out that all readers consistently ranked *Prince* as '6' more frequently than other scores.

Morphological Analysis of the Harry Potter Books and Series

According to Propp, "a tale may be termed any development proceeding from Villainy [A] or lack [a], through intermediary functions to marriage [W], or to other functions employed as a dénouement."[12] The analyst decomposes the narrative into its basic elements and tabulates all of the functions in the tale. These results can then be summarized in a symbolic string using Propp's notation for the individual functions as we did above with "The Three Bears."

As shown on the Table of Functions above, the 31 functions of the *dramatis personae* are organized in family units. Propp suggested his taxonomy of group-to-function can be likened to the biological relation of genus-to-species. Extending the biological metaphor, most functions have varieties, which Propp denoted with numeric superscripts. The function with the largest number of varieties is Villainy [A] with 19. For the purposes of this study varieties of functions were ignored.

The narratives in each book of the Harry Potter series are more complex than both traditional folktales told to children, like "The Three Bears," and formulaic genre conventions in mass-market fiction. It was essential, therefore, to establish procedures that would eliminate an analyst's idiosyncratic use of Propp's schema and forced interpretations of the narratives in the Harry Potter series. (1) Analysis, interpretation, review, critique, and revisions were conducted by a four-person research team. (2) To undertake systematic analysis *as Propp envisioned it*, Propp's assumptions and theses in the *Morphology*[13] served as the guiding criteria for interpretation of the functions in the Harry Potter stories as well as the benchmark for peer review of each team member's results. These criteria are discussed in the "Evaluation" section below. (3) The research team "calibrated" their analyses and interpretations to this shared interpretive standard. This norming procedure consisted in each team member preparing tables of the scheme for *Goblet of Fire*. The team convened to review drafts of each member's tables and arrived at a consensus on the correct decomposition of *Goblet*'s morphological structure and identification of the functions of the *dramatis personae*. (4) The remaining six books were then divided amongst the team members and analyzed. Team members reviewed and critiqued each other's draft tables and convened to amend and finalize them. Once each book in the series was analyzed, the team used each table to determine the morphological structure of the Harry Potter series of books treated as a single tale. The complete tabulated results of these analyses with detailed descriptions from

---

[12] Propp, *Morphology*, 92.
[13] Ibid., 64ff. He designates these assumptions and theses as "deductions."

the narrative for each function are included in APPENDIX II. The symbolized representation of each book in the series and the series as a whole is presented in APPENDIX III.

Evaluation

We now turn to a comparison of our findings of the aesthetic satisfaction with the individual tales in the Harry Potter series and the results of our own complete narrative analyses. Propp's approach is a data-driven typology and description of folktale morphology; therefore, it is difficult to answer normative questions about whether a given story represents a "good" instance of the folktale structure or not. What are the criteria for making a meaningful judgment with the data Proppian analyses yield?

In the discussion which follows the presentation of the 31 functions of the *dramatis personae* in the *Morphology*,[14] Propp makes several general "deductions" about the observed patterns which emerge from an examination of individual folktales "at close range." He asks, "What does the given scheme represent *in relation to the tales*?" and answers thusly: "The scheme is a measuring unit for individual tales. Just as cloth can be measured with a yardstick to determine its length, tales may be measured by the scheme and thereby defined."[15] If Propp is correct, then we should be able to "define" the tales in the Harry Potter series and the series as a whole by using their functional schemes we developed as a measuring device. However, Propp does not discuss the nature or meaning of the *quantity* which the scheme purportedly measures. For Propp,

scheme : : folktale

yardstick : : length of cloth.

We know what sort of quantity *length* is with respect to cloth; but what is the quantity with which we can "measure" the *folktale*? We know when we are measuring the length *of* cloth, we are measuring *a property* of the cloth; viz., its longitudinal extension in space. But if, as Propp's analogy asserts, we are meas-

---

[14] Propp, *Morphology*, 64ff.
[15] Ibid., 65.

uring a folktale, what is the quantity corresponding to *length* in the analogy? We are measuring what *property* of the folktale? What property is measurable with the scheme of functions? Propp does not tell us explicitly; therefore, we must identify this property or properties and corresponding quantity. There is a second problem. We can construct a concrete device—the yardstick, a material representation of the abstract unit of measure—to physically measure the quantity of length. But what sort of device can we construct from or with the folktale scheme (which is also an abstract unit of measure) to measure an as yet undefined quantity or property of a folktale? So we must identify the appropriate property and its corresponding quantity, and we must create our measuring device with the relevant units of measurement. In doing so, we desire to be guided by Propp's own vision for the use of the functional scheme in assessing folktales.

In our schematic analyses of the books in the Harry Potter series, the determination of whether a story element "fit" the functional description in the schema was conducted in a rigorous but qualitative procedure. So the first candidate for an appropriate quantity to apply to the folktale is this *fitness*, or *correspondence*, or *conformity* of the particular narrative element in the tale to the functional species in the schema. We name this quantity *Concordance*. Now, what sort of metric is defined by this quantity?

We can exclude some candidates for measuring Concordance. It would *not* be meaningful to count the number of functions present in a story and use the full slate of 31 functions in the schema as a benchmark. For example, since *Stone* had 26 unique functions, it would not make any sense to infer that its Concordance with folktale structure was therefore 84%. This is because most tales do not involve all of the functions, nor are they required to. Our example of "The Three Bears" shows this. It consists of only 6 functions (or 19% of the full slate), yet its sequential conformity to the schema is flawless; therefore, we are justified in concluding that "The Three Bears" has high Concordance because its scheme accurately exhibits the folktale structure systematized by Propp. So, Concordance does not depend on the maximal use of all the available functions in the schema, but on the appearance of the functions in the correct sequence of the schema.

When we examined the schematic analyses of the tales in the Harry Potter series, we noted those functions which did *not* fit the schema, so let us first consider the inverse quantity of the Concordance, or the *Dis*cordance of the tale. Recall that Propp's third and fourth morphological laws require that the sequence of functions is always identical and that all folktales are of one type in regard to their structure. So, more nonsequential or anomalous functions in the narrative entail greater discordance between the story and folktake structure. One possible means of determining a quantity of Discordance in a scheme, then, is to examine the number of nonsequential functions. We can normalize this quantity by dividing it by the total number of functions in the tale.[16] We thus define this number as a measure of structural *Incongruity*. Another possible means of measuring Discordance is the degree of displacement the nonsequential function departs from its "correct" schematic position. We thus define a second number as a measure of functional *Displacement*.

When we examined the nonsequential functions and computed the Incongruity and Displacement for each of the Harry Potter stories, we obtained the following results:

Measured Quantity	Stone	Chamber	Prisoner	Goblet	Order	Prince	Hallows
Incongruity (%)	14	22	0	0	10	0	2
Displacement	24	16	0	0	28	0	7

Table 3:   Summary of Discordance in the Harry Potter stories

We conservatively regard the values of Incongruity and Displacement to be relative; we do not presume that there is an absolute scale against which to interpret these quantities. We thus limit our interpretation to basic kinds of comparison. We see that *Chamber* has the largest Incongruity of the seven tales. *Stone* has the second largest Incongruity and *Order* third. We also see that *Order* and *Stone* have the largest Displacement. Let us now correlate our results for our first measurement with the results from the aesthetic satisfaction survey.

Chamber is one of the three Harry Potter stories that had the lowest aesthetic satisfaction among readers. We also recall that *Stone* was the second least aes-

---

[16] The nonsequential functions need to be normalized so that the incongruity of different tales can be metrically compared. For example, if a tale with 10 functions has one nonsequential function, then that is more significant than a tale with 50 functions with three nonsequential functions. The shorter tale has 10% incongruity compared to the longer tale which has 6% incongruity.

thetically satisfying story according to its mean score and that *Order* returned a
mode of '1' from all but Novice readers.

If we examine the other end of the spectrum, we see that *Prisoner*, *Goblet*,
and *Prince* have *no* Incongruity from folktale structure (and by entailment, no
Displacement). We recall that *Prisoner* and *Hallows* both returned a mode of '7'
from all readers, and that they were the top two aesthetically satisfying books in
the Harry Potter series according to their rank by mean score. *Prince* returned a
mode of '6' from all readers, and its mean score was third highest among all
reader groups. We arrive at our first general—and provisional—conclusion: *If a
folktale has (relatively) higher Discordance, the aesthetic satisfaction of the
reader will be (relatively) lower.* In other words, high Incongruity and Displacement is predictive of lesser aesthetic satisfaction. We cannot, however, assert the converse of our deduction; *Goblet* and *Prince* have no Discordance, yet
they were not viewed by readers as aesthetically satisfying as *Prisoner* and *Hallows*.

Let us now return to our consideration of Concordance and seek means of directly measuring this quantity. To do this, we examined more closely Propp's
general "deductions" about the observed patterns he identified in the *Morphology*. These five propositions are presented in APPENDIX IV. Our results from applying these propositions to the Harry Potter series revealed two outstanding
patterns. First, we found several unusual features that became apparent when a
book's structure and *dramatis personae* are related to the other books in the series and the series as a whole. We regard these unusual features as *Creative Exploitations of the structural phenomena described by the Propositions*. These
features exhibit the storyteller's virtuosity within the constraints of folktale
structure. Second, we identified clear *Violations of the Propositions*.

In the three books in the Harry Potter series that were identified as the least aesthetically satisfying, *Stone*, *Chamber* and *Order*, we find that there are *fewer* Creative Exploitations and *more* Violations than in the stories viewed as most aesthetically satisfying. If we examine the two books in the Harry Potter series that were identified as the most aesthetically satisfying, *Prisoner* and *Hallows*, we find that there are *fewer* Violations and *more* Creative Exploitations than in

Measured Quantity	Stone	Chamber	Prisoner	Goblet	Order	Prince	Hallows
Creative Exploitations	1	2	9	3	2	4	10
Violations	5	5	1	1	3	1	2
Concordance	-4	-3	8	2	-1	3	8

Table 4:   Summary of the Concordance to Propp's "Deductions" in the Harry Potter stories

the stories viewed as least aesthetically satisfying. Now we are in a position to quantify Concordance.[17] We define Concordance as the sum of a story's Creative Exploitations and its Violations. The results of the analysis of the Propositions gleaned from Propp's "deductions" and the computed Concordance values are shown in Table 4.

We arrive at a second general conclusion: If a folktale has (relatively) higher Concordance, the aesthetic satisfaction of the reader will be (relatively) higher; and if a folktale has (relatively) lower Concordance, the aesthetic satisfaction of the reader will be (relatively) lower. In other words, Creative Exploitations out-numbering Violations is predictive of greater aesthetic satisfaction. And the converse is true: Violations outnumbering Creative Exploitations is predictive of lesser aesthetic satisfaction.

Conclusion

We recall that Propp regards the schema of 31 functions as a "measuring unit" for folktales. We had to construct our own tools for measuring the conformity of the Harry Potter series of books to folktale morphology. We identified

---

[17] It should be pointed out that we specifically defined *Concordance* as "Concordance with Propp's Five Deductions (Propositions) from the Schema" rather than the more ambiguous "Concordance with the Schema."

two quantities, *Concordance* and *Discordance*, which we used to characterize folktale "fitness" to Propp's schema. We also identified two measures for each of these quantities: *Incongruity* and *Displacement* for Discordance, and *Creative Exploitations* and *Violations* for Concordance. We therefore constructed four independent measuring units with which to assess the relative conformity of the Harry Potter series of books to the fairy tale structure of the 31 functions of the *dramatis personae*.

When we summarize our assessments of these quantities and correlate them to the results we determined concerning the aesthetic satisfaction of readers, we obtain the following results:

Quantity	Measuring Unit	Least aesthetically satisfying books			Most aesthetically satisfying books	
		Stone	*Chamber*	*Order*	*Prisoner*	*Hallows*
Discordance	Incongruity	14	22	10	0	2
	Displacement	24	16	28	0	7
Concordance	Creative Exploitations	1	2	2	9	10
	Violations	5	5	3	1	2
	Net Concordance	-4	-3	-1	8	8

Table 5:   *Measures of Concordance and Discordance in the Harry Potter stories*

Stone, *Chamber* and *Order* have relatively discordant folktale structures whilst *Prisoner* and *Hallows* have relatively concordant folktale structures. This correlates with the respective aesthetic satisfaction reported by readers. We therefore conclude that our hypothesis is confirmed: the aesthetic satisfaction with any particular book in the Harry Potter series positively correlates to that book's fairy tale structure as enumerated in Propp's schema of 31 functions of a folktale's *dramatis personae*.

It must be pointed out, however, that we defined the quantities "measured" from the folktale schema and created the "measuring device" with the relevant units of measurement expressly for this study. The quantities and units of measure of our model need to be independently validated to obtain the desired confidence in our results and conclusions. This is one of the important outcomes of our investigation and leads to the next steps in further research using our approach and the model we devised.

The folktale structure is at least *one* of the keys to the success of the Harry Potter series. Critics who dismiss the artistic value and meaning of the series by pointing out its alleged formulaic motifs, genre tropes, normative identities, and semantic attributes derived from other forms of literary analysis often arrive at the judgment erroneously from limited familiarity with the story and its literary roots. However, the Harry Potter series of books does follow more or less closely the folktale schema as outlined by Vladimir Propp. This uniform and repetitive structure is sufficient to account for the apparent formulaic character of the Hogwarts saga. Moreover, we find that readers' aesthetic satisfaction with specific tales within the series correlates to those tales' conformity to the folktale structure. In answering the leading question *"Why has the Harry Potter series of books been so popular?"* our explanation is sufficiently robust to account for the diversity of aesthetic responses to the individual tales in the series, a result not found in other Harry Potter scholarship.

The Harry Potter series of books cast its spell over readers by closely adhering to the formal organization of folktale structure. J. K. Rowling crafted an expansive folktale that has proven to be aesthetically satisfying to readers of all ages around the world. She successfully traced an ancient and enduring "cultural script" found in folk narratives we learn from childhood and articulated this structure with "amazing multiformity, picturesqueness, and color" in her settings, characters, magical objects, and themes, producing a work rich in literary artistry.

Finally, we should consider the meaning of these results for literature beyond the Harry Potter series. First, we should regard the success of our hypothesis with due restraint. As in the empirical sciences of nature, our success is in no small measure governed by the limit of our methodological ambitions. The approach of our investigation was bounded by a very specific question: does the Harry Potter series of books conform to the narrative structure of magical folktales as enumerated by Vladimir Propp in his schema of 31 functions? To conduct our analysis as Propp envisioned it, we happily ignored everything from the social and cultural contexts. This methodological constraint eliminated entire classes of questions and disallowed other kinds of evidence. Aware of these limitations, we therefore regard our approach as an explanatory framework in which to situate the questions and evidence we have bracketed out from our work. We have shown very little about the meaning or artistry of the Hogwarts saga, but we have given a sufficient reason for its popularity, and more significantly, the relative popularity of the individual books in the series.

With these methods we have firmer contextual ground from which others can explore the literary and cultural questions which animate them. Other theoretical and methodological approaches are required to investigate such questions, but we should expect that their findings are consistent with ours. Indeed we should not be surprised that since necessity does not govern literary and cultural productions, other explanatory frameworks are effective for answering questions of meaning and artistry, and that these frameworks' linkage to ours may be obscure.

We proposed a testable hypothesis to determine whether there exists a correlation between the series' folktale structure and its popularity. Once our model has been validated, it would be of interest to determine whether our results are generalizable. With the model we have created in this study, the folktale structure of other series of books, individual works of literature, and other cultural materials can be examined along the same principles employed here. An experiment that suggests itself is to divide the tools we used in this study and analyze the folktale structure of a book or series of books, compute the Concordance and Discordance quantities, and arrive at predictions of aesthetic satisfaction. Readers' aesthetic satisfaction can then be determined by survey or interview procedures and the results of these instruments compared to the predictions.

A second experiment is to analyze the folktale structure of an incomplete series of books. If the published books in the series conform to the folktale structure, then the researchers can complete a partial scheme for the entire series. This scheme can be tested to predict the functions that should occur in the concluding book(s) in the series. These prognostications can then be evaluated against the narrative structure of the final book(s).

We have constrained our interpretation to the measurable quantities identified in this study. It was sufficient for our research to consider the values attained for Concordance and Discordance as applicable intra-series only. The applicability of these measures inter-series or across a selection of individual works by different authors can be tested. Other applications can no doubt be conceived as well.

An important unanswered question that arose during the course of this investigation of the Harry Potter series concerns the *origin* of the uniform and repetitive folktale structure. Why do folktales and other productions of different cultures and historical epochs exhibit *these* functions, *these* dramatis personae, in *this* arrangement? Propp's morphology takes the discovered functions of the *dramatis personae* as givens. But where does this script come from? This is an important question but beyond the scope of Propp's theory and this essay.

We entreat our readers that what we have here presented may be read critically and impartially. We welcome reports that supply its defects and undertake new investigations of imaginative literature and the many wondrous productions of human artistry.

Note

This investigation was undertaken with the invaluable assistance of my undergraduate research team, without whom this project would not have been possible. The author gratefully acknowledges their contributions to this study through their painstaking critical analysis of the Proppian functions in each book of the Harry Potter series and their review, corrections, and suggestions to this paper.

Works Cited

Acocella, Joan. "Under the Spell; Harry Potter explained." *The New Yorker*, July 31, 2000.

Bordwell, David. "ApProppriations and ImPropprieties: Problems in the Morphology of Film Narratives." *Cinema Journal* 27, no. 3 (1988): 5-20.

Granger, John. *How Harry Cast His Spell: The Meaning behind the Mania for J. K. Rowling's Bestselling Books*. Carol Stream, IL: Tyndale House, 2008.

Lacoss, Jann. "Of Magicals and Muggles: Reversals and Revulsions at Hogwarts." In *The Ivory Tower and Harry Potter: Perspectives on a Literary Phenomenon*. 67-88. Edited by Lana A. Whited. Columbia, MO: University of Missouri Press, 2004.

Landau, Misia. *Narratives of Human Evolution*. New Haven: Yale University Press, 1991.

Propp, Vladimir. *Morphology of the Folktale*. 2nd edition. Edited by Louis A. Wagner. Translated by Laurence Scott. Austin, TX: University of Texas Press, 1968.

—. *Theory and History of Folklore*. Edited by Anatoly Liberman. Translated by Ariadna Y. Martin and Richard P. Martin. Minneapolis, MN: University of Minnesota Press, 1984.

Venturing into the Murky Marshes
Response from Gabrielle Ceraldi

> *"You said, at the end of last term, you were going to tell me everything," said Harry. It was hard to keep a note of accusation from his voice. "Sir," he added.*
>
> *"And so I did," said Dumbledore placidly. "I told you everything I know. From this point forth, we shall be leaving the firm foundation of fact and journeying together through the murky marshes of memory into thickets of wildest guesswork."*
>
> —*Harry Potter and the Half-Blood Prince*

Why has the Harry Potter series been so popular? In posing this question and attempting to answer it, Joel Hunter is doing much more than merely taking on a challenging conundrum: he is making an argument about the purpose of studying literature. If, as Hunter argues, the diverse and multidisciplinary responses to the Harry Potter series can be summed up as attempts to answer this, and no other, question, then critical analysis of J. K. Rowling's novels must be understood to be, first and foremost, the study of human behavior. Popularity, after all, is the product of a set of behaviors: buying books, reading them, recommending them to friends. What prompts these behaviors? What is it about the Harry Potter series in particular that has prompted such widespread impulses towards buying, reading, and recommending?

One approach to the task of answering this question might focus on historical context: *Harry Potter and the Philosopher's Stone* was published in 1997, and the remaining six books, which appeared over the course of the ensuing decade, were positioned to benefit from a unique historical opportunity: Web 2.0. Melissa Anelli's book, *Harry, A History* chronicles the Harry Potter fandom, which has grown and coalesced around sites like The Leaky Cauldron (of which Anelli is webmistress). The activities that promote a book's popularity are no longer limited to buying, reading, and recommending; fans today can produce music videos, fanfiction, and artwork, disseminating their responses and ideas online. Having created a close-knit fictional world in which information is recorded on parchment and carried by owls, Rowling has benefited from Muggle technologies that allow her fans to share their enthusiasm for her novels instantaneously with other fans around the world. A social historian would thus answer Hunter's question with reference to the technologies and social behaviours that foster popularity at this particular historical moment.

Hunter, by contrast, uses the methods of Russian formalism to ground Rowling's popularity in the formal structure of her novels. Using Vladimir Propp's schema, Hunter argues that Rowling's novels have been so successful not because they contain folktale motifs but rather because those motifs are arranged in the sequence that Propp identified as essential to the folktale structure. As Hunter observes, this approach has the advantage of being "empirical and inductive," while making no attempt to hypothesize about the meaning of the story. In thus avoiding the "knotty problems of semiotics," Hunter keeps his analysis on the firm footing of established fact.

Such an approach, I cannot help but imagine, would fit nicely into the curriculum of Hogwarts itself. As a school with no arts program, Hogwarts offers a highly practical education. Students learn to brew potions and transfigure objects; there are magical counterparts to Muggle subjects such as history, chemistry, and biology. Teachers pass on to students established methods of practicing magic, and their pedagogy relies heavily on rote memorization and hands-on learning. No one at Hogwarts reads novels; wizarding students play no music, produce no plays, and—with the possible exception of the Half-Blood Prince— invent no new spells. In his notes on "The Fountain of Fair Fortune" in *The Tales of Beedle the Bard*, Albus Dumbledore indicates that Hogwarts had, at one time, a tradition of Yuletide dramatics, but the special effects proved too dangerous so, in a school that plays host, by turns, to dragons, Dementors, and three-headed dogs, the drama program was abandoned for the sake of student safety.[1]

As he is in so many other ways, however, Dumbledore proves to be the exception to the rule of empirical, fact-based education at Hogwarts. Having confided to Harry the nature of the prophecy that prompted Voldemort's attack on his parents, Dumbledore launches Harry's sixth year at Hogwarts with an invitation to a set of private lessons. Harry anticipates that these lessons will involve skills-based training of the kind he is accustomed to in Defense Against the Dark

---

[1] J. K. Rowling, *The Tales of Beedle the Bard* (London: Bloomsbury, 2008), 39.

Arts—so much so that he is surprised to find Dumbledore's office intact, with no space cleared for dueling practice.[2] After five full years of memorizing facts and practicing skills, Harry is unprepared for what Dumbledore expects of this new phase of his education: he is to move beyond the "firm foundation of fact," diving into the "murky marshes of memory."[3]

The Horcrux hunt, which is central to the plot of the sixth and seventh books of the series, seems at first glance to involve a series of factual questions. How many Horcruxes did Voldemort create? Where did he conceal them? How can they be destroyed? In that sense, the final two books of the series feature Harry, Ron, and Hermione in the detective roles they have occupied since *The Philosopher's Stone*, where they combined their considerable curiosity and resources to solve the puzzles surrounding the attempted robbery of Gringotts bank. But Dumbledore's lessons with Harry involve much more than a mere exchange of information. Dumbledore dives with Harry into the murky marshes of memory because only there can Harry begin to move beyond the safe, empirical questions into the more challenging ones; the questions that arise when we see the evil Lord Voldemort as 11-year-old Tom Riddle, sociopathic yet strangely vulnerable. The real purpose of these lessons with Dumbledore is revealed in the seventh book, not merely in Harry's success in tracking down the Horcruxes but also in the moments of pity Harry is able to achieve for his enemy.

Dumbledore's sessions with Harry are termed "lessons," yet in a very real way they are exercises in storytelling, each Pensieve memory a carefully edited narrative. After they view each memory, Dumbledore mentors Harry in the art of interpretation, calling attention to key details, hinting at the conclusions Harry might draw from what he has seen. Harry spots in these memories the shape of Helga Hufflepuff's cup, the curve of Salazar Slytherin's ring, the habit of trophy-collecting that Tom Riddle displays even in earliest childhood. The task of interpreting those memories extends beyond the confines of Dumbledore's office, however; even after the death of his mentor, Harry continues to learn from those stories, recognizing the impulses that led a young Voldemort to conceal a Horcrux at Hogwarts, the one place where he, like Harry, had found a true home.

---

[2] Rowling, *Harry Potter and the Half-Blood Prince* (London: Bloomsbury, 2005), 186.
[3] Ibid., 187.

Stories yield their meanings slowly, Rowling implies; they demand a response that is as empathetic as it is cerebral.

There is no Professor of Wizarding Literature at Hogwarts, but in *Harry Potter and the Deathly Hallows*, Rowling reveals, for the first time, that there is such a thing as wizarding folklore. The library at Hogwarts is stuffed with histories and autobiographies, how-to books filled with spells and potions recipes, but if any witch or wizard has produced a volume of fiction, Rowling makes no mention of it. Wizards may not write novels, but they do have folklore, and if, as Hunter claims, Rowling's novels are popular with readers for the same reasons that folk tales resonate with those who have retold them for generations, then "The Tale of the Three Brothers" may function as an invitation to analyze why. Why did this tale survive, to be handed down from wizard to wizard? According to Xenophilius Lovegood, the story is a source of factual information about the Deathly Hallows. According to Albus Dumbledore, however, those who seek the Hallows miss the plain meaning of the story, which cautions against any attempt to evade or defeat death.[4] Ron Weasley remembers his mother changing the details of the story to make it scarier,[5] a use of the story that emphasizes its entertainment value, its usefulness in grabbing the attention of restless children on a long winter's night. No one, however, understands the story better than Harry, who finds the Resurrection Stone only once he has realized that his role is to emulate the third brother, the one who greeted Death as a friend.

All these readers find their counterparts in the fans and foes of the Harry Potter series. Xenophilius Lovegood, who sees "The Tale of the Three Brothers" as a factual guide to the real world, might well be that bugbear of fundamentalists, the reader who uses the Harry Potter books as an introduction to the occult. Hermione, who spends many long nights poring over the runic script of *The Tales of Beedle the Bard*, has her own counterpart in the many fans who were busy mining the first six novels for clues to the outcome of the story as they waited impatiently for the publication of *The Deathly Hallows*. In Harry, however, Rowling offers us an educated reader, one who has been schooled in the art of patience and who knows that the task of interpretation requires risk and guesswork. If, as Hunter suggests, his formalist approach is a "*way to begin*" the task of answering his leading question, then I would argue that Rowling is urg-

[4] Rowling, *The Tales of Beedle the Bard*, 94.
[5] Rowling, *Harry Potter and the Deathly Hallows* (London: Bloomsbury, 2007), 330.

ing readers not to remain on that firm foundation of empirical fact. The question of meaning, which Hunter sets aside at the outset, is the very question Rowling invites us to engage. Why the books are so popular is, I think, a far less pressing issue than how they might be made meaningful, and the task of the literary critic does not end with the accumulation of numerical data but rather begins when we venture with Rowling into the murky marshes of literary meaning.

Works Cited

Anelli, Melissa. *Harry, A History*. New York: Gallery Books, 2008.

Rowling, J. K. *Harry Potter and the Deathly Hallows*. London: Bloomsbury, 2007.

—. *Harry Potter and the Half-Blood Prince*. London: Bloomsbury, 2005.

—. *The Tales of Beedle the Bard*. London: Bloomsbury, 2008.

CHAPTER 6

A Bridge To Dystopia:
Reading the Harry Potter Series
as a Collapsing Utopia
Sarah Cocita Reschan

The literary value of Young Adult literature (YA) to educators and adolescents is becoming undeniable, despite the fact that some respected professors of literature criticize this genre as being too popular to be good, too recent to stand the test of time, and too young to be respected widely.[1] These excuses may be intended to protect the hallowed American and British literary canons, but instead ignore the point that the popularity, relevance, and youth of these works are exactly what make them valuable to adolescent readers and their teachers. Making connections using pop culture is not only acceptable, but also profound if these media can open students' minds to classical literature, poetry, and drama. Rather than using its popularity to disregard YA, teachers could use it to introduce important literary terms and concepts.

In literature in general, "recent decades have seen the rise of a dystopian mood in popular culture as a whole" (Booker 1994). Within the category of YA, teen dystopia has become increasingly prevalent. Series like *The Hunger Games*, *Uglies*, and *Divergent* have captured a wide audience and turned once-reluctant readers into avid booklovers. These books engage young readers because they can relate to the teenaged protagonists and the totalitarian rule systems, often similar to the autocracies minors are subject to in schools, at home, or at first jobs. Like their canonized counterparts such as George Orwell's *1984* (1949)

---

[1] These criticisms have often been listed by Pepperdine University professor James W. Thomas as the "three Deathly Hallows for academics" that prevent them from admitting a piece of writing into conventionally accepted academic literature; this theory was published in a chapter by Karin E. Westman in *The Oxford Handbook of Children's Literature*.

and Aldous Huxley's *Brave New World* (1932), however, YA dystopias are set so far from the current world in time or space that students easily disengage from their political and social messages of awareness and activism.

One pedagogical solution to this problem of disengagement comes in the last three novels of J. K. Rowling's *Harry Potter* series. This trilogy within the series guides the reader through a tumultuous period during which the charmed world of Harry's first years in the wizarding world is stripped away and the hallmarks of dystopian society emerge. Harry himself is in the epicenter of the shift in government, law, and social convention happening all around him, at first at school (*Order of the Phoenix*), then in the Ministry of Magic (*Half-Blood Prince*), and finally in the wider wizard and Muggle worlds (*Deathly Hallows*). This is "[c]rucial to dystopia's vision in all its manifestations [because] this ability to register the impact of an unseen and unexamined social system on the everyday lives of everyday people" is what makes dystopian fiction effective (Moylan 2000). Seeing this effect on characters' lives makes readers more aware of their own historical, political, and social surroundings and better equipped to understand the events that would lead to worlds like those described in the traditional dystopian texts often assigned in schools. Readers make connections naturally as a way to process the fictional world within the context of their own realities; as teens read about fractured societies and young protagonists who fight to fix them, it is natural for them to consider the problems within their own culture and whether they have the power to affect change there. Sometimes readers will recognize patterns subconsciously, making the opportunity to work through their implications with fellow readers or the guidance of a teacher even more beneficial. This significant difference between Rowling's series and conventional YA dystopias—that Harry experiences the change as it happens—adds value to the reading of these texts: because the readers follow the slow progression from utopia to the brink of dystopia, they learn to identify signals in their own societies. The magical world when Harry is first introduced to it demonstrates few examples of tyranny, but through many minor shifts starting halfway through the series, the governing bodies around him exert more and more control over wizards' daily lives and slowly transform the society into the kind of fascist system typical to dystopias. Analyzing the development of four critical areas in the Harry Potter series—oppressive rule, "us versus them" mentality, technology or science, and resistance movements—allows young readers to see the development of a dystopia and learn to analyze individual shifts toward dystopianism within their own real worlds.

Dystopian Literature

It is part of the human condition that we dream of ways to make things better and strive toward that goal continually. Developing utopias, whether attempted in theory, in literature, or in practice, is natural and has been recorded since at least the Renaissance, when the term was first used. It was not until the twentieth century, however, that utopia's doppelgänger, dystopia, emerged. "A true opposite of utopia would be a society that is either completely unplanned or is planned to be deliberately terrifying and awful. Dystopia, typically invoked, is neither of these things; rather, it is a utopia that has gone wrong, or a utopia that functions only for a particular segment of society" (Gordin 2010). In this way dystopian literature serves as a mirror that can expose the negative results of some of our most optimistic ideas. Dystopias teach readers the Freudian idea that an ideal society is extremely unlikely due to human's innately selfish behavior and the attempt to create one, which necessitates the oppression of some individual needs, can sometimes do more harm than good. This tension between egoism and altruism causes societies built on utopian ideals like perfect equality and self-government based on an unspoken social contract to sour and become dystopic. They also remind readers to look at the whole picture, and to recognize the suffering of one group that often occurs for the benefit of another.

Both utopias and dystopias usually take place either far in the future or far in the past. This defamiliarizes the reader, making it easier to accept that the fictive society in the book is so different from the one in which the reader actually lives. "By focusing their critiques of society on spatially or temporally distant settings, dystopian fictions provide fresh perspectives on problematic social and political practices that might otherwise be taken for granted or considered natural and inevitable" (Booker 1994). This abstraction, while effective for adults because they can still connect the fictive world to the inspiration in the real world around them, can be challenging for younger readers. Adolescents often have a narrower awareness of the world, so the distance in time or space between their reality and the reality of dystopian novels can isolate the situations within literature and remove the call to action that dystopias provide.

Rowling's wizards fulfill both of these requisites of dystopian fiction. Magical society is only a small fraction of the Muggle world, but Voldemort and the Death Eaters use the Ministry of Magic to pursue wizard domination of the whole population, claiming that Magic is Might and that allowing wizards to rule the weaker Muggles would be better for everyone. And while the Harry Potter series does take place in current time and a real place, the wizarding world is removed enough from standard society, that the reader still experiences the defamiliarization necessary in dystopias.

The Beginning: A Quasi-Utopian Trilogy

The Harry Potter series is relatively utopian in the first three books. "The whole of [Harry's] first year at Hogwarts is especially a cornucopia of delights, a granting of almost everything he never had, and of much more that he never dreamt of" (Manlove 2009). Although Harry does battle the malicious forces of Lord Voldemort in books one and two, it isn't until He-Who-Must-Not-Be-Named returns to full corporeal form at the end of *Goblet of Fire* that the shift away from utopia begins. The virtuousness of children's literature is abandoned when Harry witnesses the murder of his schoolmate Cedric Diggory. This death strips Harry of much of his innocence and forces him to see the ways that evil can infect every part of a society once it begins to spread. If a dystopia is defined as "a haven corrupted by the misapplication of principles or theories or from deliberate tyranny, power-mongering, sadism, or subversion of human rights," then it could be argued that the transformation of the wizarding world under the direction of Lord Voldemort qualifies for the title (Snodgrass 1995).

Harry Potter and the Order of the Phoenix: Breaking Barriers

During the fifth book in the series, Rowling only begins to show the cracks in Harry's society. Since Harry is still young and naïve, the limited point of view only offers the reader insight into those areas of society that affect him directly, mostly at his ministry trial and at school. Since most readers, young and old alike, probably have not been witness to a murder, it important for Rowling to help them identify with Harry in other ways. Readers may not be orphans or know what it is like to see a schoolmate's death, but they will almost inevitably empathize with rules at school or in society that seem unfair or oppressive.

Harry's trial at the Ministry is important to the argument of the series as a burgeoning dystopia for many reasons. First, it pushes the adolescent out of the utopian protection of childhood by subjecting him to adult consequences for practicing magic outside of school. Second, the presence of the full Wizengamot under the leadership of Minister of Magic, instead of the Chief Warlock,[2] suggests an intensification in the way that minor misdemeanors are handled in the wake of Dumbledore's announcement that Lord Voldemort has returned. Third, this glimpse at the justice system allows the reader to contrast the treatment of Harry by a biased jury with the complete disintegration of justice that has taken place by the time Muggle-born witches and wizards to being imprisoned for "stealing magic" in *Deathly Hallows*.

At the trial, Harry witnesses the profound shift occurring within Great Britain's wizarding government based on their utter denial of the return of Lord Voldemort. Modern governments worldwide consider presumed innocence and the right to a fair, impartial trial of such importance that most developed countries have written these ideals into their laws, but Harry's trial and all of its proceedings undermine the defendant, his integrity, and his reputation. The time and location of the hearing are changed so suddenly that Harry barely makes it to the courtroom to defend himself. This only reinforces the prejudiced opinions that many members of the Wizengamot have about Harry as they question him in ways that demonstrate their belief in his deceitfulness even before he has had the opportunity to properly contest the charges against him. Even the Minister of Magic himself, Cornelius Fudge, asks Harry several leading questions but then refuses to listen to Harry's explanations when they don't support the version of the story the Minister wants to believe. He also attempts to violate Wizengamot procedure and deny Harry the right to a witness for his defense saying, "We haven't got time to listen to more taradiddles, I'm afraid [...] I want this dealt with quickly" (Rowling 2003).

Fudge's subversive behavior foreshadows darker times ahead for justice and impartiality when future witches and wizards are accused of crimes. While Harry is frustrated by his experience at the trial, though, he does not pursue the issue

---

[2] The Chief Warlock is the head of the Wizengamot, the judicial branch of magical government. The Minister of Magic is the executive head. This indicates a mixing of the branches of government and a disregard for separation of powers.

any further once the charges against him are cleared. Because of his adolescent narcissism and the relief he feels once he is acquitted, Harry forgets about the implications of justice administered in this manner for more than two years. Like the young readers who would identify with him, this experience is inconvenient but not yet enough to turn him into an activist.

Harry returns to school after his trial only to find that his idyllic space has been corrupted by rumors, lies, and the Ministry of Magic itself. When he discovers that one of the more confrontational faces from the courtroom is now sitting at the Head Table in the Great Hall, it is as if the outside world has broken into Harry's utopian haven. Dolores Umbridge does not even wait until the end of the traditional Welcoming Feast on the first night to deliver a speech that causes Hermione to declare, "the Ministry's interfering at Hogwarts" (Rowling 2003). The school is the perfect place for Rowling to introduce dystopian concepts into Harry's world, especially because "schools are places where teens are subject to dress codes, have few free speech rights, and are constantly surveilled" (Westerfeld 2010). It's no wonder that students often feel the sting of establishment control and yearn to be rid of the suppressive bonds placed on them by adults. By introducing the oppressive regime of Professor Umbridge in *Order of the Phoenix*, Rowling beings the path toward dystopia with the most familiar facet of life for her characters and her readers: overbearing school rules.

Harry's experiences at this point are limited to what he sees directly around him in the castle, so the growing totalitarianism of the Ministry of Magic is focused only on the behavior of Professor Umbridge. Where Hogwarts was once a place that represented self-determination, Umbridge's appointment at Hogwarts High Inquisitor via Educational Decree Number Twenty-Three indicates that "the Ministry of Magic [has] passed new legislation giving itself an unprecedented level of control at Hogwarts" (Rowling 2003). Small restrictions of freedom, like putting the Trace on under-aged wizards or wand registration, are accepted as the trade offs for safety, and so it is with the purview of the High Inquisitor and her many Educational Decrees. In modern society it is common to accept minor impositions on civil liberties, like ubiquitous CCTV cameras or body scanners at airport security checkpoints, in exchange for the confidence that these measures prevent from unseen dangers and threats. Likewise, Umbridge must infringe on the privacy of students by reading their mail in order to protect them from predators on the outside. It is her duty to safeguard these minors from undesireables like Professor Dumbledore, Harry Potter, each other, and even themselves in these uncertain times. And so she is able to pass Educational Decree Number 24, disbanding student clubs, teams, and organizations until she can ensure that their activities do not threaten her authority or undermine the Ministry's position that Voldemort is not a current threat the wizarding community. She then expands her impact by reducing the influence of other adults in the lives of students: they are further disconnected from their families through the surveillance of all communication with people outside the castle, and then Educational Decrees Number 25 and 26 enervate teachers by giving Umbridge "supreme authority over all punishments, sanctions, and removal of privileges pertaining to the students of Hogwarts" and banning teachers "from giving students any information that is not strictly related to the subjects they are paid to teach" (Rowling 2003). Her maneuvers are slow but deliberate, so it is possible to see every step she takes as necessary to protect Hogwarts students.

However, "good dystopian fiction reminds readers to be wary of encroachments upon individual liberty, regardless of the source or its intentions, and to push back if necessary" (Luna 2009). Harry's indignation at these injustices within the school fuels his examination of the larger injustices affecting the wider wizarding world. In many ways, Hogwarts is a microcosm of the wider community of people and creatures with magical abilities. The ways in which Harry identifies problems within his own education under Professor Umbridge and takes the necessary steps to improve the situation himself is encouraging and inspiring to readers of all ages. Young people especially can identify with Harry's plight if there are injustices within their own schools and follow his example of civil disobedience to solve them. If Professor Umbridge is able to manipulate laws to grant herself power over vulnerable adolescents, to impose draconian punishments for trivial offenses (such as forcing Harry and other students to write lines with magical quills that use their blood as ink), and to isolate students from the outside world, then it is not unreasonable to assume that the Ministry is enacting similar policies and penalties on the adult population, too.

This oppressiveness is typical of dystopia. Umbridge serves to indoctrinate youths with the ideals of the new government. By limiting individual freedoms at school, she is able to ensure model citizenship from her pupils. This extends to the larger wizarding community in the form of "the quasi-omnipotence of a monolithic, totalitarian state demanding and normally exacting complete obedience from its citizens" (Claeys 2010). Just as Hogwarts students are meant to accept the new impositions on their rights without question or complaint, so all witches and wizards of Great Britain are supposed to accept the Ministry's word as truth, its maneuvers as good, and its rejection of Harry and Dumbledore as justified. In response, the of-age wizards Harry respects most rekindle the Order of the Phoenix in preparation for what they fear has already begun. Minister Fudge demands acceptance of his ideology by influencing the reports in the Daily Prophet, publically denying Dumbledore's claims that He-Who-Must-Not-Be-Named has returned, and threatening to fire anyone at the ministry who is disloyal to him or his message. His attempts are feeble, however, and many ministry employees, including Arthur Weasley, Kingsley Shacklebolt, and Tonks, are involved in the Order despite his intimidation. The Ministry of Magic is not an imposing symbol of totalitarian intimidation yet, but it has begun to move in that direction.

When Harry and his friends establish Dumbledore's Army, they are unintentionally fulfilling another role in literary dystopia, as "the singular misfit [who] finds allies and not only learns the 'truth' of the system but also enters collectively into outright opposition." (Moylan 2000). In *Goblet of Fire*, Harry doesn't just accept a warning about Voldemort's return and inherent threat to the wizarding world, he witnesses the event first hand. Exasperated by the lack of regard Professor Umbridge has for the actual education of young witches and wizards, especially in these threatening times, Hermione encourages a secret Defense Against the Dark Arts class with Harry as the appointed leader. They fly in the face of Educational Decree 24 when Umbridge outlaws student groups of three or more people. They use underground communication and develop a headquarters that no one except the members can find. This effort to find others who support his cause and form a collective resistance reminds both Harry and the reader that he is not alone. Harry, who has been feeling isolated since Cedric's death, is invigorated by the DA, a subtle suggestion for readers to get involved in causes they care about particularly when they feel powerless. Directing the DA is Harry's first opportunity to test himself as a leader and he matures through the responsibility he takes for the other members and the pride he gains from their improvement. Without realizing it, Professor Umbridge's oppressiveness at

Hogwarts gives Harry some of the tools he needs to fight tyranny in the Ministry of Magic and intimidation by Lord Voldemort later on.

Harry Potter and the Half-Blood Prince: Chaos, Ineptitude, and Rising to Adult Responsibilities

Harry Potter and the Half-Blood Prince is characterized by the instability and chaos of a changing government. In this latest installment, "[t]he opening chapter is not about Harry Potter; it is about the terror in Potter's world," as it has become impossible to deny the ramifications of Lord Voldemort's ruthless regime (Rivers 2009). Even though Death Eaters have not officially seized control of the Ministry, the witches and wizards who work there are suspicious of each other's true loyalties. Harry's daily activities return to the status quo at school, but the uncertainty of the adult world is always close at hand. "Adult supervision is less certain and less present and the safe environment that once sheltered Harry and the other students is daily made less safe and more susceptible to attack" (Rivers 2009). The Hogwarts utopia is definitely gone, despite Professor Dumbledore and the other teachers' work to ensure the protection and assurance of every student. Each day when the *Daily Prophet* arrives by owl in the Great Hall, Ron asks "in a determinedly casual voice," if anyone they know has died (Rowling 2005). This dreary attempt at lightening the mood is a pathetic alternative to Ron's traditionally carefree attitude. These teenagers are dealing with issues much deeper and more mature than they have in previous books.

Ministry officials bumble along throughout *Half-Blood Prince*, making abundant errors in judgment of how best to deal with Lord Voldemort, his followers, and the prevalence of viciousness they cause. For several months, the Ministry arrests innocent people while ignoring flagrant criminal behavior by Death Eaters because of their own fear of retribution. Relatives of many Hogwarts students go missing or are found dead. Hermione reads about a 9-year-old boy who is "arrested for trying to kill his grandparents," presumably under the influence of the Imperius Curse (Rowling 2005). Even Stan Shunpike, the affable conductor of the Knight Bus, is arrested "on suspicion of Death Eater activity" and kept imprisoned for many months (Rowling 2005).

"In the average young adult dystopia, the adolescent knows best," so it is not surprising that Harry and his friends are frustrated by the ineptitude they see in their government and many of the other adults who are meant to protect them (Hintz 2003). Parents, wary of danger and distrustful of even the highest quality defensive measures around Hogwarts, withdraw several students from school. Government officials imprison innocent people on trumped up charges and without trial. Students are forbidden to leave the castle unescorted and their excursions to Hogsmeade are cancelled. In his desperation to appear effective, the new Minister Scrimgeour even solicits the help of Harry Potter so that he may persuade the public that he and the Ministry are working together against Voldemort. Harry is insulted by Scrimgeour's attitude that "[i]t's what people believe that's important," not what the Ministry is actually doing to apprehend Voldemort and dismantle his band of followers (Rowling 2005). During such an important moment in their history, he is appalled that the adults in charge care more about appearances than the genuine safety of their community. Instead he decides that if he wants things to get better, he can't depend on the adults who are supposed to have authority, but must change things himself.

The Battle of the Astronomy Tower completes Lord Voldemort's task of breaking any barriers between himself and the impressionable minds of young witches and wizards; from within Hogwarts he could influence students and indoctrinate generations with his ideas about wizarding superiority. In a well-planned assault on Hogwarts, sixteen Death Eaters are finally able to penetrate the protection of the school, an infiltration that officially tips the scales toward dystopia, as even the most sacredly safe place in the books is invaded by Lord Voldemort's campaign for domination. The death of the school's Headmaster allows the Dark Lord to capture the school for himself, giving him at least physical access to the students within and the potential to inculcate them with his ideals.

Harry Potter and the Deathly Hallows: Destruction from Within

Rowling outlines the massive shifts taking place in wizarding society during the Meeting at Malfoy Manor at the beginning of *Deathly Hallows*. The conversation confirms that if Voldemort is not already playing the puppet master in all areas of wizarding life, he will be soon. Suspended over the proceedings, spellbound, is Hogwarts professor of aMuggle Studies Charity Burbage. Although news reports claim that she resigned from her post at the school voluntarily, it is clear that she has been abducted by Death Eaters for her tolerance of non-magical humans and what Lord Voldemort calls, "corrupting and polluting the minds of Wizarding children" by teaching that Muggles "are not so different" from wizards (Rowling 2007). For her transgression, Voldemort himself kills her with the Avada Kedavra curse. This brutal treatment of those who would oppose the crusade for Pure-blood Supremacy is indicative of the "use of 'total terror' … to intimidate the population and ensure complete loyalty," a common characteristic of the totalitarian governments typical to dystopias (Claeys 2001). Voldemort's ruthlessness is on display in this scene, but it is not the only purpose for this particular murder; when term resumes at Hogwarts, Muggle Studies is a requirement for all students and the revised curriculum indoctrinates youth against Voldemort's chosen "other"—any non-magical or non-Pure Blood beings—by teaching about Muggles' resemblance to animals, their low levels of intelligence, and their high levels of cruelty that forced wizards into hiding.

One of the first and most important policies of the new order at the Ministry is the implementation of drastic legal subjugation of muggle-born wizards and non-human magical races. Throughout the series Rowling develops a hierarchy that all humans are born into, whether they believe in the superiority of pure-blood lineage or not. Muggles, who have no magical power, are at the bottom. Then come muggle-borns, squibs, half-bloods, and pure-bloods. These stations are fixed. Like any dystopian caste system, there is absolutely nothing a Muggle or Squib can do to earn the power of magic and thus advance his or her position. In this way magic itself plays the part that technology and science often fulfill in dystopian literature: it is a power reserved for the few, inaccessible by any but the most elite members of society, and often used to subdue the lower classes. In modern society, "any sufficiently advanced technology is indistinguishable from magic" and so it is that Rowling places those who have the power of magic in an echelon over those who do not, just like those who can access and understand science or technology may be above the uneducated masses in another dystopia (deGrasse Tyson 2010). Even while Rowling clearly presents prejudice based on Pure-blood status as wrong, "Muggles are represented as different from the wizards—and that difference, let us be clear, is constituted by a lack of ability" (Blake 2009). Under the direction of Lord Voldemort, this hierarchy is enforced even more brutally. The Muggle-Born Registration Commission forces many wizards into hiding and imprisons many others for the crime of "stealing" magic. According to an article about the organization, the Ministry is interested in learning more about how humans without magical ancestors have developed magical abilities, as they believe no one with such inferior genes could possibly have gained magical powers through any means excluding "theft or force." Thus, "[t]he Ministry is determined to root out such usurpers of magical power" by inviting all Muggle-born witches and wizards to "present themselves for interview," a twist on the reality of rounding up muggle-borns in order to punish them for obtaining magical power illegally (Rowling 2007). This frightening prospect is only one step in the movement toward eradicating all but those of the purest wizarding lineage. In Voldemort's quest for complete domination, he is willing to eliminate large numbers of detractors and dissenters, a quality common to dystopias that often reminds us of other ritual "cleansings" that have been used to "justify" genocide throughout history.

While the *Daily Prophet* and its radio partner, the *Wizarding Wireless Network News*, both effectively ignore truly newsworthy events that would expose the reality of these racist policies in the Ministry, several resisters develop their own clandestine radio program, Potterwatch, to keep the magical community abreast of what is really happening in their world. It is here that Harry hears that "a Muggle family of five has been found dead in their home… More evidence, as if it were needed that Muggle slaughter is becoming little more than a recreational sport under the new regime" (Rowling 2007). Both the information and the method of delivery are significant here: Death Eaters are killing Muggles indiscriminately with no fear of repercussions, but there is a resistance force determined to keep the wizarding world informed and to continue the fight against these destructive practices. As the announcers remind those wizards who wonder if they should perhaps leave Muggle deaths to the concern of Muggles, "it's one short step from 'Wizards first' to 'Pure-bloods first'," and it is important that all living souls—being, beast, magical, and not—pull together to save society from this virulent thinking.

Harry, Ron, and Hermione spend much of *Deathly Hallows* on the run, desperately seeking ways to undermine Voldemort's campaign, continue the resistance, and ultimately reverse the progress toward desolation. They discover that Death Eaters have seized complete control of Hogwarts, drastically changing policies that govern students in an effort to eliminate dissent. In a shift from traditional policy, "[a]ttendance [becomes] compulsory for every young witch

and wizard [...] This way, Voldemort [can] have the whole Wizarding population under his eye from a young age" (Rowling 2007). Snatchers are deputized
to pick up any muggle-borns, blood-traitors, or truant students they find hiding
in forests and other deserted areas in exchange for gold. Voldemort even uses the
advantage of magic to place a taboo on his own name in order to trace the location of anyone who dares to speak it aloud. This ultimate surveillance prevents
sedition at the primary level. Since those who are brave enough to use Lord
Voldemort's name, rather than an alias like "You-Know-Who" or "He-Who-
Must-Not-Be-Named," have always been those who were also willing to stand
firmly in opposition of the man himself, this method of rooting out defiance
proves extremely fruitful, even succeeding in locating Harry Potter.

Perhaps the most important feature in the journey of Rowling's series toward
dystopia is the fierce resistance that Harry, his friends, and the wizarding community eventually ignite against Lord Voldemort's regime. When Harry feels
overwhelmed by the depth and breadth of Voldemort's influence over society, he
is continually surprised by the individual acts of rebellion going on around him:
several members of Dumbledore's Army endure painful punishments in order to
defy their Death Eater professors and headmaster; professors resist Headmaster
Snape in order to protect students and the integrity of the school; Aberforth
Dumbledore risks the wrath of Death Eaters patrolling the streets of Hogsmeade
to hide Harry, Ron, and Hermione; and innumerous under-aged students sneak
back into the castle to defend their community and their school when Voldemort
launches an unmitigated attack on Hogwarts.

Conclusion

In most adult dystopias the "narrative runs aground when the power structure
crushes the resistant dissenter—ending the text on a note of resignation" (Moylan 2000). Alternatively, the protagonists in Young Adult literature are more likely to recognize tragic flaws in the construction of so-called "perfect worlds" and
do what is necessary to return them to balance, justice, and goodness. The wizarding world is brought to the brink of total desolation during the Final Battle of
Hogwarts: Voldemort announces his own victory in a grim speech designed to
demoralize his opposition and convert hostages into followers. Many dystopias
end in just this way, with the protagonist finally caving to the power of the es-

tablishment (*1984*) or else abandoning the society for something else (*Farenheit 451*, *The Giver*). This sense of hopelessness during the denouement often leaves readers, especially adolescents, feeling disheartened and impotent. But the primary difference between traditional fiction and that written for young adults is, as children's author Monica Hughes puts it, "You may lead a child into the darkness, but you must never turn out the light" (Hintz 2003). Even when Voldemort believes he has finally and irrefutably won, the resistance effort epitomized in the Order of the Phoenix in the adult world, Dumbledore's Army at Hogwarts, *The Quibbler* in print, and Potterwatch on radio all rise up against him. Readers learn that even they can recognize tyranny and do something about it. Most of these resisters are outcasts, underdogs, and ordinary people who don't seem powerful from the outset. Characters like Neville Longbottom, Molly Weasley, and Xenophilius Lovegood, who seemed virtually powerless when they were introduced earlier in the series, are able to enact real damage to Voldemort's cause through their efforts. While Harry may be the one who beats Voldemort himself, his triumph would not be complete without the united resistence of so many others. Readers recognize that each person plays a part in the defeat of tyranny and the restoration (or maintenance) of justice.

True literacy comprehension is the ability to compare and contrast themes and ideas in numerous literary forms. Young Adult literature allows students to connect their own thoughts and experiences to characters on their own levels. Adults have the responsibility to encourage younger generations to embrace literacy and guide them as they define their values through their reading. YA dystopia is important because it authorizes young adults to take charge of their environments. Rowling emphasizes the power of friendship, loyalty, and love throughout the Harry Potter series, and her readers connect those values to their own lives. Similarly, Harry's ability to fight tyranny is based on skills they, too, may embody. Instead of using superior magical ability, Harry's integrity, his fierce dedication to the truth, his allegiance to the people in his life who have been trustworthy and supportive, and his perseverance in the face of extraordinary circumstances are qualities that even young Muggles can emulate.

Harry is a role model for readers whose world is becoming more and more threatening. Like Harry, today's youths have grown up in societies involved in conflict and war; they must make sense of themselves in that context and find a role that fits as they determine their goals in adulthood. Rowling's series is unique within YA in that it helps readers understand not how to return from a dystopia, but how to prevent it happening in the first place. While the characters in *The Hunger Games*, *Divergent*, and other series must tear down their social constructions and start from scratch with a population that doesn't remember any other way, Harry and his friends need only remind people of the standards that existed in their society a few short years before. Similarly, today's activists do not need to build a brand new society in order to address the problems they see, rather they need to harness the courage to make small changes and see reform as possible. Young readers in particular can be inspired by Harry's righteousness and devotion to his cause, something they can emulate in their own lives for their own purposes.

Ideally, literature illuminates the human condition, clarifies the world, and connects with the reader. The dystopian aspects of the Harry Potter series not only help readers understand themselves in an unbalanced world, but encourage them to be actively involved in making their society better. As the academic respect for the Harry Potter series continues to grow, this reading of the final three installments as part of the genre of dystopia adds one more dimension to its value in education and the literary world.

Works Cited

Blake, Andrew. "The Harry Potter Books Take a Complex View of Race." In *Political issues in J. K. Rowling's Harry Potter series*. Detroit: Greenhaven Press/Gale Cengage Learning, 2009. 78-84.

Booker, M. Keith. *The Dystopian Impulse in Modern Literature: Fiction as Social Criticism*. Westport, Conn.: Greenwood Press, 1994.

Brown, Paul. "Harry Potter and the Freedom of the Press." Suite 101: Children's Books. paul-brown.suite101.com/harry-potter-and-the-freedom-of-the-press-a332287 (accessed October 14, 2011).

Claeys, Gregory. "The Origins of Dystopia: Wells, Huxley and Orwell." In *The Cambridge Companion to Utopian Literature*. Cambridge: Cambridge University Press, 2010. 107-31.

Gordin, Michael D.. *Utopia/Dystopia Conditions of Historical Possibility*. Princeton, N.J.: Princeton University Press, 2010.

"Harry Potter Wiki." Harry Potter Wiki. http://harrypotter.wikia.com/wiki/ (accessed December 13, 2011).

Hintz, Carrie, and Elaine Ostry. *Utopian and Dystopian Writing for Children and Young Adults*. New York: Routledge, 2003.

Jenkinson, Clay. "From Milton to Media: Information Flow in a Free Society." Center for Media Literacy. http://www.medialit.org/reading-room/milton-media-information-flow-free-society (accessed February 12, 2011).

Luna, Erik. "Criminal Justice and the Public Imagination." *Ohio State Journal of Criminal Law* 7: 71 (2009): 71-147. moritz-law.osu.edu/osjcl/Articles/Volume7_1/Luna-FinalPDF.pdfâ€Ž (accessed January 20, 2012).

Manlove, Colin. "The Literary Value of the Harry Potter Books." In *Hog's Head Conversations: Essays on Harry Potter*. Allentown, PA: Zossima, 2009. 1-21.

McGrath, Charles. "Teenage Wastelands." *The New York Times*, February 19, 2011. http://www.nytimes.com/2011/02/20/magazine/20FOB-WWLN-t.html (accessed October 12, 2001).

Moylan, Tom. *Scraps of the untainted sky: science fiction, utopia, dystopia*. Boulder, Colo.: Westview Press, 2000.

Rivers, Nathaniel. "The Harry Potter Books Refect an Increasingly Dangerous World." In *Political Issues in J. K. Rowling's Harry Potter Series*. Detroit: Greenhaven Press/Gale Cengage Learning, 2009. 104-7.

Rowling, J. K. *Harry Potter and the Sorcerer's Stone*. New York: A.A. Levine Books, 1998.

—. *Harry Potter and the Chamber of Secrets*. New York: Arthur A. Levine Books, 1999.

—. *Harry Potter and the Prisoner of Azkaban*. New York: Arthur A. Levine Books, 1999.

—. *Harry Potter and the Goblet of Fire*. New York: Arthur A. Levine Books, 2000.

—. *Harry Potter and the Order of the Phoenix*. New York: Arthur A. Levine Books, 2003.

—. *Harry Potter and the Half-Blood Prince*. New York: Arthur A. Levine Books, 2005.

—. *Harry Potter and the Deathly Hallows*. New York: Arthur A. Levine Books, 2007.

Snodgrass, Mary Ellen. "Dystopia." In *Encyclopedia of Utopian Literature*. Santa Barbara, Calif.: ABC-CLIO, 1995. 179-80.

Soter, Anna O. *Young adult literature and the new literary theories: developing critical readers in middle school*. New York: Teachers College Press, 1999.

"Stephen Colbert Interviews Neil deGrasse Tyson at Montclair Kimberley Academy - 2010-Jan-29 - Transcript Vids." Transcript Vids. http://transcriptvids.com/v/YXh9RQCvxmg.html (accessed February 29, 2012).

Westerfeld, Scott. "Breaking Down the "System"." *The New York Times*, December 27, 2010. http://www.nytimes.com/roomfordebate/2010/12/26/the-dark-side-of-young-adult-fiction/breaking-down-the-system (accessed September 25, 2011).

Westman, Karin E. "Blending Genres and Crossing Audiences: Harry Potter and the Future of Literary Fiction." In The Oxford Handbook of Children's Literature, edited by Julia Mickenberg and Lynne Vallone, 93-112. Oxford: Oxford University Press, 2011.

Harry Potter and the Dystopia After Tomorrow
Response from Amy H. Sturgis

In "A Bridge to Dystopia: Reading Harry Potter as a Collapsing Dystopia," Sarah Reschan justly draws attention to parallels between the Harry Potter series and the tradition of Young Adult (YA) dystopian fiction—a tradition that predates J. K. Rowling herself, thanks to the dystopian "juveniles" of the 1950s by Robert A. Heinlein, Andre Norton, and Poul Anderson, among others. During the publication of the Harry Potter series in the late 1990s and early 2000s, however, YA dystopian fiction experienced an unprecedented explosion in both the number of works produced and their popularity, a phenomenon that continues well into the second decade of the twenty-first century. This YA dystopian explosion has confirmed trends that counter the older patterns Reschan describes and shed different light on comparisons with the Harry Potter saga.

Reschan argues that "the primary difference between traditional fiction and that written for young adults" is one of tone; adult dystopias may choose the bleaker endings of disillusionment, defeat, or survival by retreat, but YA works require more hope, agency, and the promise of a happy (or happier, relatively speaking) ending. While this appears to be true for some of the earlier works in the decades-old YA dystopian tradition, this is a trend that has been seriously challenged, especially during the Harry Potter era. Farah Mendlesohn, author of 2009's *The Inter-Galactic Playground: A Critical Study of Children's and Teens' Science Fiction*, describes "anti-survivalist" themes in dystopian YA works that emphasize the immediacy and finality of the choices that face the next generation: "if you don't act, the world is doomed." Works published as early as Rosemary Harris's *A Quest for Orion* in 1982, Gudrun Pausewang's *The Last Children of Schewenborn* in 1983, and Robert Swindell's *Brother in the Land* in 1984, Mendlesohn notes, carry the message to young readers that "one can only screw up once, there is no chance at redemption" (Mendlesohn 2005).

The bleaker thread in the YA dystopian tapestry is strongly represented in Harry Potter-era YA dystopias. An illustrative contrast makes this clear. In

Heinlein's classic *Starman Jones* (1953), for example, the worst-case scenario for the young protagonist was that he would lead a subsistence existence without the promise of respite from his toils or the opportunity to pursue his dreams for a career in the stars; this seems almost luxurious compared to the best-case scenarios presented in recent works. M. T. Anderson's *Feed* (2002) depicts the futility of resistance against the mass culture; the only teenage character who actively fights the system not only fails, but also signs her own death warrant in the process. The single goal of the young protagonists in Andrea White's *Surviving Antarctica: Reality TV 2083* (2005) is simply living through their ordeal. The corrupt and oppressive regime in Gillian Philip's *Bad Faith* (2008) leaves only the option of retreat and escape—if they are lucky—for the youthful heroes. As Mendlesohn bluntly puts it, many of these YA works "have in common a certain helplessness in the face of the future and an attitude, to put it crudely, of 'the adults have fucked up and you are going to suffer'" (Mendlesohn 2009). This attitude may not be wholly apologetic, either; Noga Applebaum, in her perceptive study *Representations of Technology in Science Fiction for Young People* (2010), posits that some of these works reflect more resentment of the next generation than anxiety for it.

This context—in which YA protagonists do not always have the opportunity of making their troubled world a better place or even of surviving its danger—may have heightened the climactic sense of peril surrounding the conclusion of the Harry Potter series. Of course J. K. Rowling herself already had proven willing to kill off major characters before the publication of the concluding installment in the series, *Harry Potter and the Deathly Hallows*. Surely, however, the darker, less optimistic tone of other YA works contributed to the sense of many readers that Ron Weasley's, Hermione Granger's, and even (or especially) Harry's survival, not to mention success in thwarting Lord Voldemort and righting the wizarding world, was not a conclusion to be taken for granted.

Reschan also notes that "YA dystopias are set so far from the current world in time or space that students easily disengage from their political and social messages." This may have been true for the far-future setting of, for instance, Norton's *Star Man's Son, 2250 A.D.* (a.k.a. *Daybreak, 2250 A.D.*, 1952) or Anderson's *Vault of the Ages* (1952), but it cannot be said of contemporary YA dystopian novels. "Day after tomorrow" dystopias are a key feature of the recent explosion in the literature, and illustrative works often go to great pains to show young readers how society moved from Point A to Point B, from the present day to the dystopian nightmare.

Neil Shusterman's *Unwind Dystology* series (2007-2014 thus far) spells out how a U.S. Civil War could hinge on the issue of legalized abortion; Saci Lloyd's *Carbon Diaries* novels (2008-2010) take place in 2015 and 2017, respectively, after the United Kingdom implements mandatory carbon rationing; Kristen Simmons' *Article 5* trilogy (2012-2014) depicts the replacement of the U.S. Bill of Rights by a repressive "Moral Statutes." David Patneaude, in *Epitaph Road* (2010), goes so far as to spell out the immediate problems with today's society in a textbook from the not-so-distant future that is created by said problems, describing 2010 as a "world of poverty and hunger and crime and disease and greed and dishonesty and prejudice and war and genocide and religious bigotry and runaway population growth and abuse of the environment and immigration strife and you-get-the-leftovers educational policies and a hundred other horrors" (Patneaude 2010).

These works follow in the footsteps of critically acclaimed, successful YA dystopian series such as the *Tomorrow* series (1993-1999) by John Marsden and *The Shadow Children* sequence by Margaret Peterson Haddix (1998-2006), which solidified a trend toward instantly recognizable, contemporary dystopian settings with immediate lessons to offer. The publication dates of these series— the first four books of Marsden's series predated *Harry Potter and the Philosopher's Stone*, and the first novel in Haddix's series appeared the year after *Philosopher's Stone*—suggest that Rowling represents less a direct influence on this pattern than a highly-visible example of an emerging Zeitgeist.

One of the YA dystopias most notable for offering Reschan's "political and social messages" clearly through a distinctly contemporary setting is *Little Brother* (2008) and its sequel, *Homeland* (2013), by Cory Doctorow. In this duology, tech-savvy and innocent teens are mistaken for terrorists after a new attack on the United States, and the Department of Homeland Security proves to be the biggest threat to the citizens it supposedly exists to protect. The teen characters not only observe their world changing for the worse (a trait Reschan points out in the Harry Potter novels) as factors such as constant surveillance and state intimidation become commonplace, and fight back using their superior technological know-how, but they also learn about the recent past, as well, putting current ominous developments in historical perspective, connecting the dots of cause and effect, plotting the path to dystopia.

The process of education, enlightenment, and understanding described in *Little Brother* and *Homeland* is not unlike Harry Potter's discovery of the recent past of the wizarding world, including the actions and sacrifices of members of the Order of the Phoenix, in particular. This relates to Reschan's assertion that the Harry Potter series represents a crumbling utopia. There is, in fact, little utopian in the magical world Harry encounters. From the very start, it's a world reeling from the after-effects of a recent and terrible conflict, in which many noble witches and wizards gave their lives or sanity (including Harry's and Neville Longbottom's parents). It's a world fraught with inequality, corruption, and the abuse of power, as even the first novels show through the example of the Malfoys, among other characters. And it's a world a hair's breadth from new and deadly conflict.

What we do encounter in the novels and their ever-more sober and subtle tone, rather than a crumbling utopia, is the development and maturation of Harry's perspective as the point-of-view character. The more he grows and the more he comprehends in general, the more he recognizes the dystopian features of the world he has inherited. Harry's slow and steady disillusionment (symbolized so brilliantly by the use of the Dislliusionment Charm on him in *Harry Potter and the Order of the Phoenix*) allows him to be alert and prepared for the final harbingers of the coming showdown with Lord Voldemort and the Death Eaters, events such as the "capture" and transformation of the Ministry of Magic. This is not an ideal world gone wrong; it is history repeating with a vengeance.

The *Harry Potter* novels, in their very real sense of peril and their relatively identifiable setting, share features with many works that exemplify the contemporaneous explosion of YA dystopian fiction. It is in Harry's heroism and efficacy as an agent of positive change—in Reschan's words, his ability to "recognize tyranny and do something about it"—that the *Harry Potter* novels most resemble more traditional YA dystopian fare. Author and critic Jo Walton has noted that the remarkably dark settings of Heinlein's classic juveniles served as springboards for the plucky young heroes of his tales (Walton 2008). Despite their bleakness, Heinlein's problematic futures did not offer greater challenges than the youthful protagonists could handle and ultimately, heroically, overcome.

Rather than surrendering to hopelessness or being satisfied with mere survival or retreat, Harry Potter stands with the classic YA heroes and heroines and their later echoes as an inspiration and a role model. He's not only the boy who lived, but also the boy who changed his broken world for the better. Reschan is right to underscore how fiction such as the Harry Potter saga can "authorize young adults to take charge of their environments" and emulate the qualities of the protagonists. If young readers learn the lessons embedded in such tales, we have reason to have hope for our "day after tomorrow."

Works Cited

Applebaum, Noga. *Representations of Technology in Science Fiction for Young People*. New York: Routledge, 2010.

Doctorow, Cory. *Homeland*. New York: Tor Teen, 2013.

—. *Little Brother*. New York: Tor Teen, 2008

Heinlein, Robert A. *Starman Jones*. New York: Scribners, 1953.

Lloyd, Saci. *The Carbon Diaries 2015*. London: Hodder Children's Books, 2008.

—. *The Carbon Diaries 2017*. London: Hodder Children's Books, 2010.

Marsden, John. *The Tomorrow Series* (*Tomorrow, When the War Began; The Dead of the Night; The Third Day, The Frost; Darkness, Be My Friend; Burning for Revenge; The Night Is for Hunting; and The Other Side of Dawn.*) Sydney: Pan Macmillan Australia, 1993, 1994, 1995, 1996, 1997, 1998, and 1999.

Mendlesohn, Farah. *The Inter-Galactic Playground: A Critical Study of Children's and Teens' Science Fiction*. Jefferson, North Carolina: McFarland & Company, 2009.

—. "We Are All Doomed: Rosemary Harris, A Quest for Orion." *The Inter-Galactic Playground*. February 10, 2005. <http://farah-sf.blogspot.com/2005/02/we-are-all-doomed-rosemary-harris.html> accessed January 5, 2014.

Patneaude, David. *Epitaph Road*. New York: EgmontUSA, 2010.

Rowling, J. K. *Harry Potter and the Order of the Phoenix*. New York: Arthur A Levine Books, 2003.

Shusterman, Neal. *The Unwind Dystology Series* (*Unwind, UnWholly, UnSouled, and Undivided*). New York: Simon & Schuster Books for Young Readers, 2007, 2012, 2013, and 2014.

Simmons, Kristen. *The Article 5 Trilogy* (*Article 5, Breaking Point, and Three*). New York: Tor Teen, 2012, 2013, and 2014.

Walton, Jo. "The Dystopic Earths of Heinlein's Juveniles." *Tor.com*. August 5, 2008. <http://www.tor.com/blogs/2008/08/juviedystopias> accessed January 5, 2014.

The Canonization of Neville Longbottom:
The Development of Identity in
Rowling's Supporting Cast
Timothy Bartel

In J. K. Rowling's *Harry Potter* saga, few supporting characters are as lovable—or pitiful—as Neville Longbottom, the "round-faced and accident prone and boy with the worst memory of anyone Harry had ever met."[1] While the heart of *Harry Potter* scholarship will always be Harry and Harry's journey, attention to the peripheries of the massive arc of Rowling's narrative can illuminate the width and depth of her art. These peripheries include both the supporting cast that surrounds the principle characters—out of which Neville has proven a perennial favorite—as well as the settings and themes that surround those central to the plot of each book and main arc of the saga as a whole. In this essay, I hope to reveal why Neville is such a fascinating character through illustrating and tracing the care with which Rowling slowly and intentionally constructs and develops his identity across the entire series. In order to do this I will attempt to answer a question: who is Neville Longbottom? I will show that in books 1–6 several possible answers to this question are presented, and that in book 7 Neville is revealed in his mature identity. I conclude by considering the two dominant interpretations of this mature identity—the simpleton theory of Matthew Dickerson and David O'Hara, and the Christian discipleship theory of John Granger—and offer suggestions for further developing and particularizing each theory.

If the critical literature upon the Potter saga as a whole is still quite thin, the critical interaction with the character of Neville is even thinner. One of the first and only concentrated considerations of Neville as a character is in John Granger's *How Harry Cast his Spell*, in which Granger—with characteristic

---

[1] J. K. Rowling, *Harry Potter and the Chamber of Secrets* (London: Bloomsbury, 1998), 68.

illumination—analyses Neville's name and draws out the ambiguity in his identity. "Neville," Granger writes, can mean either "No-city" or "New city." [2] But which is he: no-city or new-city? Who's there: somebody or nobody?

More recently Kathleen McEvoy, in her 2011 essay "Heroism at the Margins," considers Neville's emergence from his early role as a "simpleton" into a mature identity as the "most interesting" of "all the marginal heroes present in the novels." [3] This interest in Neville's shifting and developing identity is not confined to the secondary literature, for Rowling herself includes, in books 1–6, several questions about Neville's identity, posed either by Neville himself, or by Harry. These questions are: *Is Neville a Gryffindor? Is Neville a Squib? Is Neville Peter Pettigrew? Is Neville Harry? Is Neville Nobody?* and most importantly *Is Neville the true son of his parents?*

Who is Neville Longbottom?

In *Harry Potter and the Philosopher's Stone*, after we are introduced to Neville as "a round-faced boy who was saying, 'Gran, I've lost my toad again,'" [4] we observe Neville in the sorting ceremony, where the hat takes a while to decide before placing him in Gryffindor. In the first of many moments of slapstick comedy involving him, Neville then runs off still wearing the Sorting Hat. [5] But is Neville truly a Gryffindor? Neville expresses his doubts that he deserves to be in Gryffindor house after failing to stand up to Malfoy's taunts and torments, including the latter's theft of Neville's rememberall. Harry and Ron assure Neville that he is "worth twelve of Malfoy." [6] Still, does this mean that Neville is

---

[2] John Granger, *How Harry Cast His Spell* (New York: Tyndale, 2009), 115. Granger also explores Neville's last name, explaining that Longbottom most obviously means something like "big-buttox." But *bottom*, Granger reminds us, also can mean courage or bravery. Though Granger does not explicitly mention Shakespeare here, I cannot but associate the name Longbottom with Bottom the Weaver, the ass-headed amateur sage of *A Midsummer's Night's Dream*, who bumbles his way toward comic profundity, and is named after the object around which the weaver's thread is wound.

[3] Kathleen McEvoy, "Heroes at the Margins," in *Heroism in the Harry Potter Series* (London: Ashgate, 2011), 216. In calling Neville a "simpleton," McEvoy draws on the terminology of Dickerson and O'Hara, who see Neville as a "modern incarnation of the 'fairytale simpleton'" (McEvoy, 216). More on this later.

[4] J. K. Rowling, *Harry Potter and the Philosopher's Stone* (London: Bloomsbury, 1997), 71.

[5] Ibid, 90.

[6] Ibid, 160.

Gryffindor material? Though this question is not fully answered until the end of *Deathly Hallows* when Neville pulls the sword of Gryffindor out of the Sorting Hat, Neville's true virtue begins to be demonstrated, to somewhat comic effect, just before the climax of *Philosopher's Stone*, when he stands up to Harry, Ron, and Hermione in the Gryffindor common room.

Though Neville's actions at the end of *Philosopher's Stone* might at first seem to be a mere annoyance, Dumbledore sets us straight in the final chapter, awarding Neville the winning ten points of the house cup for his bravery in standing up to his friends. These are the first points Neville ever wins, and, as McEvoy points out, Dumbledore presents the housepoints in such a way that it is Neville, not Harry, Ron, or Hermione, who scores the winning points. Thus, at this early stage, McEvoy argues, we see that "Neville clearly has a well of bravery inside of him."[7] The first question about Neville's identity, then, is raised and answered in *Philosopher's Stone*; Neville is indeed a Gryffindor, if only barely. He admires the trinity of Harry, Ron, and Hermione, but no one, not even Dumbledore, mistakes him for being at their level.

Neville does not play as important a role in *Chamber of Secrets* as he does in *Philosopher's Stone*. Still, as *Chamber* is the book that introduces us to the many varieties of wizard and muggle based on blood, Neville does, once again, worry out loud about his identity in this context, for he calls himself "almost a squib,"[8] referring back, perhaps, to the story in *Philosopher's Stone* of his very late demonstration of magical potential. Ron, too, does not think so highly of Neville's abilities, saying, "Look at Neville Longbottom, he's pure-blood and he can hardly stand a cauldron right way up!"[9] This doubt about his magical ability and potential makes Neville unsure of which classes to sign up for in his coming third year.[10] The question of whether Neville is, in fact, "almost a squib" is not answered in *Chamber of Secrets*. He is established as pure-blood, but such a fact does not seem to do him much good.

In *Prisoner of Azkaban*, Harry begins to think about Neville more, and this causes the question of Neville's identity to become more pronounced. When

---

[7] McEvoy, 217.
[8] Rowling, *Chamber of Secrets*, 139.
[9] Ibid., 89.
[10] Ibid., 186–187.

Harry, on the run from Privet Drive, boards the Knight Bus, he says that his name is "Neville Longbottom."[11] And Harry dreams about Neville twice in *Prisoner of Azkaban*: first he dreams that Peter Pettrigrew looks like Neville,[12] and second he dreams that Neville replaces him as seeker in the final Quidditch match.[13] The dream wherein Pettrigrew looks like Neville makes some sense, for *Prisoner of Azakaban* is the book in which Harry begins to interpret himself and his friends through the lens of his father, James, and James's friends. In both friend groups, Neville and Prettigrew are, in Granger's words, "hangers-on" who exist in a liminal space just outside the core community of their respective friends.[14] Of course, for re-readers of the book, this identification of Neville and Pettigrew is alarming, for Pettigrew is the betrayer of the Potter family to Voldemort. And Neville too, seems to inadvertently betray Hogwarts to Sirius Black by losing his list of passwords to the Gryffindor common room, which Sirius finds and uses. In the end, of course, we learn that it is Crookshanks who steals the list, not Neville who loses it. In a recent article, Emily Asher-Perrin has made much of the Neville-Pettigrew connection, arguing that "Harry and company need Neville in the exact way that James and Lily and the Order of the Phoenix needed Peter. The difference is that Neville is more than up to the task."[15] In Asher-Perrin's view, Neville's choices not only distinguish his own personal fate from that of Pettigrew, but also enable Harry's whole generation to succeed where James's generation failed.

In the next three books, the predominant identity question that Neville faces is whether he will uphold his family legacy, whether he is truly a Longbottom. In *Goblet of Fire* we see this early on, when Neville says that his Grandmother would want him to join the Triwizard tournament to "uphold the family honor."[16] What exactly the "family honor" means is fully revealed in *Order of the Phoenix*, when Harry meets Neville and his parents at St Mungo's Hospital and

---

[11] J. K. Rowling, *Harry Potter and the Prisoner of Azkaban* (London: Bloomsbury, 1999) 31.

[12] Ibid., 158.

[13] Ibid., 223.

[14] Granger, 16.

[15] Emily Asher-Perrin, "Neville Longbottom is the Most Important Person in Harry Potter—And Here's Why," http://www.tor.com/blogs/2013/11/neville-longbottom-is-the-most-important-person-in-harry-potter.

[16] J. K. Rowling, *Harry Potter and the Goblet of Fire* (London: Bloomsbury, 2000), 168.

sees first-hand the permanent toll that being tortured has taken upon Neville's parents. Even in this scene, Neville seems somewhat embarrassed to be seen with his parents, and is chided by his grandmother:

> "You should be *proud*, Neville, *proud*! They didn't give their health and their sanity so their only son would be ashamed of them, you know!"
>
> "I'm not ashamed," said Neville, very faintly…
>
> "Well, you've got a funny way of showing it!" said Mrs Longbottom.[17]

Soon after this scene, Neville begins to change. Whereas at the beginning of the book Neville tells Luna Lovegood that he is "nobody,"[18] after he receives the news that his parents' torturers have escaped from Azkaban, Neville—who has already begun to develop his rudimentary magical skills in Dumbledore's Army before Christmas[19]—is transformed: "The news of his parents' attackers' escape had wrought a strange and even slightly alarming change in him […] [he] worked relentlessly on every new jinx and counter-curse that Harry taught them, his plump face screwed up in concentration and working harder than anyone else in the room."[20] In the preceding four books, we have seen Neville show great feeling and steadfastness of spirit, but at times laughably underdeveloped skills. It is here, in *Order of the Phoenix*, that Neville begins to add real, magical skill to that spirit, preparing him not only for the coming battle in the Department of Mysteries, but also the larger battles at Hogwarts that will end books 6 and 7.

After fighting ably in the Department of Mysteries beside Harry, and gaining a little media attention, Neville tells Harry, "Gran […] says I'm starting to live up to my dad at long last."[21] Neville further proves his bravery and skill in the battle at the end of *Half-Blood Prince*, wherein he is the first to charge up the astronomy tower stairs in pursuit of the death eaters (for which he is badly injured). If Neville's story ended with *Half-Blood Prince*, we might see him as

---

[17] J. K. Rowling, *Harry Potter and the Order of the Phoenix* (London: Bloomsbury, 2003), 566.

[18] Ibid., 208.

[19] This skill development includes his first successful use of *Expelliarmus*, first on Harry, then Hermione. Ibid. 349, 352.

[20] Ibid., 609–610.

[21] J. K. Rowling, *Harry Potter and the Half Blood Prince* (London: Bloomsbury, 2005), 131.

another, less impressive Harry, who just bloomed a little later. After all, he was born on the same day, the lost prophecy could have applied to either of them, both lost their parents due to Voldemort, and both are Gryffindors. But Rowling does not allow Neville to become merely a Harry Potter-clone, for in *Deathly Hallows* he becomes a more particularized figure.

Neville's Mature Identity

In what is possibly the most surprising scene in *Deathly Hallows*, Harry, Ron, and Hermione, desperate to enter Hogwarts, are bewildered to see a badly-bruised Neville emerging from a secret tunnel in the Hog's Head Inn:

> The longer Harry looked at Neville, the worse he appeared: one of his eyes was swollen, yellow and purple, there were gouge marks on his face, and his general air of unkemptness suggested that he had been living rough. Nevertheless, his battered visage shone with happiness as he let go of Hermione and said again, "I knew you'd come! Kept telling Seamus it was a matter of time!"[22]

Neville explains that he has been beaten and tortured by the Death Eaters who teach at Hogwarts for his many defiances, including refusing to torture other students, standing up for non-pure-bloods, and carrying on Dumbledore's Army. He explains that his pure-blood status has kept him alive: "They don't want to spill too much pure blood, so they'll torture us a bit if we're mouthy, but they won't actually kill us."[23] Neville goes on to explain that his Grandmother is now on the run from Death Eaters, and is proud of him: "She sent me a letter […] telling me she was proud of me, that I'm my parent's son, and to keep it up."[24] Here Neville has come into his own, and is particularized. He is not Harry, solving mysteries and destroying Horcruxes; he is the faithful follower of Harry who, though others doubt it, firmly believes that Harry will return. John Granger has described Neville's "heroic resistance" in *Deathly Hallows* as an "example of Christian discipleship."[25] This seems quite true—Neville is the one who never doubts that Harry will return, and encourages others to believe in Harry as well.

---

[22] J. K. Rowling, *Harry Potter and the Deathly Hallows* (London: Bloomsbury, 2007), 460.
[23] Ibid., 462.
[24] Ibid., 464.
[25] Granger, 203.

In Granger's reading, Harry is the Christ-figure and Neville the disciple who stays true to his absent master.

But when he meets Harry, Ron, and Hermione in the tavern, Neville is far from finished with his journey. He still awaits his final test, which is presented in the last chapter of the series. While before he resisted with bravery Voldemort's servants, he is at last confronted and tortured by Voldemort himself. And Neville Longbottom proves in that moment that he is not only faithful to Harry and Dumbledore, but also a true Gryffindor, a true Longbottom, and a Horcrux-destroyer to boot:

> Someone had broken free of the crowd and changed at Voldemort: Harry saw the figure hit the ground, disarmed, Voldemort throwing the challenger's wand aside and laughing…
>
> "We need your kind, Neville Longbottom."
>
> "I'll join you when hell freezes over," said Neville, "Dumbledore's Army!" he shouted, and there was an answering cheer from the crowd.[26]

Unlike in the film's version of events, Neville is instantly recognized by Voldemort as admirable and brave, and even a desirable ally. Nevertheless, when tempted with a final renunciation, Neville names Dumbledore, and proves himself to be faithful to the end. For this he is cruelly tortured by Voldemort:

> [Voldemort] pointed his wand at Neville, who grew rigid and still, then forced the Hat onto Neville's head, so that it slipped down below his eyes […]
>
> "Neville here is now going to demonstrate what happens to anyone foolish enough to oppose me," said Voldemort, and with a flick of his wand, he caused the Sorting Hat to burst into flames.
>
> Screams split the dawn, and Neville was aflame, rooted to the spot, unable to move, and Harry could not bear it: he must act –[27]

Just as Neville was earlier tortured by Voldemort's servants for his defiance at Hogwarts, he is now tortured—with more deadly intentions—by the Dark Lord himself. This repeated subjection to torture by the Death Eaters and Voldemort

---

[26] Rowling, *Deathly Hallows*, 585.
[27] Ibid., 585–586.

in book 7 can be read as a more advanced form of the torment that the sons of death eaters—especially Malfoy, Crabbe and Goyle—subject Neville to from time to time throughout the series. But something has changed in the previously pitiful Neville, and indeed, in the whole Potter world since Harry sacrificed himself for his friends:

> In one swift, fluid motion Neville broke free of the Body-Bind Curse upon him; the flaming Hat fell off him and he drew from its depths something silver, with a glittering, rubied handle –

> The slash of the silver blade could not be heard over the roar of the oncoming crowd [...] With a single stroke, Neville sliced off the great snake's head, which spun high into the air, gleaming in the light flooding from the Entrance Hall, and Voldemort's mouth was open in a scream of fury that nobody could hear, and the snake's body thudded to the ground at his feet –[28]

At the last, Neville joins the ranks of Horcrux destroyers (which includes Harry, Ron, Hermione, and Dumbledore), slicing off the head of Nagini in an act reminiscent of Saint George himself.[29] And his ability to pull out the sword of Gryffindor in particular confirms his true identity as a member of Gryffindor house, which had been in question ever since book 1. Travis Prinzi has also added another interpretation to this scene: Neville, like Harry and Ron before him, takes on an Arthurian role in his ability to access the Sword of Gryffindor—an analogue of Excalibur—in his time of need.[30] Given Dumbledore's repeated insistence that such a feat confirms one's status as a true Gryffindor, reading "Gryffindor" as an analogue of Arthurian knighthood—or even kingship— elevates Neville to a very high level indeed. He is fit, Prinzi implies, not just to fight, but to rule.

In addition to Prinzi's description of Neville as an Arthurian figure, there are two other major views so far expressed in the critical literature about what to call Neville's mature identity. The first, proposed by Dickerson and O'Hara and supported by McEvoy, that Neville is a *simpleton*, an "oft recurring character [who] doesn't appear smart or clever, and yet he has some other important vir-

---

[28] Ibid., 586–587.

[29] Investigation of Rowling's use of Spencer's *Faerie Queen* in the Potter saga would prove, I think, fruitful and illuminating. I have chosen to avoid discussion of dragon slaying imagery in *Harry Potter*, as it deserves its own, focused study.

[30] Travis Prinzi, *Harry Potter and Imagination: The Way Between Two Worlds* (Allentown, PA: Zossima Press, 2009), 87.

tue, usually moral virtue, or perhaps wisdom rather than craftiness, and as a re-sult of that wisdom or virtue becomes the successful hero [...] In many stories, the simplicity of the simpleton is exaggerated by contrast with others (frequent-ly, siblings) who appear shrewder, craftier, more intelligent, or in some other ways more gifted. Yet the simpleton still proves the hero."[31] While Dickerson and O'Hara applied this role to Neville before the seventh book came out, McEvoy extends their argument to Neville's Role in *Deathly Hallows*:

> By the close of the series, Neville has moved far beyond the fearful, clumsy boy readers met on Platform Nine and Three-Quarters [...] In the Great Hall following the final battle, Harry sees "Neville [...] surrounded by a knot of fervent admirers" (DH, p. 597). Neville ultimately becomes Professor of Herbology at Hogwarts, a hero with friends who love and respect him. Not bad for a "simpleton."32

Both Dickerson and O'Hara and McEvoy use the term "hero" for Neville's ma-ture identity. And both see his heroism rising out of a seemingly simple and bumbling exterior. The factor, according to Dickerson and O'Hara, that changes a simpleton like Neville into a hero is an "important virtue" that is initially hid-den, especially when the simpleton is compared to his peers, but results in the eventual, successful heroism of the character. While neither Dickinson and O'Hara nor McEvoy explicitly single out a particular cardinal or theological virtue that results in Neville's eventual heroism, Marcus Schulzke has recently suggested that Neville's characteristic virtue, slowly emerging throughout the series, is *courage*: "Neville is, despite his faults, a symbol of courage, who rises to greatness because he takes the initiative to act."[33] If we apply Schulzke's claim to Dickerson and O'Hara's concept of the simpleton, then we have a read-ing of Neville's journey as one wherein it is moral courage in particular that leads Neville to become, in the end, a simpleton-hero.

---

[31] Matthew T. Dickerson and David O'Hara, *From Homer to Harry Potter* (Grand Rap-ids, MI: Brazos Press, 2006), 138–139.

[32] McEvoy, 218.

[33] Marcus Schulzke, "Politics and Political Activtion in *Harry Potter*," in *J. K. Rowling: Harry Potter* (London: Palgrave MacMillan, 2012), 118. One could argue that McEvoy's repeated use of the word "bravery" in descriptions of Neville's heroism is an indication that she would agree with Schulzke's that Neville's characteristic cardinal virtue is cour-age.

A second but by no means contrary reading of Neville's mature identity is that of John Granger, who, as we saw above, calls the Neville of *Deathly Hallows* a "model of Christian discipleship."[34] Granger here fits Neville into his larger read of Rowling's characters as distinctively *Christian* types and figures. Harry is Granger's Christ figure; therefore it makes good sense that Neville, as the one who looks up to Harry, imitates Harry, fights for Harry, carries on Harry's vision for Dumbledore's army in Harry's absence, and still believes that Harry will return when those around him lose hope, is indeed a model of the disciples of Christ who also look up to, follow, imitate, and wait in hope for Christ—as well as bumble, stumble, and fail—all throughout the New Testament Gospels and Acts.

But by way of conclusion, I would like to push Granger's interpretation a little further, using Schulzke's theory about Neville's charcteristic virtue. If Neville is indeed a model of the Christian disciple, and if the cardinal virtue that renders Neville heroic is courage, then we could say that Neville is a type of Christian disciple characterized by courage in particular. As we have seen in our exploration of Neville's identity journey throughout Rowling's saga, Neville is continually faced with torments and tortures. In the early books these are usually torments from former Death Eaters, like Snape, or the children of Death Eaters, like Malfoy, Crabbe, and Goyle. In the later books, especially the last, Neville faces out-and-out torture from proper Death Eaters, and finally from Voldemort himself.

It is the virtue of fortitude—the older word for courage—that allows Neville to stand up under these torments and tortures, that allows him to remain true to what he believes, to even defiantly confess his loyalty to Harry and to Dumbledore in the throes of torture. Thus, I would like to suggest that we can further particularize Granger's read of Neville as a Christian disciple and call Neville a model of a Christian *confessor*. The term *confessor* was first used in the third century as a "title of honor to designate those [...] who had confessed Christ publicly in time of persecution and had been punished with imprisonment, torture, exile, or labor in the mines"[35] under the Roman Emperor Decius.[36] The

---

[34] Granger, 203.
[35] "Confessor", *Catholic Encyclopedia*, http://www.newadvent.org/cathen/04215a.htm.

term became a common title in the first millennium, and was used to designate the particular character of those saints who had undergone torture. Famous confessor-saints of the Christian tradition include St Maximus the Confessor, St Theophilus the Confessor of Bulgaria, and St Edward the Confessor. Such saints stand as exemplars of a Christian tradition that honors not only those who die for the faith, but also those who live for the faith when such a life is agony, those who stay true through the great pain of persecution and torture, who are never afforded the mercy of a quick death.

Though it may seem arbitrary to single out fortitude in the face of torment and torture as the distinguishing attribute of Neville in his mature identity, I believe it fits well with another key aspect of Neville's maturation, namely his becoming the true son of his parents. For Neville is the son of confessors; Frank and Alice Longbottom, we remember, were tortured to the point of insanity by Bellatrix Lestrange, but they never betrayed the Order of the Phoenix. Thus they fit the classic definition of the confessor as one who is tortured for their beliefs, but never recants. Neville proves himself their true heir by facing with fortitude the tortures of the Death Eater teachers at Hogwarts, but never betraying Harry. It is for this, perhaps, more than Neville's greater proficiency with magic or growing leadership abilities, that his Grandmother calls him, in her letter, his "parents' son." Training under Harry in Dumbledore's Army developed Neville's skill at magic, but it is that deeper element—the virtue of fortitude—that Neville draws upon in imitation of his parents.

Neville's swerving path, maturation, and particularization reveal an ongoing act of care and craft on Rowling's part as an author. Even as she maintains a main focus on Harry, Ron, and Hermione, Rowling keeps Neville in view, giving us glimpses of his growth in the face of each book's villains and challenges. We might call this a quality of—to coin a term—*polyoptics* on Rowling's part, a quality shared by many of the great fantasy writers of the twentieth century. Rowling, like Tolkien before her, can see, and thus keep in view for her readers,

---

[36] For a standard early account of this persecution, see Eusebius' *History of the Church*, VI.39–46. I do not mean to suggest that Rowling is, herself, well versed in the history and terminology of the early church—though she may be, for all I know. I mean, instead, to further develop and lend nuance to Granger's interpretation of Rowling's characters in terms of Christian types and figures.

the many concomitant maturations taking place within her vast world and timeframe. Just as Rowling sees and shows us that Harry avoids several possible grim fates and false identities, so she sees and shows this in Neville—he overcomes the belittling taunts of Malfoy and Snape, who treat him like a squib and a coward, to become an accomplished wizard, herbologist, and Gryffindor. More importantly, she sees and shows Neville avoid the Judas-like fate of Pettigrew and inherit instead the job of Dumbledore's Army Leader and Horcrux destroyer. My hope is that Rowling's saga may go on, that it may be studied with increasing depth and insight, and that Harry himself may become the cultural symbol and archetype he deserves to be. But I also ask that we not forget a round-faced, forgetful boy named Neville, who became, through faith and fortitude, a confessor-saint at Hogwarts.

Works Cited

Asher-Perrin, Emily. "Neville Longbottom is the Most Important Person in Harry Potter—And Here's Why." http://www.tor.com/blogs/2013/11/neville-longbottom-is-the-most-important-person-in-harry-potter.

Dickerson Matthew T., and David O'Hara. *From Homer to Harry Potter*. Grand Rapids, MI: Brazos Press, 2006.

Eusebuis, *The History of the Church*. Translated by G.A. Williamson. London: Penguin Books, 1989.

Granger, John. *How Harry Cast His Spell*. New York, NY: Tyndale, 2009.

McEvoy, Kathleen. "Heroes at the Margins." *Heroism in the Harry Potter Series*. London: Ashgate, 2011.

Prinzi, Travis. *Harry Potter and Imagination: The Way Between Two Worlds*. Allentown, PA: Zossima Press, 2009.

Rowling, J. K. *Harry Potter and the Philosopher's Stone*. London: Bloomsbury, 1997.

—. *Harry Potter and the Chamber of Secrets*. London: Bloomsbury, 1998.

—. *Harry Potter and the Prisoner of Azkaban*. London: Bloomsbury, 1999.

—. *Harry Potter and the Goblet of Fire*. London: Bloomsbury, 2000.

—. *Harry Potter and the Order of the Phoenix*. London: Bloomsbury, 2003.

—. *Harry Potter and the Half Blood Prince*. London: Bloomsbury, 2005.

—. *Harry Potter and the Deathly Hallows*. London: Bloomsbury, 2007.

Schulzke, Marcus. "Politics and Political Activation in *Harry Potter*." *J. K. Rowling: Harry Potter*. London: Palgrave MacMillan, 2012.

The Importance of Neville Longbottom
Response from Maria Nilson

In Timothy Bartel's thought provoking and interesting article, we meet the lovable and pitiful Neville Longbottom and follow his development throughout the *Harry Potter* books. In my response, I want to focus on two things: how Neville's development from a clumsy and timid boy to the brave young man he is in the final book is an excellent example of how Rowling empowers her young characters, and on Neville as part of the supporting cast. I argue that the importance of Neville is that he is part of a community that not only supports Harry in his quest to overcome Voldemort, but makes Harry's success possible. Neville, along with Hermione and Ron, goes beyond being support. They are characters in their own right. Bartel asks in the final paragraph of his article that we don't forget Neville when we continue to analyze the *Harry Potter-* books. I would go one step further and say that we can't possibly understand Harry as a character without Neville, along with Hermione, Ron, Luna, and so on. In leaving the solitary hero behind her and letting the limelight, so to speak, shine on more than Harry Potter, Rowling demonstrates that not only is she willing to transcend and blend genre conventions but that she is also part of today's popular culture.

Last year, one of my students had an epiphany. She came up to me and argued that almost all of the examples of children's literature that we had studied together was about children who in the beginning of the story was powerless and without control, but who eventually learned to gain control and who was empowered before the story ended. This is true of both traditional fairy tales and of a great deal of modern literature for children. A lot of these stories are about empowerment. Sarah Margaret Kniesler sees Neville Longbottom as an excellent example of how Rowling empowers her young characters.

> Consider Neville Longbottom's transformation from the tearful boy wailing about his lost toad (Rowling 1997,104) to the Gryffindor recognized by Professor Dumbledore for the courage to 'stand up to your friends' (Rowling 1997, 306) to the hero who successfully destroys the final horcrux after he "broke

free of the Body-Bind Curse" and "with a great glittering rubied handle [...] sliced off the great snake's head" (Rowling 2007,587).[1]

Neville is, as Bartel clearly shows, an underdog that develops into a hero. But what kind of hero is he? Bartel convincingly argues that Neville is not a "Harry-clone." I would like to add a perspective to his analysis, as I have been one of many who has written about the Harry Potter-books from a gender perspective. In one way, we can see Neville as a character that overcomes the gender differences in the books that Rowling has been critiqued for. Boys act and girls read, says Charles Elster in "The Seeker of Secret: Images of Learning, Knowing and Schooling"[2]; and even if that is an oversimplification, I do think it rings true for some characters in the *Harry Potter* books. Neville, however, is a character that breaks that pattern. He is portrayed as a reader, but he also acts. Bartel argues that it is in *Harry Potter and the Deathly Hallows* that Neville in many ways comes into his own. Neville is loyal to Harry, he is able to hope, which is a valuable commodity, and he is courageous. He is also willing to do something and being able to act is itself sometimes heroic. Marcus Schulzke says in "Wizard's Justice and Elf Liberation: Politics and Political Activism in *Harry Potter*" that Neville becomes a leader in this book. "The choice of leader is important. Neville is, despite his faults, a symbol of courage who rises to greatness because he takes the initiative to act."[3] In Neville, we have not only a character who matures and develops and is empowered, but also a character that combines "reading with doing."

If Neville is a hero, what kind of hero is he? In her article "Neville Longbottom: The Hero with a Thousand Faces" Martha Wells argues that Neville, as well as Harry of course, is portrayed as a "typical" hero as read through the lens of Joseph Campbell's classic work *The Hero with a Thousand Faces* from

---

[1] Sarah Margaret Kniesler, "Alohomora! Unlocking Hermione's Feminism," *Hermione Granger Saves the World. Essays on the Feminist Heroine of Hogwarts*, ed. Christopher E. Bell (London: McFarlands, 2012), 90.

[2] Charles Elster, "The Seeker of Secrets: Images of Learning, Knowing and Schooling," *Harry Potter's World. Multidisciplinary Critical Perspectives*, ed. Elizabeth E. Heilman (London: Routledge, 2003), 208.

[3] Marcus Schulzke, "Wizard's Justice and Elf Liberation: Politics and Political activism in Harry Potter," *J. K. Rowling. Harry Potter*, ed. Cynthia J. Hallet & Peggy J. Huey (New York: Palgrave MacMillan, 2012), 118.

1949.[4] It is entirely possible to see Neville in this light, but I would argue that Neville is more of an "atypical" hero, as his place is not in the limelight. The quest he partakes in is *not* his quest but Harry's. Neville is an extraordinarily well-developed sidekick and interestingly not the only example of this in the *Harry Potter* series. What does it mean to give the supporting cast such an important role in the story? In his introduction to *Hermione Granger Saves the World: Essays on the Feminist Heroine of Hogwarts*, Christopher E. Bell argues that one of the main topics in the *Harry Potter* books is that "no one succeeds alone."[5] Neither Neville nor indeed Harry can be understood solely through Campbell's idea of the hero. They don't stand alone. They are both part of a larger community that together manages to defeat evil. I have tried to find a different word than support cast as this phrase doesn't really grasp Neville's or Hermione's or Ron's roles. Neville is more than support. As he destroys Nagini and defies Voldermort, he is a hero in his own right, and not just a follower of Harry's. Thus I am more inclined to agree with Bartel than with Granger, as I do think Neville is much more than a disciple.

William V. Thompson points out in the article "From Teenage Witch to Social Activist. Hermione Granger as Female Locus" that Rowling both uses traditional genres and changes them. She borrows from fairy tale tropes, but has no problem with leaving the fairy tale formula and allows her characters to develop and mature in a way that fairytale characters never do. She also uses heroic fantasy, but takes liberties with the genre. In a great deal of heroic fantasy the focus is on one hero who may or may not have a fortress of solitude, but who generally is both male (!) and alone in the final struggle. There may be supporting characters, but they are usually not well developed. Thompson says that: "Clearly not satisfied with the limitations of the genre in which she was writing, Rowling creates a character in Hermione that operates in such a way to both resists and undercut the overarching limitations of heroic fantasy."[6] I would argue that Ne-

---

[4] Martha Wells, "Neville Longbottom: The Hero with a Thousand Faces", *Mapping the World of the Sorcerer's Apprentice. An Unauthorized Exploration of the Harry Potter Series Complete Through Book Six*, ed. Mercedes Lackey (Dallas: Benbella, 2005).

[5] Christopher E. Bell, "Introduction," *Hermione Granger Saves the World. Essays on the Feminist Heroine of Hogwarts*, ed. Christopher E. Bell (London: McFarlands, 2012), 7.

[6] William T. Thompson, "From Teenage Witch to Social Activist. Hermione Granger as Female Locust," *Hermione Granger Saves the World. Essays on the Feminist Heroine of Hogwarts*, ed. Christopher E. Bell (London: McFarlands, 2012), 184.

ville, as well as Ron, has the same role to play. Instead of writing a series of books in which a young boy develops and matures and finally is able to overcome the obstacles in his way and successfully complete his quest, the *Harry Potter* books "is really much more of a tale in which the individual becomes part of a community or a social whole."[7] Rowling may have written a fantasy story about good and evil, but a major part of the books are about relationships. The *Harry Potter* books are not just about how Harry, or Neville, matures and develops their own identities; they are also about finding your place in a community and how difficult it is sometimes to interact with other people.

At Linnæus University, we have an undergraduate course focusing on the Harry Potter phenomena and we always have lively discussions on why the books and the films are so popular. One of the most compelling arguments is in my view, that Rowling creates a "hybrid." She uses traits from many different genres and combines them into something both new and familiar. She is also seen as modern. In today's popular culture fantasy and science fiction shows have learned their lesson from success stories like *Buffy the Vampire Slayer*[8] and combine action and adventure with characters that develops and acts together. The importance of Neville is not just how he overcomes his fear and is able to kill Nagini, it is also his role in the "Scooby gang" at Hogwarts. The books may be called the *Harry Potter* books, but without characters like Neville, they would in all likelihood not be the phenomena they are today.

[7] Robert T. Tilly Jr., "The Way of the Wizarding World: *Harry Potter* and the Magical *Bildungsroman*", *J. K. Rowling. Harry Potter*, ed. Cynthia J. Hallet & Peggy J. Huey (Palgrave MacMillan: New York 2012), 41.
[8] Cf. Rhonda Wilcox, *Why Buffy Matters: The Art of Buffy the Vampire Slayer* (New York: I.P. Tauris & Co).

Works Cited:

Bell, Christopher E. Introduction to *Hermione Granger Saves the World. Essays on the Feminist Heroine of Hogwarts*, ed. Christopher E. Bell. London: McFarlands, 2012.

Elster, Charles, "The Seeker of Secrets: Images of Learning, Knowing and Schooling." In *Harry Potter's World: Multidisciplinary Critical Perspectives*, ed. Elizabeth E. Heilman. London: Routledge, 2003.

Kniesler, Sara Margaret. "Alohomora! Unlocking Hermione's Feminism." In *Hermione Granger Saves the World: Essays on the Feminist Heroine of Hogwarts*, ed. Christopher E. Bell. London: McFarlands, 2012.

Schulzke, Marcus. "Wizard's Justice and Elf Liberation: Politics and Political activism in Harry Potter." In *J. K. Rowling. Harry Potter*, ed. Cynthia J. Hallet & Peggy J. Huey. New York: Palgrave MacMillan, 2012.

Thompson, William T. "From Teenage Witch to Social Activist. Hermione Granger as Female Locust." In *Hermione Granger Saves the World. Essays on the Feminist Heroine of Hogwarts*, ed. Christopher E. Bell. London: McFarlands, 2012.

Tilly Jr., Robert T. "The Way of the Wizarding World: *Harry Potter* and the Magical *Bildungsroman*." *J. K. Rowling. Harry Potter*, ed. Cynthia J. Hallet & Peggy J. Huey. New York: Palgrave MacMillan, 2012.

Wells, Martha. "Neville Longbottom: The Hero with a Thousand Faces." *Mapping the World of the Sorcerer's Apprentice. An Unauthorized Exploration of the Harry Potter Series Complete Through Book Six*, ed. Mercedes Lackey. Dallas: Benbella Books, 2005.

Wilcox, Rhonda. *Why Buffy Matters: The Art of Buffy the Vampire Slayer*. New York: I.P. Tauris & Co, 2005.

CHAPTER 8

Towards a Pattern of Paternal Atonement: The Role of Snape in *Harry Potter*
Joshua C. Richards

L ess a reading or an interpretation, this essay does not propose any answers or even begin outlining a solution to the rather thorny issue of Snape's role in Rowling's work. The purpose here is to sketch out a pattern, an observation, really, regarding the character of Snape and his function in the story.

First, I think it might be safely asserted that the Harry Potter novels are filled with a variety of paternal figures: James Potter, the actual, initially idealized, and absent father; Sirius Black, the beneficent godfather; Hagrid, the bumbling, comic father; Dumbledore, the all-father of the school—and examples could be multiplied. It might also be possible to argue for all of these figures to have some sort of atonement associated with them. Harry, after all, must come to terms with James Potter's very real faults, and he undergoes something like the Jungian *enantiodromia* with Sirius Black. Additionally, let me note that I myself have no interest in biographical speculation; whether or not there is some personal element behind this pattern is a matter for another study and another scholar.

Yet, it is, perhaps, a bit more contentious to argue that Severus Snape fits this pattern of paternal atonement, but I think an examination of the novels will render this at least plausible. Now, before proceeding further, some terminology will be necessary. For this, I am using Joseph Campbell's *The Hero with a Thousand Faces*, a steady feature in Potter studies, it seems; however, one does not, I think, need to buy into the applicability of Campbell or Jung to *Harry Potter* for my argument here to function. Because Campbell's phrasing is both expedient and beautiful, it will be employed here but divorced from its psychoanalytic underpinnings. In other words, I am treating Campbell as a describer of literary and mythological *topoi* instead of a purveyor of truth about the nature of mythology. My argument is that the resemblance exists—not why it comes about, nor am I arguing that Rowling deliberately created this dynamic; such ideas are universal enough to have arisen from her education in classics or elsewhere.

In the series' metanarrative, as it were, it seems to me that Snape, in particular, functions as the ogre-father, the wrath-bearing patriarch to be defeated. In Campbell's words,

> the ogre-aspect of the father is a reflex of the victim's own ego [...] sealing the potentially adult spirit from a better, more realistic view of the father, and therewith of the world. Atonement (at-one-ment) consists in no more than the abandonment of that self-generated double monster—the dragon thought to be God (super-ego), and the dragon thought to be Sin (repressed id). But this requires an abandonment of the attachment to ego itself; and that is what is difficult. One must have a faith that the father is merciful, and then a reliance on that mercy. (Campbell 120)

While I am uninterested in Campbell's Freudian cast, there are a couple of interesting facets to this idea. First, it is that the atonement with the father represents a change in perspective *only* in the hero, a change from an overly idealized view of the father-figure to one that recognizes the faults and complexity in him. Second, that this idealization can be either positive or negative. The hero can look upon the father with, as it were, rose-colored glasses and eventually have to realize the negative aspects. It would be speculation to say that this occurs with James Potter, but it is at least possible. Yet, I believe that Snape is the second, the ogre whom the hero must come to recognize as father. Indeed, this seems to be Snape's role in the meta-narrative—Harry begins by viewing him as villain and must come to accept that he and Snape are very much alike in some ways.

While this kind of paternal atonement may suggest an unseemly and overly Freudian reading of the series, I think there is some justification for pursuing it from a mythopoeic angle. After all, is not the Elder Wand passed down like the title of the King of the Wood in Frazer's *The Golden Bough* wherein each possessor defeating his predecessor (Frazer I.i.2-3)?[1] A full treatment of the Elder

---

[1] Several devices like the tabooing of names but particularly the external soul (horcrux) and its origins in folklore are delineated in *The Golden Bough*. While such ideas are commonplace enough to approach being *scènes à faire* and there is no direct evidence of

Wand and paternal atonement is beyond the scope of this essay, but it should at least render the presence of such themes in the series plausible. Additionally, consider Campbell's comment that

> The traditional idea of initiation combines an introduction of the candidate into the techniques, duties, and prerogatives of his vocation with a radical readjustment of his emotional relationship to the parental images. The mystagogue (father or father-substitute) is to entrust the symbols of office only to a son [...] for whom the just, impersonal exercise of the powers will not be rendered impossible by unconscious (or perhaps even conscious and rationalized) motives of self-aggrandizement, personal preference, or resentment. (Campbell 125-6)

Compare this to Dumbledore's discussion of Harry's worthiness to obtain the Hallows in the King's Cross chapter in *Deathly Hallows*, that strange *katabasis* and *nekyia* scene where Harry communes with Dumbledore. He states:

> Maybe a man in a million could unite the Hallows, Harry. I was fit only to possess the meanest of them, the least extraordinary. I was fit to own the Elder Wand, and not to boast of it, and not to kill with it. I was permitted to tame and to use it, because I took it, not for gain, but to save others from it.

> But the Cloak, I took out of vain curiosity, and so it could never have worked for me as it works for you, its true owner. The stone I would have used in an attempt to drag back those who are at peace, rather than to enable my self-sacrifice, as you did. You are the worthy possessor of the Hallows. (*Deathly Hallows* 720)

In short, because Harry will not misuse their powers and as such is worthy of them, Dumbledore, as mystagogue, entrusted the Hallows to his care—an idea previously seen in the mechanism for obtaining the Philosopher's Stone from the Mirror of Erised. This seems at least to be an instance of the father-atonement *topos*, as Campbell has phrased it, appearing in the novel. Thus, I think it justified to suppose that other instances may possibly exist.

Proving that such a pattern of paternal atonement exists would be impossible in a book chapter, but, I hope that we can at least ascertain if this pattern bears out broadly. First, we need to see if Snape seems to be portrayed as father-figure, even if a distinctly negative one. Second, we need to see if there is evidence of atonement between Harry and Snape; to this end, we will examine both the parallel atonements with James Potter and Snape in *Order of the Phoenix* and the

---

Rowling having gone to Frazer specifically, there are two stories of a seven-part external soul, in particular one involving a snake, in Frazer LXVI.16.

metanarrative of *Half-Blood Prince*. Third, we need to examine Snape's death and the epilogue of *Deathly Hallows* in particular to see if the ending of the macrocosm[2] bears out this pattern of paternal atonement.

Now, if Snape is, indeed, a father figure in the metanarrative, there should be some presence of this *topos* in Book I as I believe that the whole series is inchoate within it. Thus, any theme in the metanarrative should find some existence in *Philosopher's Stone*,[3] and, while subtle, I think there is some evidence of Snape as a sort of negative father-figure in Book I. Consider Dumbledore's conversation with Harry at the novel's end while he is in the hospital wing at the novel's end.

> "Yes, [Snape] – Quirrell said he hates me because he hated my father. Is that true?"
>
> "Well, they did rather detest each other. Not unlike yourself and Mr. Malfoy. And then, your father did something Snape could never forgive."
>
> "What?"
>
> "He saved his life."
>
> "What?"
>
> "Yes..." said Dumbledore dreamily. Professor Snape couldn't bear being in your father's debt. ...I do believe he worked so hard to protect you this year because he felt that would make him and your father even. Then he could go back to hating your father's memory in peace. ..." (*Philosopher's Stone* 300)

There are three matters for consideration in this passage. The first is the reason for Snape's hatred, the second is the *in loco parentis* nature of his actions, and the third is the analogy between Harry and Draco. On the first point, notice that Dumbledore does not actually answer Harry's question as to *why* Snape hates him. He says that Snape and James Potter hated each other, leaving Harry, and the reader, to make the inference. As *Deathly Hallows* proved, this isn't the reason at all. Yet, Dumbledore's explanation, though probably a lie to fulfill his promise to Snape of never revealing the truth to Harry, does have an aspect of

---

[2] Macrocosm throughout this essay refers to the plot of the series as a whole, microcosm the individual books. These terms refer to the action of characters and plot as distinct from metanarrative.

[3] It is, after all, only in Book I and in the macrocosm that Harry himself undergoes a complete hero's journey in the Campbellian sense.

truth (*Deathly Hallows* 679). Snape is still protecting Harry in place of his father, though for the love of his mother. As for the third, I hardly need to remind the reader that Dumbledore's analogy is misleading, as the reader would come to find out. In this comparison, it seems that Draco Malfoy is not Snape but James Potter—the popular bully going about hexing others for fun—thus, aligning Harry with Snape in the previous generation, an idea explicit in "The Prince's Tale" in Book 7.

The above alignment is worth examining in some detail as it is one of the clearer indications of a broader pattern of paternal atonement. In this instance, the atonement with Snape occurs in tandem, though not as prominently, as that of James Potter. While the focus is on this movement with James, the parallel action with Snape is important as this begins the slow slide to full atonement completed in *Deathly Hallows*. Until the chapter "Snape's Worst Memory" in *Order of the Phoenix*, Harry had valiantly defended this idealized version of his father. As mentioned earlier, paternal atonement is the movement from an unrealistic conception of the father to a more realistic. Whereas Snape is the ogre-father with whom one must learn to identify, James is the heroic father whom one must learn to be less than what you thought. By seeing his father being a bully, Harry ceases to identify with and idolize him as much. He asserts that

> For nearly five years, the thought of his father had been a source of comfort, of inspiration. Whenever someone had told him he was like his father James, he had glowed with pride inside. And now... now he felt cold and miserable at the thought of him. (*Order of the Phoenix* 654)

Here, we see the sudden shattering of Harry's image of his father, but this is disappointment, not necessarily atonement. Yet, later, Harry asserts that he had "simply learn[ed] to live with the memory of what his father had done on a summer's day more than twenty years ago" (*Order of the Phoenix* 667). This is the atonement with the actual father in James Potter. Harry had come to terms with the reality of who his father was. Additionally, this follows even more strictly Campbell's pattern. As above, Campbell states that atonement with the positively idealized father that "consists in no more than the abandonment of that self-generated double monster—the dragon thought to be God (super-ego)" (Campbell 120). For our purposes here, the super-ego can be thought of as an ideal for emulation, an ambition. Here, as expected, Harry asks, "but did he want to be like his father anymore?" (*Order of the Phoenix* 667). Yet, where is Snape in all this? It is important to note that the *initial* reaction to the memory is not revulsion from his father's behavior, but kinship with Snape, as follows:

> What was making Harry feel so horrified and unhappy was [...] that he know how it felt to be humiliated in the middle of a circle of onlookers, knew exactly how Snape had felt as his father taunted him, and that judging from what he had just seen, his father had been every bit as arrogant as Snape had always told him. (*Order of the Phoenix*, 650)

At the same time that seeing Snape's memory distances him from his real father, Harry begins to have his wholly negative view of Snape shaken as well by seeing the kinship in their situations. This is another instance of the atonement with the father-atonement *topos* with Snape as Harry begins to identify himself with the hated teacher.

Aside from the fact that Snape was devotedly in love with Harry's mother, a point that hardly requires examination, the best evidence of Snape's role as father-figure is found in *Half-Blood Prince*. The metanarrative aspect of the Half-blood Prince's book shows the pattern of paternal atonement most succinctly. Admittedly, I am highlighting the salient points; it is not clear how precisely Rowling intended the Half-Blood Prince's book to function metanarratively; the effect is wonderfully polyvalent but whether that was created intentionally or not would be speculation. After all, Snape's career-goal was always to be the Defense Against the Dark Arts instructor, and Harry's goal is to be an auror, a defender against the dark arts. Yet, it is Advanced Potions that stands between Harry and his goal, and Snape has historically been the potions master. Harry succeeds in the subject by the virtue of the Half-Blood Prince's book *i.e.* Snape's own textbook.

In other words, to fulfill a goal they both share, Harry must overcome Snape's subject, or in Campbell's phrasing, "[the heroic task] passes spiritually into the sphere of the father—who becomes for his son, the sign of the future task" (Campbell 125). Harry accomplishes this task by internalizing, unknowingly, Snape's teaching recorded in the book. Given the influence of the book, really his obsession with it, and Harry's adoption of *Expelliarmus* and *Sectumsempra*, there is at least some suggestion that, in Campbell's metaphorical view, "[the son] has become himself the father" (Campbell 126). In an admittedly glib summary, the meta-narrative pattern in *Half-blood Prince* seems to be that the son must internalize the father to defeat the father that he might fulfill the father's goal.

This fact is most obviously seen in Snape's first lesson as Defense Against the Dark Arts professor. At the conclusion of the lesson, Harry begins to rant, saying,

> "Did you hear [Snape] talking about the Dark Arts? He loves them! All that *unfixed, indestructible* stuff—"
>
> "Well," said Hermione, "I thought he sounded a bit like you."
>
> "Like *me*?"
>
> "Yes, when you were telling us what it's like to face Voldemort. You said it wasn't just memorizing a bunch of spells, you said it was just you and your brains and your guts—well, wasn't that what Snape was saying? That it really comes down to being brave and quick-thinking." (*Halfblood Prince* 180-1).

In other words, Harry and Snape both teach Defense Against the Dark Arts in the same way—a similar approach to being an auror. The path to being one is known to Snape as he immediately concludes from the list of Harry's courses that they are "[a]ll the subjects, required, in short, for an auror," though the same list of courses is also the requirement for St Mungo's[4] (*Half-blood Prince*, 320). The assumption is telling. Rowling does not elaborate further on this point and why she does not would be speculation. It is possible that the connection was being downplayed to highlight other themes; it is also possible that Rowling was not explicitly aware of it. All that we can conclude is that it is another incident in an ongoing pattern.

Let me briefly capitalize on the two aforementioned spells, *Expelliarmus* is a spell that becomes Harry's signature, so much so that the Death Eaters track which Harry is the real one, and when Harry defeats Voldemort, it is *Expelliarmus* that he uses. Yet, it is a spell that he learned from Severus Snape in Book 2, when Snape dueled Gilderoy Lockhart in "The Dueling Club" chapter.[5]

While it probably goes without being said, let me remind the reader of the Latin wordplay in the phrase *Sectumsempra*. It seems to be a composite of two

---

[4] Cf. *Order of the Phoenix*, 656.
[5] I am indebted to John Pazdziora for reminding me of this.

Latin words. While Sempra is obviously a faint variation of *semper*, "always," the *sectum* is a bit more complicated; *sectus* is the past participle of *seco*, a verb meaning to mutilate, to carve meat—fitting given the spell's violent effect. Thus, in a sort of squinting Latin, *Sectumsempra* could be "forever maimed," but in Latin *secta* is also "way of life" "code of conduct," "a philosophy of being." Thus, the use of the spell may carry an implication of *morés* as well that Harry has taken into himself—after all, in moments of desperation in Book 6, when facing Snape or the *Inferi*, *Sectumsempra* is the spell Harry lashes out with. In short, Harry fights with Snape's own weapons—a fact that Snape himself points out in their duel at the end of Book 6.

However, the pattern of paternal atonement has its clearest, overall expression in *Deathly Hallows*, that is at the end of the macrocosm. The most obvious elements suggesting a pattern of paternal atonement are the details of Snape's death and those of the epilogue.

Before examining the precise phrasing of Snape's death, it is interesting to examine the resemblance between Snape's death and that of Beowulf. In this instance, both die from a bite to the neck from a giant snake and a dragon respectively. In Beowulf's case, it's explicitly the poison that he dies from and it isn't clear the cause in Snape's case, either poison[6] or exsanguination would be possible, but neither Beowulf nor Snape die from the physical wound itself. Additionally, both are alone except for one person. Beowulf has Wiglaf, while in the case of Snape, Ron and Hermione are both under the cloak with Harry, but they are not mentioned for over 7 pages prior with one exception, and that particular sentence, "A flask conjured from thin air, was thrust into his shaking hands by Hermione," has the passive voice minimize her action (*Deathly Hallows*, 657). If the reader is inclined to dismiss that as prescriptivist claptrap, it is sufficient to note that they are still under the invisibility cloak. In this analogy, Harry would correspond roughly to Wiglaf, whose bravery places him as an heir to Beowulf (*Beowulf*, lines 2800-1). Whether Rowling intended this comparison or if it is even a meaningful resemblance is, as yet, unclear, but it is another possible clue.

---

[6] While it would be surprising if it were otherwise, Nagini is directly mentioned as being poisonous in *Order of the Phoenix*, 507.

As for the atonement in the scene itself, Snape's last words, "Look at me" are crucial. Remember that paternal atonement is about the hero recognizing the similarity and kinship between the ogre-father and the self. In Campbell's words, "[the hero] beholds the face of the father, understands—and the two are atoned" (Campbell 135). This seems to be what happens here. Snape asks for understanding, and after viewing the memory, the enmity Harry holds toward Snape is dissolved. Consider the following passage: "[Harry] did not know why he was doing it, why he was approaching the dying man: He did not know what he felt as he saw Snape's white face, and the fingers trying to staunch the bloody wound at his neck. Harry took off the Invisibility Cloak and looked down upon the man he hated" (*Deathly Hallows* 657). Here, the hatred is presented in the past tense, but after he views the memories, he defends Snape in his dialogue with Voldemort, and in the epilogue, Harry refers to Snape as "probably the bravest man I ever knew" (*Deathly Hallows*, 740-1, 758). There is an interesting echo in this compliment. When Harry confronts Snape in his flight from Hogwarts after killing Dumbledore in *Half-Blood Prince*, the accusation of cowardice by Harry is the one that provokes Snape to shrieking rage. Thus, the reference to Snape's bravery in particular seems an inversion, or, as might be the case, an atonement, a recognition of the full complexity of the situation. This, then, seems to be an instance of paternal atonement: Harry's view of Snape as villain lingering from the first book has passed into one that embraced Snape's tacit bravery, flagrant mistakes, and unrequited love of Lily.

There is a more subtle aspect of atonement in the epilogue of the novel, and that is the character Albus Severus Potter. The concatenation of details suggests that he may, in some way, be said to embody the father-atonement *topos*. Aside from the obvious issues of being named for Snape, his name, Albus Severus Potter, recapitulates the intended path of the Elder Wand. In the aforementioned King's Cross chapter in *Deathly Hallows*, Harry states to Dumbledore, "'If you planned your death with Snape, you meant him to end up with the Elder Wand, didn't you?' 'I admit that was my intention,' said Dumbledore, 'but it did not work as I intended, did it?'" (*Deathly Hallows* 721). The Elder Wand was supposed to pass from Dumbledore to Snape, then presumably to Harry, as is implied in Dumbledore's statement in the King's Cross scene.[7] In this way, Albus Severus Potter's name seems a recapitulation and, in some sense, a restoration. He is also an atonement in that as the child who bears Severus's name, he "[a]lone of Harry's three children, [...] had inherited Lily's eyes" (*Deathly Hallows* 758). Additionally, he is the one who may or may not end up in Slytherin, Snape's old house—a possibility that Harry himself rejected. Whether Albus Potter enters Slytherin or not is irrelevant; it is Harry's acceptance of this with Snape as the quoted example that indicates the atonement, the acceptance and realization of whom Snape *is* that seems to exemplify paternal atonement.

In conclusion, I think there are enough singular occurrences of what Campbell calls the atonement with the father to at least suggest a pattern. The goal of this essay was never to prove Rowling's intentions and conclude this argument, but by a preponderance of evidence prove this one possible role for Snape plausible. A full study of paternal atonement in the novels would be a book-length critical study and must likely wait for Rowling's *oeuvre* to be complete. At the last, Snape's overall role in the *Harry Potter* books is still something of an enigma, and the suggestion that Snape serves as some sort of a father figure may still be incendiary, but I think we may comfortably consider this uncomfortable proposition at least worthy of further discussion.

---

[7] The fact that Harry gives a different explanation of Dumbledore's intentions to Voldemort does not necessarily invalidate the observation.

Works Cited

Campbell, Joseph. *The Hero With a Thousand Faces*. Princeton: Princeton UP, 2004.

Frazer, James. *The Golden Bough Pt. I: The Magic Art*. 3rd ed. Vol. I. New York, NY: St. Martin's, 1976.

Frazer, James. *The Golden Bough Pt. VII: Balder the Beautiful*. 3rd ed. Vol. II. New York, NY: St. Martin's, 1976.

Rowling, J. K. *Harry Potter and the Deathly Hallows*. New York, NY: Arthur A. Levine, 2007.

—. *Harry Potter and the Half-Blood Prince*. New York, NY: Arthur A. Levine, 2005.

—. *Harry Potter and the Order of the Phoenix*. New York, NY: Arthur A. Levine, 2003.

—. *Harry Potter and the Philosopher's Stone*. London: Bloomsbury, 1997.

How the Dreaded Snape Enchants
Response from Amy Sonheim

In the previous chapter, "Towards a Pattern of Paternal Atonement: The Role of Snape in *Harry Potter*," Joshua Richards strikes at the heart of what I love best and like least in Rowling's Potter series: her plot twists. I love Rowling's plot twists because they make for page turners. Yet, toward the middle of the series, I found myself, book in hand, sighing, "The prevalence of the twists have made them predictable." In its 1997 debut, *Harry Potter and the Philosopher's Stone* proved sensational, in no little part, because we readers were frightfully surprised when the supposedly good Professor Quirrell turned villainous and the presumably villainous Professor Snape turned good. Then, the twists seemed to grow formulaic. With such a conflicted response as mine, what might Richards' observation that Snape works as Harry's ogre-father, a type of formula or pattern in itself, have to offer Potter studies? Since Richards bases his observation on Joseph Campbell's study of mythic formulas in *The Hero with a Thousand Faces*, Richards' embracing the formula of the ogre-father for Snape offers a fresh vantage point for judging the Potter series' literary merit.

Interestingly, while Richards embraces Campbell's mythic formula, he does not endorse *The Hero*'s "psychoanalytic underpinnings." While admittedly re-taining Campbell's psychoanalytic terms (relying heavily, for example, on "ego" and "super-ego"), Richards chooses to repurpose Campbell's psychoanalytic terms for literary purposes alone, choosing to sever Campbell's Freudian and Jungian premises from their themes. Forgive the pun, but such a severance for Snape is unwarranted. Psychoanalytic theory is precisely what Rowling employs to flesh out her characters. Since Richards invites us to reflect further on Snape as the ogre-father, I wish to explore further this question: if we *were* to accept Campbell's psychoanalytic theories informing Snape's role as ogre-father, how might such an acceptance nuance our readings of Snape and Harry?

Most notably, in the big picture, Rowling invites her readers to understand Harry by the psychoanalytic examining of how this son relates to his parents. Indeed, the macrocosm of Harry Potter, what Richards defines as "the plot of the

series as a whole," is a textbook coming-of-age narrative imbued with predicta-
bly psychoanalytic patterns for Harry.

For example, when we first meet Harry as an abandoned infant, Freud's theory of attachment explains both his status as outcast with the Dursleys and his
longed-for status of insider with his mates at Hogwarts. With the moniker "The
Boy Who Lived" and the scar to prove it, Harry is more than once motivated
throughout his adventures by his fear of death. And, closer to Richards' point,
when as an adolescent Harry learns that his father James was a bully, Harry follows the Freudian pattern of transferring his parental affection to Dumbledore
and, unbelievably, even to Snape. Freudian patterns of anxiety motivate Snape,
as well. As Richards duly notes, we finally understand why Snape protects Harry
when we understand that Snape, also abandoned as a boy, yearns for Lily's love.

It would seem, then, that Rowling's Snape is dramatized from the same
script as Sophocles' Laius. In *The Hero,* in its section entitled "Atonement with
the Father," Campbell describes the ogre-father relating to his son the way
Sophocles relates Laius to Oedipus. Campbell explains that "the Oedipal aggres-
sion of the elder generation" prompts the "patricidal impulse of the younger"
(139). To a degree, Snape and Harry illustrate this relationship. Richards has
already established many ways Harry identifies with Snape, not the least of
which, Potter aficionada Ellen Eubanks points out, was "their mutual status as
outcasts." With Snape pining for Harry's mother, the relationship might very
well be described as Oedipal. Although it seems a bit heavy handed to call Harry's relationship to Snape "Oedipal," it is easier to see now that Richards has
explained in such detail that Harry works as Snape's surrogate son and finally
emulates Snape to also work as a sacrificial father himself. In fact, the whole
Potter series culminates with Harry paralleling Snape in offering himself as a
sacrifice to save others.

In the final volume *Harry Potter and the Deathly Hallows,* after a ritualistic
communion with Snape, Harry, the initiate, takes on Snape's role: he willingly
offers his own life to Voldemort to save Hogwarts. Richards cites the preparato-
ry scene of Harry's atonement, when the dying Snape turns to Harry and says,
"'Look... at... me...'" (658). Richards reads this scene as "Snape [asking] for
understanding. " Yet, this scene might also be read in Campbell's psychoanalytic
parlance as the "self-giving aspect of the archetypal father" (140). For, in *The*

Hero, Campbell illustrates the Atonement of the Father with the Christian ritual of the Eucharist. In Campbell's context, the sacrifice of the father incites the son to drink his father's blood for "at-one-ment" with the father. I think Rowling invites such a parallel reading. Snape's "Look… at… me…'" to Harry could echo Christ's "Remember me" to his apostles at their Last Supper, asking his initiates to heed his example, share his life and death, follow in his footsteps. Of course, Harry does not drink Snape's blood, but he does siphon off Snape's liquid memories to resurrect them through the Pensieve. Alluding to Christian iconography, Rowling entitles the chapter in which Harry begins to perceive his unity with the dreaded Snape as "King's Cross" (708). Ironically, Rowling entitles the chapter in which Harry emulates Snape to vanquish Voldemort "The Flaw in the Plan" (724-49). So, we are as dumbfounded as Voldemort is that Snape, who seemed to serve the Dark Lord, was actually serving the Good Headmaster, but even more so that Harry becomes a good man by emulating the dreaded Snape, the latter twist unforeseen.

In "Cruel Heroes and Treacherous Texts: Educating the Reader in Moral Complexity and Critical Reading in J. K. Rowling's Harry Potter Books," Veronica Schanoes has written how such a culminating twist engages the reader morally. Rowling's Snape enchants us because his double identity stretches our ability to discern. Schanoes writes,

> Rowling forces her reader to distinguish between nastiness and wickedness, between subjective hatred and objective evil. She forces her reader to think beyond herself and her private identification with Harry to develop an awareness of the alliances necessary in order to do the right thing. This kind of distinction is one that few texts produced for adult consumption make; Shakespeare may remind us that a man may smile and smile and yet be a villain, but there is no corresponding line noting that a man may go out of his way to humiliate us and yet be a hero. (132)

Richards ably explains why Snape functions as both hero and foe to Harry, intimating how richly Rowling complicates the ethics of the world of Hogwarts.

In fact, by inventing the world of Hogwarts with magic, but without religion, Rowling creates a world concerned with human ethics. In *The Hero*, for the section "Atonement with the Father," Campbell seeks to justify the ways of culturally diverse gods to culturally diverse men, opening with Jonathan Edwards' sermon "Sinners in the Hands of an Angry God"; continuing with stories of Hindi, Navaho, Greek, and African divinities; and ending with *Job*. Using the same mythic patterns, Rowling plumbs the ways of Muggles from the vantage point of wizards.

In this way, Rowling's formulaic writing works compellingly, if you define "compelling" as I do to mean "transformative." Other children's literary critics, however, wonder if Rowlings' conventions don't pander to Western societies' lowest cultural desires to maintain the status quo.

Co-authors Carrie Hintz and Eric Tribunella noted this pandering in their 2013 book *Reading Children's Literature: A Critical Introduction.* Hintz and Tribunella attribute the sky-rocketing success of the Potter series, in part, to its endorsement of America's bigoted status quo: the acceptable sexism of Hermione's role, the acceptable classism of wizard culture, and even the working racism expressed toward house-elves and Muggles (9). Hintz and Tribunella note that Rowling also follows conventions of marketable genres, such as "fantasy, realism, the school story, adventure" (9). However, in considering these conventions, Hintz and Tribunella agree with Schanoes on Rowling's literary merit. Ultimately, they conclude that, in creating a wizard world to parallel our human one, Rowling achieves in the end a praiseworthy "moral ambiguity" (450).

Jack Zipes, on the other hand, does not concur. He deplores Rowling's formulaic writing. Working as a Marxist critic on children's literature for over thirty years, Zipes judges the value of a work's literary merit, in part, by how it is produced, calculating the work's cultural mores by the rate of exchange between the bourgeoisie and the book industry. When Rowling's wizard-dom was selling at an unprecedented price, Zipes raised more than an eyebrow. While the middle-class smelled success (which, I think, must smell like a barrel full of Bertie Bott's Beans), Zipes smelled a rat. In his 2001 *Sticks and Stones: The Troublesome Success of Children's Literature from Slovenly Peter to Harry Potter,* Zipes writes of the Harry Potter phenomenon,

> What appears unique conceals the planned production of commonality, and undermines the autonomy of judgment. A phenomenon can sway us from ourselves. We become dizzy and delirious.
>
> In the case of the Harry Potter books, their phenomenality detracts from their conventionality, and yet their absolute conformance to popular audience expectations is what makes for their phenomenality. (175-76)

To Zipes, the Harry Potter series was a best seller for years because its sales were fired up by a mechanized entertainment industry running on filthy lucre.

At the time *Sticks and Stones* went to press in 2001, Zipes denounced the first four Potter books as formulaic, saying, "if you've read one, you've read them all" (176). Though he does not reference Campbell by name, Zipes describes Rowling's formula as Campbell's monomyth: Harry is caught, summoned, tested, and brought home (176-77). Granted, Zipes allows that a narrative's being formulaic does not preclude its being good, noting that the four Harry Potter books "resemble the structure of a conventional fairy tale" (177). For Zipes, however, a book's being a Rockefeller money maker *does* prohibit its being a good book in the sense that a good book is justly created to challenge the imagination. While not against mythic structures per se, Zipes finds the Potter mythic structures are driven by commercialism, which proliferates the sale of all things "magic" from wands to motion pictures. To Zipes, P-O-T-T-E-R spells "money."

In the end, unlike Zipes, I find Harry transformed by Snape's surprising sacrifice as his ogre-father. In the series' finale, the moral failing of Dumbledore and moral victory of Snape so complicate Harry's perceptions of good and evil that I, too, was challenged to change my mind about both men. I conclude that the full story of Harry delivered over the seven volumes through various mythic patterns enables mine and other readers' views to be transformed in a manner not possible for commercial tripe. I would go so far to wager that it is Snape's double-identity as ogre-father, described so well by Richards, that endows Rowling's series with its real magic: the possibility for brave self-sacrifice on Harry's part. For, if we follow through with the sound argument Richards has begun, then the dreaded Snape atoning for Harry enables the younger wizard to remarkably become a man.

Works Cited

Campbell, Joseph. *The Hero With a Thousand Faces.* Princeton: Princeton UP, 1949.

Eubanks, Ellen. E-mail message to author. April 28, 2014.

Hintz, Carrie and Eric L. Tribunella. *Reading Children's Literature: A Critical Introduction.* Boston, MA: Bedford/St. Martin's, 2013.

Rowling, J. K. *Harry Potter and the Deathly Hallows.* New York, NY: Arthur A. Levine, 2007.

Schanoes, Veronica L. "Cruel Heroes and Treacherous Texts: Educating the Reader in Moral Complexity and Critical Reading in J. K. Rowling's Harry Potter Books." In *Reading Harry Potter*, edited by Giselle Liza Anatol, 131-145. Westport, CN: Praeger, 2003.

Zipes, Jack. *Sticks and Stones: The Troublesome Success of Children's Literature from Slovenly Peter to Harry Potter.* New York, NY: Routledge, 2001.

CHAPTER 9

What about the Dursleys?
A Re-reading of Fantastical Intrusions
in *Harry Potter*
Rebecca Langworthy

'I always value bravery... Yes, boy, your parents were brave... I killed your father first and he put up a courageous fight... but you mother needn't have died... she was trying to protect you...' [1]

His last fleeting glimpse of the living room was of Mr. Weasley blasting a third ornament out of Uncle Vernon's hand with his wand, Aunt Petunia screaming and lying on top of Dudley, and Dudley's tongue lolling around like a great slimy python. [2]

The quintessential example of maternal sacrifice in the *Harry Potter* series is the sacrifice of Lily Potter for her son Harry. The scene, however, is paralleled within our world, played out by Lily's sister Petunia at the beginning of *Harry Potter and the Goblet of Fire*, and the threatening wizard is not Voldemort but Arthur Weasley. The protective mother staying with her child when she has the opportunity to flee, and the fight between father and wizard, are strong elements in both episodes. While clear parallels exist between these scenes, the Dursleys' fight is shown to be humorous and their reactions to Mr. Weasley's magical assistance are patently ridiculous to the reader and Harry. The persistent mockery and punishment of the Dursleys, of which this scene is emblematic, forms the basis of this chapter, questioning our view of the magical world and its interaction with the real world.

---

[1] J. K. Rowling, *Harry Potter and the Philosopher's Stone* (London: Bloomsbury, 1997), 213. Referenced as PS hereafter.

[2] J. K. Rowling, *Harry Potter and the Goblet of Fire* (London: Bloomsbury, 2000), 48. Referenced as GoF hereafter.

That these parallels have hitherto been overlooked is understandable. The reader is aligned with the wizarding world rather than the real world through their association with Harry. Rowling isolates the reader from their primary reality in the Harry Potter series. Readers want to be wizards. The marketing surrounding the Harry Potter brand swallows up the readers, allowing them to buy wands and house robes and visit Hogsmead and the Three Broomsticks. With the launch of Pottermore, readers can be sorted into houses, brew potions, and become further immersed in the narrative. This is predicated upon readers behaving as, and desiring to become, wizards: part of a secondary and alien world. In terms of the books, readers are Muggles, part of the primary world.[3] The reader must believe in the wizarding world while reading the books, but by carrying this desire to belong in a fantasy world into the primary reality an intriguing phenomenon is created, in light of the treatment of Muggles.

A closer look at the treatment of the Dursleys displays the problems of the wizard-Muggle relationship. Escalating levels of violence from the magical world are contrasted with the reader's, and Harry's, amusement at these interactions between primary and secondary worlds. Fantastic intrusions take the form of various attacks upon the Dursleys that function as punishment for their lack of affection towards Harry.[4]

Philosopher's Stone
Harry left on the Dursleys' doorstep.
Letters from Hogwarts chase the Dursleys from their home.
Hagrid forces the Dursleys to recognise Harry is a wizard.
Dudley is given a pig-tail.

Chamber of Secrets
Harry threatens Dudley with magic
Dobby breaks pudding and owls scare off Mr. and Mrs. Mason, destroying Uncle Vernon's business deal.

---

[3] J. R. R. Tolkien discusses the significance of Primary and Secondary worlds in his essay 'On Fairy-Stories' in *Tree and Leaf* (London: Alan & Unwin, 1975), 40-41.

[4] This concept of intrusion as fantastic punishment is mentioned in Colin Manlove, *The Order of Harry Potter: Literary Skill in the Hogwarts Epic* (Cheshire, CT: Winged Lion Press, 2010), 5.

Prisoner of Azkaban
   Harry threatens to reveal his magical status to Aunt Marge to blackmail Uncle Vernon.
   Aunt Marge is inflated when Harry loses his temper.
   Harry threatens Uncle Vernon with his wand.

Goblet of Fire
   The Weasleys arrive to take Harry to the Burrow, destroying the living room.
   Dudley eats a Ton-Tongue Toffee.
   Aunt Petunia protects her son while Uncle Vernon confronts Mr. Weasley, paralleling accounts of Voldemort's attack on the Potters.

Order of the Phoenix
   Dementors attack Harry and Dudley.
   Owls arrive at the house.
   First discussion between Harry and the Dursleys regarding the magical world.
   The Dursleys are lured out of the house while Harry leaves with members of the Order of the Phoenix.

Half-Blood Prince
   Dumbledore visits Privet Drive and uses magic to enforce social norms, intimidating the Dursleys.

Deathly Hallows
   Harry's second discussion about the wizarding world with the Dursleys: he persuades them of the threat posed to their lives by Voldemort
   Members of the Order arrive and the Dursleys leave the house, for the last time, with only wizards left inside.

There is a sinister and unpleasant bent to the fantastical intrusions, and an escalating level of violence towards the primary world in the *Harry Potter* series, that becomes apparent when the fantastic intrusions are listed like this. Within the context of the novels, however, the humor of seeing the Dursleys punished for their mistreatment of Harry subverts any perception of violence. The punishment of the Dursleys by the magical world is encouraged in the texts. By the end of *Philosopher's Stone* Harry is prepared to use the threat of magic to manipulate them and the use of magic remains a threatening focus within the relationship. The language used in Uncle Vernon's discussions with Harry shows the perception of this threat. Terms of hate are attached to descriptions of Uncle

Vernon's speech, but physical descriptions show fear rather than hate from the moment Harry's first letter arrives

> 'Who'd be writing to you?' sneered Uncle Vernon, shaking the letter open with one hand and glancing at it. His face went from red to green faster than a set of traffic lights. And it didn't stop there. Within seconds it was the grayish white of old porridge.
>
> 'P-P-Petunia!' He gasped. (PS, 30-31)

Uncle Vernon's fear of magic remains evident in his later conversations with Harry, though often ignored or glossed over within the text by the bullying of Harry, which accompanies it. Colin Manlove suggests that Harry's perspective dominates the narrative:

> Was it possible that what we had here was a style that changed from book to book to reflect a boy growing up? In such a case the picture of the Dursleys in *The Philosopher's Stone* would be quite other than a lapse or an aberration. It would be a picture made by the boy hero, not simply by the author.[5]

Manlove's suggestion that Harry's perspective and age are influencing the view we have of the Dursleys is helpful, but does not explore the reader's engagement with Harry and the wizarding world over and above the primary, Muggle, reality. The reader's wizarding perspective allows the fantastic intrusion to be funny, rather than threatening, when attacking the characters whom we, as readers most resemble. The reader is biased by Harry's mediation as someone based primarily in the secondary world. From *The Chamber of Secrets* onwards, his reconciliation with his relations is stunted by magical intrusions and by the end of the series he has become fully integrated into the magical world, leaving the Dursleys behind.

A useful external interpretative literary form to examine this relationship, in terms of the role of Muggles in the *Harry Potter* books, is the Germanic folkloric tradition and literary representations of magical creatures that intrude into the home. Parallels between Harry and the mythology surrounding Kobolds (the Germanic forerunner of other domestic magical creatures such as the Scottish Brownie, Scandinavian Nis, and English Hobgoblin, along with *Harry Potter's* House Elves) allow an exploration of the text without the problematical relation-

---

[5] Manlove, 3.

ship between the reader and the magical world.[6] All of these creatures perform domestic chores but can behave in an aggressive fashion towards the inhabitants of the household if not treated with respect. Indeed, "Dobie" is a Yorkshire term for a clownish brownie-like creature, indicating a strong link between house elves and the fairy tale tradition in Rowling's work.[7] Harry is a magical being who performs domestic duties but is also the reason why unpleasant magical events happen in the home. The Germanic Kobold is more closely associated with negative supernatural occurrences than the more domesticated Brownie. By seeing Harry as a magical household being such as the Kobold rather than looking at Harry's tale as a modern Cinderella, as Ximeno Gallardo-C. and C. Jason Smith do, the readers are distanced from Harry and are able to maintain the distinction between Muggles and wizards.[8] This perspective places Cinderella, a normal girl who is mistreated by her extended family, in a different situation from Harry, a magical entity who is mistreated by his family. Harry unlike Cinderella can defend himself. The magical intrusions upon the Dursleys are not the action of a separate person such as a Fairy Godmother, but rather see Harry as a catalyst at the center of these events who can act through his own magical powers:

> Uncle Vernon yelped and released Harry as though he had received an electric shock. Some invisible force seemed to have surged through his nephew, making him impossible to hold.[9]

Harry Potter's magical status provides an innate level of self-defense that not only manifests in this episode but in a number of minor domestic tricks such as breaking Aunt Marge's glass. Though these are easily overlooked in favor of the more dramatic magical intrusions, like the dementor attack which follows Harry's physical tussle with Uncle Vernon in *Order of the Phoenix*, these incidents set Harry apart from the muggle world; the domestic nature of much of Harry's

---

[6] Thomas Keightley, *The Fairy Mythology Illustrative of the Romance and Superstition of Various Countries* (London, G.H. Bohn, 1850), 239.
[7] Katherine Briggs, *The Fairies: in English tradition and Literature* (London: Bellew Publishing Company, 1989), 216.
[8] Ximeno Gallardo-C. and C. Jason Smith, "Cinderfella: J. K. Rowling's Wily Web of Gender" in *Reading Harry Potter: Critical Essays*. Ed. Gisell Liza Anatol. (Westport. CT: Praeger Publishers, 2003), 191-206.
[9] J. K. Rowling, *Harry Potter and the Order of the Phoenix* (London: Bloomsbury, 2003) Referenced as OotP hereafter, 10.

own magical behavior suggests parallels with domestic folkloric creatures such as Kobolds.

While Harry does little to promote any form of friendship between himself and his family, Rowling does provide reconciliation between Dudley and Harry in *Deathly Hallows*. Dudley leaves cups of tea out for Harry, paralleling the cousins' relationship to the folklore surrounding Kobolds, who are traditionally appeased by the house's owner placing a bowl of milk outside their front door. The Kobold's tricks upon the occupants of a home create a similar tension to that which we find played out between Harry and the Dursleys. While Brownies are benign household helpers, the Kobold will engage in trickery and malevolent behavior towards the householder if they prove ungrateful for its presence. When Harry is abused by the Dursleys he is avenged by the magical world. From the perspective of the primary world there is undoubtedly a fairytale element to Harry's life at Privet Drive, beginning with him being left on the doorstep by magical beings. Harry, however innocently, brings the secondary world into the primary world of the Dursleys. Opening a space for the wizarding and Muggle worlds to interact, this space is one of fear and violence for the Dursleys.

The magical perpetrators do not see the attack on the Dursleys as malicious, displaying the magical world's disregard of Muggles. The fantastic intrusions fall into three categories. First, as a form of amusement, as when Fred and George feed Dudley a Ton-Tongue Toffee, or Hagrid gives him a tail. These act primarily to amuse the wizards with little consideration for the Dursleys' status as magical victims. Second, magic is used in response to the Dursleys' behavior, for example, the blowing up of Aunt Marge, who has taunted Harry all week, or the escalating number of letters from Hogwarts in *The Philosopher's Stone*. The third category of fantastic intrusion into the Dursley's world sees the damage suffered by the Dursleys viewed as collateral damage of the magical world's practices. The Dursleys are in the wrong place at the wrong time, for example when the Dementors attack Harry and Dudley, the destruction of the living room by Arthur Weasley and of course when Harry persuades them to leave Privet Drive in case Voldemort's forces attack them. The Dursleys' fear of Harry's presence in their home is unsurprising—they are overlooked victims of magic—but as the narrative is delivered from Harry's and the wizarding world's perspective they are shown as harboring a malicious and irrational hatred of Harry and magic.

The treatment of the Dursleys does not excuse their behavior. As Dumbledore points out:

> "You have never treated Harry as a son. He has known nothing but neglect and often cruelty at your hands."[10]

This line of questioning does, however, provide some rationale for their behavior. There is a level of fear associated with Harry as the representative of a magical world that threatens, and has intruded upon, their lives ever since he arrived upon the doorstep. Harry's status as a wizard within the Muggle world is reflected in his treatment of the magical creatures he meets, especially those who are sentient, such as house elves. Harry's first meeting with Dobby shows them as equals:

> "Offend Dobby!" choked the elf. "Dobby has *never* been asked to sit down like a wizard—like an equal."[11]

Harry and Dobby are magical servants in their respective households, mistreated by their families, and parallels can be drawn between their treatment. The equality expressed between Harry and other magical creatures diminishes as Harry becomes further assimilated into the magical world; Dobby, as a free elf, is rejected by wizards and house elves for wanting pay, while Harry becomes less sympathetic towards magical creatures. In *Goblet of Fire*, Harry threatens merpeople. He, Ron, and Hermione manipulate the centaurs within the forest to get rid of Professor Umbrage in *Order of the Phoenix*. And by the end of the series Harry sees the enslaved Kreacher as willingly participating in his servitude, marking Harry's full immersion into the wizarding attitudes.[12] The parallels between Harry and the Germanic literary tradition of Kobolds offer a useful perspective upon Harry's place within the Dursleys' family and goes some way to

---

[10] J. K. Rowling, *Harry Potter and the Half-Blood Prince* (London: Bloomsbury, 2005), 57. Referenced as HBP hereafter.

[11] J. K. Rowling, *Harry Potter and the Chamber of Secrets* (London: Bloomsbury, 1998), 16. Referenced as CoS hereafter.

[12] The treatment of House elves and other sentient magical creatures is a much larger issue than I can deal with here, but remembering Harry's place within the folklore of magical creatures may aid reading of other chapters of this book.

expressing the relationship between the primary and secondary worlds from a real world perspective, rather than through the eyes of a wizard. This perspective also demonstrates how Harry's relationship with magical creatures degrades as he becomes a full part of the magical world.

While looking closely at folkloric parallels reveals a great deal about the interaction of the primary and secondary worlds, the magical world's response to Muggles should also be reviewed as it provides some of the motivation for the Dursleys' treatment of Harry. Questions also need to be raised regarding the treatment of other Muggles by wizards; it is difficult to find a positive representation of a Muggle, owning in part to the wizarding perspective placed upon them by the text. This argument will not be looking at the anti-Muggle stance held by the Death Eaters or indulging in discussion of the purity of blood within the magical world. Rather, it will show that even those who appear to be pro-Muggle in the magical world or are on Harry's side politically demean and subjugate non-magical people. The magical world's disregard of Muggles is one of the reasons for the Dursleys' reaction to Harry. The magical community's view of non-wizards and their world is introduced in *The Philosopher's Stone* by Hagrid, who implies that Muggles are inferior to wizards in the first chapter of the book: "But I c-c-can't stand it—Lilly an' James dead—an' poor little Harry off ter live with Muggles" (PS, 17). It seems that Harry being placed in the care of non-magical relatives is part of the tragedy to Hagrid's mind. His derisive attitude towards Muggles is demonstrated when he uses the term negatively while explaining its meaning to Harry:

> "A Muggle," said Hagrid. "It's what we call non-magic folk like them. An' it's your bad luck you grew up in a family o' the biggest Muggles I ever laid eyes on." (PS, 43)

This leads readers, very early on in the book, to take on the perspectives of the magical world, particularly as we have been faced with a family who spoil their son and neglect their nephew. Hagrid's attitude is particularly troubling: his half-giant parentage and expulsion from Hogwarts place him on the fringes of the wizarding world. Negative attitudes towards Muggles are subtly expressed through unexpected characters, for example Stan Shunpike's first meeting with Harry:

"How come the Muggles don't hear the bus?" said Harry.

"Them!" said Stan contemptuously. "Don' listen properly, do they? Don' look properly either. Never notice nuffink, they don."[13]

Stan's contempt stems from the idea that Muggles are stupid for not seeing magical intrusions into their world. The likelihood that the Knight Bus is protected by the same magic which makes post boxes and lampposts move out of its way indicating that Stan's contempt of Muggles for not seeing the bus is misplaced. Mr. Weasley echoes this contempt:

> "Just Muggle baiting," sighed Mr. Weasley. "Sell them a key that keeps on shrinking to nothing so they can never find it when they need it... Of course, it's very hard to convict any one because no Muggle would admit their key keeps shrinking- they'll insist they just keep losing it. Bless them, they'll go to any lengths to ignore magic, even if it's staring them in the face... but the things our lot have taken to enchanting, you wouldn't believe—" (CoS, 34)

Here, contempt is replaced by pity. The fact that wizards are engaging in "Muggle baiting" indicates that some of the magical world seek amusement from Muggles' ignorance but this is seen as a nuisance to the magical world rather than as a serious problem with the attitudes displayed between magical and non-magical communities. Depictions of Muggles within the texts are fleeting, and almost always humorous. Mr. Roberts, the campsite owner at the Quiddich world cup is shown as distinct from wizards: "Harry knew at a glance that this was the only real Muggle for several acres" (GOF, 71). There is a casual acceptance that he is having his memory wiped by the Ministry of Magic "ten times a day" (GOF, 72). The magical world's, and the readers', disregard for Mr. Roberts is challenged when the Death Eaters use the Roberts family as puppets. Rather than express sympathy for the family, Mr. Weasley merely says "He'll be alright." Any damage to the Muggles is overlooked or removed through memory charms. The wizarding world that seeks to control Mr. Roberts and modify his memory is just as much a puppet master over him as the Death Eaters to which it is opposed.

---

[13] J. K. Rowling *Harry Potter and the Prisoner of Azkaban* (London: Bloomsbury, 1999), 32.

The objectification of Muggles is found in unlikely places. When we see Sirius Black's teenage bedroom in *The Deathly Hallows* we are confronted with Muggle paraphernalia:

> There were many pictures of Muggle motorcycles, and also (Harry had to admire Sirius's nerve) several posters of bikini-clad Muggle girls; Harry could tell they were Muggles because they remained quite stationary within their pictures, faded smiles and glazed eyes frozen on the paper.[14]

Harry's admiration of Sirius' display of sexualized Muggle women to annoy his family is indicative of Harry viewing Muggles from a wizarding perspective. His amusement at Sirius' selection of posters stems not from their sexual nature but from their blood—a wizarding objectification of Muggles, paralleled by their sexual objectification. Sirius also objectifies motorcycles; they become crossover objects between the Muggle and wizarding worlds, and his motorbike delivers Harry to Privet Drive in *Philosopher's Stone* and removes him from Privet Drive. Muggles are a tool, used by Sirius to assert his independent identity within the Black family, and this assertion is also evident in his ownership of a motorbike. The Muggle providence of the bike is displaced enchanting the bike to fly, distancing the magical and Muggle worlds.

It is only once Harry is firmly positioned within the magical world that a more positive view of Muggles can be found. Arthur Weasley, with his hobbyist enthusiasm for Muggle paraphernalia, shows enthusiasm that on occasion contravenes the law, and conflicts with his job in the Misuse of Muggle Artifacts office. When Fred and George give Dudley a Ton-Tongue Toffee, it is Arthur who objects because Dudley is non-magical:

> Harry and the Weasleys roared with laughter again.
>
> "*It isn't funny!*" Mr. Weasley shouted. "That sort of behavior seriously undermines wizard-Muggle relations! I spend half my life campaigning against the mistreatment of Muggles, and my own sons—"
>
> "We didn't give it to him because he was a Muggle!" said Fred indignantly.
>
> "No we gave it to him because he's a great bullying git," said George. "Isn't he Harry?"

---

[14] J. K. Rowling, *Harry Potter and the Deathly Hallows* (London: Bloomsbury, 2007), 148.

"Yea, he is, Mr Weasley," said Harry earnestly.

"That's not the point!" raged Mr Weasley. (GoF, 50-51)

Within this conversation, there is a clear idea that wizard-Muggle relations are not about attempting to build an equitable relationship between the magical and Muggle communities, but about protecting Muggles from interaction with magic. This attitude is reflected in Arthur's rather patronizing tone when describing Muggle baiting and his objectification of the Muggle world through collecting Muggle artifacts.

While Arthur infantilizes and wishes to protect Muggles from magic, Dumbledore is willing to engage with them and their world on a more equal basis. Dumbledore reads their newspapers; this is how he finds out that Frank Bryce has been killed in *The Goblet of Fire*. His approach to Muggles is very much an exception to the attitudes of the wizarding world, in that he is shown not only interacting with them but also assimilating aspects of Muggle culture. As one of the first magical characters we meet in the series, Dumbledore blends the Muggle world with the magical through his fondness for sherbet lemons (PS, 13-14). This Muggle element is brought into the wizarding world by making it the password to his study (CoS, 152). Dumbledore's willingness to employ Dobby and Winkie, free house elves, at Hogwarts shows an acceptance of all magical creatures and his relations with the Muggle world indicates an acceptance of Muggles within that philosophy. The relationship between Dumbledore and the Dursleys shows a trust in them as carers for Harry. While predicated upon a the magical protection of blood, Dumbledore also believes that Privet Drive is 'the best place for him' as it will allow Harry to grow up away from the fame of defeating Voldemort (PS, 15-16). Upon his return to Privet Drive in *The Half-Blood Prince* he tells the Dursleys of his original hope and expectation of them:

> "The day when I left him upon your doorstep fifteen years ago, with a letter explaining his parents' murder and expressing the hope that you would care for him as though he were your own." (HBP, 57)

This is a key difference between Dumbledore and other pro-Muggle wizards: while Arthur Weasley collects Muggle artifacts to bewitch or hide in his garden shed, Dumbledore is prepared to treat Muggles as equals. This equality is further displayed in the introduction to *Quiddich Through the Ages* where, although Dumbledore is willing to share the texts, Madame Pince is not: "Indeed, when I told her it was to be made available to Muggles, she was rendered temporarily speechless and neither moved nor blinked for several minutes."[15]

Readers are explicitly the Muggles of the Potter series. Our desire to become aware of the wizarding world and to engage with its paraphernalia is played with by Rowling. Although the readers are Muggles their sympathies lie with the wizarding world with which they wish to engage. Dumbledore is set up as an advocate for the Muggle readership of the Potter series. The lengthy description of Madame Pince's attempts to maintain the privacy of the wizarding world by not providing the text leave the reader feeling that access to magical ephemera is a privilege the wizarding world has condescended to allow. This also builds up the distinction between the readers and the magical inhabitants of the secondary world. Dumbledore becomes the only link between the magical and Muggle worlds as Harry assimilates wizarding perceptions of Muggles throughout the series.

Knitting provides a case study of the integration of Muggle culture in the magical world. Dumbledore expresses an interest in knitting patterns in *Half-Blood Prince*, Hermione learns to knit to make elf hats in *Goblet of Fire*, Hagrid knits on the London underground in *Philosopher's Stone*, and Mrs. Weasley sends homemade Christmas jumpers to her children every year. While knitting is a Muggle pastime Hermione suggests that it can also be done through magic.

> "They're hats for house-elves. I did them over the summer. I'm a really slow knitter without magic but now I'm back at school I should be able to make lots more," (OotP, 230).

Knitting becomes a crossover activity between the magical and non-magical worlds. This is shown when Dumbledore takes a Muggle magazine of knitting patterns at the beginning of *Half-Blood Prince*. Although magic can help with knitting, Muggle knitting is also used by Hermione and Hagrid and, though not explicitly mentioned in the books, Mrs. Weasley's knitting is portrayed as magical in the film adaptation of *Chamber of Secrets*. Hagrid, as a non-magic-user, is using a Muggle art form in the Muggle way, which distinguishes him from other

---

[15] J. K. Rowling, *Quiddich Through the Ages* (London: Bloomsbury. 2001), xvi.

wizards but is still a socially acceptable activity, as a magical form of knitting exists. It is interesting to note that when Hagrid knits on the underground train: "People stared more than ever on the train. Hagrid took up two seats and sat knitting what looked like a canary-yellow circus tent" (PS, 52). As the people are staring more at a giant knitting than at a giant walking around London, it suggests that knitting is not usual or socially acceptable in the way that Hagrid's knitting is accepted within the wizarding world. Thus, even though Hagrid is engaging in a Muggle activity, and believes he is behaving in a socially accepta- ble way, he is following wizarding conventions, causing Muggle attention to focus upon him. Just as Hagrid is part giant, he can also be seen as only partially magical and partially Muggle. This leaves him ultimately unable to live up to any social conventions of normal behavior. The ambiguous status of Hagrid within the magical world only serves to problematise his dismissal of Muggles.

The difference between what is considered socially acceptable to Muggles and wizards is shown in the expectations placed upon the Dursleys by Arthur Weasley and Dumbledore. There is an expectation of equality in Dumbledore's attitude to the Dursleys, shown through his ability to approach their house via the front door, but once inside their home he becomes a dominating and threat- ening presence through the casual use of magic to enforce social conventions:

> He drew his wand so rapidly that Harry barely saw it; with a casual flick, the sofa zoomed forwards and knocked the knees out from under all three of the Dursleys so that they collapsed upon it in a heap. Another flick of the wand and the sofa zoomed back to its original position.

> "We may as well be comfortable," said Dumbledore pleasantly. (HBP, 50)

Dumbledore uses magic to intimidate the family, bringing to mind Arthur Wea- sley's arguments for the protection of Dudley from magic and making the case for the necessity of Muggle protection. Dumbledore provides the most progres- sive view of wizard-Muggle relations within the series, but even he ends up us- ing magic to bully the Dursleys and enforce his expectations of hospitality.

The reader empathizes with the wizarding world. Going beyond that, every child who has grown up with the Harry Potter series will recall that dreadful eleventh birthday when the long awaited owl from Hogwarts failed to arrive. Why, then, do readers associate themselves more with wizards despite their ob- vious feeling of superiority over Muggles, rather than the Dursleys, who are more like us and represent a distinctly middle-class suburban family? J. K. Rowling has recently discussed her conceptualization of the Dursleys as a boring and unlikable family, but when she visited the film sets she discovered Four Privet Drive to be one of her childhood homes:

> Although I describe the Dursleys' house as big and square, as befitted Uncle Vernon's status as a company director, whenever I wrote about it I was unconsciously visualising the second house I lived in as a child, which on the contrary was a rather small three-bedroomed house in the suburb of Winterbourne, near Bristol.[16]

It is, however, her former class that Rowling is inadvertently criticizing by aligning the reader with the wizarding world and the constant magical punishment of the Dursleys. Rowling has intentionally created characters that we will not like, but they are representative of her own life, serving only to compound the tension that exists between the reader and wizards, as wizards are shown to be superior to Muggles.

The concept of magical superiority is displayed in the magical use of Muggle artifacts, which are all improved in some way; motorbikes and Ford Anglias fly, knitting is enchanted to knit itself. Magic makes everything Muggle better. Perhaps that goes some way to explaining why millions of readers want to eat magical sweets and own the various souvenirs available from the magical world, and to why the majority of The Wizarding World of Harry Potter, the movie-based theme park in Orlando, is devoted to various shops. Readers do not want to participate in the Muggle world but in a magical one, by aspiring to be wizards and reject the middle-class suburbia of the Dursleys with their glossy kitchen, new cars, and private school educations.

The superiority of wizards over Muggles is nowhere expressed so clearly as 'The Other Minister' chapter in *Half-Blood Prince* where we see the Muggle prime minster being bullied by his magical counterpart. Although all readers share a smirk at the thought of the latter-day figure of Tony Blair being approached in this way, again we also see the tacit superiority of the magical world over the Muggle one, and the unsettling control that it exerts. This indicates that, while Rowling has focused upon the middle-class Dursleys as primary world

---

[16] J. K. Rowling, 'Number four Privet Drive' *Pottermore*
http://www.pottermore.com/en/book1/chapter1/moment1/number-four-privet-drive

characters, the treatment of Muggles by the wizarding world transcends the boundaries of class. Travis Prinzi discusses how the *Harry Potter* books' cultural impact will work against bigotry and intolerance.[17] Although these arguments work within the magical world when examples of wizard-Muggle relations within the series are viewed, an uncomfortable reality must be faced. The Muggles are systematically overlooked or mistreated and the readership wishes to reject their primary world and become wizards. This problematizes Rowling's desire to use the books to combat intolerance.[18] The *Harry Potter* series may well lead readers to combat intolerance, but they do so predicated upon a desire to become part of the magical world that is better than our own, and yet discriminates against Muggles.

This leads back to the primary and secondary worlds. Readers do not readily associate with their world but instead mock and lampoon it through the presentation of the Dursleys. Reading Harry as a threatening magical presence similar to a Kobold or Brownie shows that if by returning attention to the real world and attendant Muggle status when reading these books, a series of uncomfortable inferences are made about the readership as close-minded, blind fools who are unknowingly relying upon, and controlled by, something beyond our understanding. The wish to be a wizard is a desire to attain a position of control and power, but that power is denied by relying upon the magical other world. When reading the books and laughing at Muggles and the control wizards exert over their lives, readers are making a disturbing commentary regarding their own place in society. By behaving like wizards, are readers placing themselves in a perceived position of power over others when addressing social injustice in our world that has parallels in the magical world? Readers, like Hagrid, become trapped between worlds, Muggles with knowledge of magic. The promise of a

---

[17] Travis Prinzi, *Harry Potter & Imagination: The Way Between Two Worlds*, (Allantown, PA: Zossima, 2009), 211-212.

[18] Rowling is quoted as saying: "The Potter books in general are a prolonged argument for tolerance, a prolonged plea for an end to bigotry, and I think it's one of the reasons that some people don't like the books, but I think that it's a very healthy message to pass on to younger people that you should question authority and you should not assume that the establishment or the press tells you all of the truth." ("J. K. Rowling at Carnegie Hall Reveals Dumbledore Is Gay; Neville Marries Hannah Abbott, and Much More," The Leaky Cauldron (fan website transcript), October 20, 2007. http://www.the-leaky-cauldron.org/2007/10/20/j-k-rowling-at-carnegie-hall-reveals-dumbledore-   is-gay-neville-marries-hannah-abbott-and-scores-more/page/6.)

magical world filled with familiar objects made 'better' through magic is allur-
ing to us and is exploited through the development of the Harry Potter brand. As
Professor McGonagall says of the Dursleys: "You couldn't find two people who
are less like us" (PS, 5). It is all too easy to forget that we are the Muggles of the
books, and the wizarding world does not view or treat Muggles as equals: we
cannot be wizards. By thinking about the mistreatment of the Dursleys, the magical secondary world of the *Harry Potter Series* is questioned and the consumer
culture surrounding the wizarding world is shown to be a form of escapism. So
rather than running out to buy a plastic wand and packet of Bertie Bott's Every-
Flavour Beans, perhaps readers should look at the world they live in and explore
why living within a magical fantasy that controls and disregards non-magical
people is so desirable.

Works Cited

Briggs, Katherine *The Fairies: in English tradition and Literature*. London: Bellew Publishing Company, 1989.

Gallardo-C., Ximeno and C. Jason Smith. 'Cinderfella: J. K. Rowling's Wily Web of Gender' in *Reading Harry Potter: Critical Essays*. Edited by Gisell Liza Anatol. Westport. CT: Praeger Publishers, 2003, 191-206.

Keightley, Thomas. *The Fairy Mythology Illustrative of the Romance and Superstition of Various Countries.* London: G.H. Bohn, 1850.

Manlove, Colin. *The Order of Harry Potter: Literary Skill in the Hogwarts Epic.* Cheshire, CT: Winged Lion Press, 2010.

Prinzi, Travis. *Harry Potter & Imagination: The Way Between Two Worlds*. Allantown, PA: Zossima, 2009.

Rowling, J. K. *Harry Potter and the Philosopher's Stone.* London: Bloomsbury, 1997.

—. *Harry Potter and the Chamber of Secrets*. London: Bloomsbury, 1998.

—. *Harry Potter and the Prisoner of Azkaban*. London: Bloomsbury, 1999.

—. *Harry Potter and the Goblet of Fire.* London: Bloomsbury, 2000.

—. *Quiddich Through the Ages*. London: Bloomsbury. 2001.

—. *Harry Potter and the Order of the Phoenix*. London: Bloomsbury, 2003.

—. *Harry Potter and the Half- Blood Prince*. London: Bloomsbury, 2005.

—. *Harry Potter and the Deathly Hallows*. London: Bloomsbury, 2007.

—. 'Number four Privet Drive', Pottermore.com
http://www.pottermore.com/en/book1/chapter1/moment1/number-four-privet-drive

—. "J. K. Rowling at Carnegie Hall Reveals Dumbledore Is Gay; Neville Marries Hannah Abbott, and Much More," The Leaky Cauldron (fan website transcript), October 20, 2007. See http://www.the-leaky-cauldron.org/2007/10/20/j-k-rowling-at-carnegie-hall-reveals-dumbledore- is-gay-neville-marries-hannah-abbott-and-scores-more/page/6.

Tolkien, J. R. R. "On Fairy-Stories." In *Tree and Leaf*. London: Alan & Unwin, 1975. 11-79.

The Other Minister

Response from Travis Prinzi

The Dursleys are being mistreated? Can this be possible? We're supposed to feel sympathy for the cruel family that has abused Harry his entire life? Well, based on the very ideals of the Harry Potter series, yes. Rebecca Langworthy is correct, although I believe a few caveats are in order.

While reading this chapter, my hope was that Langworthy would land on "The Other Minister," chapter one of *Half-Blood Prince*, as a primary example. Indeed, she did, although the article did not have space to explore it thoroughly. I would like to do so in the small space provided here.

First, however, the caveat. One subject that needs careful nuance and exploration is that of the Wizarding World's position with the Muggle world. Langworthy has convincingly demonstrated that the Wizarding World uses its magical power over the Muggle world. Much of the Wizarding World does think the Muggle world is inferior and treats them as such. Where possible, the Wizarding community uses its magical ability to make fun of and even bully the Muggle world. Examples are enumerated in this chapter and more could be given.

It also needs to be remembered that their response to the Muggle world is reactionary *against* oppression. The Wizarding World is not a group of people simply placed on equal footing with the rest of the world. In fact, it has to pretend that it doesn't exist in order to survive. For all their magical power, no Wizarding community would be able to stand against the overwhelming force of massive Muggle armies. The Wizarding World cannot simply live freely in the world. They are not free people. They are not enslaved to the Muggle world, but they have to act as though they are invisible: not a people, not real.

So while, there is much to say about the problem of fighting subjugation with subjugation, it seems to me that we're dealing with something different than, say, Wizarding subjugation of women, other magical brethren, and the like. Rowling ably demonstrates how an oppressed group can create its own levels of oppression within itself. But taking the broader perspective, worldwide, the

Wizarding community is not oppressing the Muggle world; it's just the opposite. Dumbledore stands out as an example of one who wants to resolve this subjugation with love, not with opposing power plays. Beedle the Bard would be the other notable example, particularly in "The Wizard and the Hopping Pot."

That said, let us explore the one place where it seems to me that Wizards have found a way to completely turn the tables on the Muggle world: the Prime Minister's relationship with the Muggle Prime Minister. Here we see not only a condescending attitude toward Muggles, memory charms, and the like. We see a clear usurpation of power, to the point of the Muggle world being subject to the wars and whims of the Wizarding World. Problems are introduced into the Muggle world that cause mass chaos, political turmoil, death, and tragedy, and the Muggle world is completely powerless against it. In fact, they can't even name it and understand it so that they can protect themselves against it. Consider the following conversation:

> "Difficult to know where to begin," muttered Fudge, pulling up the chair, sitting down, and placing his green bowler upon his knees. "What a week, what a week..."
>
> "Had a bad one too, have you?" asked the Prime Minister stiffly, hoping to convey by this that he had quite enough on his plate already without any extra helpings from Fudge.
>
> "Yes, of course," said Fudge, rubbing his eyes wearily and looking morosely at the Prime Minister. "I've been having the same week you have, Prime Minister. The Brockdale Bridge... the Bones and Vance murders... not to mention the ruckus in the West Country..."
>
> "You—er—your—I mean to say, some of your people were—were involved in those—those things, were they?"[1]

This sums it up well. All of these tragedies were the result of a Wizarding World war that was being hidden from Muggles—except that its effects were not unnoticed or unfelt by Muggles. The Wizarding World seems to be perfectly comfortable leaving the Muggle world powerless against real threats. It is not that Fudge, Scrimgeour, and others actually *want* the Muggle world to be hurt; they want the war to end. But they are removing from the Muggle world their own

---

[1] J. K. Rowling, *Harry Potter and the Half-Blood Prince* (New York: Arthur A. Levine Books (Scholastic), 2005), p. 4.

freedom to protect themselves. Fudge's excuses are simply not good enough. His pleas that the Wizarding World tried to stop it but couldn't are not good enough. The Muggle world is being left powerless to defend itself, and when Scrimgeour arrives it becomes clear that will not be changing. Scrimgeour is brief, uncaring, and dismissive, and informs the Prime Minister they've already been making his decisions for him. On the whole, apart from some added security for the Prime Minister so he doesn't end up with an Imperius Curse, the Muggle world is simply going to be left powerless until the Wizarding World can get control over its own war. Muggles are collateral damage of Wizarding violence.

One might be tempted to turn this back around on the Muggles. In an ideal world, Muggles would not be so afraid of magical people that they put them on trial and burn them alive. This might be seen as the longstanding unintended consequences of past measures the Muggle world took to keep itself "safe" from magical people, whom they feared. Muggles have created their own mess by forcing the Wizarding World into pretend non-existence. There may be truth in that, but Langworthy has pointed out well that there is clear hypocrisy, even with the "good guys," who talk of love and tolerance and still treat Muggles as second class citizens, inferior, and deserving of mockery or at best, pity.

I do not think this undermines Rowling's message. Rowling wrote a messy world, much like our own. We get one seven-year slice of its complicated history. I believe it would have been an insult to the complex problems of subjugation to wrap it all up in seven years and give us an ideal of Muggle/Wizard relationships at the end. But especially in the character of Dumbledore, and in Harry's being a liminal figure between two worlds, I think she has shown us a way forward for the kind of very valuable and eye-opening conversations Langworthy has started here.

RING

{ completed circles
  events in parallel
  echos

Rowling kills off + preserves characters
according to the demands of her story forms
+ structures

~~Story~~ form → plot points
                what happens
                when it happens

The World Turned Inside-Out and Right-Side Up: What *Harry Potter* Teaches us About Reading, Writing, and Literary Criticism
John Granger

T he questions serious readers of our time are obliged to confront are "Why are these *Harry Potter* novels so popular?" and "Why do we love these books the way we do?" My answer for these readers" consideration is simple: Harry Potter has more to teach us about literary criticism than conventional literary criticism does about Harry Potter. I want to argue that playful chiasm by discussing three points of discovery I've made about the Hogwarts Saga on the road less travelled. The three points are the more and the less obvious Christian content and symbolism of the series, its literary alchemy, and Ring Composition.

The first Harry Potter talk I gave was at a C. S. Lewis Society meeting and that was a meaningful origin. I think now these three insights I've had are natural consequences of two traditional ideas that were championed most eloquently by Lewis in his critical works and communicated most successfully via his fiction. The first of these ideas is the one Lewis said he learned from Coleridge scholar Owen Barfield, namely that the "universal is mental." What Lewis and Barfield meant, I believe, is that the principle of our thinking, the *logos*, is also the Creative Principle, what brings everything visible and invisible into existence moment to moment. As Lewis put it, our logic is nothing other than "our participation in a cosmic *logos*."[1]

---

[1] [C. S. Lewis, *Surprised by Joy: The Shape of My Early Life* (New York: Harcourt, Brace, Jovanovich, 1955), pp. 208-9. Cited in James Cutsinger, "C. S. Lewis as Mystic," undated, Cutsinger.Net,http://www.cutsinger.net/pdf/lewis_as_apologist_and_mystic.pdf]
"In the second place, [Barfield] convinced me that the positions we had hitherto held left no room for any satisfactory theory of knowledge. We had been, in the technical sense of the term, "realists"; that is, we accepted as rock-bottom reality the universe re-

The second idea is a point of emphasis within the first. Lewis affirms, most clearly in his essay "The Seeing Eye," that Thomistic adage *duo sunt in homine*[2] and that of these two things, the essential one is conscience. Lewis's idea of conscience, though, is less nagging echo of our upbringing or cultural metanarrative, than the *logos* within us. He describes it as "continuous with the unknown depth,"[3] the fabric of reality, and transpersonal; conscience is less an individual faculty, as the word's etymology makes clear, than a "shared knowing." There is within us, in other words, a faculty or power that is not our own, per se, but as the Greek word for conscience suggests—*suneido* or "shared vision"—an "eye of the heart" that is continuous with if not identical not only to this power in every other person but the source *Logos* that creates all things.

What Lewis, after Coleridge and Cardinal Newman, calls "conscience" or "imagination," is more traditionally the heart (or inner heart and "eye of the heart," *lev* in the Old Testament, *kardia* in the New), and then *nous* in Greek and *intellectus*, through the Middle Ages and Renaissance. The distinguishing characteristic of this faculty, whatever it is called, is its kinship or continuity with the *Logos* principle beyond Being creating existence.

I offer these two perennialist and Orthodox ideas for the serious reader's reflection because they are at the root *both* of all three unconventional insights I

---

vealed by the senses. But at the same time we continued to make, for certain phenomena of consciousness, all the claims that really went with a theistic or idealistic view. We maintained that abstract thought (if obedient to logical rules) gave indisputable truth, that our moral judgment was "valid", and our aesthetic experience not merely pleasing but "valuable". . . . Barfield convinced me that it was inconsistent. If thought were a purely subjective event, these claims for it would have to be abandoned. . . . I was therefore compelled to give up realism. . . . I must admit that mind was no late-come epiphenomenon; that the whole universe was, in the last resort, mental; that our logic was participation in a cosmic *Logos.*

[2]   Thomas   Aquinas,   "Commentary   on   Psalm   50,"   undated,   DHSPriory.org<http://dhspriory.org/thomas/PsalmsAquinas/ ThoPs50H51.htm>

Section (f): *Item nota, quod **in homine duo sunt**; scilicet culpa, ex qua dignus est poena, et natura, ex qua habet congruitatem ad gratiam: et ideo petit ut non prospiciat culpam, sed naturam, et ideo dicit, Ne proiicias me.*

Cf.,   James   Cutsinger,   "Behind   Yourself," 14   September   2008,   Cutsinger.net <http://www.cutsinger.net/wordpress2/?p=139>

[3] C. S. Lewis, "The Seeing Eye," *The Timeless Writings of C. S. Lewis,* (New York: Bristol Park Books, 2008) p. 292

want to share *and* of the books' popularity, which I hope will help us understand what Harry Potter has to teach us about reading, writing, and literary criticism.

The question is "Why are these books so popular?" One answer worth exploring is Mircea Eliade's aside in *The Sacred and the Profane*. He wrote there that in a secular culture, reading serves a mythic or religious function,[4] which, is to say, in a world where God and the sacred have been chased to the far periphery of the Public Square, men and women who are designed for a greater reality or life than their individual and accidental ego-existence, will find the means to transcendence where they can.

Literary alchemy, Christian symbolism, and ring composition in imaginative fiction are sure means to that. As Ralph Wood has written,[5] fantasy fiction is not an escape from reality but an escape *into* reality, even the most real. What I call the Eliade Thesis is simply that the books delivering the most powerful means to this transcendence – that do so without waking the sleeping dragons of resistance to anything like religion -- will be the most popular books. They do what readers want most from books, even from life.

Christian Symbolism

Let us begin with the implicit and explicit Christian symbolism Ms. Rowling employs in all her books, some of which is obvious, some not so obvious, all of which escapes most readers, from Christian Harry Haters to their academic fellow travelers.

Ms. Rowling, on her 2007 Open Book Tour, shared in an MTV interview that she the Christian symbolism of her stories was "obvious."[6] I think with respect to the magic of her books and the specific traditional symbols this is, if anything, an understatement. The magic of the Hogwarts world within a world, however problematic it was and remains for many Christians, requires a Christian cosmology to work. There are two principal types of literary magic, the invocational or "calling down" sorcery of works like *Doctor Faustus* and the hag

---

[4] Mircea Eliade, *The Sacred and The Profane: The Nature of Religion* (New York: Harvest Books, 1968), 204-205.
[5] Ralph Wood, *The Gospel According To Tolkien: Visions of the Kingdom in Middle Earth* (New York: Westminster John Knox Press, 2003), xvii
[6] Shawn Adler, "Harry Potter Author J. K. Rowling Opens Up About Books' Christian Imagery," 17 October 2007 <http://www.mtv.com/news/articles/1572107/jk-rowling-talks-about-christian-imagery.jhtml>

of Aslan's How in *Prince Caspian*, in which demons, devils, and spirits are brought in to work their craft, and the incantational or "singing along with," harmonizing magic of spoken spells and music.[7] This magical speech or song, often accompanied by wands and staffs, can only work if the fabric of reality being reshaped is also somehow verbal, or "mental" as in Lewis's description of the universe as "cosmic *logos*." The wizard in story as image of God in harmony with His word or *logos* is able to work magic by speaking the fitting word or words. Back to *Prince Caspian*, his blowing Susan's horn, though it is music rather than speech, has its effect because Aslan brings that sub-creation into existence by his song.[8] Lewis shows the qualitative difference between the two magics in having this horn's summoning trump the hag's invoking of the departed White Witch.

If Ms. Rowling thinks of her magic as Christian symbolism and that was part of what she was referring to in her statement about this being "obvious" to her, I'd have to agree. The question she was asked, though, by the MTV reporter in 2007 was about the Calvary elements of Harry's sacrificial death in *Deathly Hallows*" final scenes: Narcissa's nails "piercing his flesh," the thorns in the several wands he carries in the finale, and the supernatural "King's Cross." Her response about having "always thought" the Christian symbolism obvious points to the previous books' Christian content as well. I think it not unlikely that she was thinking of the several traditional stand-ins for Christ that appear in every novel.

There's the Gryffindor or "Golden Griffin" from Dante's *Purgatorio*, the golden lion of the house symbol as Lion of Judah (and hat tip to Aslan, no doubt), the Phoenix or "Resurrection Bird" of lore, the Unicorn from tapestry and legendary tradition, the White Stag of St. Godric and other holy men, the Hippogriff from *Orlando*, and the Philosopher's Stone of alchemy (which we will discuss below). Harry's annual resurrection from his near death experience features one or more of these symbolic figures of Christ from the traditional Christian menagerie.[9] Which is not to mention the appearance of the Grail in *Goblet of Fire*, and the theme of redemptive and protective blood sacrifice, from

---

[7] John Granger, *How Harry Cast His Spell* (Carol Spring: Tyndale, 2009), 1-12.
[8] C. S. Lewis, *The Magician's Nephew* (New York: Harper Collins, 1994) 112-126.
[9] Granger, *How Harry Cast His Spell*, 91-108

the bleeding Unicorn in *Stone's* Forbidden Forest to Harry's heroic trip into "The Forest Again" in *Hallows*.

And then there are the snakes. Serpents are not an especially obscure Christian symbol; they're the bad guys from the opening chapters of the first book in the Bible to its finish. In *Harry Potter*, with the exception of the grateful, bored boa in *Stone*, the serpents, basilisks, anguilline Dark Lord and his familiar Horcrux, Nagini, are all "bad guys." That's forgetting the sibilant Slytherins with the ophidian names of Severus Snape and Draco Malfoy that, if not evil, are not anyone's first choice for friends, either.

As interesting as these obvious symbols may or may not be, I don't think they are the ones that help explain the effect Harry's adventures have on readers around the world. It's the not-so-obvious, subliminal transparencies that deliver the goods. I want to note here that symbolism is not an aspect of literature but the whole business of literature, even, perhaps, of life. To get the power of *Harry Potter*, we need to review how symbols work, what they are. Northrop Frye in his *Anatomy of Criticism* explains via his continuum or spectrum of story that the defining extremes are mythology, stories about otherworldly gods, and absolute realism, tales of the nitty-gritty sense perceptions of mundane existence. Effective story telling he argues is sufficiently realistic at least in its opening to invite the reader in and foster the suspension of her disbelief.[10] The power of the story is when the reading heart is able to experience the mythological aspects of story through the more or less realistic qualities of characters and events. These are symbols, which is to say, story transparencies through which we are able to see and know supernatural referents and qualities. If the suspension of disbelief is sufficient and the symbolism apt enough, the window clear, the spiritual faculty or heart, the *logos* within us, transcends the world and enters a greater reality.[11] Which, in brief, is the art of literature. No symbolism, no transcendence.

Ms. Rowling's magical world has a surfeit of Christological symbols, as we've noted, and this is an important part of their power. I think, though, that her use of the Soul Triptych in her set of lead characters, Harry, Ron, and Hermione, especially Harry's symbolic role, is her greatest symbolic artistry. The Soul triptych, in brief, is a story icon of every individual's three soul faculties,

---

[10] Northrup Frye, *Anatomy of Criticism: Four Essays* (Princeton: Princeton University Press, 1957) 131-239.

[11] John Granger, *Spotlight: The Artistry and Meaning of Stephenie Meyer's Twilight* Saga (Allentown: Zossima Press, 2009), 7-20.

the passions, most closely tied to the physical body, the mind or will, the less carnal, more formal aspect of the person, and the "heart" or "eye of the heart," the transpersonal even transcendent human faculty.[12] We usually call them "Body-Mind-and-Spirit" and it isn't much of a challenge to figure which faculties the Terrible Trio each represent: Ron the body, Hermione mind, and Harry the heart.

Ms. Rowling doesn't make this up, of course, if her use is now the new standard reference. The first triptych of note is the charioteer in Plato's *Phaedrus*,[13] and probably the best modern instance is Dostoevsky's *Brothers Karamazov*, whose Dmitri is the passions, Ivan the tortured reason, and Alyosha the incarnation of loving spirit.[14] This triptych has become something of a cross medium and genre fiction commonplace. The trios of Jules Verne's *Journey to the Center of the Earth* and *Around the World in Eighty Days*, for instance, are evident triptychs as are the three Hobbits on Mount Doom in the *Lord of the Rings*, the three astronauts and Martian species in Lewis's *Out of the Silent Planet*, Bones, Spock, and Captain Kirk on the original *Star Trek* television series, and Han Solo, Princess Leia, and Luke Skywalker of the first *Star Wars* films.

This is Christian symbolism in the sense that Tertullian meant when he said "all souls are Christian souls." The noetic or spiritual faculty is the *logos* that "comes into the world in every man" (John 1:9), of which Word Christ is the perfect incarnation. The soul's other aspects naturally align themselves in the right-side-up person in obedience to the "inner heart" we've been discussing. The power of this triptych symbolism over readers is that when the reader "suspends disbelief" he becomes the reading, imagining heart and identifies with the story character representing same. His other faculties, at least while reading, align themselves as do the characters standing in for those soul capacities with respect to the heart. "Suspension of disbelief" means identification with the transpersonal "heart." In *Harry Potter*, this means as long as Harry makes the big decisions, especially in crisis, Hermione offers the mind's best guidance in service to the heart, and Ron carries baggage with more or less enthusiasm for

---

[12] John Granger, *The Deathly Hallows Lectures* (Allentown: Zossima Press, 2008), 151-189.

[13] *Phaedrus* 246b-254c-e; see also *Republic* 441e-442b

[14] John Granger, "The Story Within the Story," *The Great Books Reader: Excerpts and Essays on the Most Influential Books in Western Civilization* Ed. John Mark Reynolds (Minneapolis: Bethany House Publishers, 2011), 605-608.

both mind and heart, all is right with the world. Our souls are rightly aligned with the Word and with one another. We become the human person as designed in elision with the terrible trio so long as they are in right alignment.

Of course, the triptych sometimes falls out with one another. Ron especially has a hard time—with Hermione in *Prisoner*, Harry in *Goblet*, and Harry and Hermione in *Hallows*—and turns the soul bottom side up or upside down. These are, as a rule, the most painful reading experiences of the books. I suggest these break-ups are as painful and the reunions as joyous as they are because the reader's heart *enjoys* its experience right side up and *suffers* in the reversed imaginative posture. Either up or down, though, it is the alchemical elision of heart and story-*logos* in the referent Principle that is the source of the powerful reading experience.[15]

Literary Alchemy

Stanton Linden in *Darke Hieroglyphicks,* his survey of the use of alchemical symbols and themes in English literature from Chaucer to the Restoration, defines positive, as opposed to satirical, literary alchemy as "specialized vocabulary and individual images in the allegorization of transmutation subjects in light of Christian doctrine."[16] This use, especially in Shakespeare and the Metaphysical poets, derives from esoteric or medieval alchemy rather than exoteric or Renaissance hermeticism. The one, a Dumbledorean sacred science, is focused on the spiritual perfection of the adept; the other pursues individual longevity and material wealth, which are obviously the goals of Death Eater charcoal burners and modern chemists.

Poets, playwrights, and novelists have drawn from the former to express ideas of apotheosis and to move readers and audiences to some experience of the same from the Bard's plays in his circular Globe theatre, which Frances Yates writes was built on alchemical principles to foster said effect, to C. S. Lewis's *Ransom* and *Narniad* novels and, as I'll discuss in a moment, Ms. Rowling's *Potter* series. Why and how this is so requires that we understand "knowledge"

---

[15] Granger, *Deathly Hallows Lectures*, op. cit.; see especially the exegesis of the Dumbledore-Harry exchange at King's Cross that Rowling has said is "the key to the whole series."

[16] Stanton J. Linden, *Darke Hieroglyphicks: Alchemy in English Literature from Chaucer to the English Restoration* (Lexington: University Press of Kentucky, 1996), 241.

or *scientia* differently than we do and that we think of gold as more than a valuable element on the Periodic Table.

The esoteric alchemist or Dumbledore believed that the universe is mental and our logic or thinking was our participation via our *logos*-heart with the cosmic *logos*. Hence, knowledge to an alchemist is less knowing data a subject has about a distinctly "other" object or artifact than it is a perception of an object's inner essence or *logos* had from his *logos'* penetration of this object's material wrapping and recognizing its reflection in the *logos* aspect there. As Coleridge explained it, "all knowledge rests on the coincidence of an object with a subject,"[17] much as we experience when standing in front of a mirror (hence the importance of mirrors in fantasy works). Knowledge or "science" is less an acquisition than an elision. Gold (and silver to a lesser degree) in this traditional view was not just a metal for currency but solid light, the perfect metal in its being a fully realized or perfect incarnation of the *logos* as Creative Principle, understood as the "light of the world." Lead, conversely, is hard darkness or a fallen, stillborn metal. The purification of the one to the other and the generation of the Philosopher's Stone, then, was a process quite literally of "enlightenment." The Dumbledorean alchemist was not as interested in the generation of the Stone per se, however, as he was in the spiritual purification and illumination of his *logos* or inner heart. This end, because of the elision of subject and object in knowing, was both a necessary aspect and consequence of lead's enlightenment into gold and Stone.

Shakespeare's use of alchemical language, symbols, and stages in his work I believe derives from the common sense observation that the hermeticist's goals of elision and enlightenment in the laboratory are also the aim of the playwright. An audience within the Bard's thespian crucible identifies with the hero of his drama and in this imaginative elision experiences the purification or *katharsis* Aristotle describes in the *Poetics*. It has been in near continuous use since in authors as varied as Donne, Blake, Dickens, Joyce, and Charles Williams for the simple empirical reason that it works.[18]

The details of literary alchemy—the peculiar symbols and stages derived from alchemical lore—are a life study, as is evident in the host of guides and

---

[17] S. T. Coleridge, "From *Biographia Literaria*," in *Critical Theory Since Plato*, ed. Hazard Adams (New York: Harcourt Brace Jovanovich, 1971), 476-480.

[18] John Granger, *Unlocking Harry Potter: Five Keys for the Serious Reader* (Wayne: Zossima Press, 2007), 47-117.

dictionaries that are available today.[19] I look for five touchstones or markers of literary alchemy, though, when I suspect what I am reading has hermetic ambitions for my imagination:

1)   There must be a set of over-arching contraries that are in conflict and which seem resistant to all attempts at resolution – think "Montagues" and "Capulets.'

2)   The work should have three distinct stages marked by colors: the black or nigredo in which the principal is broken down by fire to his defining essence or prime matter, the white or albedo in which he is purified by ablutionary waters, and the red or rubedo in which by crisis he is restored to his Edenic perfection.

3)   There will be a "Quarreling Couple," a pair of characters representing the feminine and intellectual pole of existence or "Mercury" and the masculine and passionate "Sulphur," which couple act as catalysts in their strife to the hero's transformation. Think of "Mercutio" and "Tybalt" and the effect their duel to the death has on fair Romeo.

4)   The Red King and White Queen will be married between the white and red stages of the work, which Alchemical Wedding and congress plant the seeds for the birth of the "philosophical orphan" or Philosopher's Stone.

5)   Most importantly, the hero or heroine should die to self and ego sacrificially and in love, experience illumination after this death, often but not necessarily with a resurrection of sorts, both of which together resolve the contraries defining the drama. Think of the golden statues set up in Verona to commemorate the deaths of Romeo and Juliet and the end of strife between their two houses.

Alchemy in Harry Potter

Ms. Rowling announces her alchemical intentions in the title of her first work, the changing of which to *Sorcerer's Stone* she has said is her only regret in the process of publishing the books and making the movies.[20] If we put on the

---

[19] I recommend Lyndy Abraham's *Dictionary of Alchemical Imagery* (Cambridge: Cambridge University Press, 1998) for its encyclopedic coverage, ease of use, and myriad literary citations.
[20]<http://www.urbandictionary.com/define.php?term=Harry%20Potter%20and%20the%20Philosopher%27s%20Stone>
Question from Gabriela Baez: Does it bother you that in America they changed the names of your books?

glasses of literary alchemy through which we can see the five markers I've described, they stand up like the pages of a child's pop-up book.

1)   Harry's world at home, at school, and within are defined by the parallel contraries of Magic vs Muggle, Gryffindor against Slytherin, and Harry's prophesied antagonism with the Dark Lord.

2)   Alchemy is a seven cycle work in every one of which cycles are its colored stages of dissolution to black, purification in white water, and perfection in crucible and crisis as red. Each of the Harry Potter books has a black time with the Dursleys and at school with Snape, a white in the school whose Headmaster is named Albus or "white," and a red stage in which Harry's lessons learned are revealed in conflict with Death Eaters or the Dark Lord. Every Potter book except *Goblet*, for reasons I'll explain, has a predominant stage coloration, most obviously Phoenix as nigredo, Prince as albedo, and Hallows as rubedo. In addition to the substance of these books paralleling the stage of the work they represent and a host of color markers—think of the color of Harry's dates' hair in each of the books (Cho's black, Luna's blonde, and Ginny's red)— Rowling marks the end of each of these books-as-stages with the death of characters whose name is or includes the color in question (Black, Albus, and F-Red).[21]

3)   Harry complains with justification that his two best friends are a Quarreling Couple in each and every book. That Hermione is feminine and intellectual marks her as the Mercury cipher, not to mention that her name is the feminine of Hermes, another name for Mercury, her initials are Hg and her parents are dentists. Ron Weasley, of course, is her dead opposite, a choleric transparency Rowling highlights by giving him the middle name "Bilius."

4)   Hyper-masculine Bill Weasley, part-wolf after his bravery at the end of Prince, and supermodel Fleur de la Couer, genetically part-Veela, are the Red King and White Queen that are married between the White and Red novels. Remus and Tonks are married, then, too, and alas, it is that alchemical wedding between lupine wizard and metamorphmagus that ends in death and philosophical orphan.

JK Rowling: They changed the first title, but with my consent to be honest, I wish I hadn't agreed now but it was my first book, and I was so grateful that anyone was publishing me I wanted to keep them happy.

"Red Nose Day" Online Chat Transcript, BBC Online, 12 March 2001, <http://www.mugglenet.com/books/bbcchat1.shtml>

[21] The first three books are these cycles in reverse, an aspect of the echoing implicit to the ring structure of the series.

5)   Harry's "saving people thing" leads him in every book to offer himself as a willing sacrifice made in love for his friends and against evil. In every book except the last, he dies a figurative death and rises from the dead in the presence of a symbol of Christ. In the last book, he rises from his least figurative death after the most intentional of sacrifices as a figure of Christ himself, a resurrection that vanquishes the power of Death Eaters and the Dark Lord and resolves, if only for a time, the great Gryffindor-Slytherin divide.[22]

If you have your doubts from this risibly brief introduction to literary alchemy and its place in the Hogwarts Saga, a 1998 interview with Ms. Rowling was discovered in early 2007 in which she said in answer to the question, "Did you ever want to be a witch?":

> I've never wanted to be a witch, but an alchemist, now that's a different matter. To invent this wizard world, I've learned a ridiculous amount about alchemy. Perhaps much of it I'll never use in the books, but have to know in detail what magic can and cannot do in order to set the parameters and establish the stories" internal logic.[23]

I don't believe that confirmation or denial by an author closes the door on interpretation of a text one way or another, but certainly this statement suggests strongly that the textual evidence of alchemical artistry needs to be taken very seriously.

Which invites the questions "why" and "how." "Why do authors use this scaffolding?" and "how does it work?" Literary alchemy, the use of hermetic symbols and stages as story scaffolding, only survives because it works—writers are notoriously lazy and practical with respect to artifice—and only works because of what might be called the "alchemy of literature." Samuel Taylor Coleridge, I think, is our best guide for grasping this as he was with *logos* epistemology. Coleridgean "suspension of disbelief" and entry into or elision with poem or story in an "act of poetic faith" means the more or less total disregard of our individual critical faculties and the corresponding awakening of the "heart. This heart, as we've discussed, is that imaginative faculty Coleridge held to be the *logos* within us, "the living Power and prime Agent of all human Perception, and [...] a repetition in the finite mind of the eternal act of creation in

---

[22] Granger, *Lectures, Unlocking*, op.cit.

[23] Anne Simpson, "Face to Face with J K Rowling: Casting a spell over young minds," *The Herald*, 7 December 1998 <http://www.accio-quote.org/articles/1998/1298-herald-simpson.html>

the infinite I AM."[24] As the alchemist's *logos* or heart did with the inner essence or *logos* of fallen metal, so the reader's "heart" perceives its reflection in text, identifies with same, and experiences *katharsis* and transformation alongside the hero alchemically by elision. Which experience in reading, of course, is nonsensical or, at best, incomprehensible from the materialist and empiricist perspective which by definition maintains that known objects and knowing subjects remain distinct. Literary critics as notable as Northrup Frye and George Steiner and Michael Ward, however, argue for just such an anti-nominalist reading of literature a la Ruskin and Dante, which is to say, reading iconologically or sacramentally for an experience in text of greater reality referents through the transparencies of story. Theirs, of course, is very much a minority view not often taught even in schools that are nominally (*sic*) Christian.

Ring Composition

I first read about Ring Composition in Sanford Schwartz's book *Final Frontier* about C. S. Lewis's *Ransom Trilogy*, a series I was researching because of its several links to Ms. Rowling's traditional choices, most notably Lewis's alchemical symbolism and soul triptych. Prof. Schwartz noted that Lewis's three novels were each rings in conformity with the structure described by anthropologist Mary Douglas in her *Thinking in Circles: An Essay on Ring Composition* (Yale, 2007).[25] I studied the *Frontier* charts of the chapter correspondences in each *Ransom* book and the story scaffolding described by Prof. Douglas in *Thinking*. I remembered that Brett Kendall at Fordham University had argued that *chiasmus*, an Old Testament scholar's preferred name for Douglas's ring, was the structure of the Hogwarts *series* as early as 2005,[26] but had not heard any discussion that each book was built on this model.

---

[24] S. T. Coleridge, "Biographia Literaria," *Complete Works of Samuel Taylor Coleridge, Volume III* (New York: Harper and Brothers, 1868), 363.

[25] Sanford Schwartz, C. S. Lewis on the Final Frontier: Science and the Supernatural in the Space Trilogy (Oxford, Oxford University Press, 2009), 9.

[26] M. Brett Kendall, "X Marks the Spot: The Goblet of Fire and Literary Chiasm," January 2006 < http://mugglematters.blogspot.com/2006/01/x-marks-spot-goblet-of-fire-and-chiasm.html> and "Merlin's Manifesto: Further Support of Chiasm in the Harry Potter series," June 2007 <http://mugglematters.blogspot.com/2007/06/merlins-manifesto-further-support-of.html>

With Prof. Douglas" list of ring qualities and Prof. Schwartz" charts as something of a guide, I re-read the seven novels looking for these four characteristics:[27]

1) A Ring: the beginning and end of a story must meet-up by some type of repetition, usually place, characters, and answer to the question posed at the start;

2) Story Center and Turn: the middle of the story should also resonate somehow with beginning and end while acting as a turning point in the narrative direction;

3) Parallel Analogies: the chapters on each side of the story turn should mirror their reflections, as straight echoes, question and answer, or inversions, across the story axis; and

4) Rings within Rings: there are often smaller rings inside larger compositions.

Douglas is one of the few anthropologists I have ever read, so I confess to being startled by the surety with which she argued in her book that this structure, a turtleback if visualized, was the universal story scaffolding of the biblical, classical, medieval, and modern eras, and one that was the commonplace narrative format of poets and story tellers of all kinds from East and West. Though taken aback by the scope of her assertions, I was, of course, most interested in seeing if Ms. Rowling, as her name suggests, was writing in circles.

Forgive me for noting that I would *not* be telling you about this if she were *not* a Ring writer. Like the prophets of the Old Testament and the Evangelists of the New, as Homer, Virgil, and Dante, like books as varied as *Tristam Shandy, Around the World in Eighty Days, Kidnapped,* and Lewis's *Ransom novels* and most if not all of the seven *Narniad* pieces, *Harry Potter* is a ring composition as a series and in each of its seven parts.

Ring Composition in *Harry Potter*

As I mentioned, Brett Kendall and others had already noted the *chiasmus* structure of the series. *Philosopher's Stone* and *Deathly Hallows* have more than forty story echoes and parallels, many of which are also featured in the story-

---

[27] Mary Douglas, Thinking in Circles: An Essay on Ring Composition (New Haven: Yale University Press, 2007), 31-42.

turn *Goblet of Fire*.[28] The second and next-to-last books, *Chamber* and *Half-Blood Prince*, are parallel analogies, most obviously in being stories centered on revelations of the life of the young Tom Riddle, Jr. The third and fifth book, *Prisoner* and *Phoenix*, too, reflect one another across the *Stone-Goblet-Hallows* axis, here in revealing the life of Harry's god-father, Sirius Black.[29]

William Sprague has argued, I think convincingly, that the seven books are in fact parallel analogies of the three stages of the alchemical work, with *Stone* and *Hallows* as red books, *Chamber* and *Prince* as albedo's, *Prisoner* and *Phoenix* as Black books, and *Goblet* with its three TriWizard tasks as centerpieces a picture of the whole work in itself.[30] There are problems with this simple outline, most notably the many reflections of *Stone* in *Order of the Phoenix* and of *Prisoner of Azkaban* with *Deathly Hallows*.[31] These seeming exceptions to the "turtle-back" picture of a ring, however, are easily resolved if the series is drawn as an asterisk with *Goblet* at the center rather than the top of the circle, a picture which clarifies that book's place in every relationship among books in the series. That is described in an essay I contributed to Travis Prinzi's *Harry Potter for Nerds*.[32] As fascinating as I find the series structure, though, what is mind-boggling is coming to terms with *each book* as a Ring Composition unto itself. I don't have the time here to do more than make that assertion, offer seven examples, one from each book, and urge you to read my Ring lecture notes and survey the charts I've made available in anticipation of a book I'm writing on the subject.[33]

 The assertion is this: Every one of the seven *Harry Potter* novels has a beginning and end that meet, a story-turn resonant with that conjunction and acting

[28] Granger, *Lectures*, 265-67; *Harry Potter* as *Ring Composition and Ring Cycle* (Constantia: Unlocking Press, 2010), 112-115.

[29] Joyce Odell, "Second Guessing," undated < http://www.redhen-publications.com/2ndguessing.html> and Granger, *Ring Composition*, 115-119.

[30] William Sprague, "Guest Post: The Connection of Ring Composition and Literary Alchemy in the Layout of the Seven Book Harry Potter Series," 20 August 2011, <http://www.hogwartsprofessor.com/guest-post-the-connection-of-ring-composition-and-literary-alchemy-in-the-layout-of-the-seven-book-harry-potter-series/>

[31] Odell, op.cit.; Granger, *Ring*, 123-124.

[32] John Granger, "On Turtleback Tales and Asterisks," in *Harry Potter for Nerds: Essays for Fans, Academics, and Lit Geeks*, ed. Travis Prinzi, 37-81 (Oklahoma City: Unlocking Press, 2011).

[33] Granger, *Ring*, 67-91.

as pivot for the chapters on either side of it, and, this is the wonder, every chapter of each book has a parallel analogy or reflection across or along that axis.

1)   *Philosopher's Stone*: In something of a hat-tip, I think, to C. S. Lewis's The Lion, the Witch, and the Wardrobe, Ms. Rowling's first book in her seven book series is also a 17 chapter ring with a decided story-turn in chapter 9. The most striking parallel analogy in the six chapter sets are Harry and Ron's first meeting and conversation on the Hogwarts Express and their equally revealing confrontation that Christmas in front of the Mirror of Erised.

2)   *Chamber of Secrets*: Dobby appears in only three chapters of the second book: the first, center, and last chapters. Best chapter resonance? Harry and Ron's great adventures with the Ford Anglia, first on their flight to Hogwarts and, in the car's only other appearance, escaping the grove of the hungry Acromantulas.

3)   *Prisoner of Azkaban*: Ms. Rowling marks her story bracketing in the third book by titling the first and last chapters, "The Owl Post" and "The Owl Post Again." The cleanest parallel between chapters, I think, is Harry's receiving the Marauder's Map from Fred and George in chapter ten and the crisis about the Map in the chapter immediately opposite it over the story centerline in 14, "Snape's Grudge," in which the Potions Master interrogates Harry about the Map's origins.

4)   *Goblet of Fire*: The story and series center is chapter 19, "The Hungarian Horntail," in which we find Harry out at midnight under the Invisibility Cloak and dangerously out of bounds – just as he is in Philosopher's Stone's turning point and in Deathly Hallows.[34] I love the parallel analogy found in chapters 13 ('Mad-Eye Moody') in which Faux-Alastor saves Harry and punishes Draco and 25 ('The Egg and the Eye') in which the Death Eater under cover again saves Harry and treats Snape to a demeaning dressing down.

5)   *Order of the Phoenix*: A toss-up for best analogous chapter sets: it's either the Bond of Blood pairs, the second and next to last chapters in which Harry first learns of Dumbledore's communication with his Aunt Petunia and then the details of that exchange – or – its Sirius" closing the curtain over a murderously insane female relation in Chapter 4, "Number 12, Grimmauld Place," and his being murdered and punched through the Veil by another at least as insane female relation in the Department of Mysteries in Chapter 25, "Through the Veil.'

---

[34] Note, too, that the date is 22 November or 11/22, a marker that we are at the half way point (1/2) between 12 and 2 am that morning (12-1-2).

6)   *Half-Blood Prince*: *Prince* and *Hallows* both feature twin sets of begin-
       ning, middle, and end chapters. *Prince*'s has a set of Rufus Scrimgeour
       chapters, his only three appearances in the book at start, center, and fin-
       ish, and chapters focusing on the relationship of Severus Snape, Albus
       Dumbledore, and the Dark Lord. The best echo in the chapter pairs,
       perhaps the best of the whole series, is Dumbledore's "You are with me,
       Harry" in chapter 4 as they leave to find Prof. Slughorn and its trusting
       chiasmus, "I am with you" to Harry as they leave the Cave of the Inferi
       in chapter 26.

7)   *Deathly Hallows*: The two axis chapter sets are the three chapters about
       Albus Dumbledore's "Life and Lies" that end with Harry learning the
       real story at King's Cross and the Severus Snape under cover three-
       some. The most interesting parallel chapter pairs are the Dark Lord-
       Harry confrontations in chapters 4 and 34, the mirror reflection
       Polyjuice powered invasions of an underground magical stronghold in
       search of a Horcrux with the invaluable help of a suddenly friendly
       magical creature (Ministry and Gringotts, Kreachur and Griphook), and
       the Dickens-esque absurdly coincidental echoes of characters and cir-
       cumstance in chapters 15 and 22, in which the trio hear about their
       friends and Hogwarts via Extendable Ears and Wizard Wireless.

Prof. Douglas does not offer an explanation for the universality or the evident
power of the story structure in play here. I suggest it is the formal vehicle of the
circular hero's journey, a story shape and resolution of contraries. A circle, because it is the set of points equidistant from a point of origin or center, is defined
by that origin, usually invisible. The completion of a circle is to arrive at its defining point because in the completed circle, the center is revealed. Hence the

power of the circular story and of the Ring Composition. The circle's center is
an "inside greater than its outside" being its origin or cause; arriving in the non-
local place brings us to some imaginative experience of the point without extension and time without duration, the metaphysical center.

     Eliade describes the relationship of the story and the center in *The Myth of
Eternal Return: Cosmos and History*:

> The center, then, is pre-eminently the zone of the sacred, the zone of absolute
> reality. Similarly, all the other symbols of absolute reality (trees of life and im-
> mortality, Fountain of Youth, etc.) are also situated at a center. The road leading
> to the center is a "difficult road" (durohana) and this is verified at every level of
> reality, difficult convolutions of a temple (as at Borobodur); pilgrimage to sa-
> cred places (Mecca, hard war, Jerusalem); danger ridden voyages of the heroic
> expeditions in search of the seeker for the road to the self, to the "center" of his
> dig, and so on. The road is arduous, fraught with perils, because it is, in fact, a
> rite of passage from the profane to the sacred, from the ephemeral and illusory

to reality and eternity, from death to life, from man to the divinity. Attaining the center is equivalent to a consecration, an initiation: yesterday's profane and illusory existence gives to a new, to a life that is enduring, real and effective.[35]

That *Harry Potter* is such a "rite of passage" to the metaphysical center cannot be proven discursively, of course, but Ms. Rowling suggests this trip to the center is the point (*sic*) of her artistry in having Harry's adventure climax at a story center or "inner chamber" in which he learns the answers he must have for his survival and eventual apotheosis; he defeats death in each. The formal ring structure and the plot points of the narrative line work in tandem so we readers experience both consciously and with the heart the light of the world at the center revealed by the cross.

In *Stone*, this "inner chamber" is the circular room miles beneath Hogwarts in which he confronts Quirrelldemort in front of the Mirror of Erised. He gets the Stone and rises from his near death after three days in the Hospital Wing. In *Chamber*, Harry confronts the Dark Lord in his teenage form and destroys the Basilsk and his first Horcrux before being saved by the salvific tears of Fawkes, the Resurrection Bird. In *Prisoner*, Harry survives his first meeting with Sirius and Severus in the Shrieking Shack and saves himself and his friends from Dementor attack with his white stag Patronus. In *Goblet*, Harry fights his way to the center of the maze only to travel by Portkey to the Hangleton graveyard and his toe-to-toe wand duel with the Dark Lord, in which Phoenix Song and golden light save him. In *Phoenix*, Harry battles the Death Eaters in the Department of Mysteries and its spinning circular room, hidden chamber of love, and Veiled Arch. Fawkes saves Dumbledore and Harry again in the Dumbledore and Voldemort duel by the Fountain of Magical Brethren. In *Prince*, Harry and Dumbledore travel to the Cave of the Inferi; Harry is saved from a watery death by the Headmaster, who has risen from a seeming death to vanquish the living dead with fire and light. In *Hallows*, Harry goes to the Forest again and after

---

[35] Mircea Eliade, *The Myth of Eternal Return: Cosmos and History* (Princeton: Bollingen, 1971), 17-18, 31. See also Whithall Perry: The non-manifested "abode" of the supreme Principle or Universal Spirit; omniscient Self, Atma, a "point without extension" or "moment without duration," but centric and axial to all existences, where complementaries and oppositions are contained in principal equilibrium is metacosmically...equatable with the Heavenly Jerusalem or City of God, or again, the Holy Palace n the Kabbala, sanctuary of the Shekhinah. (Treasury of Traditional Wisdom [New York: Harper & Row, 1986], 814)

sacrificing himself to the ultimate inner chamber, King's Cross, for his conversation with Albus.

There is clearly a power greater than death in Rowling's inner chambers, a power she represents symbolically with her menagerie of Christ tokens. I think this narrative point in each book is buttressed by the formal ring structure that brings the reading "eye of the heart" to a point of beginning-middle-end and chapter pair resolution and recognition of Itself, the interior *logos*, in this defining origin.[36]

I wish there were more time to share Ms. Rowling's fun with circles throughout the books that point to this ring artistry.[37] As intriguing as these interior and exterior signs are, I think the strongest proof of Ms. Rowling's Ring Composition artistry is the popularity of her books. They do, quite simply, what books are supposed to do, which is to say after Eliade, that they "serve a mythic a religious function."

Conclusion

To close chiastically, then, I think it is true that *Harry Potter* has more to teach us about literary criticism than postmodern literary criticism has to teach us about *Harry Potter*. The "given" of my argument is that the never approached heights of success that the Hogwarts Saga has enjoyed nigh on universally is a marker that what it does is what readers want, what writers should be striving to deliver, and what literary critics used to explain, namely the symbolic, allegorical, and sublime artistry and meaning of a poem, play or novel. What *Harry*

---

[36] Cf., John Granger, "How Does a Ring Composition Work Anyway?," 29 November 2010 <http://www.hogwartsprofessor.com/ring-composition-25-off-on-cyber-monday-how-does-ring-composition-work-anyway/> and "The Cross and Chiasmus in Ring Composition: Some Notes," 14 April 2012 <http://www.hogwartsprofessor.com/is-the-hymn-of-the-resurrection-a-ring-composition/>

[37] Harry's round glasses through which we see much of the story, the Triangular Eye of the Deathly Hallows symbol that is a representation in figure of a Ring Composition, Moody's Trunk, like the ring quality of the series, has seven parts, each of which is a trunk unto itself that does upset the integrity of the enclosing trunk, the Ravenclaw Door questions in Deathly Hallows, both of which are pointers to the metaphysical center, and Ms. Rowling's interview comments on the Deathly Hallows, Part 2, DVD extras, three of which confirm her conscious conformity to ring structure parameters Hagrid's survival, Lupin's death, and Narcissa's saving Harry as "closing circle" and necessary plot points, see Granger, "Does Rowling Publicly Confirm Ring Composition? Pretty Much," 14 November 2011 <http://www.hogwartsprofessor.com/rowling-publicly-confirms-ring-composition-pretty-much/>

Potter does is provide, using literary alchemy, traditional Christian symbolism of the heart and Christ, and ring composition, an experience of the alchemical or transformative power of literature.

Specifically, this is an experience of the Inside-Out, the metaphysical center that is greater than the circle it defines and causes, and of the human soul turned right side up, heart directing will or mind and the desires. Modern literary tools tell us precious little about this experience because, designed by secular fundamentalists who understand human beings as principally somatic or the mask of ego rather than the wearer of the mask, the tools are designed only to explore the surface meanings of text and the ego's experience of same.

I believe that *Harry Potter* teaches us that reading fosters in us a dynamic empathy with everything created and everyone, not to mention with the Creative Principle of God, because reading, if disbelief is suspended, is an activity of Coleridge's imagination or the *logos* within us. Writing, from this view, is best when it is a conscious or unconscious setting of pieces, reagents, and catalysts for the alchemical transformation of the reader. Imagination in combination with story symbols reacts because of the effect of the supernatural realties passing through the transparencies and translucencies of the work. A writer unaware of or unwilling to use traditional symbols, scaffolding, and story structures or sequencing will not affect a reader as will the writer who does.

Literary criticism that is not about this work, forgive me, is deservedly the subject of satire. I urge you, then, as serious readers, earnest writers, and best of literary critics, to turn your attention to what your heart already knows from recognizing its reflection and its destiny in Harry's story. Eliade was right and we neglect our experience within the Hogwarts Saga if we resist this insight to the magic of literature.

Works Cited

Abraham, Lyndy. *Dictionary of Alchemical Imagery.* Cambridge: Cambridge University Press, 1998.

Adler, Shawn. "'Harry Potter' Author J. K. Rowling Opens Up About Books' Christian Imagery." 17 October 2007. MTV News. 10 April 2011 <http://www.mtv.com/news/articles/1572107/jk-rowling-talks-about-christian-imagery.jhtml>

Aquinas, Thomas. "Commentary on Psalm 50." Undated. DHSPriory.org <http://dhspriory.org/thomas/PsalmsAquinas/ThoPs50H51.htm>

Coleridge, S.T. "Biographia Literaria." In *Complete Works of Samuel Taylor Coleridge, Volume III.* New York: Harcourt Brace Jovanovich, 1971.

Coleridge, S.T. "From *Biographia Literaria.*" In *Critical Theory Since Plato.* Ed. Hazard Adams. New York: Harcourt Brace Jovanovich, 1971.

Cutsinger, James. "Behind Yourself." 14 September 2008, Cutsinger.net <http://www.cutsinger.net/wordpress2/?p=139>

Cutsinger, James, "C. S. Lewis as Mystic." Undated. Cutsinger.Net. http://www.cutsinger.net/pdf/lewis_as_apologist_and_mystic.pdf

 Douglas, Mary. *Thinking in Circles: An Essay on Ring Composition.* New Haven: Yale University Press, 2007.

Eliade, Mircea. *The Myth of Eternal Return: Cosmos and History.* Princeton: Bollingen, 1971.

Eliade, Mircea. *The Sacred and The Profane: The Nature of Religion.* New York: Harvest Books, 1968.

Frye, Northrup. *Anatomy of Criticism: Four Essays.* Princeton: Princeton University Press, 1957.

Granger, John. *Spotlight: The Artistry and Meaning of Stephenie Meyer's Twilight Saga.* Allentown: Zossima Press, 2009. 7-20.

—. *The Deathly Hallows Lectures.* Allentown: Zossima Press, 2008., 151-189.

—. "The Story Within the Story." In *The Great Books Reader: Excerpts and Essays on the Most Influential Books in Western Civilization.* Edited by John Mark Reynolds. Minneapolis: Bethany House Publishers, 2011.

—. *Harry Potter's Bookshelf.* New York: Penguin, 2009.

—. *Unlocking Harry Potter: Five Keys for the Serious Reader*. Wayne: Zossima Press, 2007.

—. "On Turtleback Tales and Asterisks," in *Harry Potter for Nerds: Essays for Fans, Academics, and Lit Geeks*. Edited by Travis Prinzi. 37-81. Oklahoma City: Unlocking Press, 2011.

—. "How Does a Ring Composition Work Anyway?" 29 November 2010 <http://www.hogwartsprofessor.com/ring-composition-25-off-on-cyber-monday-how-does-ring-composition-work-anyway/>

—. "The Cross and Chiasmus in Ring Composition: Some Notes," 14 April 2012   http://www.hogwartsprofessor.com/is-the-hymn-of-the-resurrection-a-ring-composition/

—. "Does Rowling Publicly Confirm Ring Composition? Pretty Much," 14 November 2011 <http://www.hogwartsprofessor.com/rowling-publicly-confirms-ring-composition-pretty-much/>

—. *Harry Potter* as *Ring Composition and Ring Cycle*. Constantia: Unlocking Press, 2010.

—. *How Harry Cast His Spell*. Carol Spring: Tyndale, 2009.

Kendall, M. Brett. "Merlin's Manifesto: Further Support of Chiasm in the Harry Potter series," June 2007 <http://mugglematters.blogspot.com/2007/06/merlins-manifesto-further-support-of.html>

—. "X Marks the Spot: *The Goblet of Fire* and Literary Chiasm," January 2006 <http://mugglematters.blogspot.com/2006/01/x-marks-spot-goblet-of-fire-and-chiasm.html>

Lewis, C. S. *The Magician's Nephew*. New York: Harper Collins, 1994.

—. "The Seeing Eye." In *The Timeless Writings of C. S. Lewis*. New York: Bristol Park Books, 2008.

—. *Surprised by Joy: The Shape of My Early Life*. New York: Harcourt, Brace, Jovanovich, 1955., pp. 208-9.

Linden, Stanton J. *Darke Hieroglyphicks:Alchemy in English Literature from Chaucer to the English Restoration*. Lexington: University Press of Kentucky, 1996.

Perry, Whithall. *Treasury of Traditional Wisdom*. New York: Harper & Row, 1986.

Odell, Joyce. "Second Guessing." Undated. <http://www.redhen-publications.com/2ndguessing.html>

Plato, *Phaedrus*; *Republic, in Collected Works of Plato.* Princeton: 441e-442b

Rowling, J. K. Harry Potter and the Sorcerer's Stone. New York: Scholastic, 1997.

—. Harry Potter and the Chamber of Secrets. New York: Scholastic, 1998.

—. Harry Potter and the Prisoner of Azkaban. New York: Scholastic, 1999.

—. Harry Potter and the Goblet of Fire. New York: Scholastic, 2000.

—. Harry Potter and the Order of the Phoenix. New York: Scholastic, 2003.

—. Harry Potter and the Half-Blood Prince. New York: Scholastic, 2005.

—. Harry Potter and the Deathly Hallow. New York: Scholastic, 2007.

—. "Red Nose Day." Online Chat Transcript, BBC Online, 12 March 2001, http://www.mugglenet.com/books/bbcchat1.shtml

Schwartz, Sanford. *C. S. Lewis on the Final Frontier: Science and the Supernatural in the Space Trilogy.* Oxford, Oxford University Press, 2009.

Simpson, Anne. "Face to Face with J K Rowling: Casting a spell over young minds," *The Herald*, 7 December 1998 <http://www.accio-quote.org/articles/1998/1298-herald-simpson.html>

Sprague, William. "Guest Post: The Connection of Ring Composition and Literary Alchemy in the Layout of the Seven Book Harry Potter Series," 20 August 2011 http://www.hogwartsprofessor.com/guest-post-the-connection-of-ring-composition-and-literary-alchemy-in-the-layout-of-the-seven-book-harry-potter-series/

Wood, Ralph. *The Gospel According To Tolkien: Visions of the Kingdom in Middle Earth.* New York: Westminster John Knox Press, 2003.

On Tickling Dragons
Response from Josephine Gabelman

O ne of the fundamental rules of fantasy, as every reader knows, is: "dragons are not to be disturbed." Bilbo creeps into Smaug's lair desperate that the sleeping dragon remains so. Charlie Weasley and his friends subdue the dragons for the Triwizard Tournament with a Sleeping Draught from which, with great trepidation and stunning spells at hand, they must wake them. J. K. Rowling's first words to her reader are a warning on the Hogwart's Crest: "Draco Dormiens Nuquam Titillandus" (Never Tickle a Sleeping Dragon). With these sage words in mind, we venture into the pages of fantasy literature.

In his essay, John Granger references C. S. Lewis's well-known discussion of "steal[ing] past those watchful dragons" of a "rationalist suspicion of religious ideas."[1] The phrase expresses Lewis's desire to communicate certain aspects of the Christian message in his writing without overt religious symbolism lest the reader become aware of an apologetic agenda.[2] Clearly Lewis does use symbolism within his worlds, but as Vander Elst points out he does so "always in the most natural and unforced way, for it must again be emphasized that [his books] were not conceived or written with a didactic purpose."[3] Lewis, like Rowling, succeeds in this endeavour, and the majority of readers of these fantasies enjoy the stories with little or no awareness of subliminal, or indeed as Granger points out, "explicit Christian symbolism."

One may suppose that without a conscious appreciation of religious imagery the catechistic potential of the book comes to nothing and that it is therefore important to expose and draw out moments of symbolic communication.

---

[1] Alister E. McGrath, *The Intellectual World of C. S. Lewis*, (London: Wiley, 2014), 140.

[2] C. S. Lewis, *Of Other worlds: Essays and stories* (CA: Harcourt, 1967), 37: "But supposing that by casting all these things into an imaginary world, stripping them of their stained-glass and Sunday school associations, one could make them for the first time appear in their real potency? Could one not thus steal past those watchful dragons? I thought one could."

[3] Philip Vander Elst, *C. S. Lewis: An Introduction* (London: Continuum, 1996), 95.

Granger's exposition is extremely insightful, but I want to question his assertion: "no symbolism, no transcendence." Granger suggests that providing "the symbolism [is] apt enough" then the *logos* within us is able to experience a transcendence into a greater spiritual reality. I want to gesture to the possibility that the theological potential within fantasy literature is, at least in some ways, unrelated to any religious symbolism that may be present in the text. I intend to take the motto of Hogwarts very seriously and creep past the dragons of conscious awareness to reach the unchartered territory of the imagination.

This point seems similar to what Granger refers to as the "Eliade Thesis": "that the books delivering the most powerful means to this transcendence—that do so without waking the sleeping dragons of resistance to anything like religion." Fundamental to reading Harry Potter is the reader's capacity to think in terms that contradict or unsettle the governing principles of the familiar world. This seems to be a distinctly theological activity even though I do not believe that specific events like getting on to Platform 9¾ are intended to be emblematic of anything religious. Fantasy literature requires the reader imaginatively to overstep the boundaries of the possible just as religious believers do in their daily struggle to accept by faith that which reason and empiricism has deemed impossible.

The experience of reading *Harry Potter,* as Granger observes, requires an imaginative disturbance of everyday restrictions of the possible; we suspend our disbelief in order to enjoy the story. I wonder, though, if any aspect of this imaginative playfulness remains when the book is closed. We could allude to Coleridge's description of Wordsworth's poetry as representative of literature's transformative potential: "to give the charm of novelty to things of every day, and to excite a feeling analogous to the supernatural."[4] One of Rowling's most clever inventions is her magical re-invention of everyday objects. For example ordinary items such as sellotape, marbles, jellybeans, and chess undergo a magical transformation and become "spellotape", "gobstones", "Bertie Botts every flavour bean", and "wizard's chess." By using mundane objects but recasting them in a fantastical light, we can see how the experience of reading Harry Potter "gives the charm of novelty to things of everyday." There is no religious symbolism present, but the sense of wonder experienced by the reader as the

---

[4] S. T. Coleridge, *Biographia Literaria*, 314.

familiar is made strange hints at the Christian practise of seeing the marvellous in the mundane.

Of course, for the reader of *Harry Potter* this is all a game of make-believe. We *willingly* suspend our imagination, knowing full well that the sellotape we use has no magical properties. Yet this habit of make-believe, which is foundational for reading fantasy literature, is another example of engaging in religious thinking without recourse to religious symbolism. It is not, however, immediately clear why make-believe is applicable to a religious conviction, since it carries connotations of frivolity and pretence. It seems likely that Christians would want to claim that Christ's miracles are authentic, not just mere play. However, David Miller, writing from a Christian perspective, puts forward the view that "[f]aith is make-believe. It is playing as if it were true."[5] Miller goes on to explain that it is not that religion is therefore false, but that faith is acting "as if" the unseen were seen. If we consult the biblical outline of faith—"the belief of things hoped for, the evidence not seen"—make-believe can become a helpful approach to thinking theologically because it involves a creative abstraction from the seen reality and Christianity believes that the reality of creation is mysteriously other than how it appears.

C. S. Lewis acknowledges that make-believe is a natural aspect of the growth of a child—"that is why children's games are so important," he writes, "the pretence of being grown-up helps them to grow up in earnest."[6] Christian make-believe, like the child's game, is not about escaping, but, rather, about a fuller mode of becoming. Religious make-believe is therefore fixed on a *telos* outside itself. "Let us pretend," explains Lewis, "in order to make the pretence into a reality."[7]

I am by no means suggesting that reading Harry Potter presents the reader with a religious interpretation of reality. However, as Granger indicates, perhaps the popularity of the books is linked to an intuitive human desire for the wondrous. An alternative way of expressing this lingering sensation of our longing for the marvelous would be to describe it as a sort of "homesickness." Alison Milbank notes how the objective of certain fantasy writers is "to awaken in the

---

[5] David Miller, *Gods and Games: Toward a Theology of Play* (New York: World, 1969), 168.
[6] C. S. Lewis, *Mere Christianity* (London: HarperCollins, 2002), 193.
[7] Ibid.

reader this feeling of homesickness for the truth."[8] I do not think the Potter books awake a feeling of "homesickness for the truth," but they do invoke a sense of homesickness for the fantastic, a sort of yearning after the wondrous. They transport the reader back to their own childhood when the world was strange and mystical. Perhaps this is just a homesickness for the youth we can never recapture; however, the recollection and re-enactment of childhood's sense of the fantastic can also be seen as an endeavour that endows the reader with the ability to conceive of an alternative version of reality, which is a vital component to the Christian imagination.

To conclude, I have suggested that perhaps we ought not to be overly scrutinising the extent to which the books correspond to Christian symbolism, but, instead considering the very real way by which they engage in something akin to religious thinking. In order to enter the world of Harry Potter at all, the reader must exercise a willed lack of scepticism and practice some of the central characteristics of faith: including the transgression of the possible, wonder and make-believe. When we read a story we engage in a type of play-faith; we pretend as if it were true if only for the sake of the narrative. As we engage in this innocuous playfulness the sleeping dragons of sceptical rationalism remain dormant since we are, after all, only pretending. Yet as we have intimated there seems to be some significant resemblance between the imaginative process of reading fantasy literature and willing assent to the Christian message.

---

[8] Alison Milbank, "Apologetics and the Imagination: Making Strange," in *Imaginative Apologetics*, ed. by Andrew Davidson (Grand Rapids: Baker, 2012), 33. Milbank is referring specifically to the Romantic project of Novalis.

Works Cited

Coleridge, S. T. *The Major Works*, edited by H. J. Jackson. Oxford: Oxford University Press, 2008.

Lewis, C. S. *Mere Christianity*. London: HarperCollins, 2002.

—. *Of Other worlds: Essays and stories.* CA: Harcourt, 1967.

McGrath, Alister E. *The Intellectual World of C. S. Lewis*. London: Wiley, 2014.

Milbank, Alison. "Apologetics and the Imagination: Making Strange," in *Imaginative Apologetics*, ed. by Andrew Davidson. 31-45. Grand Rapids: Baker, 2012.

Miller, David. *Gods and Games: Toward a Theology of Play*. New York: World, 1969.

Vander Elst, Philip. *C. S. Lewis: An Introduction*. London: Continuum, 1996.

Appendix I

Survey of Readers' Aesthetic Satisfaction with each book
in the Harry Potter Series

Have you read all 7 books in the Harry Potter series?
- ○ Yes
- ○ No

How many times have you read the Harry Potter series?
- ○ Once
- ○ More than once, but no more than 5 times
- ○ More than 5 times, but no more than 10 times
- ○ More than 10 times

On a scale from 1 - 7, with 1 (one) being your LEAST favorite book in the series and 7 (seven) being your favorite, rank each book in the series.

Harry Potter and the Sorcerer's [Philosopher's] Stone

	1	2	3	4	5	6	7	
Least favorite	○	○	○	○	○	○	○	Favorite

Harry Potter and the Chamber of Secrets

	1	2	3	4	5	6	7	
Least favorite	○	○	○	○	○	○	○	Favorite

Harry Potter and the Prisoner of Azkaban

	1	2	3	4	5	6	7	
Least favorite	○	○	○	○	○	○	○	Favorite

Harry Potter and the Goblet of Fire

	1	2	3	4	5	6	7	
Least favorite	○	○	○	○	○	○	○	Favorite

Harry Potter and the Order of the Phoenix

	1	2	3	4	5	6	7	
Least favorite	○	○	○	○	○	○	○	Favorite

Harry Potter and the Half-Blood Prince

	1	2	3	4	5	6	7	
Least favorite	○	○	○	○	○	○	○	Favorite

Harry Potter and the Deathly Hallows

	1	2	3	4	5	6	7	
Least favorite	○	○	○	○	○	○	○	Favorite

Appendix II

The Folktale Structure of the Individual Harry Potter Tales
and the Series as a Whole

Complete Tabulated Data of the Functions
of the Dramatis Personae

Functions of the Dramatis Personae for *The Philosopher's Stone*

Symbol	Function Name	Main Narrative	Move	Move
α	Initial Situation	The main character, Harry Potter, is introduced.		
β	Absentation	Harry's parents are dead.		
γ	Interdiction	Harry forbidden to speak or act "strange" (owls, magic, etc.); Harry is told not to go to Hogwarts.		
δ	Violation	Incident at the zoo; Harry goes to Hogwarts; as protector of the Philosopher's Stone, Dumbledore is the victim hero; hero status gets transferred to Harry as the seeker hero.		
ε	Reconnaissance	Reverse: Harry tries to obtain information about the villain, who is trying to obtain the Stone.	Voldemort seeks information about the whereabouts of the Stone.	
ζ	Delivery	Harry receives information that Voldemort is trying to use the Stone to come back.	Voldemort receives information on the whereabouts of the Stone from Quirrell.	
η	Trickery	Quirrell has Voldemort on the back of his head and pretends to have a stutter and be timid.	Voldemort deceives Dumbledore and makes him believe that Quirrell is trying to protect the Stone.	
θ	Complicity	Harry believes that Quirrell is a normal professor which makes him think Snape must be trying to steal the Stone.	Dumbledore believes that Quirrell is trying to protect the Stone.	
A	Villainy	Voldemort, seeking immortal life, uses Quirrell to try to burgle the Philosopher's Stone.		Someone is killing unicorns in the Forbidden Forest.
a	Lack			
B	Mediation; The Connective Incident	Someone attempts to break into Gringotts; Harry discovers the trapped door being guarded; Harry learns Voldemort is the one trying to obtain the Stone.		Hagrid tells Harry, Herminone, Neville, and Malfoy about the unicorns.
C	Beginning Counteraction	Harry decides to try to stop Voldemort from getting the Stone.		Harry serves detention in the Forbidden Forest with Hagrid.
↑	Departure	Harry leaves the castle for Hagrid's hut.		They enter the Forbidden Forest from the castle grounds.

Symbol	Function Name	Main Narrative	Move	Move
D	The First Function of the Donor	Hagrid is cryptic and withholds information about Fluffy and the person who sold him the egg.		(a) *Harry shops at Ollivander's.* (b) *Harry is given the cloak as anonymous present for Christmas.* (c) Harry has detention in the Forbidden Forest with Hagrid; he is sent to go search for unicorns with Malfoy.
E	The Hero's Reaction	Harry manipulates Hagrid into telling him the information.		(a) *Harry makes a connection with the wand that shares a phoenix feather with Voldemort's wand.* (b) *Harry uses the invisibility cloak.* (c) Harry, Malfoy and Fang go in search of the unicorns.
F	Provision or Receipt of a Magical Agent	Information on how to get past Fluffy.		(a) *Wand* (b) *Invisibility Cloak* (c) Firenze
G	Spatial Transference Between Two Kingdoms, Guidance	Harry, Ron and Hermione go to the forbidden corridor to prevent Snape from getting the Stone.		
H	Struggle	Physical struggle between Harry, Voldemort and Quirrell over the Stone.	Dumbledore and Voldemort join in combat.	Voldemort tries to attack Harry; Firenze saves him.
J	Branding, Marking	Scar burning, realizes the connection between the scar burning and the presence of Voldemort.		Harry's scar burns.
I	Victory	The Stone goes to Harry through the Mirror of Erised; Quirrell overcome by Harry.	Dumbledore protects Harry from Voldemort causing him to flee.	Harry escapes and learns of Voldemort's intentions to retrieve the Stone.
K	Misfortune Liquidated	Harry possesses the Stone and thus prevents Voldemort from obtaining and using the Stone.	The Stone is safe.	They find the unicorn and learn that Voldemort was killing them.
→	Return			
Pr	Pursuit, Chase			
Rs	Rescue			
o	Unrecognized Arrival			
L	Unfounded Claims			

Symbol	Function Name	Main Narrative	Move	Move
M	Difficult Task		Dumbledore and Nicholas Flamel must decide whether and how to dispose of the Stone.	
N	Solution		They destroy the Stone.	
Q	Recognition	Harry, Hermione, Ron and Neville are awarded house points for the roles they played and secure Gryffindor the House Cup.		
Ex	Exposure	Quirrell revealed as the villain, Snape exculpated.		
T	Transfiguration	Harry a true wizard, not just "The Boy Who Lived."		
U	Punishment	Quirrell has died so Voldemort is helpless again; Voldemort flees.		
W	Wedding	Harry returns to the Dursley's.		

Functions of the Dramatis Personae for *The Chamber of Secrets*

Symbol	Function Name	Main Narrative	Move
α	Initial Situation	Harry re-introduced at the Dursley's.	
β	Absentation	Ron and Hermione do not contact Harry.	
γ	Interdiction	(a) Standing Dursley and Ministry interdictions on magic; (b) Dobby warns Harry not to return to Hogwarts and solidifies Platform 9-3/4 portal.	
δ	Violation	(a) Dobby performs magic at Dursley's; (b) Harry and Ron fly Ford Anglia to Hogwarts.	
ε	Reconnaissance	(a) *Diary planted on Ginny;* (b) *Reverse: Hermione elicits history of Chamber from Prof Binns;* (c) *Reverse: Trio use Polyjuice Potion to acquire information about the heir of Slytherin.*	
ζ	Delivery	*Riddle-Diary learns about Harry and Hogwarts activity from Ginny; the Diary comes into Harry's possession.*	
η	Trickery	Riddle-Diary claims to have apprehended the last person who opened the Chamber.	
θ	Complicity	Harry visits Riddle's memory and sees Hagrid apprehended and expelled.	
A	Villainy	(a) The monster from the Chamber attacks students; (b) Harry is shunned as the suspected "heir of Slytherin;" (c) Fudge arrests Hagrid; (d) Lucius Malfoy has Dumbledore suspended as headmaster.	Ginny is abducted.
a	Lack		
B	Mediation; The Connective Incident	Hagrid hints to Harry and Ron to "follow the spiders."	Harry and Ron overhear Hogwarts faculty discuss Ginny's disappearance.
C	Beginning Counteraction	Harry and Ron decide to follow the spiders.	Harry and Ron decide to help Lockhart, solve the crime and clear Hagrid.
↑	Departure	Harry and Ron leave Hogwarts and enter the Forbidden Forest under the invisibility cloak.	Harry and Ron enter the second-floor girl's lavatory, the entryway into the Chamber.
D	The First Function of the Donor	The spiders capture Harry and Ron and bring them to Aragog, who commands the spiders to kill Harry and Ron.	Myrtle interrogates them ("What do you want this time?")
E	The Hero's Reaction	Harry and Ron plead with Aragog to spare their lives since they are Hagrid's friends; they ask Aragog about the Chamber and the monster	Harry asks Myrtle about her death.

Symbol	Function Name	Main Narrative	Move
F	Provision or Receipt of a Magical Agent	which lives there. Aragog informs Harry and Ron that the victim of the monster was found in a toilet.	(a) Myrtle shows them the secret entrance to the Chamber; (b) Fawkes delivers himself and the Sorting Hat (with the Sword of Gryffindor inside).
G	Spatial Transference Between Two Kingdoms, Guidance		Harry and Ron travel through the pipe tunnels to the Chamber.
H	Struggle		Harry fights the basilisk and the Tom Riddle shade.
J	Branding, Marking		Harry wounded by basilisk fang.
I	Victory	c	Harry kills the basilisk with the Sword of Gryffindor and the Riddle-Diary with the basilisk fang.
K	Misfortune Liquidated		Ginny is restored; later, the petrified students, Mrs. Norris, and Sir Nicholas are restored.
→	Return		Fawkes brings Harry and others back to Hogwarts.
Pr	Pursuit, Chase		
Rs	Rescue		
o	Unrecognized Arrival		
L	Unfounded Claims		Lucius Malfoy denies knowledge of how Ginny came to possess the Diary.
M	Difficult Task		Repay and liberate Dobby.
N	Solution		Malfoy throws sock to Dobby, freeing him.
Q	Recognition		400 points for Gryffindor who wins the House Cup.
Ex	Exposure		Lockhart exposed as false hero during end of year banquet.
T	Transfiguration		Harry not the heir of Slytherin; "only a true Gryffindor" could have triumphed in the Chamber.
U	Punishment		(a) Malfoy sacked from the Board of Governors; (b) Reverse: Hagrid returns from Azkaban.
W	Wedding		Harry returns to the Dursley's.

Functions of the Dramatis Personae for *The Prisoner of Azkaban*

Symbol	Function Name	Main Narrative	Move
α	Initial Situation		Harry re-introduced at the Dursley's.
β	Absentation		
γ	Interdiction	Reverse: Sirius Black chosen as Secret-Keeper for the Potters.	Standing Dursley and Ministry interdiction on magic.
δ	Violation	Peter Pettigrew obtains Secret-Keeper status from Sirius.	Harry blows up Aunt Marge.
ε	Reconnaissance	Pettigrew spies on the Potters for Voldemort.	Harry seeks information about Sirius.
ζ	Delivery	Pettigrew informs Voldemort of the Potters' whereabouts.	Harry learns Sirius is his godfather and is pursuing him.
η	Trickery	Pettigrew "disappears" by framing Sirius for a violent crime; Pettigrew is an animagus, transfiguring himself into Scabbers the rat.	Sirius is an animagus, transfiguring himself into Padfoot the dog, and uses this ability to track Harry.
θ	Complicity	The Ministry convicts the wrong person (Sirius) for the crime, leaving Pettigrew at large.	Harry does not connect the "Grim" (Padfoot) to Sirius.
A	Villainy	(a) Pettigrew betrays the Potters to Voldemort, leading to their deaths; (b) Pettigrew successfully frames Sirius, who is convicted of murder and sent to Azkaban.	Harry is susceptible to attacks by Dementors.
a	Lack		
B	Mediation; The Connective Incident		
C	Beginning Counteraction		
↑	Departure	As Padfoot, Sirius escapes from Azkaban and arrives at Hogwarts.	
D	The First Function of the Donor	Sirius must get close to Ron, Hermione and Harry in order to expose Pettigrew-Scabbers.	Harry faces the Boggart-Dementor in Defense Against the Dark Arts class and is attacked by Dementors during the Quidditch match against Hufflepuff.
E	The Hero's Reaction	Sirius-Padfoot must gain Crookshanks' trust.	Lupin teaches Harry the Patronus charm.
F	Provision or Receipt of a Magical Agent	Crookshanks aids Sirius-Padfoot.	Harry masters the Patronus charm.
G	Spatial Transference Between Two Kingdoms,	Crookshanks chases Pettigrew-Scabbers to Sirius-Padfoot.	Harry and Hermione follow Ron and Padfoot under the Whomping Willow to the Shrieking Shack.

Symbol	Function Name	Main Narrative	Move
	Guidance		
H	Struggle	Harry is torn by his trust in Lupin between identifying Sirius or Scabbers as his real enemy.	
J	Branding, Marking		
I	Victory	Scabbers is forced to transfigure back into Pettigrew, who confesses that he betrayed the Potters but was coerced to do so by Voldemort; Harry refuses to agree to his execution by Sirius, preferring to show Pettigrew mercy.	
K	Misfortune Liquidated	Pettigrew is apprehended.	
↓	Return	The trio, Lupin, and Sirius return to Hogwarts grounds with Pettigrew in custody and an unconscious Snape in tow.	
Pr	Pursuit, Chase	Lupin transforms into a werewolf; Sirius-Padfoot is wounded protecting the trio from him; he and Harry are attacked by Dementors.	
Rs	Rescue	An unknown person ("future" Harry) rescues Harry and Sirius from the Dementors.	
o	Unrecognized Arrival		
L	Unfounded Claims		
M	Difficult Task		Dumbledore proposes to Harry and Hermione that they use the time-turner to help save Sirius and Buckbeak.
N	Solution		(a) Harry and Hermione succeed in saving Sirius and Buckbeak (and the "past" Harry)—retro sequence to Rs (b) They return back to the present time and the sequence continues to the end.
Q	Recognition	Sirius is exonerated and recognized as the true friend of the Potters and enemy of Voldemort.	
Ex	Exposure	Pettigrew is exposed as a traitor and accomplice to Voldemort.	
T	Transfiguration	Sirius takes up his role as Harry's godfather.	
U	Punishment	Pettigrew is a fugitive.	
W	Wedding	Sirius is free, though still regarded as a fugitive by the Ministry.	

Functions of the Dramatis Personae for *The Goblet of Fire*

Symbol	Function Name	Main Narrative	Move	Move	Move	Move
α	Initial Situation	Harry re-introduced at the Dursley's.				
β	Absentation					
γ	Interdiction	(a) Standing Dursley and Ministry interdictions on magic; (b) Vernon resists allowing Harry to leave early to attend the World Cup.				
δ	Violation	Weasley's arrive at the Dursley's to collect Harry for the World Cup.				
ε	Reconnaissance	Out-of-sight, Voldemort (or his agents) seek information about the upcoming Triwizard Tournament and Harry's activities.				
ζ	Delivery	Voldemort (or his agents) acquire this information from Bertha Jorkins.				
η	Trickery	Barty Crouch, Jr. impersonates Mad-Eye Moody.				
θ	Complicity	Harry trusts the false Mad-Eye Moody.				
A	Villainy	Harry's name is selected by the Goblet of Fire (Voldemort plans to use the opportunity of the Triwizard Tournament to abduct Harry).	Task 1: Dragons	Task 2: Open the egg to find out what the challenge will be.	Task 3: Maze and obstacles	
a	Lack	Harry is compelled by Ministry rules to participate in the Tournament and face the three tests.				
B	Mediation; The Connective Incident	Harry complies with the "binding contract" of competing as one of four Triwizard champions.				
C	Beginning Counteraction					
↑	Departure					
D	The First Function of the Donor		Hagrid reveals the dragons to Harry; Moody coaches him.	Cedric advises Harry how to solve the egg puzzle; Dobby provides Gillyweed.	Moody coaches Harry.	
E	The Hero's Reaction		Harry learns the Accio spell under	Harry accepts the Gillyweed.	Harry follows Moody's	

Symbol	Function Name	Main Narrative	Move	Move	Move
F	Provision or Receipt of a Magical Agent		Hermione's instruction; Harry tells Cedric about the dragons. Harry masters the Accio spell.	Harry will use the Gillyweed to breathe underwater.	instructions.
G	Spatial Transference Between Two Kingdoms, Guidance	Harry and Cedric are sent to Little Hangleton graveyard by the Triwizard Cup portkey.	Awaits the dragon challenge in the champion's tent; enters the dragon arena to acquire the golden egg.	Harry searches underwater for Ron and the other "abductees."	Harry enters the maze. Moody, out-of-sight, clears obstacles in the maze to the path to the Cup for Harry.
H	Struggle	Following the return of Voldemort to an autonomous physical body, he and Harry duel.	Harry battles the dragon.	Harry battles the merpeople.	Harry battles the maze obstacles: Dementor, sphinx, blast-ended skrewt.
J	Branding, Marking	Harry has been pierced with a knife to supply the blood needed for the potion that restored Voldemort.			
I	Victory	Priori incantatem enables Harry to survive the duel with Voldemort.	Harry acquires the golden egg.	Harry releases Ron and Gabrielle from their bonds and the merpeople guards.	Harry reaches the Cup.
K	Misfortune Liquidated	Harry survives the Triwizard Tournament and the showdown with Voldemort.	Harry completes the first challenge. *Move to next A (a).*	Harry completes the second challenge. *Move to next A.*	Harry completes the third challenge. *Return to G on main narrative.*
→	Return	Harry returns from the graveyard to the Hogwarts grounds with Cedric's body.			
Pr	Pursuit, Chase	Mad-Eye Moody (Barty Crouch, Jr.) whisks Harry away from the crowd and imprisons him in his office.			
Rs	Rescue	Dumbledore, Snape and McGonagall rescue Harry from the false Mad-Eye Moody.			
o	Unrecognized Arrival				
L	Unfounded Claims				
M	Difficult Task	Dumbledore and Sirius ask Harry to recount his ordeal; Harry must counter Fudge's views.			
N	Solution	Harry recounts his ordeal and refutes Fudge's interpretation.			

Symbol	Function Name	Main Narrative	Move	Move	Move
Q	Recognition	Harry is honored at the Leaving Feast for standing up to Voldemort and his veracity is confirmed by Dumbledore			
Ex	Exposure	The Mad-Eye Moody who taught Defense Against the Dark Arts that year is revealed to be Barty Crouch, Jr., agent of Voldemort.			
T	Transfiguration	By direct physical confrontation with Voldemort and his minions, Harry matures into an active opponent of the Dark Lord.			
U	Punishment	Fudge allows the Dementors to kill Barty Crouch, Jr.			
W	Wedding	Harry returns to the Dursley's.			

Functions of the Dramatis Personae for *The Order of the Phoenix*

Symbol	Function Name	Main Narrative	Move
α	Initial Situation	Harry re-introduced at the Dursley's.	
β	Absentation	Dumbledore avoids Harry.	
γ	Interdiction	(a) Standing Dursley and Ministry interdictions on magic; (b) Harry warned about his scar "dream"-connection to Voldemort.	Harry instructed by authorities to deny that Voldemort is back.
δ	Violation	(a) Harry performs the Patronus charm in the presence of Dudley against Dementors. (b) Harry does nothing to prevent the visions of Voldemort.	Harry disobeys the interdiction; speaks about it openly in Umbridge's class.
ε	Reconnaissance	Voldemort attempts to acquire the prophecy.	The Ministry seeks information about Dumbledore's and Harry's intentions.
ζ	Delivery	Voldemort learns about the "mental" connection between he and Harry.	The Ministry appoints Umbridge as High Inquisitor in addition to her duties as Defense Against the Dark Arts.
η	Trickery	Voldemort plants in Harry the vision that Sirius has been captured and is being tortured in the Ministry of Magic for information.	The Ministry disparages Harry's and Dumbledore's veracity to discredit them in the wizarding community.
θ	Complicity	Harry wonders whether the vision shows him what is actually happening to Sirius.	The wizarding community, by and large, accepts the Ministry propaganda about Harry and Dumbledore.
A	Villainy		The Ministry prevents students from learning useful defensive magic and attempts to wrest control of Hogwarts from Dumbledore.
a	Lack	Harry lacks assurance of Sirius' safety; he also desires to know the "secret weapon" sought by Voldemort.	
B	Mediation; The Connective Incident	Harry learns from Kreacher that Sirius is missing.	Hermione surmises that Umbridge's appointment is an attempt by the Ministry to gain control of Hogwarts.
C	Beginning Counteraction	Harry decides to rescue Sirius.	The trio decide that Harry will give practical instruction in Defense Against the Dark Arts to select students.
↑	Departure	Umbridge, Harry and Hermione enter the Forbidden Forest.	Enter Hogsmeade.
D	The First Function of the Donor	(a) Grawp protects Harry and Hermione. The centaurs confront them; (b) *Snape instructs Harry in Occlumency.*	Dumbledore's Army formed.
E	The Hero's Reaction	(a) Harry and Hermione freed from Umbridge's custody; (b) *Harry disregards Snape's instructions and lessons.*	Harry agrees to teach them.
F	Provision or Receipt of a Magical Agent	(a) – (b) *Harry peers into Snape's Pensieve.*	The DA use the Room of Requirement for lessons and training.

Symbol	Function Name	Main Narrative	Move
G	Spatial Transference Between Two Kingdoms, Guidance	(a) Thestrals whisk Harry and students to the Ministry of Magic in London; (b) *Harry views Snape's "worst memory," learning about his father's confrontations with Snape during their time in Hogwarts.*	
H	Struggle	Harry, the DA, and the Order battle the Death Eaters over the prophecy; Harry confronts Voldemort in person but Dumbledore intervenes; Voldemort "possesses" Harry.	
J	Branding, Marking		
I	Victory	Harry's love expels Voldemort.	
K	Misfortune Liquidated	Harry acquires the prophecy, denying Voldemort the "weapon."	
→	Return	Harry returns to Hogwarts.	
Pr	Pursuit, Chase		
Rs	Rescue		
o	Unrecognized Arrival		
L	Unfounded Claims		
M	Difficult Task	Harry learns that he must be the one to confront and defeat Voldemort; the death of Sirius means he will again be without family.	
N	Solution	Harry accepts his fated task.	
Q	Recognition	Harry is vindicated in his earlier claims about Voldemort.	
Ex	Exposure	Voldemort's return is accepted by the wizarding community and Fudge is revealed to have slandered Harry and Dumbledore.	
T	Transfiguration	Harry is transformed from outcast-villain to hero.	
U	Punishment	Umbridge is expelled from Hogwarts.	
W	Wedding	Harry returns to the Dursley's.	

Functions of the Dramatis Personae for *The Half-Blood Prince*

Symbol	Function Name	Main Narrative	Move	Move
α	Initial Situation		Fudge calls on the Muggle Prime Minister of Britain.	
β	Absentation			
γ	Interdiction			
δ	Violation			
ε	Reconnaissance			
ζ	Delivery			
η	Trickery			
θ	Complicity			
A	Villainy	Dumbledore is mortally wounded in his attempt to destroy the Gaunt-Slytherin ring.		
a	Lack		Knowledge of Voldemort's understanding of horcruxes needs to be ascertained.	
B	Mediation; The Connective Incident		(a) Dumbledore writes to Harry requesting his help; (b) Dumbledore uses Harry to persuade Slughorn to become the Defense Against the Dark Arts teacher at Hogwarts.	
C	Beginning Counteraction		Harry agrees to accompany Dumbledore.	
↑	Departure		(a) Harry leaves the Dursley's with Dumbledore; (b) Harry leaves Slughorn's house with Dumbledore to go back to Hogwarts.	
D	The First Function of the Donor		(a) Harry must win a Potions competition to obtain the Felix Felicis prize; (b) Harry must obtain Slughorn's unadulterated memory; Slughorn refuses Harry's requests.	
E	The Hero's Reaction		(a) Harry wins the competition with the aid of	

Symbol	Function Name	Main Narrative	Move	Move
			the Half-Blood Prince's textbook; (b) Harry uses the Felix Felicis in an attempt to acquire the memory from Slughorn.	
F	Provision or Receipt of a Magical Agent		(a) Harry obtains the Felix Felicis; (b) Harry obtains the Slughorn's true memory.	
G	Spatial Transference Between Two Kingdoms, Guidance		Harry and Dumbledore apparate to the cave once Harry gives his word to do everything Dumbledore asks of him.	
H	Struggle		Harry and Dumbledore contend with Voldemort's dark magic defenses in the cave in order to obtain the locket.	
J	Branding, Marking			
I	Victory		Harry and Dumbledore overcome all of the defenses and seize the locket.	
K	Misfortune Liquidated		Harry and Dumbledore escape from the cave with the locket.	
→	Return		Harry apparates with the weakened Dumbledore to Hogsmeade.	
Pr	Pursuit, Chase			
Rs	Rescue			
o	Unrecognized Arrival		Harry and Dumbledore return to Hogwarts, Harry under his Invisibility Cloak.	
L	Unfounded Claims			
M	Difficult Task		Harry continues to obey Dumbledore's instructions upon return to the Astronomy Tower.	
N	Solution	Dumbledore freezes Harry to prevent him from interfering with Draco's and Snape's attack.		
Q	Recognition			
Ex	Exposure	Snape appears to have been a double-agent and still a Death Eater in Voldemort's employ.		
T	Transfiguration	Harry is the Chosen One. He must now take the lead against Voldemort.		

Symbol	Function Name	Main Narrative	Move	Move
U	Punishment	Snape is banished (temporarily) from Hogwarts.		
W	Wedding	After Dumbledore's funeral, Harry returns to the Dursley's.		

Functions of the Dramatis Personae for *The Deathly Hallows*
Table A*

Symbol	Function Name	Main Narrative	Move	Move	Move	Move
α	Initial Situation	Snape and Yaxley inform Voldemort of the dates and times of Harry's transfer from the Dursley's.				
β	Absentation	Dumbledore has died; the Dursleys are evacuated from Privet Drive and go into hiding.				
γ	Interdiction	(a) Mrs. Weasley urges Harry to return to Hogwarts; (b) Hermione urges Harry to keep his "mental" connection to Voldemort closed.				
δ	Violation	(a) Harry, Ron and Hermione do not return to Hogwarts; (b) Harry allows himself to see Voldemort's thoughts.				
ε	Reconnaissance					
ζ	Delivery					
η	Trickery					
θ	Complicity					
A	Villainy				The trio are captured by Death Eaters and imprisoned in Malfoy Manor; Hermione is tortured.	
a	Lack	Harry needs to obtain all of the horcruxes.	Harry needs to know the truth about Dumbledore and obtain the Sword of Gryffindor to destroy the locket.			
B	Mediation; The Connective Incident		Harry is determined to go to Godric's Hollow.			The trio surmise that a horcrux must be in Bellatrix's vault at Gringott's.
C	Beginning Counteraction	The trio decide to infiltrate the Ministry of Magic in search of the genuine locket.	(a) – (b) Harry and Hermione decide to go to Godric's Hollow and		Harry, with the aid of Dobby, rescues the prisoners; he and Ron overcome Pettigrew and	The trio make plans to infiltrate the vault in Gringott's.

Symbol	Function Name	Main Narrative	Move	Move	Move
↑	Departure	The trio leave Grimmauld Place for the Ministry of Magic.	(c) find Bathilda Bagshot; (a) Ron leaves Harry and Hermione in the forest; (b) Harry and Hermione apparate to Godric's Hollow; (c) —	rush to rescue Hermione.	
D	The First Function of the Donor	(a) Dumbledore bequeaths the Deluminator to Ron, his copy of The Tales of Beedle the Bard to Hermione, and the snitch and the Sword of Gryffindor to Harry; (b) Umbridge wears the locket.	(a) — (b) — (c) The silver doe (Snape) catches Harry's attention.		Griphook offers a deal to the trio: his help in Gringott's for the Sword of Gryffindor.
E	The Hero's Reaction	Harry stupefies Umbridge and others.	(a) Ron regrets abandoning Harry and Hermione and desires to return to them; (b) — (c) Harry follows the doe.		Harry accepts Griphook's offer.
F	Provision or Receipt of a Magical Agent	Harry takes the locket from Umbridge.	(a) Ron uses the Deluminator bequeathed to him by Dumbledore; (b) — (c) The doe leads Harry to the Sword in a lake.		Griphook supplies the trio with the information needed to infiltrate Gringott's.
G	Spatial Transference, Guidance	The trio emerge from the Ministry dungeons to the atrium.	(a) Ron returns, guided by the Deluminator; (b) Harry and Hermione enter Bathilda Bagshot's home; (c) Harry dives into the lake.		They travel from Shell Cottage to Gringott's, descend and enter Bellatrix's vault.
H	Struggle	The trio clash with Ministry officials and attempt to escape.	(a) — (b) Bagshot-snake attacks Harry and Hermione; (c) The Voldemort soul-fragment in the horcrux attempts to drown Harry.	Harry and Ron clash with Bellatrix and Voldemort's other agents in Malfoy's house.	The burning and multiplying curses on the objects in the vault impede their effort to obtain the Hufflepuff cup horcrux.
J	Branding, Marking	Ron splinches.	(a) — (b) Harry is bitten, Hermione uses a Severing charm to		

Symbol	Function Name	Main Narrative	Move	Move	Move
			(c) detach the locket from Harry's chest, and Harry's wand is broken; The locket chain cuts his neck.		
I	Victory	The trio escape.	(a) – (b) Harry and Hermione escape Godric's Hollow before Voldemort arrives; (c) Ron pulls Harry out of the lake and removes the locket from him.	Dobby joins the struggle and subdues Bellatrix and Narcissa.	Harry overcomes the cursed objects to obtain the cup.
K	Misfortune Liquidated	Harry now possesses the genuine locket.	(a) – (b) Harry obtains information about Dumbledore from Rita Skeeter's book; (c) Harry and Ron possess the Sword, and Ron destroys the locket.	Dobby rescues the trio and Griphook; all disapparate to Shell Cottage; Dobby sustains a mortal wound.	Harry possesses the cup.
→	Return		(a) – (b) Harry and Hermione return to the forest; (c) Harry and Ron return to the tent and Hermione.		

* The *Deathly Hallows* narrative consists of seven moves; Table A presents the initial narrative and the first three moves; Table B presents the final four moves.

Functions of the Dramatis Personae for *The Deathly Hallows*
Table B*

Symbol	Function Name	Move	Move	Move	Move
α	Initial Situation				
β	Absentation				
γ	Interdiction				
δ	Violation				
ε	Reconnaissance				
ζ	Delivery				
η	Trickery				
θ	Complicity				
A	Villainy				
a	Lack				
B	Mediation; The Connective Incident	Harry has a vision that the last horcrux is at Hogwarts.	McGonagall gives Harry control of the castle.	Harry sees Voldemort's thoughts, revealing that he and Nagini are in the Shrieking Shack.	
C	Beginning Counteraction	The trio decide to go to Hogwarts together.	Harry decides to look for the Gray Lady.	The trio decide to pursue Voldemort to the Shrieking Shack.	
↑	Departure	The trio travel to Hogsmeade.		The trio fight their way out of the castle to the Whomping Willow and traverse underground to the Shrieking Shack.	
D	The First Function of the Donor	Aberforth advises Harry to stop fighting and run away.	The Gray Lady distrusts Harry and refuses to help him.	Snape is mortally wounded by Nagini.	
E	The Hero's Reaction	Harry tells Aberforth about Dumbledore's passion in the cave of the Inferi.	Harry convinces the Gray Lady that he opposes Voldemort.	Harry tries to come to Snape's aid.	Harry tells the snitch he is about to die.
F	Provision or Receipt of a Magical Agent	Aberforth agrees to help Harry and reveals a secret passage to Hogwarts.	The Gray Lady reveals the story of the lost diadem.	Before he dies, Snape gives Harry his memories which hold the key to understanding how to defeat	The snitch opens, yielding the Resurrection Stone.

Symbol	Function Name	Move	Move	Move	Move
					the headmasters in Dumbledore's office.
Ex	Exposure				The full extent of Voldemort's villainy in creating the horcruxes is revealed.
T	Transfiguration				Harry's scar no longer hurts; all of Hogwarts and the wizarding world recognize Harry as their savior hero.
U	Punishment				
W	Wedding				Harry and Ginny; Ron and Hermione.

The Epilogue ends with a β-function: Albus Severus Potter is sent away to Hogwarts; the next chapter in the Hogwarts saga begins.

Functions of the Dramatis Personae for the Complete Harry Potter series

Symbol	Function Name	Narrative Description
α	Initial Situation	Voldemort, the Dark Lord, dominates and terrorizes the wizarding world.
β	Absentation	The Potters go into hiding.
γ	Interdiction	Dumbledore offers to be the Potters' Secret-Keeper.
δ	Violation	The Potters employ Pettigrew as their Secret-Keeper.
ε	Reconnaissance	Voldemort seeks the location of the Potters.
ζ	Delivery	Pettigrew reveals the Potters' whereabouts to Voldemort.
η	Trickery	Pettigrew serves as a double agent for Voldemort, retaining the trust of the Potters.
θ	Complicity	The Potters do not suspect Pettigrew's true allegiance.
A	Villainy	Voldemort murders the Potters, attempts but fails to murder Harry, leaving Harry orphaned and physically scarred.
a	Lack	
B	Mediation; The Connective Incident	*Stone:* Harry learns that Voldemort seeks immortal life. *Chamber:* Harry learns that he shares significant traits with Voldemort (Parseltongue, an orphan, Hogwarts as "home"). *Prisoner:* Harry learns of Pettigrew's role in the Villainy. *Goblet:* Harry witnesses Voldemort's reembodiment. *Order:* Harry learns from the prophecy that either he must kill Voldemort or Voldemort must kill him. *Prince:* (1) Dumbledore sacrifices his life to maintain the illusion of Snape's treachery and prepare Harry to learn the means of defeating Voldemort. (2) Harry learns he must find and destroy all of the horcruxes in order to defeat Voldemort;
C	Beginning Counteraction	Harry resolves to find the horcruxes and destroy them rather than return to Hogwarts.
↑	Departure	Harry leaves the Dursley's for the last time, no longer under the protection of his mother's blood by relation (Petunia).
D	The First Function of the Donor	Dumbledore bequeaths the snitch to Harry.
E	The Hero's Reaction	Harry, Ron and Hermione obtain and destroy three horcruxes: the locket, the cup and the diadem. To destroy the most difficult horcrux, the one in Harry himself, he— (a) tries to come to Snape's aid; (b) enters the Forbidden Forest and tells the snitch, "I am about to die."
F	Provision or Receipt of a Magical Agent	(a) Before he dies, Snape gives Harry his memories which hold the key to understanding how to defeat Voldemort; (b) Harry obtains the Resurrection Stone, which emerges from the open snitch.

Symbol	Function Name	Narrative Description
G	Spatial Transference Between Two Kingdoms, Guidance	Harry is temporarily in the company of the shades of Harry's parents, Sirius and Lupin, who emerge from the Stone
H	Struggle	Harry struggles with himself and his internal horcrux over his resolve to sacrifice his life.
J	Branding, Marking	
I	Victory	Harry feigns a duel with Voldemort, allowing Voldemort's Killing Curse to strike him down.
K	Misfortune Liquidated	The horcrux in Harry is destroyed; he awakes in an intermediate state—King's Cross station.
→	Return	Harry's soul departs the intermediate state in King's Cross station and returns to physical existence in the Forbidden Forest.
Pr	Pursuit, Chase	
Rs	Rescue	
o	Unrecognized Arrival	Reverse: Narcissa, after checking on Harry, claims that he is dead.
L	Unfounded Claims	Voldemort announces to the combatants that he has killed Harry Potter.
M	Difficult Task	Harry must bide time to lower Voldemort's protectiveness for Nagini and then destroy Voldemort for good.
N	Solution	Neville dispatches Nagini; Harry defeats Voldemort with only defensive spells.
Q	Recognition	Harry is recognized as the victorious hero by the shades of the headmasters in Dumbledore's office.
Ex	Exposure	The full extent of Voldemort's villainy in creating the horcruxes is revealed.
T	Transfiguration	Harry's scar no longer hurts; all of Hogwarts and the wizarding world recognize Harry as their savior hero.
U	Punishment	
W	Wedding	Harry and Ginny; Ron and Hermione.

Appendix III

The Symbolized Schemes of the Individual Harry Potter Tales and the Series as a Whole

The basic components are arranged sequentially from left to right in their respective symbolized schemes. Some elements are included as needed to clarify the scheme:

- An italicized symbol or string of symbols denotes a nonsequential or otherwise anomalous function or group of functions;
- Braces { } are used to group moves or indicate the convergence or divergence of multiple narrative lines;
- Dashed lines clarify narrative lines;
- Solid lines with arrowheads show sequential development if the constraints of paper size and margins interfere with a strict linear presentation;
- Angle brackets < > indicate narrative elements that occur "off the page" and which are revealed retrospectively. Because the story does not unfold with these elements in the correct sequential order, the functions grouped in angle brackets should be regarded for information only.

Individual Schemes for the Seven Tales
in the *Harry Potter* Series

Philosopher's Stone

$$\alpha\,\beta\,\gamma\,\delta \begin{cases} <\varepsilon\,\zeta\,\eta\,\theta \\[6pt] \varepsilon\,\zeta\,\eta\,\theta \end{cases} \begin{array}{l} \text{--- HIKMN>} \\[4pt] (DEFDEF)^*\,ABC\text{----------------}\uparrow DEFGHJIKQExTUw \\ \qquad ABC\uparrow DEFGHJIK \end{array}$$

Stone is a double-move tale with two spliced Transference sequences. It is a surprisingly complex tale, with 42 functions spread over two moves. Six of these functions are out of sequence. The Reconnaissance–Complicity sequence in the upper move is Dumbledore as victim-hero and an independent axis is maintained throughout the tale. The Dumbledore axis terminates at a Solution [N]. The lower axis is Harry as seeker-hero. The presence of two distinct heroes is an unusual feature shared only with *Prisoner*.

The original villainy done to Harry and his parents is nonsequential backstory to this narrative and so is omitted in this scheme. Because the liquidation of this villainy is the primary movement driving the Harry Potter series as a whole, and because it is not resolved until *Hallows*, it will be the Preparation and Villainy of the series of books treated as a single tale. The dénouement for all but *Half-Blood Prince* and *Deathly Hallows* ends with Harry's return to 4 Privet Drive. We designate this with a lower-case 'w'.

Chamber of Secrets

$$\alpha\,\beta\,\gamma\,\delta \begin{cases} \mathcal{E}\,\zeta\,> \\ \mathcal{E}_{ret}\,\zeta \\ \mathcal{E}_{ret} \end{cases} \eta\,\theta^*\,ABC\uparrow DEF \\ \qquad\qquad\qquad\qquad <A>BC\uparrow DEFGF^*HJIK\downarrow LMNQExTUw$$

Chamber is a double-move tale that has layered sub-moves in the Preparation section, particularly among the Reconnaissance—Delivery functions. The most important pair occurs off the page and two of the three sub-moves are reverse types, an anomalous feature signified by the italicized function symbols.

Several of the functions in the Preparation section are nonsequential with respect to two of the four initial villanies. Indeed, out of 36 functions spread over two moves, eight (or 22%) do not conform to Propp's schema. The nonsequential Receipt of a Magical Agent [*F**] is Fawkes' delivery of himself, the Sorting Hat and the Sword of Gryffindor *after* Harry's Spatial Transference [G] to the Chamber.

Prisoner of Azkaban

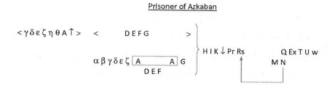

Prisoner has no moves per se, but two heroes whose axes converge. The top narrative axis of *Prisoner* has Sirius as the victim- and seeker-hero. The bracketed Preparation and Complication groups for Sirius are disclosed near the end of Harry's narrative. The bracketed Transference group < D E F G > denotes Sirius-Padfoot's collusion with Crookshanks out of Harry's sight. Harry's Preparation group is demoted below the main axis because Sirius is the hero in *Prisoner* as borne out by the Q—W dénouement. A box is shown around the Villainy [A] done to Harry—the presence and attacks of Dementors—to indicate their constant threat and multiple appearances in this section of the narrative. The Transference group below the A-box [D E F] denotes Harry's receiving instruction from Lupin in the Patronus Charm to defend himself against the Dementors.

The Victory [I] occurs in the Shrieking Shack after Sirius is vindicated and Harry shows mercy to Peter Pettigrew. The H—Rs sequence represents Sirius and Harry as temporary joint heroes. The Difficult Task [M] of rescuing both Sirius and Buckbeak (and, as it turns out, Harry himself) is given to Harry and Hermione by Dumbledore. The Solution [N] includes an endless feedback loop to the earlier [Rs] because of the use of the time-turner.

Goblet of Fire

α γ δ ε ζ η θ A B C - G H J I K ↓ Pr Rs M N Q Ex T U w
          A D E F G H I K   ↑
                    a D E F G H I K |
                              A D E F G H I K

Goblet, a tale with four moves, nevertheless has a "purer" folktale structure than any of the other tales in the series. Even with 48 functions spread over the four moves, its narrative scheme is the simplest of the seven books in the series to analyze. Harry is both the victim- and seeker-hero and he endures multiple villainies: three moves represent the three Tri-Wizard tasks and the final move is the direct conflict with Voldemort in Little Hangleton graveyard.

Order of the Phoenix

α β γ δ < ε ζ >   (D E F G)* η θ a B C ↑ D E G H I K ↓ M N Q Ex T U w
γ δ ε ζ η θ A B C ↑ D E F

Order is a double-move tale with a spliced Transference sequence. The main axis of *Order* concerns the villainy done to Harry and Sirius by Voldemort, which creates a Lack [a]. The move below the main axis concerns the complicating villainy of Umbridge and the Ministry. The out-of-order sequence in the main axis concerns the events from the founding of Dumbledore's Army through Harry's peering into Snape's "worst memory" (Chs 16-28). The double-move is neither consecutive nor concurrent; such an incongruity in the linear sequence of the tale is a notable structural anomaly.

Half-Blood Prince

< A > ⎰ - ⎱ N ⎱ Ex T U w
      ⎰   ↑ D E F   G H I K ↓ o   M ⎰
      ⎱ a B C ↑ D E F ⎰

Prince, like *Prisoner*, has no moves per se but two heroes whose axes converge. The main axis in *Prince* is Dumbledore as the victim-hero; he was mortally wounded by the villainy of the Gaunt-Slytherin ring horcrux prior to the narrative's beginning, which is shown by the initial Villainy < A >. Dumbledore is also a co-seeker-hero with Harry. Harry's secondary hero status in this tale is indicated by his action halting at the second Difficult Task [M] where it joins with the Solution [N] now governed by Dumbledore's plan coming to fruition. In the context of the entire Harry Potter series, this tale is further complicated by a third victim- and seeker-hero: Severus Snape. However, within the confines of the *Prince* narrative, his status as such is not recognized and is therefore omitted from this scheme. An interesting corollary study to the present one could examine Snape as the main hero in the Harry Potter series.

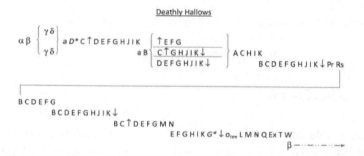

Hallows is comprised of 101 functions over seven moves. This makes *Hallows* by far the most complicated tale in the series, yet it has only two functions out of sequence. Classifying its multiple moves is complicated by the carryover of the discovery of Voldemort's horcrux creations and Dumbledore's dispatch of the trio from *Prince*. The number of moves occurring on the basis of Villainy [A] or Lack [a] internal only to the *Hallows* narrative is three; including the sequence of multiple Mediations [B] as moves, there are seven. Since these Mediation-moves lead to additional receipts of magical agents [DEF] for the purpose of completing the liquidation of all the preceding villainies, we treat these also as moves in *Hallows*.

There are several notable sequences in *Hallows*. The first Complication includes the efforts to retrieve the real locket horcrux from Umbridge. Dumbledore's bequest includes the donation of three magical agents to aid each member of the trio of heroes which are put to use at key points in the narrative. The next notable sequence is the combination of three interwoven sequences representing the efforts to acquire the Sword of Gryffindor and destroy the locket horcrux.

The remaining horcrux-artifacts are retrieved and destroyed with less complication as exhibited by the consecutive single axes for each. The [E – T] sequence in the final move of the story occurs in the Forbidden Forest and the Battle of Hogwarts. The Epilogue ends with Albus Severus Potter absenting himself from home and the next chapter in the Hogwarts saga begins.

Scheme for the Series Treated as a Single Tale

$$< \alpha \; \beta \; \gamma \; \delta \; \varepsilon \; \zeta \; \eta \; \theta \; A > B^7 \; C \uparrow D \; E \; F \; G \; H \; I \; K \downarrow o_{rev} \; L \; M \; N \; Q \; Ex \; T \; W$$

If we examine the Harry Potter series of books as a whole unit, we find the many moves in its single tales resolve into an overarching tale with one linear, sequential narrative. The Preparation group and Villainy [A] is the backstory developed and revealed in *Prisoner*, *Prince*, and *Hallows*. The Mediation [B], the misfortune made known to Harry, is gradually unfolded in the first six books of the series, and Dumbledore gradually dispatches Harry to defeat Voldemort. We note the seven occurrences of this function in the first six books of the series with the superscript. The functions subsequent to the Mediation [B] transpire within the pages of *Hallows*, starting with the Counteraction [C]: it is initiated at the beginning of the school year and it is confirmed conclusively by Harry at Dobby's grave. Harry's final test is to learn that he holds one of Voldermort's horcruxes within him and resolve to destroy it as well. For this he needs both the final guidance from Dumbledore, which he receives from the dying Snape, as well as the Snitch, the magical agent donated to him by Dumbledore [E—F]. The story returns to the main axis where the struggle with Voldemort is concluded [H—N].

Comparison to the Lacoss Schemes (2004)

First, we return to the tables for *Philosopher's Stone* and *Goblet of Fire* prepared by Jann Lacoss.[1] If we translate her table for *Stone* into its symbolic notation, we get:

---

[1] Lacoss, "Of Magicals and Muggles," 86.

β γ δ A a B C D ↑ E F G H J L M N Q Ex T U

Some critical notes are in order. First, Lacoss has the D and ↑ functions out of order in her table. Second, she identifies both a Villainy [A] and a Lack [a], but these are alternative types of one function and, according to Propp, cannot appear in the same narrative axis. Third, an initial Villainy [A] or Lack [a] is always liquidated [K], but Lacoss omits this essential function. Lastly, some of the assignations are dubious. For example, she has Branding [J] as "People notice [Harry's] scar," but the Branding function should be a consequence of the preceding combat between the hero and the villain [H]. Harry receives his scar in the prequel to the narrative and, at least in *Stone*, cannot be located at this point in the narrative. We believe the double-villainy directed at Harry within the narrative sequence of *Stone* is essential to describe correctly this story's formal structure.

If we translate Lacoss' table for *Goblet* into its symbolic notation, we get the following scheme:

```
βγδεζaBCD↑EFGHJ----------------------------HJ(IK↓)*PrRsoLExW
         CD↑EFGHJ                              ↑
              CD↑EFGHJ                         ¦
                   CD↑EFGHJ
```

Structurally, this is very similar to our reconstruction of this story. It is noteworthy that Lacoss' moves occur on the Beginning Counteraction [C] move rather than on a Villainy [A] or a Lack [a]. However, if her assignment of the Villainy on the main axis were corrected (it should be an 'A' rather than a Lack [a]), picking up the axis at the struggle with Voldemort in Little Hangleton graveyard completes that pairing at the Liquidation [K] function. The sequence (I K ↓) is misassigned to elements preceding the Struggle [H] in the graveyard. Lastly, the Unfounded Claims [L] function is misapplied; Lacoss simply names the false hero *dramatis persona*, but this does not fulfill the requirement for this narrative constant. We conclude that Lacoss has correctly identified the general structure of *Goblet*, but has incorrectly analyzed some of the key sequences of functions in the primary axis of the story.

Appendix IV

Propp's Five Propositions Bearing on the Quantity of Concordance and the Results of Applying the Propositions to the Individual Harry Potter Tale

Common Pair Arrangements

Proposition 1: "we observe that [the following functions] are arranged in pairs:"[1]

- Prohibition—Violation [γ δ]
- Reconnaissance—Delivery [ε ζ]
- Struggle—Victory [H I]
- Pursuit—Rescue [Pr Rs]

When we examine the schemes for the Harry Potter books, we find these notable results concerning their common pair arrangements:

- All of the stories, if they have one function in a pair, have both;
- Of those stories that have a Reconnaissance—Delivery [ε ζ] pair, only Stone's and Chamber's do not directly involve Harry (Stone's targets Dumbledore; Chamber's targets Ginny Weasley);
- Only Chamber has multiple Reconnaissance—Delivery pairs that are also nonsequential;
- Only Goblet has all of the pairs.

There are notable results for other books in the series, but we will limit our assessment to the books identified earlier at the extremities of readers' aesthetic satisfaction.

---

[1] Jann Lacoss, "Of Magicals and Muggles: Reversals and Revulsions at Hogwarts, in *The Ivory Tower and Harry Potter: Perspectives on a Literary Phenomenon*, ed. Lana A. Whited (Columbia, MO: University of Missouri Press, 2004), 64-5.

Task Differentiation [B, D, M]

Proposition 2 concerns what tasks the hero is given or undertakes. Propp claims that "(…) it is always possible to be governed by the principle of defining a function *according to its consequences*. (…) all tasks giving rise to a search must be considered in terms of B; all tasks giving rise to the receipt of a magical agent are considered in terms of D. All other tasks are considered as M, with two varieties: tasks connected with match-making and marriage, and tasks not linked with matchmaking."[2] When we examine the schemes for the Harry Potter books, we find these notable results concerning their task differentiation:

- *Prisoner* and *Prince* have a B task with a victim- and seeker-hero other than Harry (Sirius and Dumbledore, respectively);
- Stone has three nonsequential D tasks; Order and Hallows have one nonsequential D task;
- Hallows has a remarkable seven D tasks;
- All of the stories have an M task;
- The M task in Stone occurs off the page;
- The M task in Chamber is less urgent for resolving the narrative than the M tasks in the other books;
- The M task in Prisoner involves a time loop and a future-Harry and future Hermione co-present with their past selves;
- Hallows is the only story with an M task that ends in a wedding.

There are notable results for other books in the series, especially *Stone*, but again we will limit our assessment to the books identified earlier at the extremities of readers' aesthetic satisfaction.

Spheres of Action of the Dramatis Personae

Proposition 3: "(…) many functions join logically together into certain *spheres*. These spheres in toto correspond to their respective performers. They are spheres of action."[3] The following spheres of action are present in folktales:

- Villain [A, H, Pr]
- Donor [D, F]

---

[2] Lacoss, 67-8.
[3] Lacoss., 79-80.

- Helper [G, K, Rs, N, T]
- Princess (or sought-for person) [M, J, Ex, Q, U, W]
- Dispatcher [B]
- Hero [C, ↑, E, W]
- False Hero [C, ↑, E, L]

When we examine the schemes for the Harry Potter books, we find these notable results concerning their spheres of action:

- Only Prisoner has a villain other than Voldemort;
- Hallows has a remarkable six Donors;
- In Hallows, the seeker-hero includes the whole trio and the victim-hero includes Snape;
- Sirius is a false villain in Prisoner; Snape is the false villain in Hallows;
- Draco is the false villain (by narrative misdirection) in Chamber;
- Hallows has a villain Donor (Umbridge); Order has a false villain Donor (Snape);
- Prisoner has seven Helpers (Crookshanks, Fred & George Weasley, Dumbledore, Sirius, Harry, Hermione);
- Prisoner has two sought-for persons at cross-purposes: Sirius seeks Pettigrew and Harry seeks Sirius;
- Prisoner has no Dispatcher;
- Dumbledore serves as Dispatcher in Prince; Harry serves as a Dispatcher in Hallows.

Multiple Villainies, Interwoven and Sequential

Proposition 4: "A tale may be termed any development proceeding from villainy (A) or a Lack (a) through intermediary functions to marriage (W), or to other functions deployed as a dénouement. Terminal functions are at times a reward (F), a gain or in general the liquidation of misfortune (K), and escape from pursuit (Rs), etc. (…) This type of development is termed by us a move. Each new act of villainy, each new lack, creates a new move. (…) One move may directly follow another; but they may also interweave (…)."[4] We find these notable results concerning multiple villainies:

- All of the stories have multiple villainies;

---

[4] Lacoss., 92.

- The villainies in Chamber only indirectly affect Harry;
- Only Order has a move (Villainy) that is neither consecutive nor concurrent.

Exclusive Pairs of Functions

Proposition 5: "(…) we observe that there are two such pairs of functions which are encountered within a single move so rarely that their exclusiveness may be considered regular, while their combination may be considered a violation of this rule (…). The two pairs are the Struggle with the villain and the Victory over him [H – I] and the Difficult Task and its Solution [M – N]. In 100 tales, the first pair is encountered 41 times, the second pair is encountered 33 times, and the two combined into one move three times [Some moves exist which develop without either of these pairs.]."[5] We find these notable results concerning the exclusive pairs:

- All of the stories break the exclusionary rule and have both pairs, though the M—N pair in Stone is Dumbledore's and it occurs off the page;
- Only Goblet and Hallows have Harry in sequential and multiple H—I pairs (four and seven, respectively);
- Hallows has Harry in two sequential M—N pairs;
- Prisoner has hybrid pairs: the H—I pair involves Sirius and Harry together on the primary narrative axis whilst the M—N pair involves Harry on the move axis;
- Prince has hybrid pairs: both the H—I and M—N pairs involve Harry and Dumbledore acting together.

---

[5] Lacoss., 101-2.

Further Reading:
Bibliography of Harry Potter Criticism
Compiled by Rebecca Langworthy

Harry Potter Anthologies

Anatol, Giselle Liza, ed. *Reading Harry Potter: Critical Essays*. London: Praeger, 2003.

Anatol, Giselle Liza, ed. *Reading Harry Potter Again: New Critical Essays*. Westport: Greenwood, 2009.

Baggett, David and Klein, Shawn, eds. *Harry Potter and Philosophy: If Aristotle ran Hogwarts*. Chicago: Open Court Press, 2004.

Bassham, Gregory, ed. *The Ultimate Harry Potter and Philosophy: Hogwarts for Muggles*. (The Blackwell Philosophy and Pop Culture Series 20). Hoboken, NJ: John Wylie & Sons Inc., 2010.

Bell, Christopher E., ed. *Hermione Granger Saves the World: Essays on the Feminist Heroine of Hogwarts*. Jefferson: McFarland & Co., 2012.

Berndt, Katrin and Steveker, Lena, eds. *Heroism in the Harry Potter Series*. Aldershot: Ashgate, 2011.

Bryfonski, Dedria, ed. *Political issues in J. K. Rowling's Harry Potter Series*. Detroit: Greenhaven Press, 2009.

Dutchen, Stephanie; Lewanski, Amanda; Morris, Phyllis; and Patterson, Diana, eds. *The Laurentian Letters: Conference Proceedings of Convention Alley*. Ontario: Laurentian Normal School of Consolidated Magicks, July 2004.

Frankel, Valerie Estelle, ed. *Teaching with Harry Potter: Essays on Classroom Wizardry from Elementary School to College*. Jefferson: McFarland, 2013.

Goetz, Sharon K., ed. *Phoenix Rising: Collected Papers on Harry Potter, 17-21 May 2007*. Sedalia/Colorado: Narrate Conferences, 2008.

Granger, John, ed. *Who Killed Albus Dumbledore? What Really Happened In Harry Potter and the Half-Blood Prince? Six Expert Harry Potter Detectives Examine the Evidence*. Hadlock: Zossima Press, 2006.

Hallett, Cynthia J. and Huey, Peggy J., eds. *J. K. Rowling: Harry Potter.* Basingstoke: Palgrave Macmillan, 2012.

Hallett, Cynthia Whitney and Mynott, Debbie, eds. *Scholarly Studies in Harry Potter: Applying Academic Methods to a Popular Text.* Lewiston: Edwin Mellen Press, 2005.

Heilman, Elizabeth E., ed. *Critical Perspectives on Harry Potter. 2nd edition.* New York: Routledge, 2008.

Heilman, Elizabeth E., ed. *Harry Potter's World: Multidisciplinary Critical Perspectives.* New York: Routledge Falmer, 2002.

Lackey, Mercedes and Wilson, Leah, eds. *Mapping the World of Harry Potter: Science Fiction and Fantasy Writers Explore the Best Selling Fantasy Series of All Time.* Dallas, Texas: BenBella Books, 2006.

Morris, Phyllis and Patterson, Diana, eds. *Proceedings of Accio 2008: A Harry Potter Conference.* 25-27 July, Magdalen College, Oxford. Oxford, U.K: Accio UK, 2008.

Mulholland, Neil, ed. *The Psychology of Harry Potter: An Unauthorized Examination of the Boy Who Lived.* Dallas, Tex: BenBella Books, 2007.

Nexon, Daniel H. and Neumann, Iver B., eds. *Harry Potter and International Relations.* Lanham, Maryland: Rowman and Littlefield, 2006.

The Nimbus-2003 Programming Team, eds. *Selected Papers from Nimbus-2003 Compendium: We Solemnly Swear These Papers Were Worth The Wait.* Philadelphia, PA: Xlibris Corporation, 2005.

Thomas, Jeffrey E., ed. *Harry Potter and the Law.* Texas: Wesleyan Law Review, 2005.

Patterson, Diana, ed. *Harry Potter's World-Wide Influence.* Newcastle: Cambridge Scholars Publishing, 2009.

Prinzi, Travis, ed. *Hog's Head Conversations: Essays on Harry Potter.* Vol. 1. Allentown: Zossima Press, 2009.

Prinzi, Travis, ed. *Harry Potter for Nerds: Essays for Fans, Academics, and Lit Geeks.* Unlocking Press, 2011.

Thomas, Jeffrey E. and Snyder, Franklin G., eds. *The Law and Harry Potter.* Durham: Carolina Academic Press, 2010.

Whited, Lana A., ed. *The Ivory Tower and Harry Potter: Perspectives on a Literary Phenomenon*. Columbia, Mo: University of Missouri Press, 2002.

Wiener, Gary and Parks, Penny J., eds. *Readings on J. K. Rowling*. San Diego: Greenhaven Press, 2004.

Harry Potter as Literature

Monographs

Abate, Michelle Ann. *Bloody Murder: The Homicide Tradition in Children's Literature*. Baltimore: Johns Hopkins University Press, 2013.

Adam, Jim. *Destiny Unfulfilled: A Critique of the Harry Potter Series*. Huntersville: Gragthor Terrazin, 2010.

Agarwal, Nikita and Agarwal, Chitra. *Friends and Foes of Harry Potter: Names Decoded*. Dallas, Tex: Texas World Publishing, 2005.

Asher, Mary. *The Power of Women in Harry Potter*. Saarbrücken: Verlag Dr. Müller, 2010.

Barratt, Bethany. *The Politics of Harry Potter*. New York: Palgrave Macmillan, 2012.

Baumann, Mary C. *A Detective's Analysis of Harry Potter and the Mysteries Within*. Bloomington: Authorhouse, 2004.

Beahm, George, W. *Fact, Fiction, and Folklore in Harry Potter's World: An Unofficial Guide*. Charlottesville: Hampton Roads, 2005.

Berger, Helen A. and Ezzy, Douglas. *Teenage Witches: Magical Youth and the Search for the Self*. New Brunswick: Rutgers UP, 2007.

Berner, Amy; Card, Orson Scott; and Millman, Joyce. *The Great Snape Debate: Is Snape Innocent or Guilty?* Dallas, Tex: Benbella Books, 2007.

Blake, Andrew. *The Irresistible Rise of Harry Potter*. London: Verso, 2002.

Boyle, Fionna. *A Muggle's Guide to the Wizarding World: Exploring the Harry Potter Universe*. Toronto: 2004.

Campbell, Lori M. *Portals of Power: Magical Agency and Transformation in Literary Fantasy*. Jefferson: McFarland, 2010.

Clarnette, Lynley. *A Wizard lit master to J. K. Rowling's Harry Potter*. Ballarat: Wizard Books, 2001.

Colbert, David. *The Magical Worlds of Harry Potter*. A Treasury of Myths, Legends, and Fascinating Facts. London: 2001.

Davis, Graeme. *Exploring Beedle the Bard: Unauthorized, Pithy, Tale-By-Tale Perspectives*. Ann Arbor: Nimble Books, 2008.

Deepa, Shree and Karra, K. S. *Harry Potter and Indian Mythology*. Bloomington: Author House, 2011.

Duriez, Colin. *A Field Guide to Harry Potter*. Downers Grove: InterVarsity Press, 2007.

Eccleshare, Julia. *A Guide to the Harry Potter Novels*. Continuum, 2002.

Furst, Peter and Heilmann, Craig. *Hogwarts or hogwash? The Harry Potter phenomenon and your child*. Rozelle/N.S.W.: Lime Grove House Publishing, 2001.

Garrett, Greg. *One Fine Potion: The Literary Magic of Harry Potter.* Waco: Baylor UP, 2010.

Gierzynski, Anthony. *Harry Potter and the Millennials: Research Methods and the Politics of the Muggle Generation.* Baltimore: Johns Hopkins UP, 2013.

Granger, John. *Harry Potter as Ring Composition and Ring Cycle*. [s.l.]: Unlocking Press, 2011.

Granger, John. *Harry Potter's Bookshelf: The Great Books behind the Hogwarts Adventure.* New York: Berkley Books, 2009.

Granger, John. *The Deathly Hallows Lectures: The Hogwarts Professor Explains Harry's Final Adventure.* Allentown: Zossima Press, 2008.

Granger, John. *How Harry cast his spell: the meaning behind the mania for J. K. Rowling's bestselling books.* Carol Stream: Tyndale House Publishers, 2008.

Granger, John. *Unlocking Harry Potter: Five Keys for the Serious Reader.* Hadlock: Zossima Press, 2007.

Granger, John. *The Hidden Key to Harry Potter: Understanding the Meaning, Genius and Popularity of Joanne Rowling's Harry Potter Novels.* Hadlock: Zossima Press, 2003.

Gupta, Suman. *Re-Reading Harry Potter*. Basingstoke: Palgrave Macmillan 2003.

Houghton, John. *The Harry Potter Effect: Taking a Closer Look at the Complete Series.* Eastbourne: David C. Cook, 2007.

Houghton, John. *A Closer Look at Harry Potter: Bending and Shaping the Minds of Our Children.* Eastbourne: 2001.

Kirk, Connie Ann. *The J. K. Rowling Encyclopedia*. Westport, Conn: Greenwood Press, 2006.

Kreuter, Lisa. *Fantasy Worlds: A Comparison of "Harry Potter", "The Lord of
the Rings" and "His Dark Materials"*. Saarbrücken: VDM Verlag Dr. Müller,
2011.

Kronzek, Allan Zola and Kronzek, Elizabeth. *The Sorcerer's Companion: A
Guide to the Magical World of Harry Potter*. 2nd, extended edition. New York:
Broadway Books, 2004.

MacDonald, Joan Vos. *J. K. Rowling: Banned, challenged, and censored*. Berke-
ley Heights, NJ: Enslow Publishers, 2006.

Manlove, Colin N. *The Order of Harry Potter: Literary skill in the Hogwarts
epic*. Cheshire: Winged Lion Press, 2011.

Mayes-Elma, Ruthann. *Harry Potter: Feminist Friend or Foe?* Rotterdam:
SensePublishers, 2007.

Mayes-Elma, Ruthann. *Females and Harry Potter: not all that empowering*.
Lanham, Md: Rowman & Littlefield Publishers, 2006.

Moore, P. D. *What Every Kid Should Know About Harry Potter: Not for Muggles*. Enfield: Lux Verbi, 2003.

More, Jacques R. *Harry Potter - the catalyst*. London: Jarom Books, 2002.

Nel, Philip. *J K Rowling's Harry Potter Novels. A Reader's Guide*. New York,
London: Continuum International Publishing Group, 2001.

Prinzi, Travis. *Harry Potter & Imagination: The Way Between Two Worlds*. Allentown: Zossima Press, 2008.

Rana, Marion. *Creating Magical Worlds: Otherness and Othering in Harry Potter*. Frankfurt am Main: Peter Lang, 2009.

Saxena, Vandana. *The Subversive Harry Potter: Adolescent Rebellion and Con-
tainment in the J. K. Rowling Novels*. Jefferson: McFarland, 2012.

Schafer, Elizabeth D. *Exploring Harry Potter: The Unapproved Beacham's
Sourcebook*. Osprey, Fla: Beacham Publishing Group, 2000.

Thomas, James W. *Rowling Revisited: Return Trips to Harry, Fantastic Beasts,
Quiddich, & Beedle the Bard*. Allentown: Zossima Press, 2010.

Thomas, James W. *Repotting Harry Potter*. Allentown: Zossima Press, 2009.

Trevarthen, Geo Athena. *The Seeker's Guide to Harry Potter: The Unauthorized Course.* Winchester: O Books, 2008.

Vander Ark, Steve et al. *The Lexicon: An Unauthorized Guide to Harry Potter Fiction and Related Material.* Muskegon/Michigan: RDR Books, 2009.

Vander Ark, Steve. *In search of Harry Potter.* London: Methuen, 2008.

Villaluz, Nancy Solon. *Does Harry Potter Tickle Sleeping Dragons?* Seattle: Ramance Press, 2008.

Waters, Galadriel and Mithrandir, Astre. *Ultimate Unofficial Guide to the Mysteries of Harry Potter.* Niles, IL: Wizarding World Press, 2003.

Wesam, Ibrahim. *Linguistic Approaches to Crossover Fiction: Towards an Integrated Approach to the Analysis of Text Worlds in Children's Crossover Fantasy Fiction.* Saarbrücken: VDM Verlag Dr. Müller, 2011.

Westman, Karin E. *J. K. Rowling's Library: Harry Potter in Context.* Jackson, Miss: UP of Mississippi, 2003.

Wolosky, Shira. *The Riddles of Harry Potter: Secret Passages and Interpretative Quests.* New York: Palgrave Macmillan, 2010.

Wrigley, Christopher. *The Return of the Hero.* Lewes: Book Guild, 2005.

Theses

Aas, Grethe. "J. K. Rowling, Harry Potter, and contemporary society: The Harry Potter books as social criticism." MA Thesis, Universitetet i Oslo, 2004.

Ackman, Nicole. "Gender portrayal in J. K. Rowling's "Harry Potter and the Order of the Phoenix": A Feminist Rhetorical Criticism." M.Sc. Thesis, South Dakota State University, 2007.

Amnell, Malin. "Harry Potter and the philosopher's stone: Its place within the genre of fantasy fiction." Student Thesis, Luleå Tekniska Universitet, 2001.

Andreasen, Anne-Johanne. "Explaining Harry Potter: Development of a generic hybrid." Thesis, Center for Engelsk, Syddansk Universitet, Odense, 2004.

Angel, Will A. "An Immortal Science: Alchemy's Role in "Harry Potter and the Deathly Hallows."" MA Thesis, East Carolina University, 2011.

Angerer, Christina. "Patterns of Heroism in Harry Potter." MA Thesis, Universität Salzburg, 2010.

Arch, Wendy Michelle Ryun. "A living fire to enlighten the darkness": Allegorical interpretations of Madeleine L'Engle's "A Wrinkle in Time" and J. K. Rowling's "Harry Potter and the Sorcerer's Stone."" MA Thesis, Iowa State University, 2010.

Bader, Simone. "Magic as a phenomenon in children's books. An analysis of J. M. Barrie's Peter Pan, Roald Dahl's The Witches and J. K. Rowling's Harry Potter." MA Thesis, Universität Innsbruck, 2004.

Bakke, Kristine Ohrem. "A muggle's study of Harry Potter's magical world: J. K. Rowling's literary texts and Chris Columbus' film adaptations." MA Thesis, Universitetet i Oslo, 2004.

Baltzar, Birgit. "Power and Evil in J. K. Rowling's Harry Potter Novels." MA Thesis, Tampereen yliopisto, 2007.

Bamdas, Jo Ann Tucker. "Imagination at work: Improving Adult Literacy with the 'Harry Potter' Novels." MA Thesis, Florida Atlantic University, 2002.

Beatty, Bronwyn. "The Currency of Heroic Fantasy: The Lord of the Rings and Harry Potter from Ideology to Industry." PhD Thesis, Massey University, Auckland, 2006.

Beck, Ann Sandra. "The Power of Literacy in J. K. Rowling's Harry Potter: The Making/Unmaking of the World." PhD Thesis, University of Victoria, 2008.

Bekaan, Brigitte. "The reception of J. K. Rowling's Harry Potter in Britain and Germany: a comparative study." MA Thesis, Carl-von-Ossietzky-Universität Oldenburg, 2002.

Bertilsson, Andreas. "Freaks and Muggles - Intolerance and prejudice in Harry Potter and the Philosopher's Stone." Student Thesis, Högskolan Kristianstad, 2008.

Brown, Angela. "Harry Potter and the gender structure: Exploring gender in "The Goblet of Fire."" MA Thesis, The University of Calgary, 2008.

Brüggler, Andrea Nicola. "An analysis of the Harry Potter phenomenon." MA Thesis , Universität Salzburg, 2002.

Cantrell, Sarah K. "When Worlds Collide: Heterotopias in Fantasy for Young Adult Readers in France and Britain." PhD Thesis, The University of North Carolina at Chapel Hill, 2010.

Chappell, Shelley Bess. "Werewolves, Wings, and Other Weird Transformations: Fantastic Metamorphosis in Children's and Young Adult Fantasy Literature." PhD Thesis, Macquarie University, 2007.

Dahlén, Nova. "Severus Snape and the Concept of the Outsider: Aspects of Good and Evil in the Harry Potter Series." Thesis, Karlstad Universitet, 2009.

Daniel, Carolyn. "All that Glitters is not Gold: Reading Harry Potter." BA Honours Thesis, Victoria University of Technology, 2000.

Davies, Alison E. "Endlessly Talking: An Investigation into the Success of the Harry Potter Books by J. K.Rowling." M.Ed. Thesis, University of Melbourne, 2001.

Eilefsen, Lilly. "The life of Tom Marvolo Riddle aka Lord Voldemort: A study of the origin of evil and how it is portrayed in fantasy." Thesis, Universitetet i Agder, 2008.

Fenske, Claudia. "Muggles, Monsters and Magicians. A Literary Analysis of the Harry Potter Series." PhD Thesis, Philipps-Universität Marburg, 2008.

Flüchter, Annika. "Happily ever after. The fantasy of family in Harry Potter and Twilight." MA thesis, Leuphana Universität, 2012.

Gamweger, Philipp Werner Andre. "Magical Elements and Creatures and Their Underlying Concepts and Myths in Rowling's Harry Potter Series." MA Thesis, Universität Graz, 2013.

Gaul, Reinhard. "Language as element and mirror of complexity in literature. An investigation into the construction of complexity in "Harry Potter", volumes 1 and 4." MA Thesis , Universität Graz, 2003.

Glinsman, Melanie. "Harry Potter and the Reimagined Fairy Tale: J. K. Rowling's Use and Manipulation of Fairy Tale Narrative in the Harry Potter Series." MA Thesis, University of Nebraska at Kearney, 2011.

Gottsbachner, Birgit. "The Uncanny in "Harry Potter."" MA Thesis, Universität Wien, 2007.

Harkamp, Anna. "Othering and the Representation of Racism in Joanne K. Rowling's Harry Potter Novels." MA Thesis, Universität Graz, 2013.

Hatfield, Rachel. "Social Categorization of Op Ed Discourse in Harry Potter." MA Thesis, University of Kansas, 2010.

Heider, Marlene. "Rowling's Harry Potter and Stroud's Bartimaeus: The creation of fantastic worlds." MA Thesis, Universität Wien, 2009.

Hijazi, Skyler James. "Bodily Spectacles, Queer Re-Visions: The Narrative Lives of "Harry Potter" Slash Online." M.A. Thesis, University of Arizona, 2007.

von Hilsheimer, Tessa. "Word Magic: Defining Harry Potter's World in New Terms." MA Thesis, East Carolina University, 2011.

Hirsch, Anne-Christin. "Names and their underlying mythology in J. K. Rowling's Harry Potter-Novels." Student Thesis, Universität Leipzig, 2008.

Hirvonen, Ritva. "The Retrolutionary Fantasy in Harry Potter and the Chamber of Secrets." MA Thesis, Joensuun yliopisto, 2002.

Höberth, Ursula Eva. "Gendered heroes? Male and female hero construction in J. K. Rowling's "Harry Potter and the Philosopher's Stone" and Philip Pullman's "Northern Lights."" MA Thesis, Universität Wien, 2012.

Holmqvist, Kristina. "Rowling's use of family in Harry Potter and the philosopher's stone, Harry Potter and the chamber of secret's, Harry Potter and the prisoner of Azkaban." Student Thesis, Luleå tekniska Universitet, 2003.

Holst, Oscar. "Becoming The Chosen One: The Choice, Identity and Destiny of Harry Potter." Student Thesis, Högskolan i Kalmar, 2008.

Horsthemke, Maximilian. "Harry Potter, the Familiar Hero." BA Thesis, Ruhr-Universität Bochum, 2011.

Huber, Melanie. "Harry Potter and its success as a mass phenomenon." MA Thesis, Universität Innsbruck, 2004.

Hüls, Simone. "Disrobing the White Wizard: A Postcolonial Examination of Race and Culture in 'Harry Potter'." MA Thesis, The University of Alabama, 2004.

Hunter, Cheryl A. "Mythological Heroes and the Presence of the Hero and Journey Archetypes in "The Lord of the Rings" and "Harry Potter"." MA Thesis in Library Studies, University of New Hampshire, 2007.

Kmochová, Terezie. "Heritage of Celtic Myths, Legends, Traditions and Rituals in Harry Potter Books." BA Thesis, Univerzita Pardubice, 2007.

Lakka, Anne-Maria. "Foster Parenting in L.M. Montgomery's Anne of Green Gables and J. K. Rowling's Harry Potter Novels - Representations of Parenting in Two Classic Children's Novel Series from the Early and the Late 20th Century." MA Thesis, Tampereen yliopisto, 2009.

Lehtonen, Sanna. "Contemporary British Society in the Magic World of J. K. Rowling's Harry Potter books 1997-2000." MA Thesis, Jyväskylän Yliopisto, 2003.

Lima, Katherine. "Morality Through the Ages: A Look at Morality in J. K. Rowling's "Harry Potter and the Deathly Hallows" in Relation to Geoffrey Chaucer's "The Pardoner's Tale."" MA Thesis, California State University, 2010.

Limbach, Gwendolyn. "Conjuring Her Self: Hermione's Self-Determination in Harry Potter." Senior Honors Thesis, Pace University/Pforzheimer Honors College, 2007.

Mayes-Elma, Ruthann Elizabeth. "A Feminist Literary Criticism Approach to Representations of Women's Agency in Harry Potter." PhD Thesis, Miami University, 2003.

McGee, Chris. "The Mysterious Childhood: The Child Detective from the Hardy Boys to Harry Potter." PhD Thesis, Illinois State University, 2004.

McKeever, Alison Elisabeth. "Dickensian Characters in J. K. Rowling's "Harry Potter."" MA Thesis, University of Arkansas, 2012.

Mintzer, Conor Andrew. "Growing Up in Time: Mapping a Theory of Temporal Navigation Through the Bildungsromane of Charles Dickens and J. K. Rowling." MA Thesis, Georgetown University, 2010.

Mukhopadhyay, Malini. "Harry, England and St. George: An analysis of J. K. Rowling's use of merrie England and New Britain in the Harry Potter series." Senior Honors Thesis, Dartmouth College, 2011.

Muller, Cathleen. "Harry Potter and the Rescue from Realism: A Novel Defense of Anti-Realism about Fictional Objects." PhD Thesis, Ohio State University, 2012.

Napolitano, Marc Philip. "Of Waifs and Wizards." MA Thesis, Villanova University, 2006.

Noren, Mary Elizabeth. "Beneath The Invisibility Cloak: Myth and The Modern World View in J. K. Rowling's Harry Potter." MA Thesis, Wright State University, 2007.

Pääkkönen, Eeva-Liisa. "Hero myth and elements of de- and remythologisation in J. K. Rowling's Harry Potter." MA Thesis, Oulun yliopisto, 2006.

Pawley, Daniel W. "Popular Privation: Suffering in Fan Cultures." PhD Thesis, The University of Edinburgh, 2007.

Posch, Katharina. "The portrayal of good and evil in two cult books for children. J. K. Rowling's Harry Potter novels and J. M. Barrie's "Peter Pan."" MA Thesis, Universität Wien, 2002.

Powers, Andrea R. "Magical Triumph or Miserable Illusion? Gender and Race Constructions in "Harry Potter and the Sorcerer's Stone" and "Harry Potter and the Chamber of Secrets."" MA Thesis, University of Colorado at Boulder, 2007.

Reading, Jill. "Critical Literacy in a Global Context: Reading Harry Potter." PhD Thesis, Edith Cowan University, 2006.

Renath, Katharina. "Location, characters and education in contemporary school stories. "The prime of Miss Jean Brodie", "Dead poets society" and "Harry Potter."" MA Thesis, Universität Wien, 2008.

Rhymes, Martha Young. "The Phenomenal 'Harry Potter' Books: A Cultural Study of Corporate Influence on Reading Instruction and Image-Making." EdD Thesis, Georgia Southern University, 2003.

Ronkainen, Essi-Lotta. "Rewriting the school series: Formulaic elements in J. K. Rowling's Harry Potter series." MA Thesis, Turun yliopisto, 2006.

Rybråten, Kristine. "Harry Potter: Tradition and innovation." MA Thesis, Universitetet i Oslo, 2004.

Samuelsen, Kjersti Riise. "Fantasy and magic in children's literature: an analysis of The Lion, the Witch and the Wardrobe, Matilda and Harry Potter and the Chamber of Secrets." MA Thesis, Universitetet i Bergen, 2007.

Santoso, Yokhebed. "A Study of the Dominant's ideology and its hegemony over the marginal in Joanne Kathleen Rowling's Harry Potter Series." BA Thesis, Petra Christian University, 2005.

Silva, J. Rodolfo. "The Cat Who Reads the Map: Posthumanism and Animality in Harry Potter." BA Thesis, Universidade Federal de Santa Catarina, 2009.

Skartveit, Brit Elin. "" ... a witch in the family!": Sexist language in the chronicle of Narnia and the Harry Potter series." MA Thesis, Universitetet i Bergen, 2005.

Skoglund, Kristin Flaten. "The war between good and evil in children's literature: A study of children's fiction by C.S. Lewis, Roald Dahl and J. K. Rowling." MA Thesis, Universitetet i Bergen, 2003.

Soares Faria, Paula. "The Journey of the Villain in the Harry Potter series: An Archetypal Study of Fantasy Villains." MA Thesis, Universidade Federal de Minas Gerais, 2008.

Spitzer, Drennan C. "Models of Medievalism in the Fiction of C.S. Lewis, J.R.R. Tolkien and J. K. Rowling." PhD Thesis, University of California, 2005.

Stolz, Michaela. "Neologisms and xenisms in selected novels by J. K. Rowling and J. R. R. Tolkien." MA Thesis, Universität Graz, 2005.

Taylor, Jeanne Zanussi. "The Symbolic Order of the Phoenix: The Fracturing of the Family Romance and the Quest for the Real in J. K. Rowling's "Harry Potter" Series." MA Thesis, Tennessee State University, 2011.

Tellefsen, Tonje Holtan. "Killing time: The uses of violence in the Potter books." MA Thesis, Høgskolen i Agder, 2006.

Ward, Renee Michelle. "Cultural Contexts and Cultural Change: The Werewolf in Classical, Medieval, and Modern Texts.' PhD Thesis, University of Alberta, 2009.

Watts, Robin. "The Secret World of Harry Potter. The Literary Laws of Fantasy Applied to the Novels by J. K. Rowling." Student Thesis, Institutionen för genus, kultur och historia, Södertörns högskola, 2007.

Waugh, Kirsty. "Mixing Memory and Desire: Recollecting the Self in Harry Potter and His Dark Materials." MA Thesis, Massey University, 2009.

van der Wey, Amanda Leanne. ""Harry Potter and the Philosopher's Stone": Shifting Centres, Margins, and Publics." MA Thesis, Trent University, 2011.

Wilkes, Hannah Meleney. ""All was well": "Harry Potter" in the Medievalist Tradition." MA Thesis, The University of Alabama, 2011.

Winterink, Heiltje. "Harry Potter through the years: A reception study of American and Dutch reviews." MA Thesis, Universiteit Utrecht, 2008.

Wolfbauer, Irmtraud Maria. "Constructions of Good and Evil in J. K. Rowling's Harry Potter Books." MA Thesis, Universität Graz, 2010.

Articles

Adney, Kristine Karley. "From Books to Battle: Hermione's Quest for Knowledge in Harry Potter and the Order of the Phoenix." Topic: The Washington and Jefferson College Review 54 (2004): 103-112.

Alderson, Brian. "Harry Potter, Dido Twite, and Mr. Beowulf." The Horn Book Magazine 76:3 (2000): 349-352.

Algeo, John. "A Fancy for the Fantastic: Reflections on Names in Fantasy Literature." Names: A Journal of Onomastics 49:4 (Dec 2001): 248-253.

Arden, Heather and Lorenz, Kathryn. "The Harry Potter Stories and French Arthurian Romance." Arthuriana. The Journal of Arthurian Studies 13:2 (2003): 54-68.

Barfield, Steven. "Fantasy and the Interpretation of Fantasy in Harry Potter." Topic: The Washington and Jefferson College Review 54 (2004): 24-32.

Barton, Julie. "Fantasy World, Realistic Issues: Contemporary Socio-Political Imagery in Harry Potter." The Journal of Children's Literature Studies 5:1 (2008): 53-67.

Battis, Jes. "Transgendered Magic: The Radical Performance of the Young Wizard in YA Literature."The Looking Glass: An On-line Children's Literature Journal 10:1 (2006).

Beach, Sara Ann and Willner, Elizabeth Harden. "The Power of Harry: The Impact of J. K. Rowling's Harry Potter Books on Young Readers." World Literature Today (Winter 2002): 102-106.

Beck, Bernard. "The Sunny Side of Life: Harry Potter, K-PAX, Bandits and the Forces of Good in a Wicked World." Multicultural Perspectives 4:3 (2002): 21-24.

Behr, Kate. "'Same-as-Difference': Narrative Transformations and Intersecting Cultures in Harry Potter." Journal of Narrative Theory 35:1 (Winter 2005): 112-132.

Berman, Lauren. "Dragons and Serpents in J. K. Rowling's Harry Potter Series: Are They Evil?" Mythlore: A Journal of J. R. R. Tolkien, C. S. Lewis, Charles Williams, and Mythopoeic Literature 27:1-2 (2008): 45-65.

Bérubé, Michael. "Harry Potter and the Power of Narrative."The Common Review 6:1 (2007): 15-20.

Billone, Amy. "The Boy Who Lived. From Carroll's Alice and Barrie's Peter Pan to Rowling's Harry Potter." Children's Literature 32 (2004): 178-202.

Black, Rena. "Privation and Perversion: The Nature of Evil in J. K. Rowling's Harry Potter Series." Tolle Lege (Mount Saint Mary's University Emmitsburg, Maryland) 2 (2008): 35-43.

Black, Sharon. "Harry Potter: A Magical Prescription for Just about Anyone." Journal of Adolescent and Adult Literacy 46:7 (2003): 540-544.

Black, Sharon. "The Magic of Harry Potter: Symbols and Heroes of Fantasy." Children's literature in Education 34:3 (2003): 237-247.

Blackford, Holly. "Private Lessons from Dumbledore's 'Chamber of Secrets': The Riddle of the Evil Child in Harry Potter and the Half-Blood Prince." Lit: Literature Interpretation Theory 22:2 (2011): 155-175.

Blake, Andrew; Carretero-González, Margarita; and Marquez-Linares, Carlos F. "... And then came the Fall: on the nature of evil in J.R.R. Tolkien's and J. K. Rowling's arch-villains."Perspectives on Evil and Human Wickedness 1:3 (2003): 170-181.

Butler, Rebecca R. "Harry Potter and the Politics of Oppression." The Journal of Children's Literature Studies 5:1 (2008): 68-87.

Byam, Paige. "Children's Literature or Adult Classic? The Harry Potter Series and the British Novel Tradition." Topic: The Washington and Jefferson College Review 54 (2004): 7-13.

Caldecott, Léonie. "Harry Potter and the Culture of Life." Chesterton Review: The Journal of the G. K. Chesterton Institute 27:1-2 (2001): 119-123.

Canton, Jeffrey. "Harry Potter, Instant Classic." The Looking Glass: An On-line Children's Literature Journal 4:2 (2000).

Casares, Allyson J. "The Effect of Book Banning on Child Culture: A Close Look at the Harry Potter Series." The Looking Glass: An On-line Children's Literature Journal 8:3 (2004).

Cecire, Maria. "Harry Potter and the Poetics of Paranoia in the Oxford School of Children's Literature." The Journal of Children's Literature Studies 5:1 (2008): 88-109.

Chappell, Drew. "Sneaking Out After Dark: Resistance, Agency, and the Postmodern Child in JK Rowling's Harry Potter Series." Children's Literature in Education 39:4 (2008): 281-293.

Chappell, Shelley. "Contemporary Werewolf Schemata: Shifting Representations of Racial and Ethnic Difference." International Research in Children's Literature 2 (2009): 21-35.

Cherland, Meredith. "Harry's girls: Harry Potter and the discourse of gender." Journal of Adolescent and Adult Literacy 52:4 (2008): 273-282.

Chevalier, Noel. "The Liberty Tree and the Whomping Willow: Political Justice, Magical Science, and Harry Potter." The Lion and the Unicorn 29:3 (2005): 397-415.

Croft, Janet Brennan. "Naming the Evil One: Onomastic Strategies in Tolkien and Rowling." Mythlore: A Journal of J. R. R. Tolkien, C. S. Lewis, Charles Williams, and Mythopoeic Literature 28 (2009): 149-163.

Croft, Janet Brennan. "The Education of a Witch: Tiffany Aching, Hermione Granger, and Gendered Magic in Discworld and Potterworld." Mythlore: A Journal of J. R. R. Tolkien, C. S. Lewis, Charles Williams, and Mythopoeic Literature 27 (2009): 129-142.

Cummins, June. "The Secret World of Harry Potter." Michigan Quarterly Review 39:3 (2000): 661-666.

Curthoys, Ann. "Harry Potter and historical consciousness: Reflections on history and fiction." History Australia 8:1 (2011): 7-22.

Dendle, Peter. "Cryptozoology and the Paranormal in Harry Potter: Truth and Belief at the Borders of Consensus." Children's Literature Association Quarterly 36:4 (2011): 410-425.

Devlin-Glass, Frances. "Contesting Binarisms in Harry Potter: Creative Rejigging, or Gender Tokenism?" English in Australia 144 (2005): 50-63.

Diffendal, Lee Ann. "Questioning Witchcraft and Wizardry as Obscenity: Harry Potter's Potion for Regulation." Topic: The Washington and Jefferson College Review 54 (2004): 55-62.

Dodd, Antony N.; Hotta, Carlos T.; and Gardner, Michael J. "Harry Potter and the prisoner of presumption." Nature 437 (15 September 2005): 318.

Doniger, Wendy. "Can You Spot the Source?" London Review of Books (17 February 2000): 26-27.

Downes, Daragh. "Harry Potter and the Deathly Hollowness: A Narratological and Ideological Critique of J. K. Rowling's Magical System." International Research in Children's Literature 3 (2010): 162-175.

Eagleton, Mary. "The Danger of Intellectual Masters: Lessons from Harry Potter and Antonia Byatt." Revista Canaria de Estudios Ingleses 48 (2004): 61-75.

Edwards, Owen Dudley. "Harry Potter and History." Chesterton Review: The Journal of the G. K. Chesterton Institute 27:1-2 (2001): 112-119.

Farmer, Joy. "The Magician's Niece: The Relationship between J. K. Rowling and C. S. Lewis." Mythlore: A Journal of J. R. R. Tolkien, C. S. Lewis, Charles Williams, and Mythopoeic Literature 23:2 [88] (Spring 2001): 53-64.

Fife, Ernelle. "Wise Warriors in Tolkien, Lewis, and Rowling." Mythlore: A Journal of J. R. R. Tolkien, C. S. Lewis, Charles Williams, and Mythopoeic Literature 25:1-2 [95-96] (2006): 147-162.

Fitzsimmons, Rebekah. "Testing the Tastemakers: Children's Literature, Bestseller List, and the "Harry Potter Effect." Children's literature 40 (2012): 78-107.

Flaherty, Jennifer. "Harry Potter and the Freedom of Information: Knowledge and Control in Harry Potter and the Order of the Phoenix." Topic: The Washington and Jefferson College Review 54 (2004): 93-102.

Fleming-Fido, Penelope. "'Well—are girls like boys, then?' Genre and the Gender Divide in School Stories." New Review of Children's Literature and Librarianship 10:1 (2004): 79-89.

Fry, Michele. "Heroes and heroines: myth and gender roles in the Harry Potter books." The New Review of Children's Literature and Librarianship 7 (2001): 157-167.

Galway, Elizabeth A. "Reminders of Rugby in the Halls of Hogwarts: The Insidious Influence of the School Story Genre on the Works of J. K. Rowling."Children's Literature Association Quarterly 37:1 (2012): 66-85.

Garbe, Gabriele and Siebold, Jörg. "Harry Potter and the World of Wizards and Dragons." Fremdsprachenunterricht 44/53 (2000): 317-318.

Goatly, Andrew. "Corpus Linguistics, Systemic Functional Grammar and Literary Meaning: A Critical Analysis of Harry Potter and the Philosopher's Stone." Ilha do Desterro: A Journal of English Language, Literatures in English and Cultural Studies 46 (2008): 115-154.

Gómez Pascual, Natalia. "A Bridge between Two Different Worlds: On the Reflection and Fracture of Stereotypes in the Harry Potter Novels." Anuario de Investigación en Literatura Infantil y Juvenil 5 (2007): 91-108.

Green, Amy M. "Interior/Exterior in the Harry Potter Series: Duality Expressed in Sirius Black and Remus Lupin." Papers on Language and Literature 44:1 (2008): 87-108.

Green, Lelia, and Guinery, Carmen. "Harry Potter and the Fan Fiction Phenomenon." M/C Journal 7:5 (12 November 2004), http://journal.media-culture.org.au/0411/14-green.php.

Haas, Heather A. "The wisdom of wizards - and muggles and squibs: Proverb use in the world of Harry Potter." The Journal of American Folklore 124 (2011): 29-54.

Hall, Jordana. "Embracing the Abject Other: The Carnival Imagery of Harry Potter." Children's Literature in Education 42:1 (2011): 70-89.

Harris, Marla. "Is Seeing Believing? Truth and Lies in Harry Potter and the Order of the Phoenix." Topic: The Washington and Jefferson College Review 54 (2004): 83-92.

Hess, Mary E. "Resisting the Human Need for Enemies, or What Would Harry Potter Do?" Word and World 28:1 (2008): 47-56.

Hiquiana, Alfonso M. "Harry Potter's Analogical World." Diliman Review 49:3-4 (2001): 66-75.

Hoppenstand, Gary. "The not-so-age-old debate." The Journal of Popular Culture 37:3 (2004): 375-379.

Horne, Jackie C. "Harry and the Other: Answering the Race Question in J. K. Rowling's Harry Potter." The Lion and the Unicorn 34:1 (2010): 76-104.

Hutcheon, Linda. "Harry Potter and the Novice's Confession." The Lion and the Unicorn 32:2 (2008): 169-179.

Innocenti, Orsetta. "The Magic of Make-Believe: Reading, Plots and Protagonists in the Harry Potter Series". LiCuS. Journal of Literary Theory and Cultural Studies 3 (2008): 35-52.

Jacobs, Alan. "Harry Potter's Magic." First Things 99 (January 2000): 35-38.

Jacobs, Dawn Ellen. "Tolkien and Rowling: Reflections on Reception." Topic: The Washington and Jefferson College Review 54 (2004): 46-54.

Jacoby, Kathryn. "Harry-Is That Potter, Percy or Plantagenet? A Note on Shakespeare's 1 Henry IV in the Transitional Novels of J. K. Rowling." Borrowers and Lenders: The Journal of Shakespeare and Appropriation 2:1 (2006).

Jones, Jo. "The Nostalgic Appeal of Harry Potter: Regressive or Radical?" English in Australia: The Journal of the Australian Association for the Teaching of English Inc.140 (2004): 47-54.

Kidd, Dustin. "Harry Potter and the Functions of Popular Culture." The Journal of Popular Culture 40 (2007): 69-98.

Kidd, Kenneth. "Outing Dumbledore." Children's Literature Association Quarterly 33:2 (2008): 186-206.

Köhler, Ulrike Kristina. "Harry Potter - National Hero and National Heroic Epic." International Research in Children's Literature 4:1 (2011): 15-28.

Langford, David. "Hogwarts Proctology Class: Probing the End of Harry Potter." New York Review of Science Fiction 20:2 [230] (2007): 1, 8-11.

Lankshear, Colin John and Knobel, Michele. "Harry Potter: A boy for all seasons." Journal of Adolescent and Adult Literacy 44:7 (2001): 664-666.

Le Lievre, Kerrie Anne. "Wizards and Wainscots: Generic Structures and Genre Themes in the Harry Potter Series." Mythlore 24:1 (2003): 25-36.

Lockman, Darcy. "The fantastic Harry Potter." Instructor 110:1 (2000): 53.

Loidl, Sonja. "Constructions of Death in Young Adult Fantastic Literature." International Research in Children's Literature 3 (2010): 176-189.

MacGreevy, Ann Loftus. "Under her spell: an analysis of the creativity of JK Rowling." Gifted Education International 19:1 (2004): 34-41.

McCarron, Bill. "Basilisk Puns in Harry Potter and the Chamber of Secrets." Notes on Contemporary Literature 36:1 (Jan 2006): 2.

McCarron, Bill. "Power vs. Authority in Harry Potter and the Order of the Phoenix." Notes on Contemporary Literature 34:5 (2004): 8-10.

McCarron, Bill. "Literary Parallels in Harry Potter and the Chamber of Secrets." Notes on Contemporary Literature 33:1 (2003): 7-8.

McCay, M.A. "Harry Potter: Literature or the Rubbish Heap of Literature?" New Orleans Review 26:3/4 (2000): 168-178.

McDaniel, Kathryn N. "Harry Potter and the Ghost Teacher: Resurrecting the Lost Art of Teaching." The History Teacher 43:2 (2010): 289-297.

McEvoy, Kathleen. "Aesthetic Organization: The Structural Beauty of J. K. Rowling's Harry Potter Series." Topic: The Washington and Jefferson College Review 54 (2004): 14-23.

McIlroy, Thad. "Harry Potter and the Sustainable Forest." The Seybold Report 7:15 (2007): 6f.

Mendlesohn, Farah. "Crowning the King: Harry Potter and the Construction of Authority." Journal of the Fantastic in the Arts 12:3 (2001): 287-308.

Mikulan, Krunoslav. "Harry Potter through the Focus of Feminist Literary Theory: Examples of (Un)Founded Criticism." Uluslararası Sosyal Araştırmalar Dergisi / Journal of International Social Research 2 (2009): 288-298.

Mikulan, Krunoslav. "The Archaic Attraction of Harry Potter." LiCuS - Journal of Literary Theory and Cultural Studies 1:1 (2006): 31-48.

Miller, Karl. "Magic in the Air." Changing English 8:1 (2001): 29-34.

Miller, Karl. "Harry and the Pot of Gold." Raritan: A Quarterly Review 20:3 (Winter 2001): 132-140.

Mills, Alice. "Harry Potter and the Terrors of the Toilet." Children's Literature in Education 37:1 (2006): 1-13.

Mullen, Alexandra. "Harry Potter's Schooldays: Tom Brown, Harry Potter, and other Schoolboy Heroes." The Hudson review: A magazine of literature and the arts 53:1 (2000): 127-135.

Mynott, Glen. "Harry Potter and the public school narrative." The New Review of Children's Literature and Librarianship 5/1999: 13-27.

Natov, Roni. "Harry Potter and the Extraordinariness of the Ordinary." The Lion and the Unicorn 25:2 (2001): 310-327.

Nilsen, Alleen Pace and Nilsen, Don L. F. "Six Literary Functions of Name-Play in J. K. Rowling's Harry Potter Books." Onoma: Journal of the International Council of Onomastic Sciences 40 (2005): 65-81.

Norman, Emma R. "International Boggarts: Carl Schmitt, Harry Potter and the Transfiguration of Identity and Violence." Politics & Policy 40:3 (2012): 403-423.

Norman and Delfin. "Wizards under Uncertainty: Cognitive Biases, Threat Assessment and Misjudgments in Policy Making." Politics & Policy 40:3 (2012): 369-402.

Nylund, David. "Reading Harry Potter: Popular Culture, Queery Theory and The Fashioning of Queer Identity." Journal of Systemic Therapies 26:2 (2007): 13-24.

Ormes, Sarah. "The strange case of Harry Potter and the invisible Marijuana." Multimedia information & technology 25:4 (1999): 325-333.

Oziewicz, Marek: "Representations of Eastern Europe in Philip Pullman's 'His Dark Materials', Jonathan Stroud's 'The Bartimaeus Trilogy', and J. K. Rowling's 'Harry Potter' Series." International Research in Children's Literature 3:1 (2010): 1-14.

Patkin, Terri Toles. "Constructing a New Game: J. K. Rowling's Quidditch and Global Kid Culture." Reconstruction: Studies in Contemporary Culture 6:1 (2006). http://reconstruction.eserver.org/061/toles-patkin.shtml

Payne, Michael. "Hogwarts and the Austere academy: Reviving the school story." Bookbird 41:2 (2003): 20-24.

Pennington, John. "From Elfland to Hogwarts, or the Aesthetic Trouble with Harry Potter." The Lion and The Unicorn 26:1 (2002): 78-97.

Perry, Tonya. "Taking Time: Harry Potter as a Context for Interdisciplinary Studies." English Journal 95:3 (2006): 100-103.

Petrina, Alessandra. "Forbidden Forest, Enchanted Castle: Arthurian Spaces in the Harry Potter Novels." Mythlore: A Journal of J. R. R. Tolkien, C. S. Lewis, Charles Williams, and Mythopoeic Literature 24:3-4 [93-94] (2006): 95-110.

Phipps, Alison. "Languages, Identities, Agency: Intercultural Lessons from Harry Potter." Language & Intercultural Communication 3:1 (2003): 6-19.

Pond, Julia. "A Story of the Exceptional: Fate and Free Will in the Harry Potter Series." Children's Literature 38 (2010): 181-206.

Prewitt, Janice C. "Heroic Matriculation: The Academies of Spenser, Lewis, and Rowling." West Virginia University Philological Papers 53 (2006): 25-34.

Pugh, Tison and Wallace, David L. "Heteronormative Heroism and Queering the School Story in J. K. Rowling's Harry Potter Series." Children's Literature Association Quarterly 31:3 (2006): 260-281.

Pugh, Tison and Wallace, David L. "A Postscript to 'Heteronormative Heroism and Queering the School Story in J. K. Rowling's Harry Potter Series.'" Children's Literature Association Quarterly 33:2 (2008): 188-192.

Purkiss, Diane. "From Bedford Falls to Pottersville: Harry Potter, consuming narratives, and bad writing." The Journal of Children's Literature Studies 5:1 (2008): 110-134.

Radigan, Winifred M. "Connecting the Generations: Memory, Magic, and Harry Potter." Journal of Adolescent & Adult Literacy 44 (2001): 694.

Rafer, David. "Symbols for the Post-Mythical Society: Myth-Making in J. K. Rowling's Harry Potter Series." Critical Engagements: A Journal of Criticism and Theory 1:1 (2007): 188-210.

Rana, Marion. "'The less you lot have ter do with these foreigners, the happier yeh'll be': Cultural and National Otherness in J. K. Rowling's Harry Potter Series." International Research in Children's Literature 4:1 (2011): 45-58.

Rauhofer, Judith. "Defence against the Dark Arts: How the British Response to the Terrorist Threat Is Parodied in J K Rowling's 'Harry Potter and the Half Blood Prince'." International Journal for Liability and Scientific Enquiry 1:1/2 (2007): 94-113.

Reiss, Ellen. "Nature, Romanticism, & Harry Potter." The Right of Aesthetic Realism to Be Known 1420 (21 June 2000): 1-2.

Robbins, Ruth Anne. "Harry Potter, Ruby Slippers and Merlin: Telling the Client's Story using the Characters and Paradigm of the Archetypal Hero's Journey." Seattle University Law Review 29:4 (Fall 2006): 767.

Robertson, Judith P. "What Happens to our Whishes: Magical Thinking in Harry Potter." Children's Literature Association Quarterly 26:4 (2001/2002): 198-211.

Rollin, Lucy. "Harry and Frodo: From page to screen and back again." The Five owls 16:3 (2002): 52-53.

Rollin, Lucy. "Among School Children: The Harry Potter Books and the School Story Tradition." South Carolina Review 34:1 (2001): 198-208.

do Rozario, Rebecca-Anne C. "Harry Potter and the Adults." The Journal of Children's Literature Studies 5:1 (2008): 32-52.

Saltman, Judith; Denton, Peter H.; and Opar, Tamara. "Understanding the Harry Potter Frenzy and Furor." Journal of Youth Services in Libraries 15:3 (2002): 24-35.

Saltman, Judith. "Harry Potter's Family Tree." Journal of Youth Services 15:3 (Spring 2002): 22-26.

Sattaur, Jennifer. "Harry Potter: A World of Fear." The Journal of Children's Literature Studies 3:1 (2006): 1-14.

Schmid, Hannah and Klimmt, Christoph. "A magically nice guy: Parasocial relationships with Harry Potter across different cultures." International Communication Gazette 73:3 (2011): 252-266.

Semaan, Ingrid Leyer. "Harry Potter and the Proverbial Armenian Merchant." The Haigazian Armenological Review 20 (2002): 295-430.

Siegel, Lee. "Harry Potter and the Spirit of the Age: Fear of Not Flying." New Republic. A Journal of Politics and the Arts (22 November 1999): 40.

da Silva, Maria Carolina and Paraíso, Marlucy Alves. "The Harry Potter's Syllabus: Representations of School and Syllabus in Children's and Adolescent Literature." Educação: Teoria e Prática 22:39 (2012): 99-116.

Silva, Roberta. "The Risk of Conformity: Representing Character in Mass Market Fiction and Narrative Media." International Research in Children's Literature 3 (2010): 75-91.

Simmons, Amber M. "Fusing Fantasy Films and Traditional Adolescent Texts to Support Critical Literacy: The Harry Potter Series and The Giver." Signal Journal: The Journal of the International Reading Association's Special Interest Group 34:2 (2011): 25-30.

Stevenson, Iain. "Harry Potter, Riding the Bullet and the Future of Books: Key Issues in the Anglophone Book Business." Publishing Research Quarterly 24:4 (2008): 277-284.

Stone, Jim. "Harry Potter and the Spectre of Imprecision." Analysis 70:4 (2010): 638-644.

Storck, Inez Fitzgerald. "J. K. Rowling: A Wounded Imagination." Chesterton Review: The Journal of the G. K. Chesterton Institute 27:1-2 (Feb-May 2001): 103-106.

Stover, Lynne Farrell. "Library at Hogwarts: Classification, Alliteration, Imagination and Prolongation." School Library Media Activities Monthly 17:6 (2001): 28-29.

Strait, Daniel H. "____." Chesterton Review: The Journal of the G. K. Chesterton Institute 27:1-2 (Feb-May 2001): 99-123. Special section.

Strimel, Courtney B. "The Politics of Terror: Rereading 'Harry Potter'." Children's literature in Education 35:1 (2004): 35-52.

Sturgis, Amy H. "Harry Potter Is A Hobbit: Rowling, Tolkien, and The Question of Readership." CSL. The Bulletin of The New York C.S. Lewis Society 401 35:3 (May/June 2004): 1-10, 12-13.

Stypczynski, Brent. "Wolf in Professor's Clothing: J. K. Rowling's Werewolf as Educator." Journal of the Fantastic in the Arts 20 (2009): 57-69.

Sutton, Roger. "What Hath Harry Wrought?" The Horn Book Magazine 88:3 (2012): 10-16.

Talamo, Joseph A. "Harry Potter and the Hauted Prophet." Psychological Perspectives: A Quarterly Journal of Jungian Thought 52:3 (2009): 335-346.

Tambovtsev, Yuri; Tambovtsev, Ludmila; and Tambovtsev, Juliana. "Some Stylistic Typological Distances between the Prose of Some British Writers." Studia Anglica Posnaniensia: An International Review of English Studies 39 (2003): 247-261.

Tigner, Steven S. "A Right Imagination." Chesterton Review: The Journal of the G. K. Chesterton Institute 27:1-2 (2001): 102f.

Tucker, Nicholas. "The Rise and Rise of Harry Potter." Children's Literature in Education 115:4 (1999): 221-234.

Virole, Benoît. "Harry Potter's Cauldron: The Power of Myth and the Rebirth of the Sacred." Queen's Quarterly 111:3 (Fall 2004): 371-379.

Waetjen, Jarrod and Gibson, Timothy A. "Harry Potter and the Commodity Fetish: Activating Corporate Readings in the Journey from Text to Commercial Intertext." Communication and Critical Cultural Studies 4:1 (2007): 3-26.

Wannamaker, Annette. "Men in Cloaks and High-heeled Boots, Men Wielding Pink Umbrellas: Witchy Masculinities in the Harry Potter novels." The Looking Glass: An On-line Children's Literature Journal 10:1 (2006): http://www.lib.latrobe.edu.au/ojs/index.php/tlg/article/view/96/81

Webb, Caroline. "'Abandoned boys' and 'pampered princes': Fantasy as the journey to reality in the Harry Potter sequence." Explorations into Children's Literature 18:2: 15-21.

Westman, Karin E. "'The Weapon We Have Is Love'." Children's Literature Association Quarterly 33:2 (2008): 193-199.

Westman, Karin E. "Perspective, Memory, and Moral Authority: The Legacy of Jane Austen in J. K. Rowling's Harry Potter." Children's Literature 35 (2007): 145-165.

White, Gertrude M. "Harry Potter and the Spell of Love." Chesterton Review: The Journal of the G. K. Chesterton Institute 27:1-2 (2001): 106f.

Whited, Lana. "1492, 1942, 1992: The Theme of Race in the Harry Potter Series." The Looking Glass: An On-line Children's Literature Journal 10:1 (2006): http://www.lib.latrobe.edu.au/ojs/index.php/tlg/article/view/97/82.

Whited, Lana A. "McGonagall's Prophecy Fulfilled: The Harry Potter Library." The Lion and the Unicorn 27:3 (2003): 416-425.

Willson-Metzger, Alicia and Metzger, David. "But Is He Really Smart? Gardner's Multiple Intelligences Theory in the World of Harry Potter." Popular Culture Review 14:2 (2003): 55-61.

Winters, Sarah Fiona. "Bubble-wrapped children and safe books for boys: the politics of parenting in 'Harry Potter'." Children's Literature 39 (2011): 213-233.

Wood, Andelys. "Quidditch Rules: Sport in the Postmodern School Story." Journal of Kentucky Studies 21 (Sept 2004): 155-160.

Woodford, Donna C. "Disillusionment in Harry Potter and the Order of the Phoenix." Topic: The Washington and Jefferson College Review 54 (2004): 63-72.

Wu, Yung-Hsing. "The Magical Matter of Books: Amazon.com and The Tales of Beedle the Bard." Children's Literature Association Quarterly 35 (2010): 190-207.

Wyler, Lia. "Harry Potter for Children, Teenagers and Adults." Meta - Traduction pour les enfants 48:1-2 (2003): 5-14.

Yaggi, Miranda Maney. "Harry Potter's Heritage: Tolkien as Rowling's Patronus against the Critics." Topic: The Washington and Jefferson College Review 54 (2004): 33-45.

Yeo, Michelle. "Harry Potter and the Chamber of Secrets: Feminist Interpretations/Jungian Dreams." Studies in Media & Information Literacy Education 4:1 (2004): 1-10.

Zimmerman, Virginia. "Harry Potter and the Gift of Time." Children's Literature 37 (2009): 194-215.

Chapters

Andrade, Glenna. "Hermione Granger as Girl Sleuth." in Nancy Drew and Her Sister Sleuths: Essays on the Fiction of Girl Detectives, edited by Michael G. Cornelius, Melanie E. Gregg, 164-178, Jefferson: McFarland, 2008.

Arden, Heather and Lorenz, Kathryn. "The Ambiguity of the Outsider in the Harry Potter Stories and Beyond." in The Image of the Outsider in Literature, Media, and Society: Selected Papers, 2002 Conference, Society for the Interdisciplinary Study of Social Imagery, edited by Will Wright and Steven Kaplan, 430-434, Pueblo, Colo.: Society for the Interdisciplinary Study of Social Imagery, University of Southern Colorado, 2002.

Arendt, Elycia. "The Great Harry Potter Debate." in *Braveheart and Broomsticks: Essays on Movies, Myths, and Magic*, edited by Elycia Arendt, 73-86, Haverford, PA: Infinity Publishing.com, 2002.

Blackford, Holly. "Private Lessons from Dumbledore's 'Chamber of Secrets': The Riddle of the Evil Child in Harry Potter and the Half-Blood Prince." in *The "Evil Child" in Literature, Film and Popular Culture*, edited by Karen J. Renner, 87- 107, London: Routledge, 2013.

Blackford, Holly Virginia. "The Riddle of Féminine Écriture in J. K. Rowling's Harry Potter and the Chamber of Secrets (1998)." in *The Myth of Persephone in Girls' Fantasy Literature*, edited by Holly Virginia Blackford,181-198, New York: Routledge, 2011.

Brude-Firnau, Gisela. "From Faust to Harry Potter: discourses of the centaurs."*Goethe's Faust: Theatre of Modernity*, edited by Hans Schulte, John Noyes and Pia Kleber, 113-128, Cambridge, New York: Cambridge UP, 2011.

Burger, Alissa. "Magical Learning and Loss: Hermione Granger and the Female Intellectual in Harry Potter." in *Supernatural Youth: The Rise of the Teen Hero in Literature and Popular Culture*, edited by Jes Battis, Lanham: Lexington Books, 2011.

Campbell, Lori M. "J. R. R. Tolkien and the Child Reader: Images of Inheritance and Resistance in The Lord of the Rings and J. K. Rowling's Harry Potter." in *How We Became Middle-Earth: A Collection of Essays on The Lord of the Rings*, edited by Adam Lam, Nataliya Oryschchuk and Howard McNaughton, 291-310 Zollikofen: Walking Tree, 2007.

Carretero-González, Margarita. "A Tale as Old as Time, Freshly Told Anew: Love and Sacrifice in Tolkien, Lewis and Rowling." in *Myth and Magic: Art according to the Inklings*, edited by Eduardo Segura and Thomas Honegger, 241-265, Zollikofen: Walking Tree, 2007.

Carretero González, Margarita. "A Male Cinderella: Heritage and Reception of the Harry Potter Books." in *A Life in Words. A Miscellany Celebrating Twenty-Five Years of Association between the English Department of Granada University and Mervyn Smale (1977-2002)*, edited by Margarita Carretero González et al., 51-58, Granada: Editorial de la Universidad de Granada 2002.

Caselli, Daniella. "Reading Intertextuality: The Natural and the Legitimate. Intertextuality in 'Harry Potter'." in *Children's Literature: New Approaches*, edited by Karin Lesnik-Oberstein, 168-188, Basingstoke: Palgrave Macmillan, 2004.

Christensen, Jørgen Riber. "Certain Regressive Tendencies in Rowling and Tolkien." in *Marvellous Fantasy,* edited by Jørgen Riber Christensen , 45-57, Aalborg: Aalborg Universitetsforlag, 2009.

Corinth, Jacqueline. "Food Symbolism in Three Children's Literature Texts: Grahame's The Wind in the Willows, Dahl's Charlie and the Chocolate Factory and Rowling's Harry Potter Novels," in *You Are What You Eat: Literary Probes into the Palate,* edited by Annette M. Magid, 260-283, Newcastle: Cambridge Scholars Publishing, 2008.

Coward, Jo. "The Harry Potter challange to children's literature." in *Seriously playful: Genre, performance and text,* edited by Sharyn Pearce and Kerry Mallan, 239-246, Flaxton/Qld: Post Pressed, 2004.

Crabtree, Sara. "Harry the Hero? The Quest for Self-Identity, Heroism, and Transformation in the 'Goblet of fire'," in *From Colonialism to the Contemporary: Intertextual Transformation in World Children's and Youth Literature,* edited by Lance Weldy, 61-75, Newcastle-upon-Tyne: Cambridge Scholars, 2007.

Cronn-Mills, Kirstin and Samens, Jessica: "Sorting heroic choices: green and red in the Harry Potter septology." in *Millennial Mythmaking: Essays on the Power of Science Fiction and Fantasy Literature, Films and Games,* edited by John Perlich and David Whitt, 5-31, Jefferson: McFarland & Co., 2010.

Cummins, June. "Hermione in the bathroom: menarche, the grotesque, and female development in Harry Potter and The Philosopher's Stone." in *The Gothic in children's literature: Haunting the borders,* edited by Anna Jackson, Karen Coats and Roderick McGillis, 177- 194, New York: Routledge, 2007.

Dendle, Peter. "Anglo-Saxonism in the Harry Potter Series." in *Critical Insights: Contemporary Speculative Fiction,* edited by M. Keith Booker, 86-99, Ipswich: Salem Press, 2013.

Desilet, Gregory E. "Deconstructing Harry Potter: The Hidden Cultural Costs of the Most Popular Children's Fantasy." in *Transformative Communication Studies: Culture, Hierarchy, and the Human Condition,* edited by Omar Swartz, 161-189, Leicester: Troubador, 2008.

Desilet, Gregory E. "Epic/Serial Melodrama: Star Wars, Harry Potter, and Lord of the Rings." in *Our Faith in Evil: Melodrama and the Effects of Entertainment Violence,* edited by Gregory E. Desilet, 265-275, Jefferson: McFarland, 2006.

Doughty, Amie E. "Just a Fairy, His Wit, and Maybe a Touch of Magic: Magic, Technology, and Self-Reliance in Contemporary Fantasy Fiction." in *Chil-*

dren's Literature and Culture, edited by Harry Edwin Eiss, 53-76, Newcastle upon Tyne: Cambridge Scholars, 2007.

Eccleshare, Julia. "'Most Popular Ever': The Launching of Harry Potter." in *Popular Children's Literature in Britain,* edited by Julia Briggs, Dennis Butts and M. O. Grenby, 287-300, Aldershot: Ashgate, 2008.

Ehnenn, Jill R. "Queering Harry Potter." in *Queer Popular Culture,* edited by Thomas Peele, 229-256, New York: Palgrave Macmillan, 2011.

Falconer, Rachel. "Harry Potter, Lightness and Death." in *The Crossover Novel: Contemporary Children's Fiction and its Adult Readership,* 43-72, New York: Routledge, 2009.

Field, Hana S. and Weech, Terry. "'Book Banning and Boggarts:' Harry Potter and Issues of Accessibility to Children's Literature." in *Providing Access to Information for Everyone: Proceedings of the 16th BOBCATSSS Symposium, 28-30 January 2008, Zadar, Croatia,* edited by Petra Hauke, 49-55, Bad Honnef: Bock+Herchen, 2008.

Gibson, Michelle and Meem, Deborah T: "Performing Transformation: Reflections of a Lesbian Academic Couple." in *Lesbian Academic Couples,* edited by Michelle Gibson and Deborah T. Meem, 107-128, New York: Harrington Park, 2005.

Gillis, Stacy. "The Brand, the Intertext, and the Reader: Reading Desires in the 'Harry Potter' Series." in *Popular Children's Literature in Britain,* edited by Julia Briggs, Dennis Butts and M. O. Grenby, 301-315, Aldershot: Ashgate, 2008.

Goodman, Robin Truth. "Philosopher's Stoned: Harry Potter's Public." In: *World, Class, Women: Global Literature, Education, and Feminism,* by Robin Truth Goodman, 53-94, New York: Routledge Falmer, 2004.

Griesinger, Emily. "The search for 'deeper magic': J. K. Rowling and C.S. Lewis." in *The gift of story: Narrating hope in a postmodern world,* edited by Emily Griesinger and Mark A. Eaton, 317- 332, Waco, Tex: Baylor UP, 2006.

Hayles, Dianne. "Nonhuman Animals, Inclusion, and Belonging in Harry Potter and the Philosopher's Stone." in *Knowing their Place? Identity and Space in Children's Literature,* edited by Terri Doughty and Dawn Thompson, 187-199, Newcastle upon Tyne: Cambridge Scholars, 2011.

Hibbs, Thomas. "Virtue, Vice, and the Harry Potter Universe." in *The Changing Face of Evil in Film and Television,* edited by Martin F. Norden, 89-99, Amsterdam: Rodopi, 2007.

Hochbruck, Wolfgang. "'Vulchanov! Volkov! Aaaaaaand Krum!' Joanne K. Rowling's 'Eastern' Europe." in *Facing the East in the West: Images of Eastern Europe in British Literature, Film and Culture*, edited by Barbara Korte, Eva Ulrike Pirker, and Sissy Helff, 233-244, Amsterdam: Rodopi, 2010.

Hofmann, Annette R. "From Tom Brown's school days to Harry Potter. The role of sport in English literature." in *Sport and Education in History: Proceedings of the 8th ISHPES Congress, Urbino, Italy*, edited by Gigliola Gori and Thierry Terret, 417-422, Sankt Augustin: Academia-Verlag, 2005.

Johnson-Haddad, Miranda. "Harry Potter and the Shakespearean Allusion." in *Reimagining Shakespeare for Children and Young Adults*, edited by Naomi J. Miller, 162-170, New York: Routledge, 2003.

Jordan, Timothy. "Security in the social: Gardens and Harry Potter." in *Security: Sociology and social worlds,* edited by Simon Carter, Timothy Jordan, and Sophie Watson, 17-46, Manchester: Manchester UP, 2008.

Kennedy, Valerie. "In Search of the 'Imaginative Golden Age in Time or Space': Narrative Form in Tanglewreck, Harry Potter and the Philosopher's Stone, and The Golden Compass." in *Winterson Narrating Time and Space*, edited by Mine Özyurt Kılıç and Margaret Sönmez, 139-154, Cambridge: Cambridge Scholars Publishing, 2009.

Lurie, Alison. "The Perils of Harry Potter." in *Boys and Girls Forever: Children's Classics from Cinderella to Harry Potter,* written by Alison Lurie, 113-123, London 2003.

Mayes-Elma, Ruthann. "Got Agency? Representations of Women's Agency in Harry Potter." in *Kinderculture: the corporate construction of childhood.* 2nd edition, edited by Shirley R. Steinberg and Joe L. Kincheloe Boulder, 181-206, Colorado: Westview Press, 2004.

McDaniel, Kathryn N. "The Elfin Mystique: Fantasy and Feminism in J. K. Rowling's Harry Potter Series." in *Past Watchful Dragons: Fantasy and Faith in the World of C. S. Lewis,* edited by Amy H. Sturgis, 183-207, Altadena, CA: Mythopoeic, 2007.

McGavock, Karen."In Pursuit of the Golden Snitch: Harry Potter and the representation of adulthood." in *Children's Fantasy Fiction: Debates for the Twenty First Century*, edited by Nickianne Moody and Clare Horrocks, 75-90, Liverpool: The Association for Research in Popular Fictions and Liverpool John Moores University, 2005.

McWilliams, Susan. "The Crisis of Slavery in Harry Potter." in *Damned if you do: Dilemmas of action in literature and popular culture*, edited by Margaret S. Hrezo and John M. Parrish,137-164, Lanham: Lexington Books, 2010.

Orbaugh, Sharalyn. "Girls Reading Harry Potter, Girls Writing Desire: Amateur Manga and Shojo Reading Practices." in *Girl Reading in Japan*, edited by Tomoko Aoyama and Barbara Hartley, 174-187, London: Routledge, 2010.

Orgelfinger, Gail. "J. K. Rowling's Medieval Bestiary." in *Defining Medievalism(s),* edited by Karl Fugelso, 141-160, Cambridge: D.S. Brewer, 2009.

Pedersen, Lene Yding. "Harry Potter and the Ending Hallows." in *Marvellous Fantasy*, edited by Jørgen Riber Christensen, 17-44, Aalborg: Aalborg Universitetsforlag 2009.

van Peer, Willie. "The Secret of Harry Potter." in *Textual Secrets. The Message of the Medium. Proceedings of the 21st PALA-Conference, April 12-15, 2001,* edited by Judit Zerkowitz and Szilvia Csabi, 84-89, Budapest: Eötvös Loránd UP, 2002.

Pennington, John. "Peter Pan, Pullman, and Potter: Anxieties of Growing Up." in *J. M. Barrie's Peter Pan In and Out of Time: A Children's Classic at 100,* edited by Donna R. White and Anita C. Tarr, 237-262, Lanham, MD: Scarecrow, 2006.

Petrina, Alessandra. "One Thousand Magical Herbs and Beasts: Medieval Elements in the Harry Potter Saga." in *Children's Fantasy Fiction: Debates for the Twenty First Century*, edited by Nickianne Moody and Clare Horrocks, 161-174, Liverpool: Association for Research in Popular Fiction, 2005.

Pharr, Mary F. "From the Boy Who Lived to the Girl Who Learned: Harry Potter and Katniss Everdeen." in *Of Bread, Blood and The Hunger Games: Critical Essays on the Suzanne Collins Trilogy*, edited by Mary F. Pharr and Leisa A. Clark, 219-228, Jefferson: McFarland, 2012.

Pinsent, Pat. "Theories of Genre and Gender: Change and Continuity in the School Story." in *Modern Children's Literature. An Introduction,* edited by Kimberley Reynolds, 8-22, Basingstoke: Palgrave Macmillan, 2005.

Pinsent, Pat. "From Tyke Tiler to Harry Potter: Recent Variations on the School Theme." in *School Stories from Bunter to Buckeridge,* edited by Nicholas Tucker, 8-22, Lichfield: Pied Piper Publishing, 1999.

Polk, Bryan. "The Medieval Image of the Hero in the Harry Potter Novels." in *The Image of the Hero in Literature, Media, and Society: Selected Papers, 2004 Conference, Society for the Interdisciplinary Study of Social Imagery*, edited by Will Wright and Steven Kaplan, 440-445, Pueblo, Colo: Colorado State University, 2004.

Pütz, Babette. "Harry Potter and Oedipus: Heroes in Search of their Identities." in *Super/Heroes: From Hercules to Superman,* edited by Angela Ndalianis, Chris Mackie, and Wendy Haslem, 225-235, Washington, DC: New Academia Publishing, 2007.

Rothman, Ken. "Hearts of Darkness: Voldemort and Iago, with a Little Help from Their Friends." in *Vader, Voldemort, and Other Villains: Essays on Evil in Popular Media,* edited by Jamey Heit, 202-217, Jefferson: McFarland, 2011.

Routledge, Christopher. "Harry Potter and the Mystery of Ordinary Life." in *Mystery in children's literature,* edited by Adrienne E. Gavin and Christopher Routledge, 202-207. New York 2001

Saxena, Vandana and Multani, Angelie. "Plotting Hogwarts: Situating the School Ideologically and Culturally." in *Literature for Our Times: Postcolonial Studies in the Twenty-First Century,* edited by Bill Ashcroft et al., 469-484, Amsterdam: Rodopi, 2012.

Starrs, D. Bruno. "Quidditch: J. K. Rowling's Leveler." in *Playing the Universe: Games and Gaming in Science Fiction,* edited by David Mead and Pawel Frelik, 77-85, Lublin: Wydawnictwo Uniwersytetu Marii Curie-Skłodowskiej w Lublinie, 2007.

Thompson, Deborah L. "Deconstructing Harry: Casting a critical eye on the witches and wizards of Hogwarts." in *Beauty, brains, and brawn: The construction of gender in children's literature,* edited by Susan Lehr, 42-50, Portsmouth, NH: Heinemann, 2001.

Totaro, Rebecca Carol Noel. "Suffering in Utopia: Testing the limits in young adult novels." in *Utopian and dystopian writing for children and young adults,* edited by Carrie Hintz and Elaine Ostry, 127-138, New York: Routledge, 2002.

Velazquez, Maria. "The Occasional Ethnicities of Lavender Brown: Race as a Boundary Object in Harry Potter." in *Critical Insights: Contemporary Speculative Fiction,* edited by M. Keith Booker, 100-114, Ipswich: Salem Press, 2013.

Ward, Renee. "Remus Lupin and Community: The Werewolf Tradition in J. K. Rowling's Harry Potter Series." in *The Year's Work in Medievalism,* edited by Gwendolyn A. Morgan, 26-40, Eugene/OR: Wipf and Stock, 2006.

Węgrodzka, Jadwiga. "Harry Potter and the Motif of the Book." in *The Lives of Texts: Exploring the Metaphor,* edited by Katarzyna Pisarska and Andrzej Sławomir Kowalczyk, 115-128, Newcastle upon Tyne: Cambridge Scholars, 2012.

Westman, Karin E. "Blending Genres and Crossing Audiences: *Harry Potter* and the future of Literary fiction." in *The Oxford Handbook of Children's Literature*, edited by Julia Mickenberg and Lynne Vallone, 93-113, Oxford: Oxford UP, 2010.

Wilcox, Rhonda. "When Harry Met Buffy: Buffy Summers, Harry Potter, and Heroism." in *Why Buffy matters: The art of Buffy the Vampire Slayer,* edited by Rhonda Wilcox, 66-78, London: I.B. Tauris, 2005.

Winters, Sarah Fiona. "Good and Evil in the Works of Diana Wynne Jones and J. K. Rowling." in *Diana Wynne Jones: An Exciting and Exacting Wisdom,* edited by Teya Rosenberg, Martha P. Hixon, Sharon M. Scapple, and Donna R. White, 79-95, New York: Peter Lang, 2002.

Wygant, Amy. "The Golden Fleece and Harry Potter." in *The Meanings of Magic: From the Bible to Buffalo Bill*, edited by Amy Wygant, 179-198, New York: Berghahn Books, 2006.

Zipes, Jack. "The Phenomenon of Harry Potter, or Why All the Talk?" in *Sticks and Stones: The Troublesome Success of Children's Literature from Slovenly Peter to Harry Potter*, by Jack Zipes, 170-189, New York, London: Routledge, 2001.

Zock, Hetty. "Cultural Anxieties in Harry Potter and the Half-Blood Prince. Evil and the magic of human abilities." in *At the Crossroads of Art and Religion: Imagination, Commitment, Transcendence,* edited by Hetty Zock, 101-116, Leuven: Peeters, 2008.

Harry Potter in the Classroom

Monographs

Belcher, Catherine L. and Stephenson, Becky Herr. *Teaching Harry Potter: The Power of Imagination in Multicultural Classrooms*. New York: Palgrave Macmillan, 2011.

Breyer, Michelle. *A Guide for Using Harry Potter and the Sorcerer's Stone and Other Harry Potter Books in the Classroom*. Westminster: Teacher Created Materials, 2002.

Perry, Phyllis Jean. *Teaching the Fantasy Novel: From The Hobbit to Harry Potter and the Goblet of Fire*. Portsmouth, NH: Teacher Idea Press, 2003.

Potts-Klement, Edina. *Harry Potter as a Fairy Tale in the Twentieth Century: The Teaching Aspect: How to Teach a Fairy Tale?* Saarbrücken: VDM Verlag Dr. Müller, 2008.

Theses

Carter, Jeanne Noelle. "What would Captain Underpants do? A Literary Analysis of Children in School." PhD Thesis, University of Alaska, 2006.

Drouillard, Colette. "Growing up with Harry Potter: What motivated youth to Read?" PhD Thesis, The Florida State University, 2009.

L'Esperance, Jordanna M. "Harry Potter and the Transitions Group: A Developmental Curriculum." PsyD Thesis, Antioch New England Graduate School, 2006.

Hinojosa, Manuel Matthew. "Teaching outre literature rhetorically in first-year composition." PhD Thesis, The University of Arizona, 2005.

Kiesi-Talpiainen, Taija. "Using literature in the language classroom: Grade six meets Harry Potter." MA Thesis, Turun yliopisto, 2003.

Kokkonen, Tiia. "Discourse between teacher and student: The effect of teacher's style of communication on learning environment as viewed in literature and the cinema."BA Thesis, University of Jyväskylä, Finland, 2009.

Nåmdal, Torunn. "Children's literature and the child reader: A study of the ideology at work in children's fiction and its possible influence on child readers, with particular reference to texts by Lewis Carroll, Roald Dahl and J. K. Rowling." MA Thesis, Universitetet i Bergen, 2003.

Nedoma, Jeannette, and Meyer, Rebecca Elisabeth. "Harry Potter and the Philosopher's Stone - Literature in the English Classroom." Student Thesis, Ernst-Moritz-Arndt-Universität Greifswald, 2007.

Novosel, Jadranka. "The Harry Potter Phenomenon and Its Implications for Literacy Education." MA Thesis, University of British Columbia, 2010.

Simonen, Anne. "Children and their Books: Children's ideas about Harry Potter and the Philosopher's Stone." MA Thesis, Tampereen yliopisto, 2003.

Stuart, Gina Anne. "Exploring the Harry Potter Book series: A Study of Adolescent Reading Motivation." PhD Thesis, Utah State University, 2006.

Titus, Timothy Warren. "Muggle Studies 101: What magic motivates so many children to read Harry Potter?" MA Thesis, California State University, 2003.

Wheeler, Päivi. "Harry Potter: A popular book with a group of children in Amuri school in Tampere. Why?" MA Thesis, Tampereen yliopisto, 2003.

Articles

Ashton, Jean. "Barbie, the Wiggles and Harry Potter. Can Popular Culture Really Support Young Children's Literacy Development?" *European Early Childhood Education Research Journal* 13:1 (2005): 31-40.

Barr, K. "Magic and mind maps. Continuing the Harry Potter theme." *Literacy and Learning* 23 (2002): 9-13.

Barta, James and L'Ai, Linda. "Galleons, Magic Potions, and Quidditch: The Mathematics of Harry Potter." *Teaching Children Mathematics* 11:4 (Nov 2004): 210-216.

Beaton, M. J. "Harry Potter as a Context for Problem-Based Learning." *Science Scope* 27:4 (2004): 15-17.

Beaton, Tisha. "Teacher to Teacher: Harry Potter in the Mathematics Classroom." *Mathematics Teaching in the Middle School* 10:1 (2004), 23-25.

Booth, Margaret Zoller and Booth, Grace Marie. "Tips from Harry Potter for American Schools: Insights on what these books say about education." *Education Digest* 69:6 (2004): 4-11.

Booth, Margaret Zoller and Booth, Grace Marie. "What American Schools Can Learn from Hogwarts School of Witchcraft and Wizardry." *Phi Delta Kappan* 85:4 (2003): 310-315.

Brown, Molly. "Harry Potter and the Reluctant Reader: Strategies for Encouraging Reading Fluency." *Mousaion: South African Journal for Information Studies* 27:1 (2009): 47-57.

Cavilia, Francesco and Delfino, Manuela. "Harry Potter and the Quest for Knowledge: A Commonplace for Reflecting on Learning and Teaching." *L1 Educational Studies in Language and Literature* 9:3 (2009): 29-48.

Christensen, Paula. "Harry Potter, Edgar Allen Poe, and The Internet." *Technology and Teacher Education Annual* 6 (2006): 3872-3874.

Chua, Boon Liang. "Harry Potter and the Cryptography with Matrices."*Australian Mathematics Teacher* 62:3 (2006): 25-27.

Deets, Stephen. "Wizarding in the Classroom: Teaching Harry Potter and Politics." *PS, Political Science & Politics* 42:4 (2009): 741-744.

DeMitchell, Todd A. and Carney, John J. "Harry Potter and the Public School Library." *Phi Delta Kappan* 87:2 (October 2005): 159-165.

DeMitchell, Todd A. and Carney, John J. "Harry Potter, wizards, and muggles. The First Amendment and the reading curriculum." *Education Law Reporter* 173:2 (2003): 363-379.

Dickinson, Renée. "Harry Potter Pedagogy: What We Learn about Teaching from J. K. Rowling." *The Clearing House* 79:6 (2006): 240-244.

Dudink, Peter. "Harry Potter anti-hero. From mis-education to conflict mismanagement." *The New Review of Children's Literature and Librarianship* 8 (2002): 203-221.

Duffy, Edward. "Sentences in Harry Potter: students in future writing classes." *Rhetoric Review* 21:2 (2002): 170-187.

Gruner, Elisabeth Rose. "Teach the Children: Education and Knowledge in Recent Children's Fantasy." *Children's Literature: Annual of The Modern Language Association Division on Children's Literature and The Children's Literature Association* 37 (2009): 216-235.

Hallell, Pamela Esprívalo and Morton, Andrea: "Muggles, Wizards, and Witches: Using Harry Potter Characters to Teach Human Pedigrees." *Science Activities* 39 (Summer 2002): 24-29.

Howe, Roger. "Hermione Granger's Solution." *Mathematics Teacher* (Feb. 2002): 86-89.

Knudson, D. "Invite Harry Potter to Physical Education Class." *Strategies* 14:6 (2001): 36-37.

Kooy, Mary. "Riding the Coattails of Harry Potter: Readings, Relational Learning, and Revelations in Book Clubs." *Journal of Adolescent and Adult Literacy* 47:2 (2003): 136-145.

Marshall, Joanne M. "Critically Thinking about Harry Potter: A Framework for Discussing Controversial Works in the English Classroom." *The ALAN Review* 30:2 (2003): 16-19.

McShea, Betsy; Vogel, Judith; and Yarnevich, Maureen. "Harry Potter and the Magic of Mathematics." *Mathematics Teaching in the Middle School* 10:8 (2005): 408-415.

Nilsen, Alleen Pace and Nilsen, Don L. F. "Latin revived: Source-based vocabulary lessons courtesy of Harry Potter." *Journal of Adolescent and Adult Literacy* 50:2 (2006): 128-135.

Nilsen, Alleen Pace and Nilsen, Don L. F. "Lessons in the teaching of vocabulary from September 11 and Harry Potter." *Journal of Adolescent and Adult Literacy* 46:3 (2002): 254-261.

Nicola, Ruth. "Returning to Reading with Harry Potter." *Journal of Adolescent & Adult Literacy* 44 (2001): 747-750.

Rasekh, Abbas Eslami and Shomoossi, Nematullah. "The Hidden Curriculum in Children's Literature: The Hogwarts School of Witchcraft and Wizardry." *Iranian Journal of Language Studies* 2:3 (2008): 359-380.

Randall, Jessy. "Wizard Words: The Literary, Latin, and Lexical Origins of Harry Potter's Vocabulary." *Verbatim: The Language Quarterly* 26:2 (2001): 1, 3-7.

Wagner, Meaghan M. and Lachance, Andrea. "Mathematical adventures with Harry Potter." *Teaching Children Mathematics* 10:5 (2004): 274-227.

Wallace, David L. and Pugh, Tison. "Teaching English in the World: Playing with Critical Theory in J. K. Rowling's Harry Potter Series." *English Journal* 96:3 (2007): 97-100.

Chapters

Beeby, Allison. "Language Learning for Translators: Designing a Syllabus." in *Translation in Undergraduate Degree Programmes,* edited by Kirsten Malmkjær, 39-65, Amsterdam, Netherlands: Benjamins, 2004.

Bland, Janice. "Critical Education Potential with Young Adult Literature in Language Education: The Harry Potter Series in the Literature Class." in *Basic issues in EFL teaching and learning,* edited by Maria Eisenmann and Theresa Summer, 203-215, Heidelberg: Winter, 2012, 203-215.

Fisher, Douglas; Flood, James; and Lapp, Diane. "Material Matters: Using Children's Literature to Charm Readers (or Why Harry Potter and the Princess Diaries Matter)." in *Best Practices in Literacy Instruction, 2nd edition,* edited by Lesley Mandel Morrow, Linda B. Gambrell, and Michael Pressley, 167-186, New York: Guilford Press, 2003.

Fitzsimmons, John. "Speaking Snake: Authentic Learning and the Study of Literature." in *Authentic Learning Environments in Higher Education Information Science,* edited by Anthony Herrington and Jan Herrington, 162-171, Hersley: Information Science Publishing, 2006.

Harada, Naoko. "'Nothing to Worry About': Anxiety-reduction Strategies in Harry Potter's Class and Mine." in *Realizing Autonomy: Practice and Reflection in Language Education,* edited by Kay Irie and Alison Stewart, 196-209, Basingstoke: Palgrave Macmillan, 2012.

Jentsch, Nancy K. "Harry Potter and the Tower of Babel: Translating the Magic." in *The Translation of Children's Literature. A Reader,* edited by Gillian Lathey, 190-207, Clevedon, Tonawanda: Multilingual Matters, 2006.

Marshall, Joanne M. "Critically Thinking about Harry Potter: A Framework for Discussing Controversial Works in the English Classroom." in *Reflective teaching, reflective learning: How to develop critically engaged readers, writers, and speakers,* edited by Thomas M. McCann et al., 178-188, Portsmouth: Heinemann, 2005.

Harry Potter in Translation

Theses

Astrén, Johanna. "Hogwarts, Muggles and Quidditch: A Study of the Translation of Names in J. K. Rowling's Harry Potter Books." Student Thesis, Institutionen för Humaniora och språk, Högskolan Dalarna, Falun, 2004.

Eriksson-Nummela, Susanna. "Names and their translation into Finnish in the fantastic world of Harry Potter and the Philosopher's Stone." MA Thesis, Vaasan yliopisto, 2002.

Erlangga, Muzakir. "An Analysis Of Compound Sentence In J. K Rowling's Harry Potter And The Sorcerer's Stone." Thesis, University of North Sumatra, 2008.

Fernandes, Lincoln P. "Brazilian Practices of Translating Names in Children's Fantasy Literature: A Corpus-based Study." PhD Thesis, Universidade Federal de Santa Catarina, 2004.

Helgegren Sofia. "Tracing Translation Universals and Translator Development by Word Aligning a Harry Potter Corpus." BA Thesis, Linköpings universitet, Institutionen för datavetenskap/Kognitionsvetenskapliga programmet, 2005.

Hera, Oksana. "Translation strategies of Victor Morozov (as based on the Ukrainian translation of Joanne K. Rowling's "Harry Potter" book series)." MA Thesis, Department of Translation Studies and Contrastive Linguistics, Lviv University/Ucraine, 2007.

Holm, Katja Elisabeth. "Alohomora! Accessing Harry Potter's world through the magic of translation: A study of the Norwegian and Swedish translations of 'Harry Potter and the Philosopher's stone'." Student Thesis , Institutionen för litteraturvetenskap och idéhistoria, Stockholms universitet, 2005.

Kumpumäki, Petri. "Study of the names of the main characters and other central concepts and their translations in Harry Potter and the Philosopher's Stone." MA Thesis, Oulun yliopisto, 2006.

Lempinen, Satu. "Deconstructing Harry: On syntactic aspects of readability in the Finnish translation of J. K. Rowling's Harry Potter and the Goblet of Fire." Thesis, Helsingin yliopisto, 2004.

Malkki, Aila. "Reflections on innovatory translation: With special reference to quotability in two Finnish translations of British fantasy fiction." MA Thesis, Helsingin yliopisto, 2005.

McDonough, Julie. "Muggles, and Quidditch, and Squibs, Oh My! A Study of Names and Onomastic Wordplay in Translation, with a Focus on the Harry Potter Series." MA Thesis, University of Ottawa, 2004.

Mörk, Charlotte. "Using Harry Potter as a "Mirror of Erised": What can Swedish teenagers learn from reading the book series as a school project?" Thesis, Göteborgs Universitet, Sweden/The University of Sussex, 2008.

Olsen, Tora. "The Norwegian Translation of Harry Potter: Bringing Down the Magic Brick Wall?" MA Thesis, Norges teknisk-naturvitenskapelige universitet, 2010.

Roostaee, Zahra. "An Intercultural Study: The Reception of J. K. Rowling's the "Harry Potter" Book Series in Iran." MA Thesis, Université de Sherbrooke, 2010.

Sewell, Sarit. "Neologisms and Made-Up Names in the Translations of the Harry Potter Books into Hebrew: Ways of Creation in the Original Text and in the Translation with Respect to Fantasy, Ambivalence and Norms." Thesis, Bar-Ilan University Ramat-Gan 2007.

Shaio, Yah-Ying Elaine. "Bewitched or befogged in a magical world? Chinese translations of culture-specific items in a Harry Potter novel." MA Thesis, Auckland University of Technology, 2006.

Tå, Åsa. "Lost or Gained in Translation: A Comparative Study of English and Spanish Motion Verbs." Thesis, Luleå Tekniska Universitet, 2010.

Tikkanen, Anna. "Translating magic: Magic spells in the Finnish translation of J. K. Rowling's Harry Potter books." Thesis, Helsingin yliopisto, 2002.

Tsai, Ming-Ho. "Translating Children's Literature in Taiwan: The Case of "Harry Potter and the Philosopher's Stone."" MA Thesis, University of Warwick, 2002.

Vilkman, Milla. "Intralingual Translation of Children's Literature: Harry Potter Books from British to American English." MA Thesis, Turun yliopisto, 2006.

Articles

Bedeker, Laetitia and Feinauer, Ilse. "The Translator as Cultural Mediator."*Southern African Linguistics and Applied Language Studies* 24:2 (2006): 133-141.

Brøndsted, Katrine and Dollerup, Cay. "The Names in Harry Potter." *Perspectives: Studies in Translatology* 12:1 (2004): 56-72.

Burn, Andrew. "Potterliteracy: cross-media narratives, cultures and grammars." *Papers: Explorations into Children's Literature* 14:2 (2004): 5-17.

Davies, Eirlys E. "A Goblin or a Dirty Nose? The Treatment of Culture-Specific References in Translations of the Harry Potter Books." *The Translator* 9:1 (2003): 65-100.

Feral, Anne-Lise. "The Translator's 'Magic' Wand: Harry Potter's Journey from English into French." *Meta: Journal des Traducteurs/Translators' Journal* 51:3 (2006): 459-481.

Fernandes, Lincoln P. "Translation of Names in Children's Fantasy Literature: Bringing the Young Reader into Play." *New Voices in Translation Studies* 2 (2006): 44-57.

Fernandes, Lincoln P. "On the Use of a Portuguese-English Parallel Corpus of Children's Fantasy Literature in Translator Education." *Cadernos de Tradução* 20:2 (2007): 141-163.

Goldstein, Steven. "The Language of Magic." *Translorial* 26 (2004): 16-17.

Goldstein, Steven. "Translating Harry. Part II: The Business of Magic." *Translorial* 27:1 (2005): 16f.

Grindhammer, Lucille. ""Harry Potter and the philosopher's stone" in four different countries (ab Klasse 9)." *Englisch betrifft uns* 4 (2001): 12-15.

Grindhammer, Lucille. "How it all began. Listening to chapter one of "Harry Potter and the philosopher's stone" (ab Klasse 9)." *Englisch betrifft uns* 4 (2001): 29-34.

Grindhammer, Lucille, and Hall, Alexander. "The "Harry Potter" phenomenon." *Englisch betrifft uns* 4 (2001): 1.

Harper, Neil. "Farewell, Father Christmas: Marketing the British Harry Potter Trilogy to the U.S." *Language International: The Business Resource for a Multilingual Age* 12:2 (Apr 2000): 38-39.

Henningsen, Lena. "Harry Potter with Chinese Characteristics, Plagiarism between Orientalism and Occidentalism." *China Information* 20:2 (2006): 275-311.

Inggs, Judith. "From Harry to Garri: Strategies for the Transfer of Culture and Ideology in Russian Translations of Two English Fantasy Stories." *Meta - Traduction pour les enfants* 48:1-2 (2003): 285-297.

Jaleniauskienė, Evelina. "The Strategies for Translating Proper Names in Children's Literature." *Kalbų Studijos/Studies about Languages* 15 (2009): 31-42.

Jentsch, Nancy K. "Harry Potter Speaks in Tongues: Translating J. K. Rowling's Magical World." *Kentucky Philological Review* 16 (2001): 54-60.

Kamala, N. "Harry Potter/ Hari Puttar or what's in a name?" *JSL New Series II* (Autumn 2004): 4.

Lathey, Gillian. "The Travels of Harry: International Marketing and the Translation of J. K. Rowling's Harry Potter Books." *The Lion and the Unicorn* 29:2 (Apr. 2005): 141-151.

Liang, Wen-Chun. "A Descriptive Study of Translating Children's Fantasy Fiction." *Perspectives: Studies in Translatology* 15:2 (2007): 92-105.

Mazzotti, Lydia. "Garri, Ron ee Ghermeeohna - Harry Potter in Translation." *Linguist: Official Journal of the Institute of Linguists* 43:5 (2004): 148-149.

Minier, Márta. "Beyond Foreignisation and Domestication: Harry Potter in Hungarian Translation." *The Anachronist* 10 (2004): 153-174.

Moore, Miranda. "The translatability of Harry Potter." *The Linguist (Institute of Linguists)* 39:6 (2000): 176-77.

Rehling, Petra. "Harry Potter, wuxia and the transcultural flow of fantasy texts in Taiwan." *Inter-Asia Cultural Studies* (2012): 69-87.

Valero Garcés, Carmen and Bogoslaw, Laurence. "Humorous (Un)Translated Names in the Harry Potter Series Across Languages". *Babel* 10 (2003): 209-226.

Valero Garcés, Carmen. "Translating the imaginary world in the Harry Potter series or how Muggles, Quaffles, Snitches, and Nickles travel to other cultures." *Quaderns: Revista de tradució* 9 (2003): 121-134.

Willems, Klaas and Mussche, Erika. "Fred or farid, bacon or baydun ('egg'). Proper names and cultural-specific items in the Arabic translation of Harry Potter." *Meta: Journal des Traducteurs/Translators' Journal* 55 (2010): 474-498.

Wood, Carolyn. "'Feminine' speech in the Japanese Translations of Harry Pot-ter."*Griffith Working Papers in Pragmatics and Intercultural Communications* 2,1 (2009): 44-50.

Chapters

Hestermann, Sandra. "Teaching the Harry Potter 'Phenomenon' in the EFL Classroom: Harry Potter and the Prisoner of Azkaban." in *Cultural Studies in the EFL Classroom,* edited by Werner Delanoy and Laurenz Volkmann, 313-322, Heidelberg: Winter, 2006.

Holt, Margaret. "Racism in British Children's Literature, or, from Little Black Sambo to Harry Potter." in *Cultural Studies in the EFL Classroom,* edited by Werner Delanoy and Laurenz Volkmann, 337-350, Heidelberg: Winter, 2006.

Erni, John Nguyet. "When Chinese youth meet Harry Potter: Translating Con-sumption and Middle Class Identification." in *Asian Popular Culture,* edited by Anthony Y. H. Fung, 21-41, New York: Routledge, 2013.

Gundel, Jeanette K. "Clefts in English and Norwegian: Implications for the Grammar-Pragmatics Interface." in *The Architecture of Focus,* edited by Valé-ria Molnár and Susanne Winkler, 517-548, Berlin: Mouton de Gruyter, 2006.

Kansu-Yetkiner and Neslihan Oktar, Lütfiye. "Hayri Potur vs. Harry Potter: A Paratextual Analysis of Glocalization in Turkish." in *Translation Peripheries: Paratextual Elements in Translation,* edited by Anna Gil Bardají, 13-27, Bern: Lang, 2012.

Kawano, Kyohei. "Critiquing the Japanese Translation of Harry Potter in the Revisionist History of the Japanese Language Wikipedia: A Case Study of an Attempt at Language Control in Japan." in *Language under Controls: Policies and Practices Affecting Freedom of Speech. Selected Papers of the Interna-tional Conference September 23-24, 2011,* edited by Wayne H. Finke and Leonard R. N. Ashley, 81-87, East Rockaway: Cummings & Hathaway; 2012.

Kenda, Jakob J. "Rewriting Children's Literature." in *The Translator as Writer,* edited by Susan Bassnett and Peter R. Bush, 160-170, London: Continuum, 2006.

Minier, Márta. "Linguistic inventions, culture-specific terms and intertexts in the Hungarian translations of Harry Potter." in *No child is an island: The case for childrens' literature in translation,* edited by Pat Pinsent, 119-137, Lichfield: Pied Piper, 2006.

Moskowitz, Marc L. "From Warlocks to Aryans: The Slippery Slope of Cultural Nuance in Reading Harry Potter in Taiwan." in *Popular Culture in Taiwan:*

Charismatic Modernity, edited by Marc L. Moskowitz, 167-180, London: Routledge, 2010.

Mühleisen, Susanne. "American Adaptations: Language Ideology and the Language Divide in Cross-Atlantic Translations." in *Americanisms: Discourses of Exception, Exclusion, Exchange,* edited by Michael Steppat, 381-393, Heidelberg: Winter, 2009.

Valero Garcés, Carmen. "Playing Quidditch Through Languages: Relevance and Translation Strategies For New And Invented Words" in *Fifty Years of English Studies in Spain (1952-2002). A Commemorative Volume,* edited by Ignacio M. Palacios et al., 735-741, Santiago de Compostela: Universidad de Santiago de Compostela, 2003.

Harry Potter, Science, Medicine and Psychology

Monographs

Highfield, Roger. *The Science of Harry Potter: How Magic Really Works.* New York: Viking, 2002.

Markell, Kathryn A. and Markell, Marc A. *The Children Who Lived: Using Harry Potter and Other Fictional Characters to Help Grieving Children and Adolescents.* New York: Routledge, 2008.

Theses

Carlisle, Shannon Smith. "Examining the Thoughts and Actions of Harry Potter through the Lens of Erik Erikson's Psychological Stages." PhD Thesis, The University of Missisippi, 2010.

Cox, Rachel. "Freud, Lacan, and Harry Potter: Two Readings of Trauma." MA Thesis, University of South Dakota, 2010.

Engdahl, Erica. ""The foulest creatures that walk this earth." J. K. Rowling's Magical Creatures as Metaphors for Difficulties for Teenagers." B.A. Thesis, Växjö Universitet, 2008.

Garcia, Jalyn M. "The Move from Mono-Heroism to Poly-Heroism: A Look at Harry Potter and Contemporary Consciousness." PhD Thesis, Pacifica Graduate Institute, 2011.

Gerhold, Christine. "The Hero's Journey Through Adolescence: A Jungian Archetypal Analysis of "Harry Potter."" PsyD Thesis, The Chicago School of Professional Psychology, 2011.

Hippard, Victoria L. "Who Invited Harry? A Depth Psychological Analysis of the Harry Potter Phenomenon." PhD Thesis, Pacifica Graduate Institute, 2007.

Lennard, Anthony. "Harry Potter and the Quest for Values: How the boy wizard can assist young people in making choices." PhD Thesis, Australian Catholic University, 2007.

Nguyen, Kim Hong Thanh. "Imagining orphanhood post-9/11: Rhetoric, trope, and therapy." Iowa PhD Thesis, The University of Iowa, 2008.

Piippo, Taija. "The Effect of Desire on Identity in the Harry Potter novels: Deleuze and Guattari Against Psychoanalysis." MA Thesis, Tampereen yliopisto, 2006.

Schoomer, Sarah R. "The Uses of Magic: Fantasy Literature and its Effects in Pre-Adolescent Development." PsyD Thesis, The Wright Institute, 2010.

Stafford, Katherine Brooke. "Learning from Text: The Effect of the Connection of Information to a Protagonist on Readers' Content Acquisition and Motivation." PhD Thesis, Columbia University, 2006.

Tisdell, Timothy Michal. "'Harry Potter' and the World of Internal Objects: An Object Relations Analysis." PsyD Thesis, The Wright Institute, 2002.

Articles

Adami, Gian Franco. "Harry Potter and Obesity." *Obesity Surgery* 12:2 (2002): 298.

Barton, Julie. "The Monsters of Depression in Children's Literature: of Dementors, Spectres, and Pictures." *The Journal of Children's Literature Studies* 2:1 (2005): 27-39.

Bates, J. "As if by magic - A patient's ideal nurse is a cross between Harry Potter and Hercule Poirot." *Nursing Standard* 20:47 (2006): 29.

Black, Mary S. and Eisenwine, Marilyn J. "Education of the Young Harry Potter: Socialization and Schooling for Wizards."*The Educational Forum* 66:1 (2001): 32-37.

Bryan, Charles S. "Myth, Magic, and Muggles: Harry Potter and the Future of Medicine." *The Journal of the South Carolina Medical Association* 96:12 (2000): 514-518.

Conn, Jennifer Joy and Elliott, Susan Leigh. "Harry Potter and Assessment." *Clinical Teacher* 2:1 (2005): 31-36.

Conn, Jennifer Joy. "What can clinical teachers learn from Harry Potter and the Philosopher's Stone?" *Medical Education* 36:12 (2002): 1176-1181.

Corriveau, Kathleen H., et al. "Abraham Lincoln and Harry Potter: Children's differentiation between historical and fantasy characters." *Cognition.* 113:2 (2009): 213-225.

Craig, Jeffrey M.; Dow, Renee; and Aitken, Mary Anne. "Harry Potter and the recessive allele." *Nature* 436 (11 Aug. 2005): 776.

Debling, Heather. "'You Survived to Bear Witness': Trauma, Testimony, and the Burden of Witnessing in Harry Potter and the Order of the Phoenix." *Topic: The Washington and Jefferson College Review* 54 (2004): 73-82.

Denton, Peter H. "What Could Be Wrong with Harry Potter?" *Journal of Youth Services* 15:3 (Spring 2002): 24-33.

Fox, Anthony. "Harry Potter Writes." *Headache: The Journal of Head and Face Pain* 47:8 (2007): 1230f.

Frank, Andrew J. and McBee, Matthew T. "The use of Harry Potter and the Sorcerer's Stone to discuss identity development with gifted adolescents." *Journal of Secondary Gifted Education* 15:1 (2003): 33-39.

Gibson, Donna M. "Empathizing With Harry Potter: The Use of Popular Literature in Counselor Education." *Journal of Humanistic Counseling Education and Development* 46:2 (2007): 197-210.

Grynbaum, Gail A. "The secrets of Harry Potter." *San Francisco Jung Institute Library Journal* 19:4 (2001): 17-48.

Gwilym, Stephen et al. "Harry Potter casts a spell on accident prone children." *British Medical Journal* 2005, Nr. 7531: 1505-1506.

Hagen, Knut. "Harry Potter's Headache." *Headache: The Journal of Head and Face Pain* 48:1 (2008): 166.

Harris-Hendriks, Jean. "Bereavement in literature - the Harry Potter Series." *Bereavement Care Journal* 21:1 (2002): 11.

Hunt, Kathy. "'Do You Know Harry Potter? Well, He is an Orphan': Every Bereaved Child Matters." *Pastoral Care in Education* 24:2 (2006): 39-44.

Katz, Maureen. "Prisoners of Azkaban: Understanding Intergenerational Transmission of Trauma Due to War and State Terror (with Help from Harry Potter)." *JPCS: Journal for the Psychoanalysis of Culture & Society* 8:2 (2003): 200-207.

Khemlani, Sangeet S.; Sussman, Abigail B.; and Oppenheimer, Daniel M. "Harry Potter and the sorcerer's scope: latent scope biases in explanatory reasoning." *Memory and Cognition* 39:3 (2011): 527-535.

Lake, Suzanne. "Object Relations in Harry Potter." *The Journal of the American Academy of Psychoanalysis and Dynamic Psychiatry* 31:3 (2003): 509-520.

Lerer, Seth. "'Thy Life to Mend, This Book Attend': Reading and Healing in the Arc of Children's Literature." *New Literary History: A Journal of Theory and Interpretation* 37:3 (2006): 631-642.

Lewis, Donald Hershey and Andrew Hershey. "Harry Potter's Headaches." *Headache: The Journal of Head and Face Pain* 48:1 (2008): 167f.

Mayor, Alisa Gayle. "Viewpoint: Incorporating Humanities into Medical Education Harry Potter and the Silver Shield: Vaccines from a Magical Perspective." *The Journal of the American Medical Writers Association* 22:3 (2007): 121-122.

Moses, Alan C. "Commentary: Will It Take Harry Potter to Solve Diabetes? Divining the Future of Diabetes Care." *Journal of Periodontology* 78:11 (2007): 2077-2080.

Noctor, Colman. "Putting Harry Potter on the Couch." *Clinical Child Psychology and Psychiatry* 11:4 (2006): 579-590.

Noel-Smith, Kelly. "Harry Potter's Oedipal Issues." *Psychoanalytic Studies* 3:2 (2001): 199-207.

Ramagopalan, Sreeram V. et al. "Altered States - Origins of magic: review of genetic and epigenetic effects - The completion of JK Rowling's Harry Potter cycle allows geneticists to make important advances in understanding the heritability of magic." *British Medical Journal - International Edition* 335/7633 (2007): 1299-1301.

Roncone, Kelly. "The Technology of Magic: Scientific Challenges and Opportunities from Harry Potter's World." *Journal of the Minerals, Metals and Materials Society* 57:11 (2005): 30.

Rudski, Jeffrey Michael; Segal, Carli; and Kallen, Eli. "Harry Potter and the End of the Road: Parallels with Addiction." *Addiction Research & Theory* 17:3 (2009): 260-277.

Russell, J. "Harry Potter and the Psychologist's Tome." *Psychology Review* 11:4 (2005): 30-32.

Seden, Janet. "Parenting and the Harry Potter Stories: A Social Care Perspective." *Children and Society* 16:5 (2002): 295-305.

Sheftell, Fred; Steiner, Timothy J.; and Thomas, Hallie. "Harry Potter and the Curse of Headache." *Headache: The Journal of Head and Face Pain* 47:6 (2007): 911-916.

Welsh, Christopher. "Harry Potter and the Underage Drinkers: Can We Use This to Talk to Teens About Alcohol?" *Journal of Child and Adolescent Substance Abuse* 16:4 (2007): 119-126.

Welsh, Christopher J. "Harry Potter and Butterbeer." *Journal of the American Academy of Child and Adolescent Psychiatry* 43:1 (2004): 9-10.

Chapters

McNulty, William. "Harry Potter and the Prisoner Within: Helping Children with Traumatic Loss." in *Popular Culture in Counseling, Psychotherapy, and Play-Based Interventions*, edited by Lawrence C. Rubin, 25-42, New York: Springer, 2008.

Harry Potter, Philosophy and Law

Monographs

Armstrong, Ari. *Values of Harry Potter: Lessons for Muggles.* Denver: Ember, 2008.

Brown, Karen A. *Prejudice in Harry Potter's World: A Social Critique of the Series, using Allport's The Nature of Prejudice.* College Station, Tex: Virtual-bookworm.com Publishing, 2008.

Hederman, Mark Patrick. *Harry Potter and the Da Vinci code: 'Thunder of a Battle fought in some other Star'.* Dublin: Dublin Centre for the Study of the Platonic Tradition, 2007 (Platonic Centre pamphlets 2).

Holland, Nancy J. *Ontological Humility: Lord Voldemort and the Philosophers.* Albany: State University of New York Press, 2013.

Kern, Edmund M. *The Wisdom of Harry Potter: What Our Favorite Hero Teaches Us about Moral Choices.* Amherst, N.Y: Prometheus Books, 2003.

Plyming, Philip. *Harry Potter and the Meaning of Life.* Cambridge: Grove Books, 2001.

Theses

Fettke, Sarah. ""Beasts", "beings", and Everything Between: Environtmental and Social Ethics in Harry Potter." MA Thesis, University of Kansas, 2012.

Green, Covey Jordan. "Existentialism in Harry Potter." MA Thesis, Angelo State University, 2008.

Guanio-Uluru and Lykke Harmony Alara. "Best-selling Ethics: A Literary Analysis of the Ethical Dimensions of J. R. R. Tolkien's The Lord of the Rings and J. K. Rowling's Harry Potter series." PhD Thesis, Universitetet i Oslo, 2013.

Helgesen, Linnea. "Harry Potter's Moral Universe: Reading Harry Potter as a Morality Tale." MA Thesis, Universitetet i Oslos, 2010.

Articles

Barton, Benjamin. "Harry Potter and the Half-Crazed Bureaucracy." *Michigan Law Review* 104 (May 2006).

Binnendyk, Lauren and Schonert-Reichl, Kimberly A. "Harry Potter and Moral Development in Pre-adolescent Children." *Journal of Moral Education* 31:2 (2002): 195-201.

Cain, Amanda. "Books and becoming Good: Demonstrating Aristotle's Theory of Moral Development in the Act of Reading." *Journal of Moral Education* 34:2 (2005): 171-183.

Cantrell, Sarah K. "I Solemnly Swear I Am up to No Good": Foucault's Hetero-topias and Deleuze's Any-Spaces-Whatever in J. K. Rowling's 'Harry Potter' Series." *Children's Literature: Annual of the Modern Language Association Division on Children's Literature and the Children's Literature Association* 39 (2011): 195-212.

Carney, John J. and DeMitchell, Todd A. "Harry Potter v. Muggles: Literary criticism and legal challenge." *International Journal of Educational Reform,* 14 (2005): 2-16.

Horrocks, Ian. "Ontologies and the Semantic Web." *Communications of the ACM* 51:12 (2008): 58-67.

Joseph, Paul R. and Wolf, Lynne E. "The Law in Harry Potter: A System Not Even a Muggle Could Love." *The University of Toledo Law Review* 34:2 (2003): 193-202.

Karjala, Dennis S. "Harry Potter, Tanya Grotter, and the Copyright Derivative Work." *Arizone State Law Journal* 38:1 (2006): 17-40.

Macneil, William P. "'Kidlit' as 'Law-And-Lit': Harry Potter and the Scales of Justice." *Law and Literature* 14:3 (2002): 545-564.

Maza, Luisa Grijalva. "Deconstructing the Grand Narrative in Harry Potter: In-clusion, Exclusion and Discriminatory Policies in Fiction and Practice." *Politics & Policy* 40:3 (2012): 424-443.

Morriss, Andrew P. "Why Classical Liberals Should Love Harry Potter." *The Freeman: Ideas on Liberty* 50:12 (2000): 12-16.

Rutherford, Ian. "Harry Potter: Situation Ethics Candy-Coated for Kids." *New Oxford Review* 69:4 (2002): 36-37.

Schwabach, Aaron. "Harry Potter and the Unforgivable Curses: Norm-formation, Inconsistency, and the Rule of Law in the Wizarding World." *TJSL Legal Studies Research Paper No. 05-13. Roger Williams University Law Review* 309 (2006)

Striphas, Ted. "Harry Potter and the Simulacrum: Contested Copies in an Age of Intellectual Property." *Critical Studies in Media Communication* 26:4 (2009): 1-17.

Van Praagh, Shauna. "Adolescence, Autonomy and Harry Potter: The Child as Decision-Maker." *International Journal of Law in Context* 1:4 (2005): 335-373.

Wolosky, Shira. "Harry Potter's Ethical Paradigms: Augustine, Kant, and Feminist Moral Theory." *Children's Literature: Annual of The Modern Language Association Division on Children's Literature and The Children's Literature Association* 40 (2012): 191-217.

Chapters

Kleinberger, Daniel S. "Agents of the good, servants of evil : Harry Potter and the law of agency." in *Agency, partnerships, and LLCs,* written by Daniel S. Kleinberger, 575-590, New York: Wolters Kluwver Law & Business, 2012.

Pierce, Jeremy. "Destiny in the Wizarding World" in *Introducing Philosophy through Pop Culture: From Socrates to South Park, Hume to House,* edited by William Irwing and David Kyle Johnson, 89-99, Malden: Wiley-Blackwell, 2010.

Walls, Johnathan L. and Walls, Jerry L. " Beyond Godric's Hollow: Life After Death and the Search for Meaning" in *Introducing Philosophy through Pop Culture: From Socrates to South Park, Hume to House,* edited by William Irwing and David Kyle Johnson, 319-326, Malden: Wiley-Blackwell, 2010.

Rauhofer, Judith. "Defence against the Dark Arts." in *Legal, Privacy and Security Issues in Information Technology, Volume 2,* edited by Sylvia Mercado Kierkegaard, 175-200, Oslo: 2006

Tan, David. "Harry Potter and the transformation wand: fair use, canonicity and fan activity." in *Amateur Media: Social, Cultural and Legal Perspectives,* edited by Dan Hunter et al., 94-102, Abingdon, New York: Routledge, 2012.

Harry Potter and Religion

Monographs

Abanes, Richard. *Harry Potter, Narnia, and The Lord of the Rings*. Eugene, Ore: Harvest House Publishers, 2005.

Abanes, Richard. *Fantasy and Your Family: Exploring the Lord of the Rings, Harry Potter, and Modern Magick*. Camp Hill, Pa: Horizon Books, 2002.

Abanes, Richard. *Harry Potter and the Bible: The Menace Behind the Magick*. Camp Hill, Pa: Horizon Books, 2001.

Arms, Phil. *Pokemon & Harry Potter: A Fatal Attraction. An Expose of the Secret War Against the Youth of America*. Oklahoma City: Hearthstone Publishing, 2000.

Bell, Luke. *Baptizing Harry Potter: A Christian Reading of J. K. Rowling*. Mahwah: Hidden Spring, 2010.

Bridger, Francis. *A Charmed Life: The Spirituality of Potterworld*. London: Darton, Longman and Todd, 2001.

Brown, Nancy Carpentier. *The Mystery of Harry Potter: A Catholic Family Guide*. Huntington: Our Sunday Visitor Pub., 2007.

Cronshaw, Darren. *Harry Potter and the Living Stone: A Consideration of Gospel Themes in J K Rowling's Books I to V*. Hawthorn: Zadok Institute for Christianity and Society, 2003.

Dalton, Russell W. *Faith Journey Through Fantasy Lands. A Christian Dialogue With Harry Potter, Star Wars, and the Lord of the Rings*. Minneapolis: Augsburg Fortress, 2003.

Falaschi-Ray, Sonia. *Harry Potter: A Christian Chronicle*. Brighton: Book Guild, 2011.

Granger, John. *Looking for God in Harry Potter*. Carol Stream: Tyndale House, 2004.

Gray, D. J. *Harry Potter and Tolkien's Rings. A Christian perspective*. Cannon Hill: Qld 2002.

Killinger, John. *Life, Death, and Resurrection of Harry Potter.* Macon/Georgia: Mercer UP, 2009.

Killinger, John. *God, the Devil, and Harry Potter. A Christian Minister's Defense of the Beloved Novels.* New York: Thomas Dunne Books, 2002.

Krulwich, Dov. *Harry Potter and Torah.* [s. l.]: Lulu.com, 2006.

Lansdown, Andrew. *Harry Potter: Witchcraft or story-craft.* Nollamara: Life Ministries, 2002.

Murphy, Derek. *Jesus Harry Potter Christ: The Fascinating History of the Literary Jesus.* Portland: Holy Blasphemy Press, 2011.

Neal, Connie W. *Wizards, Wardrobes & Wookiees: Navigating Good and Evil in Harry Potter, Star Wars & the Chronicles of Narnia.* Downers Grove: IVP Books, 2007.

Neal, Connie. *The Gospel according to Harry Potter: The spiritual Journey of the World's Greatest Seeker.* Louisville: Westminster John Know Press, 2008.

Neal, Connie. *What's a Christian to Do with Harry Potter?* Colorado Springs: Waterbrook Press, 2001.

Neal, Connie and Bruner, Kurt et al. *Wizards, Hobbits and Harry Potter: What Your Family Needs to Know.* Little Rock: FamilyLife Publishing, 2001.

Roper, Denise. *Lord of the Hallows: Christian Symbolism and Themes in J. K. Rowling's Harry Potter.* Denver/Colorado: Outskirts Press, 2009.

Smith, Janet. *Bewitched, bedazzled & beguiled: Harry Potter and the Philosopher's Stone.* Cheltenham: Hawker Brownlow Education, 2000.

Smith, Rob. *Hogwarts, Narnia, and Middle Earth: Places Upon a Time.* Huron: Drinian Press, 2007.

Tumminio, Danielle Elizabeth. *God and Harry Potter at Yale: Teaching Faith and Fantasy Fiction In An Ivy League Classroom.* [s.l.]: Unlocking Press, 2010.

Wohlberg, Steve. *Exposing Harry Potter and Witchcraft: The Menace beneath the Magic.* Shippensburg: Destiny Image Publishers, 2005.

Wohlberg, Steve. *Hour of the Witch: Harry Potter, Wicca Witchcraft and the Bible.* Shippensburg: Destiny Image Publishers, 2005.

Zingaro, John. *Harry Potter Sermons: Biblical truths illustrated by the Harry Potter stories.* Newton NJ: John Zingaro, 2008.

Theses

Dudink, Peter. "Hoax, Parody, and Conservatism in Harry Potter." MA Thesis, University of Waterloo, 2002.

Milwee, Linda. "The Harry Potter Series: Innocent Family Fiction or Occult Black Magic?" Student Thesis, Luleå Tekniska Universitet, 2009.

Murphy, Alan C. "Inferred Religion in J. K. Rowling's Harry Potter." Honors Thesis, Tulane University, 2006.

Ozyra, Paula. "Magic or Magick? The Witchcraft Charges against the Harry Potter Series." MA Thesis, Tampereen yliopisto, 2004.

Scheffer, Susanne. ""Satanic Harry": How a Wizard Has to Fight the Church." Student Thesis, Karlstads Universitet, 2009.

Vehkanen, Johanna. "Defending the Harry Potter series from its Detractors and Defenders." MA Thesis, Tampereen yliopisto, 2006.

Articles

Ballard, S. B. "Thoughts on Harry Potter: Wizardry, Good and Evil." Anglican Theological Review 82 (2000): 173-176.

Barber, Peter John. "The Combat Myth and the Gospel's Apocalypse in the Harry Potter Series: Subversion of a Supposed Existential Given." Journal of Religion and Popular Culture 24:2 (2012): 183-200.

Birmingham, Carrie. "Harry Potter and the Baptism of Imagination." The Stone-Campbell Journal 8:2 (2005): 199-214.

Boston, Rob. "Witch Hunt. Why the Religious Right is Crusading to Exorcise Harry Potter Books from Public Schools and Libraries." Church and State 55:3 (2002): 8-10.

Briggs, Melody. "The Boy who Lived and Died for the Wizarding World: Concepts of Salvation in J K Rowling's 'Harry Potter and the Deathly Hallows'." The Journal of Children's Literature Studies 5:1 (2008): 1-21.

Caldecott, Léonie. "A Wizard's Missions - Christian Themes in Harry Potter." The Christian Century 125:1 (2008): 24.

Cockrell, Amanda. "Harry Potter and the Witch Hunters: A Social Context for the Attacks on Harry Potter." Journal of American Culture (Special issue on children and popular culture): 24-30.

O'Conaill, Sean. "Harry Potter and the Disappearing Pupil." Doctrine and Life 51:10 (2001): 627-631.

Deavel, Catherine Jack and Deavel, David Paul. "Character, Choice and Harry Potter." Logos: A Journal of Catholic Thought and Culture 5:4 (2002): 49-64.

Dooley, David. "Harry Potter: Pro and Con." Catholic Insight (Jan/Feb 2002): 37-39.

Edwards, Cliff. "Harry Potter and the Bible: Should They Both Be Banned?" Bible Review 16:3 (2000): 2.

Flesher, Paul V.M. "Being True to the Text: From Genesis to Harry Potter." The Journal of Religion and Film 12:2: (2008).

Gatta, Julia M. "Harry Potter and Friends: The Moral and Spiritual Vision of J. K. Rowling." Sewanee Theological Review 49:2 (2006): 257-263.

Gish, Kimbra Wilder. "Hunting Down Harry Potter: An Exploration of Religious Concerns about Children's Literature." The Horn Book Magazine 76:3 (2000): 262-271.

Glanzer, Perry L. "Harry Potter's Provocative Moral World: Is There a Place for Good and Evil in Moral Education? Moral Education and Harry Potter: Why do young readers find Harry Potter so compelling and moral education so often deadly dull?" Phi Delta Kappan 89:7 (2008): 525-528.

Goddard, Andrew. "Harry Potter and the Quest for Virtue." Anvil. An Anglican Evangelical journal for theology and mission 18:3 (2001): 181-192.

Granger, John. "Harry Potter and the Inklings: The Christian Meaning of The Chamber of Secrets." CSL. The Bulletin of The New York C.S. Lewis Society 392 33:6 (November/December 2002).

Griesinger, Emily. "Harry Potter and the Deeper Magic: Narrating Hope in Children's Literature." Christianity and Literature 51:3 (Spring 2002): 455-480.

Hjelm, Titus. "Between Satan and Harry Potter: Legitimating Wicca in Finland." Journal of Contemporary Religion 21:1 (2006): 33-48.

Jacobsen, Ken. "Harry Potter and the secular city: The dialectical religious vision of J. K. Rowling." Animus: The Canadian Journal of Philosophy and Humanities 9 (2004): 79-104.

Jacobson, Karl N. and Jacobson, Rolf A. "The One Who Will Be Born: Preaching Isaiah's Promises in a Harry Potter Culture." Word and World 27:4 (2007): 426-435.

Jansen, Henry. "Harry Potter and the Problem of Evil." Studies in Interreligious Dialogue 13:1 (2003): 70-85.

Johnston, Susan. "Harry Potter, Eucatastrophe, and Christian Hope." Logos: A Journal of Catholic Thought and Culture 14:1 (2011): 66-90.

Kruk, Remke. "Harry Potter in the Gulf: Contemporary Islam and the Occult." British Journal of Middle Eastern Studies 32:1 (2005): 47-74.

Masson, Margaret. "The Harry Potter Debate." Anvil: An Anglican Evangelical journal for theology and mission 18:3 (2001): 193-196.

Masson, Sophie. "So What's All This about Harry Potter?" Quadrant 44:12 (2000): 68-71.

McCarron, Bill. "Christianity in Harry Potter and the Deathly Hallows." Notes on Contemporary Literature 39:1 (2009): 10-12.

McVeigh, Dan. "Is Harry Potter Christian?" Renascence: Essays on Values in Literature 54:3 (2002): 197-214.

Ney, Philip G. "Harry Potter: The archetype of an abortion survivor." Catholic Insight (Dec 2003), http://ca.vlex.com/vid/harry-potter-archetype-abortion-survivor-56582587

Ostling, Michael. "Harry Potter and the Disenchantment of the World." Journal of Contemporary Religion 18:1 (2003): 3-32.

Pearson, Jo. "Inappropriate Sexuality? Sex magic, s/m and wicca (or 'whipping Harry Potter's arse!')." Theology & Sexuality 11:2 (2005): 31-42.

Šaric, Julia. "A Defense of Potter, or When Religion is Not Religion. An Analysis of the Censoring of the Harry Potter Books." Canadian Children's Literature 103 (2001): 6-26.

Schmidt, Gary D. "The Dangerous Harry Potter." Christian Home and School 78 (Mar/Apr 2000): 26-27.

Soulliere, Danielle M. "Much Ado about Harry: Harry Potter and the Creation of a Moral Panic." Journal of Religion and Popular Culture, 22:1 (2010): http://www.nabilechchaibi.com/resources/Soulliere.pdf .

Vineberg, Steve. "Harry Potter and The Trip." Christian Century 128:17 (2011): 43f.

Wandinger, Nikolaus; Drexler, Christoph; and Peter, Teresa. "Harry Potter and the Art of Theology: A Theological Perspective on J. K. Rowling's Novels.

Part One: Healing, Grace and Original Sin." *Milltown Studies* 52 (Winter 2003): 1-26.

Wandinger, Nikolaus; Drexler, Christoph; and Peter, Teresa. "Harry Potter and the Art of Theology 2: A Theological Perspective on J. K. Rowling's Novels-Part Two: Sacrifice and Mission." *Milltown Studies* 53 (Summer 2004): 131-153.

Chapters

Duriez, Colin. "Voldemort, Death Eaters, Dementors, and the Dark Arts: A Contemporary Theology of Spiritual Perversion in the Harry Potter Stories." in *The Lure of the Dark Side: Satan and Western Demonology in Popular Culture*, edited by Christopher H. Partridge and Eric Christianson, 182-195, London, Oakville, CT: Equinox, 2008.

Guttfeld, Dorota. "Coping with Mortality: Lewis, Le Guin and Rowling on the Inhumanness of Immortality." in *Towards or Back to Human Values? Spiritual and Moral Dimensions of Contemporary Fantasy*, edited by Justyna Deszcz-Tryhubczak and Marek Oziewicz, 198-208, Newcastle: Cambridge Scholars, 2006.

Kruk, Remke. "Harry Potter in the Gulf: Contemporary Islam and the Occult." in *Islamic medical and scientific tradition: Critical concepts in Islamic Studies*, edited by Peter E. Pormann, 209-242, London: Routledge, 2011.

Poe, Elizabeth A. "Defending Harry Potter." in *Censored Books II: Critical Viewpoints, 1985-2000*, edited by Nicholas Karolides, 206-212, Lanham, MD: Scarecrow, 2002.

Sky, Jeanette. "Harry Potter and Religious Mediatization." in *Implications of the Sacred in (Post)modern Media*, edited by Johanna Sumiala-Seppänen, Knut Lundby, and Raimo Salokangas, 235-253, Göteborg: Nordicom, 2006.

ᵗ

Other Fields

Monographs

Brown, Stephen. *Wizard! Harry Potter's Brand Magic*. London: Cyan Books, 2005.

Götz, Maya; Lemish, Dafna; Aidmann, Amy; and Moon, Hyesung. *Media and the Make-Believe Worlds of Children: When Harry Potter meets Pokémon in Disneyland*. Mahwah, N.J: Lawrence Erlbaum, 2005.

Morris, Thomas V. *If Harry Potter ran General Electric: Leadership Wisdom from the World of the Wizards*. New York: Currency/Doubleday, 2006.

Reagin, Nancy. *Harry Potter and History*. New York: Wiley, 2011.

Snir, Avichai and Levy, Daniel. *Popular Perceptions and Political Economy in the Contrived World of Harry Potter*. Atlanta: 2005.

Theses

Clark, Leise Anne. "Butterbeer, Cauldron Cakes, and Fizzing Whizzbees: Food in J. K. Rowling's Harry Potter Series." MA Thesis, University of South Florida, 2012.

Dunphy, Heather Victoria. "Trust, Friendship and Hogwarts Houses: An Ethnography of Harry Potter Fans." PhD Thesis, University of Calgary, 2011.

Lüscher, Anna. "The secret community: The magical nation-state and its borders in 'Harry Potter.'" BA Thesis, Universität Konstanz, 2002.

Merrill, Trista Marie. "Crossing Boundaries on a Bolt of Lightning: Mythic, pedagogical and Techno-Cultural Approaches to Harry Potter." PhD Thesis, State University of New York at Binghamton, 2003.

Micklitz, Bill. "The Censors' Magic Wand: The Disappearing Children's Literature." MSc Thesis, University of Wisconsin, 2006.

Moulton, Daniel Lee. "Finding Platform 9¾: Connections between Technology and Literacy." PhD Thesis, University of Calgary, 2004.

Ray, Katherine. "To Read or Not to Read: The Influence of Literature on Behavior Management." Senior Honours Thesis, Liberty University, 2009.

Articles

Alpion, Gëzim. "Images of Albania and Albanians in English literature: from Edith Durham to J. K. Rowling." BESA: Journal indépendant fondé par un groupe Albanais pour la liberté de l'Albanie 6:2 (Spring 2002): 30-34.

Bloom, Harold. "Can 35 Million Book Buyers Be Wrong? Yes." Wall Street Journal (11 July 2000): A26.

Bones, C. "A list of Resolutions for HR with a Little Help from Harry Potter." Human Resources (January 2002): 16-17.

Bristow, Alexandra. "Fragments and Links: Organizational Actor-World of the Harry Potter Phenomenon." Culture and Organization 13:4 (2007): 313-325.

Brown, Stephen and Patterson, Anthony. "Selling stories: Harry Potter and the Marketing Plot." Psychology & Marketing 27:6 (2010): 541-556.

Brown, Stephen and Patterson, Anthony. "Harry Potter and the Service Dominant Logic of Marketing: A Cautionary Tale." Journal of Marketing Management 25:5-6 (2009): 519-533.

Brown, Stephen and Patterson, Anthony. "'You're A Wizard, Harry!' Consumer Response to the Harry Potter Phenomenon." Advances in Consumer Research 33 (2006): 155-160.

Brown, Stephen. "Who moved my Muggle? Harry Potter and the marketing imaginarium." Marketing Intelligence & Planning 20/3 (2002): 134-148.

Brown, Stephen. "Marketing for Muggles: The Harry Potter Way to Higher Profits." Business Horizons 45:1 (2002): 6-14.

Brown, Stephen. "Harry Potter and the marketing mystery: A review and critical assessment of the Harry Potter books." Journal of Marketing 66:1 (2002): 126-130.

Brown, Stephen. "Torment Your Customers (They'll Love It)." Harvard Business Review 79:9 (October 2001): 82-88.

Brown Stephen. "Marketing for muggles: Harry Potter and the retro revolution." Journal of Marketing Management 17:5/6 (2001): 463-479.

Byatt, A. S. "Harry Potter and the Childish Adult." The New York Times 7 July 2003: A13.

328 Ravenclaw Reader

Czubek, Todd A. and Greenwald, Janey. "Understanding Harry Potter: Parallels to the Deaf World." Journal of Deaf Studies and Deaf Education 10:4 (2005): 442-450.

Dresang, Eliza T. "Harry Potter and Censorship." Florida Media Quarterly 27:4 (2002): 9.

Duska, Ronald F. "Harry Potter, 9/11, and Enron: Implications for Financial Service Professionals." Journal of Financial Service Professionals 56:3 (2002): 28-30.

Erni, John Nguyet. "Enchanted: Harry Potter and magical capitalism in urban China." Chinese Journal of Communication 1:2 (2008): 138-155.

Friedlander, Amy. "The Internet and Harry Potter: What Users Want." Information Outlook 7:12 (2003): 19-26.

Godwin, Mike. "Prisoners of Digital Television: A misadventure in high-tech regulatory policy-and a Harry Potter fix." Reason 34:11 (2003): 44-51.

O'Gorman, Kevin D. and Brooks, David. "Harry Potter and metaphysical hospitality." Hospitality Review 9:4 (2007): 41-47.

James, C. Renée. "The Real Stars of Harry Potter - Writer J. K. Rowling's universe of Harry Potter and associates is colorful, complicated, and punctuated by some genuinely stellar characters." Mercury - Journal of the Astronomical Society of the Pacific 36:4 (2007): 20-27.

McCafferty, Joseph. "Harry Potter and the Corner Office: Management Lessons from Unusual Sources." CFO Magazine 22:12 (2006): 32-35.

Meysman, Filip J.R., Campbell, Linda M., and Chasar, Lynda C. "Harry Potter and the Ecologist's Thesaurus: DIACES 2002." Limnology & Oceanography Bulletin 13:4 (2004): 84-86.

Nel, Philip. "Is There a Text in This Advertising Campaign? Literature, Marketing, and Harry Potter." The Lion and the Unicorn 29:2 (Apr. 2005): 236-267.

Pannell, David J. "Harry Potter and the Pendulums of Perpetual Motion: Economic Policy Instruments for Environmental Management." Connections - Farm, Food and Resources 1 (2001): 3-8.

Pfaltzgraff, Robert L. "Harry Potter in a Globalizing and Localizing World." International Studies Review 9:4 (2007): 718-720.

Rosser, Manda H. "The Magic of Leadership: An Exploration of Harry Potter and the Goblet of Fire." Advances in Developing Human Resources 9:2 (2007): 236-250.

Weber, R. "Harry Potter and the Dark Arts: With technology it's always best to consider: Just because I can, doesn't mean I should." Journal of Financial Service Professionals 61:6 (2007): 34-36

Chapters

Brown, Stephen and Patterson, Anthony. "Riddikulus! Consumer Reflections on the Harry Potter Phenomenon." in *Consuming Books: The Marketing and Consumption of Literature*, edited by Stephen Brown, 146-159, London: Sage, 2006.

Brown, Stephen. "Harry Potter and the fandom menace." in *Consumer Tribes*, edited by Bernard Cova, Robert V. Kozinets, and Avi Shankar, Avi, 177-192, Amsterdam, London: Butterworth-Heinemann, 2007.

Burn, Andrew. "Multi-text Magic: Harry Potter in book, film and videogame." in *Turning the Page: Children's Literature in Performance and the Media*, edited by Fiona M. Collins and Jeremy Ridgman, 227-249, Bern: Peter Lang, 2006.

Dawson, Melanie. "Sugared Violets and Conscious Wands: Deep Ecology in the Harry Potter Series." in *Environmentalism in the Realm of Science Fiction and Fantasy Literature*, edited by Chris Baratta, 69-89, Newcastle upon Tyne: Cambridge Scholars, 2012.

Frankel, Valerie Estelle. "More than just a hero's journey: Harry Potter, Frodo Baggins, and Captain Jack Harkness." in *Illuminating Torchwood: Essays on narrative, character and sexuality in the BBC series*, edited by Andrew Ireland, 53-65, Jefferson: McFarland & Co., 2010.

Haig, Matt. "Harry Potter: the story brand." in *Brand Royalty: How the World's Top 100 Brands Thrive & Survive* edited by Matt Haig, 57-62, London: Kogan Page, 2004.

Mayer, Uwe. "The Economic Values of Literature: Harry Potter and the Magic of Consumerism." in *Literature and Values: Literature as a Medium for Representing, Disseminating and Constructing Norms and Values*, edited by Sibylle Baumbach, Herbert Grabes, and Ansgar Nünning, 241-262, Trier: Wissenschaftlicher Verlag Trier, 2009.

Digital Resources

Coleman, Catherine, Dutchen, Stephanie, and Patterson, Diana. Eds. Proceedings of Accio 2005: The First Harry Potter Conference in the UK. University of Reading, 29-31 July 2005. CD-ROM. Reading: Accio UK, 2006.

Gunder, Anna. "As if by Magic: On Harry Potter as a Novel and Computer Game." in Level Up: Digital Games Research Conference, 4-6 November 2003, Utrecht University. edited by Marinka Copier and Joost Raessens, CD-ROM, Utrecht: Faculty of Arts, Utrecht University, 2003.

Useful Websites

www.accio-quote.org

www.hogwartsprofessor.com

www.hp-lexicon.org

www.mugglenet.com

www.pottermore.com

www.the-leaky-cauldron.org

www.thehogshead.org

A regularly updated and fully comprehensive bibliography can be found at http://www.eulenfeder.de/hpliteratur.html

Made in the USA
San Bernardino, CA
07 December 2015